Postliberal Theological Method

A Critical Study

D1518394

PATERNOSTER THEOLOGICAL MONOGRAPHS

Postliberal Theological Method

A Critical Study

Adonis Vidu

Paternoster:
thinking faith

First published 2005 by Paternoster
Paternoster is an imprint of Authentic Media
9 Holdom Avenue, Bletchley, Milton Keynes, MK1 1QR, U.K.
and
PO Box 1047, Waynesboro, GA 30830-2047, USA

11 10 09 08 07 06 05   7 6 5 4 3 2 1

British Library Cataloguing in Publication Data
A catalogue record for this book is available from the British Library.

ISBN–13: 978-1-84227-395-1
ISBN–10: 1-84227-395-7

Typeset by the Author.

Printed and bound in Great Britain
by Nottingham Alphagraphics.

Series Preface

In the West the churches may be declining, but theology—serious, academic (mostly doctoral level) and mainstream orthodox in evaluative commitment—shows no sign of withering on the vine. This series of *Paternoster Theological Monographs* extends the expertise of the Press especially to first-time authors whose work stands broadly within the parameters created by fidelity to Scripture and has satisfied the critical scrutiny of respected assessors in the academy. Such theology may come in several distinct intellectual disciplines—historical, dogmatic, pastoral, apologetic, missional, aesthetic and no doubt others also. The series will be particularly hospitable to promising constructive theology within an evangelical frame, for it is of this that the church's need seems to be greatest. Quality writing will be published across the confessions—Anabaptist, Episcopalian, Reformed, Arminian and Orthodox—across the ages—patristic, medieval, reformation, modern and counter-modern—and across the continents. The aim of the series is theology written in the twofold conviction that the church needs theology and theology needs the church—which in reality means theology done for the glory of God.

Series Editors

David F. Wright, Emeritus Professor of Patristic and Reformed Christianity, University of Edinburgh, Scotland, UK

Trevor A. Hart, Head of School and Principal of St Mary's College School of Divinity, University of St Andrews, Scotland, UK

Anthony N.S. Lane, Professor of Historical Theology and Director of Research, London School of Theology, UK

Anthony C. Thiselton, Emeritus Professor of Christian Theology, University of Nottingham, Research Professor in Christian Theology, University College Chester, and Canon Theologian of Leicester Cathedral and Southwell Minster, UK

Kevin J. Vanhoozer, Research Professor of Systematic Theology, Trinity Evangelical Divinity School, Deerfield, Illinois, USA

For Adriana

Contents

Acknowledgements   xi
Introduction   xiii

Chapter One
Textual Habitats   1
  Modernity's Prejudice against Tradition   2
  Two Ways of Recovering Vico   8
  Alasdair MacIntyre and Stanley Fish on Tradition   21
  Postliberal Notions of Setting   30
  Initial Critique   39

Chapter Two
Hermeneutics   45
  Realistic Narratives: Frei's Early Hermeneutics   45
  The Gospels as History   64
  Interpretation and Law   68
  The Later Frei   77
  Concluding Reflections   82

Chapter Three
Ontology   89
  Cultural Linguisticism: Formal Considerations   90
  World Absorption and God's Prevenience: Material
  Considerations   102
  Lindbeck, Schemes, and Content   110

Chapter Four
Justification   **117**
  Problems with Justification   118
  Justification in Narrative Theology   138

Chapter Five
Doctrine   **157**
  The Regulative View of Doctrine   157
  Against the Reification of Practice   177
  Doctrine and Ontology   182
  Conclusions   188

Chapter Six
Christology   **193**
  Christology in Conflict: Rival Christological Methods   194
  Hans Frei's Narrative Rendering of Identity   200
  Lindbeck and Grammatical Christology   217
  Christological Reference and Tradition as Habitus   232

Conclusion   **241**
Bibliography   **247**
Index   **265**

ACKNOWLEDGEMENTS

This book is a slightly modified version of a doctoral dissertation written at the University of Nottingham, England. My gratitude goes first of all to my supervisor, Prof. Anthony C. Thiselton. It is difficult to find a more charitable, generous spirit. He has been an encouragement even before I arrived at Nottingham and his always-detailed feedback was exemplary.

I am also grateful to the University of Nottingham for granting me a Research Scholarship, as well as for being a wonderful place to study and live. The Theology Department at Nottingham provided unbelievable support and a stimulating environment. The Council of Vice-Chancellors and Principals (CVCP-UK) granted me an Overseas Research Student Award. I am deeply thankful to them.

I want to thank other individuals and organisations for their financial and spiritual support: Langham Trust through its scholarship administrator, the Revd. Paul Berg; The Jerusalem Trust, who generously provided a scholarship covering my accommodation expenses, administered through Eurovangelism, of whom I would like to thank its director Gary Cox; the Revd. Chris Buss who was and is both friend and mentor; the Fellowship in the Pass Church, Beaumont, California; Woodmen Valley Chapel, Colorado Springs; Mr. and Mrs. Jimmy Thomas, Lewis and Mary Thomas; Bill Pollard.

A part of Chapter Two is also appearing in slightly revised form in *Trinity Journal* 26 NS, no. 2, Fall 2005. I would like to thank the editors for permission to use the material here.

I am deeply grateful to my parents for their unflinching support and encouragement. My theological education and formation would have been impossible without their help. Last but not least, I want to thank my wife, Adriana, for enduring so many hours of contemplative silence and absent-mindedness on my part. This book is dedicated to her.

Introduction

Since the 1980s, a group of American and British theologians, but also of German and other nationalities, started to retrieve with renewed vigour the project of situating theological and Christian reflection at the centre of the contemporary intellectual scene. The context could hardly have been more favourable. Philosophy, often theology's arch-rival, seemed to have entered a process of self-dissolution. By the mid-eighties it became a common place to level the status differences between philosophy, science, literature and the arts. Numerous theoreticians of science were questioning the objectivity of its methodology, which until not long ago supplied it with an illusion of certainty. Reason introspectively discovered its complicity with imagination and language. Universality, objectivity, legitimation and truth could no longer be secured – either as presuppositions, or as ends.

With great enthusiasm, intellectual discourses turned to their repressed 'other', discovering their entanglement with strategies of power, control and normalisation. The cultural world was slowly, sometimes hesitatingly, but steadily, discovering that it had not killed the other, but merely repressed it. Whether out of political duty, from a guilty conscience, or from ethical conviction, the majority in effect transformed the 'liberationists' into the 'empowered'. Disciplines such as theology (and even its subdisciplines) un-apologetically assumed the sufficiency and worthiness (together with the difference) of their own horizon of assumptions.

The new cultural era is not without its own perils, however. While it enables theology to recover faith in its academic respectability, the postmodern 'style' appears at times to be contradicting important Christian beliefs. The theological predicament, it might be said, is no less acute today than in any other historical age.

I have chosen to look at one particular problem which I believe haunts so-called postliberal theology. It is a problem that pertains to its theological epistemology and it may be construed as a meta-discursive contradiction between the formal assumption of a philosophical framework and certain material requirements of Christian religion, particularly God's prevenience. The pragmatist doctrine of the *epistemic priority* of the social forms of life encounters the theological conviction of the *ontological priority* of God. Postliberal writers exhibit both presuppositions. It is towards this potential contradiction that I orient my critical study: does not the narrative (here taken as the socially-pragmatic) construal of Jesus' and God's identity preclude their ontological superiority for the Christian form of life?

This issue is explored by first investigating the epistemological importance of *setting* (Chapter One), whereby two divergent trends are uncovered: a synchronic, territorial notion of background, which is prone to reification; and a diachronic, temporal view. In postliberal hermeneutics, the tendency is to reify the issues of setting by either formalising the texts, or by reifying the interpretive community (Chapter Two). The latter especially is accompanied by a denial of any serious role to criticism or rational adjudication among competing traditions. An internal corrective, this study suggests, is provided by the postliberal development of the notion of figuration.

The reification of setting is itself the consequence of a failure to grasp the relation between *truth and meaning*, as well as a result of maintaining a *dualism of scheme and content* (Chapter Three). Because meaning is the result of a practical process rather than a fixed and stable entity, traditions cannot invoke incommensurability as an exculpation before actually engaging in dialogue. The way is thus open for a good reasons approach to 'justifying' belief, rather than a *foundational* project of legitimation (Chapter Four).

Although narrative theologians claim to have appropriated holism, they appear to have done so in a piece-meal fashion. In fact, when holism is brought to bear on the issue, it no longer makes sense to permit a separation between *first and second orders of language*. This will cast doubt upon notions of grammatological theology (Chapter Five). Instead, theology should speak directly in world-involving terms, and courageously risk 'knowledge'. Finally, Chapter Six applies the critical discussion to *Christology*. It concludes that narrative rendering without ontological elucidation remains an incoherent undertaking.

Chapter One

Textual Habitats

This chapter does the job of stage-setting for the larger argument of the book. My intention is to present and critique various postliberal notions of background which involve the concepts of 'tradition' and 'church'. There will be no separate treatment of these, but they shall be treated as the two sides of the same coin, the idea that knowledge inhabits a textual world, in this case shaped by both church and tradition. In starting with a discussion of background, I am, so to speak, starting with the problem which serves as the motivation for the present work. There is a tension within narrative theology between a philosophical assumption concerning the priority of the social and the pragmatic on the one hand and the theological conviction of the ontological and epistemic priority of God's reality, on the other. The very presence of such a tension is not in itself problematic. Tensions sometimes need to be preserved in order to maintain the excitement. In this case, however, it is the manner in which the tension is worked out which will receive some critical attention. In a very strong sense, then, the proposals emerging out of this debate should be seen as in general sympathy with a lot of the postliberal suggestions, rather than as shots fired from a distance. Although at times the rhetoric may get the upper hand – which in itself should not seem offensive to narrativists – I would like to offer internal correctives rather than an outright rejection.

Having thus excused myself, I will start by pointing out that there are divergent perceptions of the significance of background. On the one hand there is the 'territorial' version, a spatial perception of the horizon of understanding which arguably tends to stress its 'artefact' character. This spatialisation predisposes theologians, religious analysts and adherents towards fideism, isolationism and insularism. Mis-applying the metaphor of language-games, it will render traditions as depositories of accomplished meanings and rules as well as – on the negative side – fields of ideological force. This type of postliberalism results from a pragmatist-rhetorical interpretation of historicism. It is effected through Lindbeck's reading of Clifford Geertz, Hauerwas' indebtedness to Stanley Fish, as well as Milbank's particular retrieval of Vico.

Vico's historicism, however, has not been retrieved exclusively along pragmatist-rhetorical lines. I would like to point out the promise of another Vichian variation, stemming from Gadamer and discernible in MacIntyre's notion of 'tradition-constituted enquiry'. Thinkers in this lineage view setting as an historical argument, an engagement with an extra-linguistic object. Setting is in this case a temporal event, or series of events, resulting in a 'sedimentation of meaning' which inscribes itself upon the agent as a disposition to interpret in a certain way.

Modernity's Prejudice against Tradition

Modernity inherits from the Enlightenment what Gadamer calls 'prejudice against prejudice itself.'[1] The project of a genealogy of modernity has become increasingly central to the postliberal agenda ever since John Milbank published *Theology and Social Theory*.[2] Milbank and some of his Radically Orthodox colleagues suggest that the origins of modernity are to be sought much earlier than Descartes, arguably as early as the thirteenth century. The reasons why such a genealogy might be important are to be sought in Milbank's critique of modern legitimation. Since modern procedures of rational justification fail, all that is left is the possibility of out-narrating a rival tradition. Tracing the genealogy of modernity is an essential part of such a process for it unmasks the arbitrary nature of modernity itself. Thus our allegiance to it becomes a matter of choice rather than some universal human duty. What Milbank in fact wishes to effect is a return to an essentially pre-modern, but at the same time post-modern Christian vision of reality as participating in God. This return becomes not only possible but also attractive once one realises, as he would want us to, that theology and philosophy took an essentially heretical step with Duns Scotus.

Before getting to Scotus, some thoughts about Aquinas are in order. A number of postliberal theologians confess to being admirers of Aquinas. Indeed, it is not only Milbank who traces the origins of modernity to the abandonment of Aquinas' *via antiqua*. For William Placher, Aquinas' precaution regarding the possibility of theological knowledge is most laudable. Knowledge of things is not independent of the knowledge of their being created by God. Creation makes theological knowledge possible, after all, since there exists a created relation between creatures and the creator. Analogical knowledge of God is given with this very relation. In this strongly participative account of theological epistemology where certainty

---

[1] Hans-Georg Gadamer, *Truth and Method*, trans. Joel Weinsheimer and Donald G. Marshall, (New York: Continuum, 1994), p. 270.

[2] (Oxford: Blackwell, 1990). Other examples of such genealogies are provided by Gavin Hyman, *The Predicament of Postmodern Theology: Radical Orthodoxy or Nihilist Textualism?*, (Louisville: Westminster John Knox, 2001); Phillip Blond, 'Introduction: Theology Before Philosophy' in Phillip Blond, ed., *Post-Secular Philosophy: Between Philosophy and Theology*, (London: Routledge, 1998); Connor Cunningham, *Genealogy of Nihilism: Philosophies of Nothing and the Difference of Theology*, (London: Routledge, 2002).

of reference obtains, caution is nevertheless exercised when one is asked to
'explain' the relation of reference. There is a qualitative ontological difference which haunts every attempt to explain theological knowledge and thus
derive a theological epistemology based on neutral explanation. For modernity, as Rorty shows, the ability to explain *how* language or thought work is
a precondition to showing *what* these refer to. Knowledge of the mental
process is a condition for achieving modern certainty.

Nothing could be more foreign to the modest medieval theologian who
believed that 'we could meaningfully use a term without really understanding how it applies.'[3] While the predicates we apply to God are *somehow* connected to the way we use the same words, we cannot *explain* what
the connection is. Aquinas denies any knowledge of the *ratio* which connects beings with God, or human words with divine referents. For this reason there can be no firm distinction between knowledge and revelation,
reason and authority, or between things as they are and their participation in
God. There can be, in other words, only a single moment, a unitary perception. Yet this is a perception of 'depth', as characters and things are discovered to have a surplus identity conferred upon them by theistic participation. Such a perception is denied to the gaze untrained by the Scriptural
narratives. Milbank revels in such a world ordered around a circular temporality, where things are repetitively returned to their created origins and to
their belonging to God. He holds that ontological difference alone makes
analogical participation possible. In such a world certainty is negotiated
necessarily in narrative terms. As Bruce D. Marshall points out, the criteria
for what is appropriate or inappropriate in this world are given intra-
textually in the Christian Scriptures.[4]

Modern thought, this genealogy goes on to say, will soon abandon this
intra-textual certainty in favour of a causal explanation of knowledge. Yet it
would be a mistake to trace this departure to Thomas who

> offered not a metaphysical system that would place God within our un-
> derstanding of the world and specify the meaning of our language about
> God, but metalinguistic rules that remind us of the limitations our lan-
> guage about God and thereby make it clear that we cannot place God
> within the world we can understand.[5]

---

[3] William Placher, *The Domestication of Transcendence: How Modern Thinking About God Went Wrong*, (Louisville: Westminster John Knox Press, 1996), p. 73.

[4] Bruce D. Marshall, *Christology in Conflict: The Identity of the Saviour in Rahner and Barth*, (Oxford: Blackwell, 1987); 'Aquinas as Postliberal Theologian', *The Thomist*, 53 (1989), 353-402.

[5] Placher, *Domestication*, p. 31.

Aquinas unequivocally assumes the horizon of the scriptural tradition. Since knowledge is analogical participation aided by revelation, its *pathos* is that of being moved by the object of reflection itself.

This mystic union between knowledge and tradition was about to be dissolved in the theology of Duns Scotus and Thomas de Vio, Cardinal Cajetan. The *via antiqua* by which knowledge of God could remain ignorant of its own mechanism appears as hopelessly incoherent for Scotus and Cajetan. Hence the 'indistinction of Being' which stipulates that Being could be indiscriminately applied to all: finite or infinite, substance or accidents.[6] In the concept of Being, theology has thus 'found' a ground for its desired univocal specification of God. If both God and creatures share in the same Being, the difference between their respective shares can be named. The world, man, and God are all placed on the great chain of Being, only at a distance. Some postliberal theologians and their Radical Orthodox colleagues stress that at this point theology itself became idolatrous. Its reliance on the third notion of Being as intervening between object and subject is suspect since this putative 'ground' is not founded in God's free and sovereign revelation. Ontological distance collapses and becomes epistemological difference. Idolatry could only be avoided by refusing to posit and master that third element which makes language about God possible, as Phillip Blond explains:

> Moreover, if one wishes to say that the relationship with God is analogous to the relationship one has with an object, then unless the source of the object or the thing (res) is understood as lying only in God then this analogy will, as Thomas pointed out, only point at some higher entity which both God and creature will have to share as derivative terms.[7]

The Thomist way, while it *believes* that we can have positive knowledge of God in virtue of the created nature of things can drive no further towards univocity simply because it is not clear what creation tells us about the actual relation between things and God. In other words, creation has no epistemological point to make. With the univocity of Being, this weakness of the knowledge disappears, in a sense.

A febrile search for a rigorous language and conceptual clarity was thus undertaken. This involved a systematisation of Aquinas' thoughts on analogy since Cajetan and Scotus both considered themselves to be interpreters of Thomas. Yet, as Eric Alliez points out, Duns' doctrine was less elaborated through contact with Thomas than with the 'contradictory dialogue

---

[6] Hans Urs von Balthasar, *The Glory of the Lord: A Theological Aesthetics*, 7 vols, ed. Joseph Fession SJ and John Riches, (Edinburgh: T&T Clark, 1982-1991), p. 16.

[7] Blond, 'Introduction', pp. 6-7.

between Averroes and Avicenna.'[8] If Placher's suggestion that Aquinas never intended a theory of analogy is right,[9] it seems that at least in one sense the turn can be called 'heretical'. Aquinas' modest proposals about theological language are replaced with a purgation of analogy of any hint of equivocity. Cajetan rejects all but the Thomist analogy of proportionality and he also denies its metaphorical use, as Placher notes.[10] He goes on to say that 'the univocist drift that analogy undergoes with Suarez and others' constitutes the first step in the domestication of transcendence.'[11]

Since theology needed a different locus for the difference between God and creation, in the hands of Cajetan and Scotus this became epistemological difference. Cajetan takes the mathematical overtones of the analogy of proportionality in an extremely literal direction. God is no longer ontologically different, but epistemologically distant from humanity. With historical hindsight, it may be said that the ironical consequence is that although the intention was a clearer discourse about God, the result banned transcendence from the realm of the nameable. As Eric Alliez comments:

> In effect, once the primary mover of continuity (the Aristotelo-Thomist principle of universal analogy) has been abandoned to the benefit of a univocal conception of Being, giving no means to creatures to distinguish themselves ontologically from God by analogically drawing near him, the distance between finite and infinite becomes infinite.[12]

This irony in fact prefigures a pattern which characterised the historical debates around the notion of certainty. There is, arguably, a certain complicity between a drive towards certainty and scepticism, nihilism, or ag-

---

[8] Eric Alliez, *Capital Times: Tales from the Conquest of Time*, trans. Georges Van Den Abbeele, (Minneapolis: University of Minnesota Press, 1996), p. 198.

[9] It seems reasonable to accept this interpretation, although it runs against classic studies such as those of Frederic Copleston. The tendency to read into Aquinas the later canonical interpretations by theologians such as Suarez and Cajetan has recently been criticised by David Burrell, *Aquinas: God and Action*, (Notre Dame: University of Notre Dame Press, 1979); Victor Preller, *Divine Science and the Science of God: A Reformulation of Thomas Aquinas*, (Princeton: Princeton University Press, 1967); Eugene Rogers, *Thomas Aquinas and Karl Barth: Sacred Doctrine and Natural Knowledge of God*, (Notre Dame: University of Notre Dame Press, 1995). Alan Torrance makes essentially the same point in *Persons in Communion: An Essay on Trinitarian Description and Human Participation, With Special Reference to Volume One of Karl Barth's* Church Dogmatics, (Edinburgh: T&T Clark, 1996), esp. p. 129. For a recent survey, see Philip Rolnick, *Analogical Possibilities: How Words Refer to God*, (Atlanta: Scholar's Press, 1993).

[10] Placher, *Domestication*, p. 73.

[11] Placher, *Domestication*, p. 75.

[12] Alliez, *Capital Times*, p. 199.

nosticism. What is at one point thought to be a solid ground for knowledge has, historically at least, dissolved as the arbitrary projection of over-enthusiastic thought. The more determined one is to secure a sure founda-tion, the more devastating the ensuing resignation. But there are also other consequences which follow from this historical departure from a narrative vision of reality. Together these open up an essentially practical aspect of our present theme.

The erection of Being as *indistinctive* amounts to the creation of a purely secular space. Being was intended by Scotus to constitute a field of pure receptivity, wherein divine knowledge could inscribe itself. Von Balthasar comments that reason attains natural knowledge of God through Scotist univocity and as a result 'it is not entirely unprepared for the Word which the free God utters.'[13] This purely secular space was the locus of meta-physics proper, as opposed to revealed theology. What must be observed is that the complicity of the will in this shift is undeniable. The creation of the secular and of Being was not unavoidable, but an arbitrary decision and a momentous one at that. A direct result of this 'will for Being' was that the difference between God and man had to be rendered in terms of proportion-ality. It may be argued that herein lies the modern and popular mispercep-tion of God as a 'huge' Being. Given this perception, creatures understood to negotiate their freedom by relating to an impossibly powerful deity. The next step was unavoidable: modernity understood its identity as self-assertion. It seems that we have come full circle: from a Thomist represen-tation of identity as participation and submission to the authority of God, legislated by the Scripture and tradition, to a modern will to self-determination as against all external authority.

The ordering of this classificatory system around Being resulted in knowledge being covertly moved away from the objects themselves to-wards the will to represent them according to genera. Alliez notes that Scotus modified the very concept of essence, placing it between the singu-larly real and the universally logical.[14] What moves the intellect to cognise is not *ipso facto* the cognised object. This leaves the way open for the legal establishment of the possibility of an intellection absolutely independent of its object.[15] The notion of object that surfaces from Scotus' metaphysics is 'so profoundly transformed that it negotiates its modernity by overtaking its ancient sense in the reduction of being to the concept of being.'[16] It is not difficult to glimpse here an anticipation of the Kantian creative spontaneity. But what happened was not short of extraordinary: knowledge became re-moved from the objects themselves and entangled with a web of concepts,

---

[13] Von Balthasar, *Glory*, p. 16.
[14] Alliez, *Capital Times*, p. 203.
[15] Alliez, *Capital Times*, p. 207.
[16] Alliez, *Capital Times*, p. 208.

employed, discovered, and managed by the will. The will, moreover, is 'de-finalised'[17] in that it is not moved by the solicitation of things.

Alliez discerns in all these shifts the emergence of a dualism between subject and object. It is the will which motivates the intellect, rather than the thing itself, which in turn becomes a verifiable object. Pretending to be in the service of the things themselves, by inscribing them on the framework of being, Scotist epistemology arguably masks its own arbitrariness. This will prove symptomatic of the rest of philosophy: metaphysics doing violence to the particular. The arbitrary act of a selective will assumes a stable and natural hierarchy of genera, species and things. Participation in the created reality is short-circuited by conceptuality, heralding a legal constitution of knowledge and enthroning a de-finalised will as the intentional force behind this knowledge.

Politically, writes Alliez, this coincided with the transition from a rural to an urban mode of community.[18] Rural will is primarily conceived as receptivity to an original divine movement ruled by myths and traditions. Time is circular in the village in that things are repetitively returned to their origin in God and they derive their meaning and telos from their beginning. Modernity, on the other hand, projects a linear time, as a production of the new rather than a recollection of the past. Urban will is synonymous with creativity and force.

So much for this particular genealogy of modernity. Its merit may consist not so much in the amount of historical detail used to substantiate its revisionist readings. Indeed, it may be strongly objected that its attack on Scotus is too vicious and distorted. Scotus is also given the dubious honour to have 'invented' the notion of Being. Rather, its value is given in its correlation with the larger Radical Orthodox critique of both secular modernity and postmodernity. Against these 'foes' of Christianity argument is pointless, as it will clearly emerge below. Theology's best hope is to tell these philosophical alternatives to simply get lost by uncovering their arbitrariness and involvement with issues of power. This is clearly a distinctive postmodern strategy as well, which should be a first clue that Milbank's relation to postmodernity is nuanced. Modernity's notion of self-assertion, of the secular, as well as the postmodern rejection of modern universality in the name of pure heterogeneity are rejected as myths, as ungrounded tales. In their place no effort should be made to erect new foundations, but rather to return with postmodern sensitivity to premodern and antique origins. The illusion offered by the notion of Being proved to have a lasting effect on Western intellectual history. In the wake of its establishment, authority had to be conceived as authoritarianism since the location of humanity on the same plane of Being with God conflicted with human identity. Against this

---

[17] Alliez, *Capital Times*, p. 211.

[18] Alliez, *Capital Times*, pp. 213-5.

Milbank argues that neither modernity's mythical ontology, nor postmodernity's philosophy of absolute difference is able to do justice to the particular. Modernity buries the particular under a conceptuality forgetful of its narrative or mythic nature, while postmodern heterologies are crippled by their ontology of original violence. It follows that neither a modern *narrative amnesia*, nor postmodern *narrative frenzy* are able to safeguard particularity. I shall argue that although the claim is right, its particular Milbankian interpretation requires a corrective.

It would appear that what Milbank and his fellow radicals suggest is a sort of realism in which the will is not involved. This would be to seriously misunderstand their distinctively postmodern negotiation of pre-modernity. The point is not the effacement of the will before the particular thing, but precisely the employment of a will to believe, the will to train one's gaze according to revelation. This will become clearer as we look at Milbank's engagement with Giambattista Vico.

Two Ways of Recovering Vico

In his effort to chart a course parallel to that of modernity, Milbank enlists the help of Vico who makes an early stand against Cartesian autonomy from tradition. Contrary to the Enlightenment's disjunction between reason and authority, especially religious authority, Vico and, later, Hamman propose their mutual implication. While for Kant enlightened identity is conceived in terms of maturity, self-assertion and the daring to know,[19] Vico finds no necessary contradiction between knowledge and revelation, maturity and belonging to a community, or between epistemic courage and modest submission.

Vico's principle of the *verum-factum* holds that we can only know with certainty that which we have made. Mathematics can be mastered with certainty not because it mirrors eternal and natural relations obtaining between numbers or forms *out there*, but for the simple reason that it was created by man. Vico appears to give this principle a sort of metaphysical primordiality, which has led some to suspect a contradiction here. A principle stating that we can only know with certainty what we have made cannot claim any such certainty for itself. It is therefore difficult to see how such a concept may be of any use in the human sciences. The contradiction recedes as soon as one realises that Vico's intention was never the derivation of a first principle, but the discovery of a historical assumption. Milbank points out that Vico coins the principle through a study of the wisdom of

---

[19] For a wonderful analysis of this Kantian notion, see Garrett Green, *Theology, Hermeneutics and Imagination: The Crisis of Interpretation at the End of Modernity*, (Cambridge: Cambridge University Press, 2000).

the ancient Italians.[20] This theological derivation of the *verum-factum* gains further importance in light of recent contradictory interpretations. While some argue that the principle was a common place in Vico's time, deriving from Ficino. Cardano, Scotus or Ockham,[21] Milbank's reading takes Vico to make a specifically theological move. The *verum-factum* was substantially different from ancient and medieval uses, themselves the result of certain religious cosmologies. Vico writes that 'the ancient philosophers of Italy thought that the true converted with the made because they thought that the world was eternal, and accordingly the pagan philosophers worshiped a God who was always operative *ad extra*, which our theology denies.'[22]

In this way Vico has in fact opened the way for another extraordinary shift in the theory of knowledge. As it turned out, however, philosophy preferred the Cartesian and Kantian autonomy, thus drastically restricting Vico's impact. In any case, Vico's change of perspective involved a move beyond the Platonic notion of knowledge as the organisation of ready-made forms. This resulted from the rejection of Platonic cosmology and ontology which restricted God's creativity to moulding a pre-existing matter. The *verum-factum* is theologically modified to suggest that there is nothing secondary about the made, as opposed to the original. We are evidently faced with a theological reconstruction of epistemology. Since it is only God that created everything, knowledge of everything depends on participation in him.

Metaphysics seeks a grounding of knowledge in pre-existing, ready-made forms, which the intellect believes it is able to 'discover'. Vico's theological theory of knowledge re-finalises will by reorienting it towards the origin of truth. Knowledge is not something to be achieved through the unprejudiced gaze at 'objects' and at their metaphysical ordering (law), but something which involves religious orientation:

> Given these opinions of the ancient philosophers concerning the true, the distinction which obtains in our religion between what is begotten and what is made, we hold the principle that since the exact truth is in the one God, we must acknowledge to be entirely true that which he has revealed to us – not inquiring after the genus, by which mode it is true, since we are wholly unable to comprehend it.[23]

---

[20] John Milbank, *The Religious Dimension in the Thought of Giambattista Vico 1668-1744*, (Lewiston/ Queenston/ Lampeter: The Edwin Mellen Press, 1992), p. 81.

[21] Isaiah Berlin, *Three Critics of the Enlightenment: Vico: Herder, Hamann*, ed. by Henry Hardy, (London: Pimlico, 2000), p. 35, n. 1.

[22] Quoted in Milbank, *Religious Dimension*, p. 82.

[23] Quoted in Milbank, *Religious Dimension*, p. 84.

This abandonment of a metaphysical quest signifies the return to a partici-
patory framework of the 'ancient days'. Since the certainty of our knowledge does not derive from an explanatory account of how words and sentences related to reality or to God, it can only be negotiated by trusting the
historically mediated revelation. The locus of such an objective divine
revelation is the *sensus communis* of past and present communities of faith.
It turns out that this is also a return to practical wisdom. Vico understands
tradition and community as mediating truth and knowledge. Access to such
truth implies an ethical disposition. Already in Vico we glimpse the con-
tours of a sociology of knowledge, and of a future linguistic turn. To understand a concept is to understand the linguistic and social history of its reception. There is no clear distinction between the mental and the practical
embodiment of ideas. Doctrines cannot be dissociated from politics or from
ethics.

Explanation has no further task to perform other than to narrate the history of an idea. The *verum-factum* implies that to know something is to
know how it has come about, which is a knowledge *per causas*. It is difficult to miss the remoteness of this *art* from Cartesian *method*. Not only the
fact that he repudiates Cartesian methodological orthodoxy at a time when
it was difficult to see around it, but also the very manner of the rejection is
notable.[24] Rather than arguing against and out-explaining Descartes position, he simply out-narrates it. Vico anticipates Gadamer's disentangling of
truth from method by clearly sensing that theoretical issues cannot be isolated from the social setting which they inhabit, or, as he would insist in his
later writings, from a network of signs.

Vico's account of knowledge also prefigures Gadamer's and Wittgenstein's wedding of meaning with application or use. A great part of the Vichian *oeuvre* analysed the possibility of historical knowledge of other cultures and peoples. Such knowledge is made possible by certain human ca-
pacities such as imagination and understanding.[25] The desire to know, to
imagine other conceptual arrangements than our own, implies that Vico
clearly sees an enduring role for the will. Knowledge is not disinterested.
It's very possibility implies something like an ethical attitude, a moral disposition. This conclusion derives from the *verum-factum*: to know something is to participate in it creatively. Yet since the principle itself is specifically Christian, the imperative itself may be considered Christian. Milbank suggests that

> 'revelation' simultaneously implies access to a truth which we did not
> originate, and also an initiation into this truth within specific historical
> time. A third component for Vico is the ethical disposition of peoples and

---

[24] Milbank, *Religious Dimension*, p. 84.
[25] Berlin, *Three Critics*, p. 131.

individuals enabling them to perceive the revelation of truth. [...] The need for the ethical dimension underscores the joining of a grasp of first principles to a particular communal ethos.[26]

So strong was Vico's regard for the importance of communal participation that he suspects *a priori* proofs of God's existence of being idolatrous.[27] The acquisition of truth is both inseparable from a certain community which mediates participation, and also organically connected to the practice of virtues.

Underlining the ethical in this way turned Vico towards legal philosophy, where he is considered to be one of the most influential figures of modernity. He denies the possibility of natural law for the same reasons he rejects *a priori* arguments for God's existence. Contrary to the popular assumption regarding a common human nature, for Vico there is no static nucleus, no unalterable minimum of this kind.'[28] Natural law theory, or jusnaturalism, doubly fails: first, in its mistaking of what is a human institution and a human argument for a natural state of affairs. This is the characteristically modern mistake and the complaint that it is inherently violent is now commonplace. Secondly, it fails in the practical implementation of law, namely in the cultivation of virtues. Law should not be isolated from the institutions which have created it, for it is therein that its truth resides, not in a correspondence to a given human nature. Vico asserts that 'the nature of institutions is nothing but their coming into being [*nascimento*] at certain times and in certain guises.'[29] This relativity of the truth of law to the social and political institutions which gave rise to it may not surprise us, but it must have done so to his contemporaries. All this leads towards an incipient doctrine of the incommensurability of paradigms in Vico. He speaks about a given collective social outlook of peoples, their *sensus communis*. Laws, it follows, are the linguistic embodiment of the collective response of a specific social group at a particular historical time.

Vico's influence on the history of legal thought is felt in the origins of Italian, chiefly Neapolitan, legal positivism. Elio Gianturco argues that Vico forges a synthesis of jusnaturalism and historicism. He suggests that Vico does not completely renounce natural law, but rather understands that it is unavailable outside its various cultural incarnations.[30] This is plausible, since Vico does not draw the conclusion that there are no natural kinds

---

[26] Milbank, *Religious Dimension*, p. 85.

[27] Berlin, *Three Critics*, p. 40.

[28] Berlin, *Three Critics*, p. 106.

[29] Quoted in Berlin, *Three Critics*, p. 106.

[30] Elio Gianturco, 'Vico in the History of Legal Thought', in Giorgio Tagliacozzo, Hayden V. White, eds., *Giambattista Vico: An International Symposium*, (Baltimore: The Johns Hopkins Press, 1969), p. 329.

from the premise that we can only know with certainty that which we have made. Vico simply would not discuss theoretical issues in isolation from their historical lives and institutional affiliation.[31] The validity of law, it follows, can only derive from its history and its enforcement, not from an adequacy to human nature, but from the law makers themselves. As an institution, it is the creation of men and it does not seek to recapitulate anything primordial. Now whether this interpretation of Vico is corect or flawed, it certainly made its way into legal positivist circles.

The possibility of a connection between Vico and the school of legal positivism may seem an unnecessary detour from our main theme. But it is only deceivingly so, especially for those who would not expect to find contingent facts about history, society or politics in a philosophical or theological argument. Vico is among the first historicist thinkers, moreover one who understood the relative nature of any conceptual outlook. It is true that, as Milbank convincingly argues, his relativism was in fact a theologically derived contextualism. Vico is convinced, for theological reasons, that to narratively and contextually perceive things does not lead to a distortion of their identity, but rather to its preservation. His instrumentalism, therefore, does not clash with his realism.[32] Tradition does not oppose reason, but makes it possible. Because human beings are not isolated individuals, both scepticism and foundationalism are closed avenues for post-Vichian thought.

Scepticism unmasks itself as the unavoidable result of an avoidable quest for certainty. Milbank, Pickstock and Ward are convinced that to see things as being illuminated by revelation is in fact to see them as they really are.[33] This is to say that since there is no direct view to reality, no mirroring of the world in the mind's eye, there is nothing suspicious about allowing our gaze to be trained by the revelation-bearing church. What Vico thus offers is not a naïve realism, but a metacritical realism, since 'the critical role in his philosophy is played by contingent linguistic categories, and not *a priori* transcendental ones.'[34] The above-named radical orthodox theologians are united in their drafting of Vico, Hamann and Herder in the service of their quest to affirm the linguistic nature of truth, the communitarian locus of true knowledge and the analogical participation in the divine. The conviction informing this project is that modernity has taken a wrong turn, inevitably leading to nihilism.[35] Following recent philosophy, they all understand Kant as the 'great delayer'[36], in the sense that his persistence in the

---

[31] Gianturco, 'Vico in the History of Legal Thought', p. 336.

[32] Milbank, *Religious Dimension*, vol. 1, p. 329.

[33] Milbank, *Radical Orthodoxy*, pp. 3, 4.

[34] Milbank, *Religious Dimension*, vol. 1, p. 333.

[35] Milbank, *Theology and Social Theory*, pp. 302-6.

[36] George Grant's phrase, Milbank, *Theology and Social Theory*, p. 279.

belief that philosophy had a privileged access to the *a priori* constitution of knowledge merely postponed the discovery of the arbitrary and cultural nature of thought. Once knowledge understands its complicity with will, it either despairs and seeks new ways of grounding itself (psychology, philosophy of language, theory of reference etc.[37]) in an exodus outside matter, corporeality and texts, or it ecstasies in the newly discovered freedom. Milbank and his colleagues, however, suggest a third alternative: a reorientation of the will towards the historical locus of divine revelation in the practices of the Christian community. If modernity should not have taken the path of an independent ontology, theology should simply return in repentance to the place it abandoned tradition and revelation.

There is within the postliberal project a constant negotiation between universality and particularity. The Christian community does not shy from offering its own master-story. But it believes that this master story guarantees the safeguarding of particularity. Its difference from rival independent ontology does not consist in the fact that it is not all-encompassing, for it is, but in the way it presents its certainty. Postliberals suggest that only Christian theology can accommodate the Other, since it alone adheres to an ontology of eternal and gifted peace.[38] But the question is whether Christian tradition is not capable of revealing a darker, more violent side by forcing itself upon the particulars?

I would like to suggest the possibility of an affirmative answer to this suspicion. This should not be taken to imply that the postliberal reaffirmation of tradition is to be discarded out of hand, but that it should make space for a proper critical attention to the possibility of ideological distortion and manipulation. Some readers may not require further demonstration of the claim that tradition may go hand in hand with oppression. However, given the fact that Vico is drafted in the service of Radical Orthodoxy, it is illustrative (and I shall leave it at that) to point out a historical connection between Vico and the Holocaust, *via* legal positivism. The Jewish connection is in fact essential to the argument of the book, as a test case for measuring the impact of the Christian meta-narrative upon the Jewish particulars (Old Testament books, Jewish historical figures and, why not, the modern Jewish nation). It is not that Vico was anti-Semitic, far from it, but he unwittingly participated in a paradigm shift which saw truth being relocated within social contexts. The truth of the law rests with the law makers. For the legal positivists there is no fact of the matter other than the particular social derivation of a given law system. But could a theology which aims to do justice to the other afford to resort exclusively to an internal justification for its actions? How might particularity, alterity and identity be preserved in face

---

[37] See Rorty's illuminating narrative in *Philosophy and the Mirror of Nature*, (Princeton: Princeton University Press, 1979), *passim*.

[38] Milbank, *Theology and Social Theory*, chapter 12.

of a 'world-absorbing' master story, albeit one recited from a non-foundational perspective? The possibility of just such an oppression seems to trouble most critics of postliberalism, especially in its Radically Orthodox guise, including some of the more sympathetic ones like Rowan Williams, who senses that 'an intellectual style that declines to engage with matters of legitimacy, or even truthfulness, if we want to be primitive, is making a strong political bid.'[39] Adolf Eichmann believed in the sufficiency of a local justification and his making use of the very ideas of legal positivism raises questions about the sufficiency of such a justification.[40] As Hannah Arendt comments in her wonderful book about Eichmann, it actually would have been immoral in his own eyes to do otherwise than as the Führer demanded. The influence of legal positivism at the end of the nineteenth century coincided with the resurgence of anti-Semitic feelings in Italy, Vienna and Berlin. Wittgenstein himself, another important partner in the present conversation, inhabited this same social atmosphere, which is not irrelevant to how his philosophy is to be understood.[41]

The point of the above 'detour' is that any appropriation of tradition, theological or otherwise, is bound to give rise to critical reservations. The historical precedent of the Holocaust shows why we must be wary of unreserved traditionalism or of the hegemony of any institution, be it the church or the state. But this very reservation might appear as itself tributary to an Enlightenment mentality. One might imagine Milbank and others asking whether this very demand of a justification which escapes the traditional and narrative constraints is not itself violent? Quite clearly, it is far from established that epistemic and political justification – which the above suspicion wants to invoke – are unblemished neutral rational procedures. Once again we find ourselves between the Scylla of a relativist occultation of the Other in the name of a local will to power, and the Charybdis of a non-narrative, putatively objective and fair legitimisation which is itself violent. Theologically the issue is whether there can truly be a mediation of the divine and of truth exclusively through local and particular languages? And if it can, is there a case to be made for a good-reasons-approach in contrast to the myopia of a 'this is what we do' attitude?

I believe a strong case must be made for the former and that the sequence of such an argument must follow an alternative direction of post-Vichian

---

[39] Rowan Williams, 'Between politics and metaphysics: reflections in the wake of Gillian Rose', *Modern Theology*, 11 (1995), 3-22, p. 4.

[40] See the excellent article by Harry Lesser, 'Political philosophy and the Holocaust', in Patrick Dunleavy and Jeffrey Stanyer, eds., *Contemporary Political Studies 1994: Proceedings of the Annual Conference Held at the University of Wales, Swansea*, 1994, pp. 663-671, in this case p. 665.

[41] Alan Janik and Stephen Toulmin, *Wittgenstein's Vienna*, (New York: Simon and Schuster, 1973), chapters 2, 6.

philosophy. This different path departs from the relativist notion of context favoured by Fish, Danto and Bloom, but also from the foundationalism they all reject. This second historical trajectory of post-Vichian philosophy, which is also a second way of recovering tradition can only be legitimated as such in practice, as we analyse in turn Hans-Georg Gadamer and Alasdair MacIntyre.

So far I have shown how modernity's self-understanding is tied to a rejection of tradition and authority in its desire to create a space of pure human autonomy. Bound with this desire is an anxiety of constraint, or what Rorty calls a philosophical urge,[42] which is the desire to ground knowledge on solid foundations. Since tradition cannot fulfil this function, it cannot be a source of truth. Gadamer rightly strives to overcome this unfortunate Enlightenment antithesis between reason and tradition. He praises Vico for returning to the *sensus communis*, but more especially for hanging on to the Roman overtones of the concept. 'For Vico, the sensus communis is the sense of what is right and of the common good that is to be found in all men; moreover it is a sense that is acquired through living in the community and is determined by its structures and aims.'[43] Theoretical and practical reason are distinct, yet they necessarily interpenetrate, argues Gadamer.[44] Being limited, theoretical knowledge solicits the help of practical wisdom, aided by rhetoric.[45] However, this does not convey the sense of a monolithic community, possessing a single practical wisdom, moving in a unitary direction, a blissful synergy of wills. The will as it is moved by the *sensus communis* will not have a single direction, but will depend upon the community itself: 'what gives the human will its direction is not the abstract universality of reason but the concrete universality represented by the community of a group, a people, a nation, or the whole human race.'[46] Gadamer describes this Vichian appeal to the *sensus communis* as having a special colouring within the humanistic tradition in that, although it serves the self-determination of the human sciences, it asserts its scientific character.

Once the sphere of the humanities is created and the principle of the *verum-factum* is applied to it, several contradictions arise.[47] The freeing of the human domain from domination by the scientific method made room for the specifically humanist concept of *fantasia*. Isaiah Berlin takes this Vichian concept to be an anticipation of the hermeneutical notion of under-

---

[42] Rorty, *Philosophy*, p. 179.
[43] Gadamer, *Truth and Method*, p. 22.
[44] Gadamer, *Truth and Method*, p. 20.
[45] Gadamer, *Truth and Method*, p. 21.
[46] Gadamer, *Truth and Method*, p. 21.
[47] Gadamer, *Truth and Method*, pp. 230ff.

standing. This is a decidedly Romantic anticipation, as Berlin further observes:

> He believed that in principle we could re-enact in our minds – 'enter' into
> by sympathetic imagination – what a class, a society, perhaps (though he
> gives no example) individuals were at; what such beings wanted, worked
> for, were after; what forwarded, what frustrated them in their search to
> satisfy their needs; the demands of social necessities and utilities in this or
> that situation; how they were affected by their own creations, cultural or
> historical.[48]

Thus *verum-factum* implied for Vico that we could know with certainty that
which we have created. And since men created history, knowledge of it was
scientifically possible. As a result, certainty is reintroduced by Vico in the
very realm where one least expected to discover it. For Dilthey and the rest
of modern historical consciousness, this amounted to a license to know
historically, because of the very historical nature of man. In Gadamer's own
words,

> Dilthey himself has pointed out that we understand historically because
> we are ourselves historical beings. This is supposed to make things easier
> epistemologically. But does it? Is Vico's oft-repeated formula correct?
> Does it not transpose an experience of the human artistic spirit to the his-
> torical world, where in the face of the course of events, once can no
> longer speak of 'making' – i.e., of planning and carrying out?[49]

There appears to be in Vico an assumption that self-mastery and self-
knowledge are possible, and it is to these assumptions that Gadamer objects. He urges that, on the contrary, 'finitude dominates not only our humanity, but also our historical consciousness.'[50] Vico thus misapprehends
the task of historical knowledge by concentrating on the *reconstruction* of
isolated mental events of creativity,[51] when in fact the actual task of historiography is *dialogue* with tradition. What for Vico can be made transparent
through its partaking in human creativity, must remain thematically undis-
closed for Gadamer, as implicit background assumptions. It is the 'non-
definitiveness of the horizon in which understanding moves,'[52] which
makes historical knowledge less assured for Gadamer than it is for Vico
and for Romantic hermeneutics. With Gadamer, tradition submerges to the
level of a subconscious condition of understanding. Vico and his avatars

---

[48] Berlin, *Three Critics*, p. 135.

[49] Gadamer, *Truth and Method*, p. 231.

[50] Gadamer, *Truth and Method*, p. 276.

[51] See Gadamer's forceful objections to Romantic hermeneutics, *Truth and Method*,
pp. 173-218.

[52] Gadamer, p. 373.

have not really solved the problem of history by positing homogeneity;[53] they in fact concealed how history becomes historicity.

In fact history does not belong to us; we belong to it. Long before we understand ourselves through the process of self-examination, we understand ourselves in a self-evident way in the family, society, and state in which we live. The focus of subjectivity is a distorting mirror. The self-awareness of the individual is only a flickering in the closed circuits of historical life. That is why the prejudices of the individual, far more than his judgements, constitute the historical reality of his being.[54]

To critics like Hans Herbert Kögler, this implies a trans-subjectivity of interpretation which is based on a 'tragic conception of what it means to belong to a tradition.'[55] The sense of tragedy derives from an alleged abandonment of the critical ability of the hermeneutical agent in the moment of interpretation. Understanding takes place in the (subconscious) interplay between the symbolic orders of agent and tradition. Kögler rightly complains that 'the subject is not in a position to bring forth *in a thematically open manner* the basic assumptions that internally determine her.'[56] He enumerates the multiple arguments by which Gadamer advances the thesis of the so-called trans-subjectivity of hermeneutics. First on this list is an argument against authorial hermeneutics.[57] Interpreting for the original intention of the author, or in order to recreate an original creative act implies trying to overcome the historical distance between past and present. It also equivalent to assuming the position of Danto's ideal chronicler,[58] and to find it impossible to perceive historical significance. Such an ideal chronicler, for instance, would be unable to specify the beginning of the Second World War, or its end for that matter, since he would lack a narrative framework which alone makes such demarcations meaningful. Gadamer correctly holds that the very meaning of a historical event, or of a linguistic sign, is given in the pattern of historically sedimented meanings which form the horizon of understanding. History and tradition are not barriers to be overcome, but they facilitate access to the truth.

Just as the author or historical agent is powerless over the meanings he manipulates, the interpreter likewise is relativised.[59] Kögler, however, sur-

---

[53] Gadamer, *Truth and Method*, p. 222.

[54] Gadamer, *Truth and Method*, pp. 276-7.

[55] Hans Herbert Kögler, *The Power of Dialogue: Critical Hermeneutics After Gadamer and Foucault*, trans. Paul Hendrickson, (Cambridge, Mass.: The MIT Press, 1996), p. 13.

[56] Kögler, *Power*, p. 25.

[57] Gadamer, *Truth and Method*, pp. 184ff; Kögler, *Power*, pp. 20-4.

[58] Arthur Danto, *Analytical Philosophy of History*, (Cambridge, 1965).

[59] Kögler, *Power*, p. 23.

mises that this argument alone does not establish the trans-subjectivity the-sis: 'the claim that 'every historian and philologist must reckon with the fundamental non-definitiveness of the horizon in which his understanding moves'[60] is nevertheless incapable of truly grounding the strong thesis of the transsubjectivity of understanding.'[61] In order to augment the thesis, Gadamer introduces a second argument which underlines the holistic char-acter of pre-understanding, 'which makes every reflective performance of the subject dependent on the symbolic context of a historical tradition.'[62] Since understanding depends on a multitude of factors, most of which are unknown and unknowable, the interpreter is in a position to have his meanings dictated to him by the tradition. However, Kögler suggests that this argument is again not able to establish such a strong ontological thesis. Although the contents of one's symbolic order may be partly (or even mostly) unconscious, there is no reason that such contents should not be presentable to consciousness.[63]

Kögler has Habermasian misgivings about the fact that one may remain subject to a tradition which is suspect of ideological manipulation. If one denies certain methodological provisions for critique, there is nothing to prevent such a manipulation. It should be pointed out that the trans-subjective character of understanding reflects as much on the self as on the other. For Gadamer this is also a way of underscoring the irreducible par-ticularity of the other. There are not two selves which have the same sym-bolic construction and which are the result of the same sociological circum-stances. Each individual is unique. But it is how this uniqueness is con-structed that prompts reservations in several ideologically sensitive readers, like Kögler, E. D. Hirsch[64], P. D. Juhl[65] and others. More recently the late Gillian Rose has expressed serious reservations against this loss of dis-crimination which she denounces as jeopardising the very project of a phi-losophy of alterity.[66] Knowledge is too hastily abandoned, she laments, following the discovery of its involvement with power and domination.

> But by renouncing knowledge as power, we are then only ale to demand expiation for total domination, for we have disqualified any possible in-

---

[60] Gadamer, *Truth and Method*, p. 373.

[61] Kögler, *Power*, p. 24.

[62] Kögler, *Power*, p. 25.

[63] Kögler, *Power*, p. 29.

[64] E. D. Hirsch, *Validity in Interpretation*, (New Haven: Yale University Press, 1967).

[65] P. D. Juhl, *Interpretation: An Essay in the Philosophy of Literary Criticism*, (Princeton: Princeton University Press, 1980).

[66] See especially *Mourning Becomes the Law: Philosophy and Representation*, (Cambridge: Cambridge University Press, 1996).

vestigation into the dynamics of the configuration and reconfiguration of power – which is our endless predicament.[67]

This is in fact a denouncing of a false dualism between a socially constructed knowledge and objectivist epistemologies fuelled by the notions of correspondence, mind, Being or whatever. Kögler's position understands and approves the hermeneutical modification of Vico's stance with respect to the 'event-ness' of understanding, yet it argues that too much is made of this from an ontological point of view. Event-ness need not imply the loss of interpretive agency. The prospect of losing agency haunts us since Vico and it seems it is carried forward by Gadamer's neglect of the critical self.

However, there may be reason to suppose that Kögler's criticism of Gadamer assumes too much about the intended strength of the latter's view of trans-subjectivity. I want to draw the attention to a few markers which point in the direction of a more optimistic Gadamer. He stresses that traditions themselves are to be sustained through the very work of interpreters. This constitutes the fulcrum of his argument against modernity's confusion of authority with authoritarianism. The former is based on acknowledgement, rather than obedience. The very connection of tradition with recognition, which also distinguished itself from the uncritical Romantic acceptance of authority,[68] implies that a critical task remains to be accomplished. If tradition is not to be reified, a notion to which we shall return later, it 'needs to be affirmed, embraced, cultivated. It is essentially preservation, and it is active in all historical change. But preservation is an act of reason, although an inconspicuous one.'[69] And again, 'we do not conceive of what tradition says as something other, something alien. It is always part of us, a model or exemplar...'[70] This is not to say that the acts of rational agents are themselves free from tradition. Georgia Warnke draws attention to the concept of *Wirkungsgeschichte*, which is 'the operative force of the tradition over those who belong to it so that even in rejecting or reacting to it they remain conditioned by it.'[71]

So it remains possible to be conditioned by something and to react to it at the same time. This does not mean that the reaction itself is fake, or illusory, but simply that the conditioning is not complete. Kögler departs from Gadamer's model on the grounds that for the latter tradition obstructs understanding. The way he conceives the model for dialogue between self and tradition un-permissively inhibits critical agency, he suspects. Yet a closer

---

[67] Rose, *Mourning*, p. 21.

[68] Gadamer, *Truth and Method*, p. 281.

[69] Gadamer, *Truth and Method*, p. 281.

[70] Gadamer, *Truth and Method*, p. 282.

[71] Georgia Warnke, *Gadamer: Hermeneutics, Tradition and Reason*, (Stanford: Stanford University Press, 1987), p. 79.

look at Gadamer's linguistic ontology suggests that perhaps such an assumption is hasty. In his appendix to *Truth and Method* entitled 'Does Language Preform Thought?' it becomes clear that to appropriately understand
his linguistic holism one must understand that he does not treat language as
a depository of accomplished meanings, which inherently limit the extent of
thought:

> To sum up, I would say that the misunderstanding in the question of the
> linguisticality of our understanding is really one about language – i.e.,
> seeing language as a stock of words and phrases, of concepts, viewpoints
> and opinions. In fact language is the single word, whose virtuality opens
> for us the infinity of discourse, of speaking with one another, of freedom
> of 'expressing oneself' and 'letting oneself be expressed'. Language is
> not its elaborated conventionalism, nor the burden of pre-schematization
> with which it loads us, but the generative and creative power to increas-
> ingly make this whole once fluent.[72]

It follows that tradition, although it conditions thought, does not constitute a
rigid, reified structure, but a flexible and agency-constituted (as well as
agency-constitutive) habitus in which tactical moves can still be made. For
this reason the very notion of relativist traditions and incommensurable
paradigms is absent in Gadamer. Such notions presuppose that meanings
are closed and determinate.[73] Herein lies the difference between Gadamer,
on the one hand, and Fish, Danto and Bloom on the other. For the later, as I
will show presently, tradition is spatialised and it is alienated from critical
selves. For Gadamer, on the contrary, tradition is historical, a temporary
engagement with a subject matter, or an object. Gadamer applies Heidegger's temporality of the *Dasein* and locates the 'structure of care'in history
itself. Hence the symbolic order presupposed by interpretation is not an
arbitrary collection of conventions and concepts which obstructs understanding, but it is a historically sedimented meaning built through a series
of engagements with the text.[74]

To conclude this engagement with Gadamer, if the transparency of tradition involves a danger of agency loss, such a danger can be alleviated[75] and

---

[72] Gadamer, *Truth and Method*, p. 549.

[73] See Warnke, *Gadamer*, p. 82.

[74] For Gadamer this historical space is also the place where bad prejudgements are
separated from the useful ones (p. 266). But see Anthony Thiselton's reservations in *The
Two Horizons: New Testament Hermeneutics and Philosophical Description with Special Reference to Heidegger, Bultmann, Gadamer and Wittgenstein*, (Grand Rapids:
Eerdmans, 1980), p. 315; also Warnke, *Gadamer*, p. 82.

[75] Kögler suggests that the monopoly of tradition may be broken in the process of en-
countering rival traditions which challenge one's own. The solution he offers is akin to
that of MacIntyre, see below.

is not endemic to Gadamer's thought as a whole. Furthermore, Gadamer's view of tradition entails that members of one tradition may successfully understand members of differing traditions.[76] It is precisely such an exercise that promises to make what was hidden and transparent into what is visible and open to scrutiny. The work of Alasdair MacIntyre carries the contemporary retrieval of tradition in an even more promising direction.

Alasdair MacIntyre and Stanley Fish on Tradition

The Enlightenment conception of autonomous reason forgets its own arbitrariness, or what Milbank prefers to call its mythic character. It abandons the locality and positivity of tradition in favour of a disembodied intellection. Yet, as MacIntyre remarks, the intellectual landscape which results from this evasion of the tradition is composed only of fragments of disembodied traditions and rationalities. His *After Virtue* takes the contemporary failure of moral discourse to be a necessary result of employing concepts removed from their social and historical settings.[77] Estranged from the original context and from a tradition of normative use, these concepts have almost degenerated into meaninglessness. The perception of this failure of modernity has led to the rediscovery of sources such as Aquinas and Vico. The resulting postmodern cultural geography undergoes something of a re-enchantment with narratives.

MacIntyre undoubtedly stands in the tradition of Vico by affirming that moral concepts do not exist apart from their social embodiment. Robert Miner rightly points out against critics who have complained about the 'confused' nature of *After Virtue* – whether it is a work of philosophy or of history – that they fail to recognise that 'any adequate comprehension of rational philosophy will exhibit it narratively, as the end product of a tradition whose roots are in the pre-rational soil of custom and myth.'[78] Indeed, the fusion between reason and narrative is perhaps MacIntyre's most interesting contribution to the contemporary philosophical debate. Yet his proposals do not amount to a relativising of truth to the various backgrounds which dispute it. Although context is constitutive of rationality, there is another, non-relativist way of describing the connection. The very way in which he understands what tradition denotes is not unrelated to the more positive proposals he makes in reference to rationality.

---

[76] Gadamer, *Truth and Method*, p. 546.

[77] Alasdair MacIntyre, *After Virtue: A Study in Moral Theory*, (Notre Dame: University of Notre Dame Press, 1984^2), pp. 6-22.

[78] Robert Miner, in an unpublished part of the book manuscript on Vico. The book was published under the title *Vico: Genealogist of Modernity*, (Notre Dame: University of Notre Dame Press, 2002).

Julia Annas points out that MacIntyre doesn't anywhere characterise tradition in general, but works with specific historical traditions from the discussion of which a certain meaning of tradition emerges.[79] This is not entirely correct, and I shall mention his own attempts at definition. The matter of definition is important in this case and the following two definitions underline subtle differences of nuance which might prove important. George Stroup writes that tradition 'refers to more than simply a collection of creeds and confessions, more than simply a museum of theological artefacts; it refers to the whole history of the church's interpretation of Scripture and therefore the living history of its understanding of faith.'[80] A slightly different orientation, perhaps idiosyncratically sociological, is visible in Timothy Luke's description of tradition as a set of conventions, a set of rules which regulate cultural and social life.[81] While Stroup conceives tradition in historical terms, Luke tends to allow a territorial element to govern the notion: tradition as a matrix of rules and conventions. This is symptomatic of a certain trend in modern philosophy to reify the background even to the point of subliminally ascribing agency to it.

For MacIntyre, on the other hand,

> A tradition is an argument extended through time in which certain fundamental agreements are defined and redefined in terms of two kinds of conflict: those with critics and enemies external to the tradition who reject all or at least key parts of the fundamental agreements, and those internal, interpretative debates through which the meaning and rationale of the fundamental agreements come to be expressed and by whose progress a tradition is constituted.[82]

One of his earlier sporadic attempts at a definition reads: 'a living tradition is an historically extended, socially embodied argument, and an argument precisely in part about the goods which constitute that tradition.' Several points of interest may be underlined. There is no trace, or at least very little mention of the conventionalism of Luke in MacIntyre. Although it is undeniable that what tradition establishes does condition what may presently and coherently be said from within that tradition, it does not legislate on the whole domain of rationality. On the other hand, MacIntyre's definitions

---

[79] Julia Annas, 'MacIntyre on traditions', *Philosophy and Public Affairs* 18 (1989), 388-415, p.389.

[80] George Stroup, *The Promise of Narrative Theology*, (London: SCM, 1984), p. 31.

[81] Timothy Luke, 'Identity, meaning and globalisation: de-traditionalisation in postmodern time-space compression', in Paul Heelas, Scott Lash, Paul Morris, eds., *De-Traditionalisation: Critical Reflections on Authority and Identity in a Time of Uncertainty*, (Oxford: Blackwell, 1996), p. 111.

[82] Alasdair MacIntyre, *Whose Justice? Which Rationality?*, (Notre Dame: University of Notre Dame Press, 1988), p. 12.

stress the argumentative rather than the arbitrary. Tradition is not simply conventional delimitation of space, but also temporal interaction with a given good. In this respect, as Miner observes, MacIntyre and Vico are once again in agreement: both wish to combine a type of historicism with a teleological ethic.[83] By anchoring tradition to the *summum bonum*, MacIntyre is providing an alternative to the contemporary relegation of tradition to myth and arbitrariness. Indeed, one of the ironies of the present discussion is that it re-imports the prejudices of the Enlightenment against tradition by failing to see its connection with truth. For MacIntyre, as well as Gadamer, tradition enables the expression of truth.

It is useful to distinguish between two levels on which tradition functions as a concept in the philosophy of MacIntyre. On an ontological level, tradition contributes to the creation of agents' identity, while on the epistemological level it determines the conditions of knowledge. To understand a text, a person, or an action involves situating that unit on the larger background:

> We cannot, that is to say, characterise behaviour independently of intentions, and we cannot characterise intentions independently of the settings which make those intentions intelligible both to agents themselves and to others. I use the word 'setting' here as a relatively inclusive term. A social setting may be an institution, it may be what I have called a practice, or it may be a milieu of some other human kind. But it is central to the notion of setting as I am going to understand it that a setting has a history, a history within which the histories of individual agents not only are, but have to be situated, just because without the setting and its changes through time the history of the individual agent and his changes through time will be unintelligible.[84]

We as selves can only make sense on the background of some setting. This is the positive function of tradition, as Gadamer also shows. A self can only relinquish tradition at the cost of losing coherence and intelligibility. Indeed, this is the fulcrum of MacIntyre's critique of both modern and postmodern thought in his *Three Rival Versions of Moral Inquiry*.[85] The self cannot be thought of apart from the roles that it is playing in the setting which it inhabits. Arguing against an atomistic conception of self, he holds that its unity is the unity of a story.[86] This view is complicated by the recognition that 'we are never more (and sometimes less) than the co-authors of our own narratives.'[87] Here the ontological function of tradition is visi-

---

[83] Miner, unpublished manuscript, p. 225.

[84] MacIntyre, *After Virtue*, p. 206.

[85] (London: Duckworth, 1990), pp. 17-216, esp. 205-10.

[86] MacIntyre, *After Virtue*, p. 205.

[87] MacIntyre, *After Virtue*, p. 213.

ble. He seems to be advocating a form of ontological constructivism such as
the one to which Kögler has reacted in relation to Gadamer. However, understanding his notion of rationality helps dispel such suspicions. Critical
agency is retained at least in part: 'I am the subject of a history that is my
own and no-one else's, that has its own peculiar meaning.'[88] Such a notion
of self is arguably indispensable for a moral philosopher of virtue, for
whom the concept of responsibility, presupposed as it is by the cultivation
of virtue, cannot simply be dispensed with. He is very careful indeed to
keep a distance from social constructivism while at the same time acknowledging a level of construction. The argument that I would like to put forward is that to grasp the temporality of tradition, in the manner in which
MacIntyre is aware of it, is to understand that it is an argument extended
through time, therefore an agent-sustained institution concerned with the
very end of that tradition. Spatial images of setting will tend to obstruct the
necessity of agency as the sustaining force of the background itself, underscoring instead the arbitrary nature of social conventions. To schematise,
this means that on the first, temporal model, tradition recedes to the background, enabling knowledge and truth, while for the second, spatial model,
it pre-forms thought and pre-determines truth and knowledge.

It is essential for MacIntyre that the traditional and social embeddedness
of arguments does not preclude their claim to truth. Both Gadamer and
MacIntyre stress the positive and enabling nature of setting, as in fact Vico
does too. For the later, as we saw, there is no knowledge which does not
presuppose human making. Truth can only be discovered in the web of rituals and in human *poiesis*. Yet, as Milbank points out, Vico never separated
this human making from its participation in divine *poiesis*. Hence, being
made is a necessary, but not sufficient condition for truth in the human
realm. *Poiesis* must be grounded in *pathos*[89] to be relevant for truth. Mac-
Intyre does not conceive tradition as a *poiesis* which undercuts all attempts
to mediate truth and reality other than the locally entrenched opinion. His
whole project for the reconstruction of rationality is geared to allow for a
strong conception of truth and realism from within a contextual and socially
sensitive rationality.

The social and traditional construction of rationality does not leave us
with mere rhetoric or manipulation. To be sure, 'there is no neutral way of
characterising either the subject matter about which they give rival accounts, or the standards by which they are evaluated.'[90] The legitimate
worry is that this leads to the disappearance of the subject matter itself. If
all our understandings of the subject matter are in fact preformed by the

---

[88] MacIntyre, *After Virtue*, p. 217.

[89] Cf. Reinhard Hütter, *Suffering Divine Things: Theology as Church Practice*, trans.
Doug Stott, (Grand Rapids: Eerdmans, 2000), p. 47.

[90] MacIntyre, *Whose Justice?*, p. 166.

symbolic orders which we inhabit, then there is nothing external to the scheme. The scheme itself cannot be put into question by anything, or if it is, the dispute will not be decided by reason, since there is no such thing as reason without authority. Furthermore, if traditions are incommensurable, we seem to be left with closed systems which legislate all possible moves within them. The notion that knowledge is local and informed by concepts which have histories does not mean that all knowledge is regulated by the sedimented rules of a given setting. To suppose this is to reify the notion of setting.

Since a tradition depends on agency and recognition for its authority, some of its beliefs are always and under certain conditions put into question.'[91] Some feeling for the difficulty of MacIntyre's position is given by the following:

> Notice also that the fact that the self has to find its moral identity in and through membership in communities such as those of the family, the neighborhood, the city and the tribe does not entail that the self has to accept the moral limitations of the particularity of those forms of community... yet particularity can never be simply left behind or obliterated. The notion of escaping from it into a realm of entirely universal maxims which belong to man as such, whether in its eighteenth century Kantian form or in the presentation of some modern analytical moral philosophers is an illusion and an illusion with painful consequences.[92]

Even while arguments can never escape the entanglements of a particular *episteme*, it does not follow that they are only intelligible from within that tradition. One of the more problematic and disputed aspects of MacIntyre's proposals is an argument for inter-traditional rationality based on the learning of a second first language. The agent, he suggests, can achieve critical distance from his own tradition (although only on specific matters and not from the entire tradition), yet this will always take place within some social context.[93] It is in the encounter between traditions that one realises the relativity of one's own and learns to perceive differently. This is obviously not a formal freedom from all tradition, but a material escape from a particular determination into a recognition of other ways of conceiving the matter. Indeed, it is in the encounter between traditions that this process of criticism takes place.[94]

---

[91] Alasdair MacIntyre, 'Epistemological Crises, Dramatic Narrative and the Philosophy of Science', *The Monist* 60 (1977), 453-472, reprinted in Stanley Hauerwas and G. L. Jones eds., *Why Narrative? Readings in Narrative Theology*, (Grand Rapids: Eerdmans, 1989), p. 147.

[92] MacIntyre, *After Virtue*, p. 221.

[93] MacIntyre, 'Epistemological Crises', p. 147.

[94] This is also Bert Kögler's argument, *Power*, pp. 159-179.

The possibility to which every tradition is always open, as I argued earlier, is that the time and place may come, when and where those who live their lives in and through the language-in-use which gives expression to it may encounter another alien tradition with its own very different language-in-use and may discover that while in some area of greater or lesser importance they cannot comprehend it within the terms of reference set by their own beliefs, their own history, and their own language-in-use, it provides a standpoint from which once they have acquired its language-in-use as a second first language, the limitations, incoherences and poverty of resources of their own beliefs can be identified, characterised, and explained in a way not possible from within their own tradition.[95]

Critique is a function of dialogue with and understanding another tradition. Members of one community can indeed understand those from other communities, through 'empathetic conceptual imagination', a notion resembling and partly inspired from Vico's *fantasia*. Both Vico and MacIntyre introduce issues that will acquire some significance in the present study. For example, one suspects that MacIntyre assumes a deficient notion of rhetoric, acquired less through contact with Vico and more through both ancient and modern prejudice. Neither, however, considers the question of truth to be irrelevant. The textual constraints imposed upon knowledge do not preclude access to what counts as reality. Needless to say that the way this access is conceived is radically revised. Both Vico and MacIntyre raise questions about the possibility of translation, a notion destined to gain importance together with the rise of the notion of background. I shall argue in later chapters that background, however ubiquitous and constructive, underdetermines reality and truth. It seems, however, that a predisposition to underline the spatial dimension of tradition leaves less room for inquiry into its legitimacy, while it will tend to over-emphasise its conventional nature.

Stanley Fish has emerged as another increasingly suggestive philosopher and literary theorist for narrative theology. His influence on the movement is felt especially in the theology of Stanley Hauerwas[96], although he is by no means the only narrativist writing under his influence. A number of postliberal thinkers such as James McClendon, David Kelsey and Nancey Murphy claim to have learned from him at one point or another. But it is especially Hauerwas who, perhaps due to a certain similarity of style and rhetoric, has introduced the work of Fish to the theological community. In *Unleashing the Scripture: Freeing the Bible from Captivity to America*,[97] Hauerwas points out the congeniality of their respective projects. Hauer-

---

[95] MacIntyre, *Whose Justice?*, p. 388.

[96] See the wonderful article of Alan Jacobs, 'A Tale of Two Stanleys', *First Things* 44 (1994), 18-21.

[97] (Nashville: Abingdon, 1993).

was' political agenda of liberating the Gospel from its idolatrous identification with 'Americanism' is theoretically consolidated with Fish's account of the political nature of interpretation.[98] The influence Fish exerts on Hauerwas, although by no means uncritical, is illustrative of the impact of what Thiselton calls socio-pragmatic hermeneutics upon biblical studies.

The hermeneutical journey undertook by Fish resembles that of Hans Frei, which I shall discuss in the next chapter. William Ray helpfully distinguishes between two emphases characteristic of different stages in Fish's writing career.[99] From an understanding of the action of the text upon the reader (formalism and reader-response) Fish came to stress the way in which the text itself is determined by the reader. An earlier textual theory, similar in some respects to Wolfgang Iser's proposal that there are formal units or gaps in the text which force the reader into certain exegetic moves, gave way to an understanding of meaning as determined by the interpretive community. Fish became increasingly aware, and with good reason, that the ontological force placed on the structures of the text as such cannot be borne by it alone. The flow of the text, its direction, its force, all these had to be recognised in order to become effective. Furthermore, such a recognition could not be imposed from within the text, but has to have an outside source. The text is therefore supplemented with external decisions which determine its meaning. However, Fish does not stop here. He further suggests that this heteronomous determination of the text is of such a degree that the text itself is lost as an object and can only be recovered as a reconstruction. We are witnessing something like a Kantian idealism in literary theory. A text depends for its stability, unity, meaning, force on the active support of the community. Stability and unity are no longer textual properties. It is in fact the text itself which turns out to be the effect of a political activity:

> That is to say, both the stability of interpretation among readers and the variety of interpretations in the career of a single reader would seem to argue for the existence of something independent of and prior to interpretive acts, something which produces them. I will answer this challenge by

---

[98] For similar accounts, see Frank Lenttrichia, *After the New Criticism*, (London: Athlone, 1980); Frank Kermode, *The Genesis of Secrecy: On the Interpretation of Narrative*, (Cambridge, Mass. and London: Cambridge, Mass. and London: Harvard University Press, 1979); Fredric Jameson, *The Political Unconscious: Narrative as a Socially Symbolic Act*, (London: Methuen, 1981).

[99] William Ray, *Literary Meaning: From Phenomenology to Deconstruction*, (Oxford: Blackwell, 1984), p. 154.

asserting that both the stability and the variety are functions of interpretive strategies rather than of texts.[100]

The pattern that may be observed is that realism comes increasingly under attack as soon as a strong and constitutive notion of background is adopted. The disappearance of the object is almost complete in Fish's version of social constructivism, yet one wonders whether the solution he offers is not unnecessarily reductionist. This is at any rate what I shall argue.

Texts do not subsist as stable entities waiting to be read and appropriated. Fish doesn't suffer from any anxiety of constraint. The task of hermeneutics does not consists in digging up the objective text in order to ground interpretation on stable ground. Returning to tradition and community relieves the anxiety. Social pragmatism construes setting as the ineluctable screen through which we perceive what is otherwise absent, or present only in myth, the myth of the given text. Reading is always 'reading as'.[101] There is no unmediated and uneducated access to the facts: interpretation goes all the way down. Our concepts are embedded in the social practices of the community in which we happen to live, they are 'institutionally nested'.[102] Three related functions of the interpretive communities deserve mention.

a) Construction of texts. Fish eventually disallowed an earlier preference for the flow of the text which draws the reader to participate creatively, and deconstructed the very notion of text. Neither texts, nor the histories of their reception are brute facts. These only become available through a strategy, as they play a part in a socially-semiotic system, in a web of practices and political interests which determine what counts as fact. This entails an anti-realist ontology.

b) Creation of meaning. An either/or approach seems to be favoured by Fish with regard to meaning: either it is discovered in the text, or it is made, created. Clearly, meaning cannot be discovered since this would assume an uninhibited access to the text itself. Nor could it be the creation of the solitary reader, who could thus construct any meaning he intends. Fish devotes lengthy discussions to refuting the notion of a radically creative reader.[103] To accept this possibility is to entertain the notion of a 'dead space'[104], where no meanings are ascribed and substance patiently awaits the imposi-

---

[100] Stanley Fish, *Is There a Text in This Class? The Authority of Interpretive Communities*, (Cambridge, Mass.: Cambridge, Mass. and London: Harvard University Press, 1980), p. 168.

[101] Fish, *Is There a Text*, p. 309.

[102] Fish, *Is There a Text*, p. 309.

[103] Fish, *Is There a Text?*, pp. 321, 342; Stanley Fish, *Doing What Comes Naturally: Change, Rhetoric and the Practice of Theory in Literary and Legal Studies*, (Durham and London: Duke University Press, 1989), pp. 11, 98.

[104] Fish, *Is There a Text*, p. 318.

tion of form. But there is no such gap between reading and ascribing meaning since the community always already fills it, tacitly supplying meanings and rules for what may count as a possible interpretation.[105]

c) Limitation of relativism. Since there is no 'dead space', the community always legislates on what is proper reading. Fish's point, not necessarily original but certainly insightful, is that relativism only makes sense on the backdrop of a dead space. But when meanings are already distributed and rules are in force, interpretation appears as less than arbitrary. Relativism thus becomes an impossible option[106] because the interpreter is not able to step outside the structure of constraints of his own community. Since there is no freedom from institutional assumptions[107] even apparently radical interpretations are only possible on the basis of a substantial agreement with and submission to communitarian hermeneutical rules. There are obvious parallels here a point made by Gadamer, namely that even in dissenting from a given tradition one is a follower of it. In short, it is the community that dictates the preferences of interpretation: 'all preferences are principled (...) but by the same token, all principles are preferences.'[108]

I want to argue that while Gadamer's and MacIntyre's notions of tradition have more resources to escape reification, Fish comes perilously close to it. In MacIntyre's opinion, traditions change during their historical interaction with what they perceive as their proper object, as well as through dialogue with other traditions. The flux of various historical interpretations contrasts sharply with the stability of the object of inquiry, the *summum bonum* of the tradition itself. The former is what gives tradition a reason for its very existence, it is its end of inquiry. Change is seen retrospectively as a result of engagement with a subject matter. It will tend to appear as a less than arbitrary process, although not an objectively legislated one. However, it must be pointed out, the transitions which a given tradition undergoes appear rational from the perspective of so-called present science. Crucially, this perspective is itself traditional and not a neutral discourse. The interpretation of historical change as less than arbitrary and putatively rational is still a historical judgment, made from the perspective of a present view on reality and on the subject matter of a tradition. This acknowledgement is pivotal in any discussion of realism, correspondence theories and representationalism, such as will be carried out in later chapters. The fact that we have no God's eye point of view on things, does indeed suggest that we have no coherent way of arguing for realism. By the same token, however, nor can we argue for non-realism. Having said this, it still has to be emphasised that even from the perspective of present knowledge (as opposed to

---

[105] Fish, *Is There a Text?*, pp. 338-55.

[106] Fish, *Is There a Text*, p. 319.

[107] Fish, *Is There a Text*, p. 321.

[108] Fish, *Doing What Comes Naturally*, p. 11.

ideal knowledge) changes of tradition are less than arbitrary and that there is a *reasonableness* attaching to what MacIntyre calls narrative shifts.

As I shall point out, Fish's account of conceptual change is entirely unsatisfactory for reasons having to do with his reification of community and his reductionist solution to the issue of unity. Before that critique it will be helpful to see how it has come about that social constructivism is so much at home in postliberal circles.

Postliberal Notions of Setting

The thinkers which have been briefly engaged have a common quarrel with the idea of an autonomous self. Related to this conception of selfhood is the view that knowledge achieves certainty when all prejudgements have been removed, when all opinion has given way to hard facts. What has been called 'anxiety of constraint' extends to secular as well as to theological knowledge. The desire to clear the ground for a univocal theological language resulted in banishing God from the realm of the speakable. Radically Enlightened thinkers such as Vico, Hamann and others realised, however, that the seeds of the ruin of modernity lie with its own roots, in a mythical postulation of Being. Conversely, theologians like Milbank have argued that nihilism becomes a prospect for modernity only once it abandons theological participation. It is possible that such arguments are but theological echoes of suggestions made by Gadamer and Rorty. Nonetheless, it is not surprising that theology, especially through the postliberal voice, has taken such an interest in the new intellectual ethos.

The awakening of theology to a sense of the background conditions of knowledge materialised in a double emphasis on 'practice' and 'rules', which are endemic to the idea of setting. Such an interest derived partly from MacIntyre's arguments in *After Virtue*, Wittgenstein's reformulation of the 'theory' of meaning, as well as from Sellars' attack on the myth of the given.[109] The common argument of these philosophers is that any account of knowledge and rationality must take into consideration the social practices, within which language and rational justification make sense. Since language is an activity, embedded in practices, meaning can no longer be defined as a mental entity, which is discovered and which forges a mysterious relation between word, concepts and things. A theologian who during his life has shown an increasing interest in Wittgenstein writes: 'the great positive gain the Wittgensteinian account offers is to show language not on the *Tractatus* model of propositions picturing clusters of atomic facts, but on a model thoroughly woven into the fabric of human (linguistic

---

[109] W. Sellars, 'Empiricism and the Philosophy of Mind' in *Science, Perception and Reality*, (New York: Humanities Press, 1963).

and other) activity.'[110] The meaning of propositions is not established by a direct relationship to the objects or states of affairs they designate, but are connected to the actions in which people use those propositions. In these activities they play specific roles and it is these roles that give their meaning. It follows that legitimising those propositions is no longer a matter of checking them against the bare facts, against reality. Since truth presupposes meaning, knowledge must always return to the practical context of life which endows sentences with meaning. 'Forms of life', another concept popularised (rather than invented) by Wittgenstein[111] defines the context of theology. Although the concept itself appears only a half a dozen times in Wittgenstein's work[112], it began to be employed with great urgency in theology, most clearly under the alias of 'practice'.

James Wm. McClendon, Jr., was perhaps one of the most neglected postliberal theologians. It is only recently that his work has started to received the attention he deserves. In one of his earlier publications, *Understanding Religious Convictions*,[113] a collaborative effort with James M. Smith, an atheist philosopher, he underscores the importance of practices for the meaning of religious assertions. This essay in religious philosophy of language, or more generally philosophy of religion, argues that the cultural setting, alongside the grammatical conventions of a given language, is crucial to the determination of meaning. He discusses the felicity of religious speech acts in the context of speech acts in general and writes: 'ethos works with language to specify the conditions of happy bread requesting.' Already in 1975, long before any sustained theological argument with speech act theory, McClendon was making serious theological use of Austin and Searle.[114] The existence of a linguistic community with its social

---

[110] James Wm. McClendon, Jr., 'Ludwig Wittgenstein: A Christian in Philosophy', *Scottish Journal of Theology*, 51 (1998), 131-161, p. 152.

[111] The concept was common place in Wittgenstein's Vienna, it was also used by Goethe and goes as far back as Schleiermacher. See Alan Janik and Stephen Toulmin, *Wittgenstein's Vienna*, (New York: Simon and Schuster, 1973), p. 230.

[112] Hans Johann Glock, *A Wittgenstein Dictionary*, (Oxford: Blackwell, 1996), p. 127.

[113] (Notre Dame: University of Notre Dame Press, 1975), p. 108.

[114] Anthony C. Thiselton has been one of the pioneers of the use of speech act theory in biblical studies. See 'Communicative Action and Promise in Interdisciplinary, Biblical and Theological Hermeneutics', in A. C. Thiselton, C. Walhout and R. Lundin, *The Promise of Hermeneutics*, (Grand Rapids: Wm. B. Eerdmans, 1999). His work was followed by that of Wolterstorff, *Divine Discourse: Philosophical Reflections on the Claim that God Speaks*, (Cambridge: Cambridge University Press, 1995) and by Thiselton's student, Richard Briggs, *Words in Action: Speech Act Theory and Biblical Interpretation: Towards a Hermeneutic of Self-Involvment*, (Edinburgh: T&T Clark, 2001), among others.

practices is what guarantees the stability of meaning for McClendon. Practices are the bedrock of our speech and communication. Speech, knowledge and practice involve each other in a holistic web. Such reflections helped bring theology closer to the general philosophical climate of a disenchantment with what may be called a 'pernicious mentalism', to echo Quine. Several philosophical developments together contributed to this change of atmosphere: Wittgenstein's post-Tractarian reflections, the general resurgence of American pragmatism, inspired as it was by its encounter with Continental logical positivists exiled to the United States, as well as developments in philosophy of language, not least of which was speech-act theory. While all of these denounced earlier modes of philosophising, the particular lesson taught by speech-act theory was that speaking is just another form of action.[115] The erasure of a hard distinction between performatives and constatives,[116] opens the possibility for a more promising approach which treats all utterances as kinds of actions,[117] having the sort of linguistic liability and linguistic asset which performative acts have been taken to possess. The concept of practice therefore acquires a double force: meanings take shape on the background of practice and, secondly, speaking is also a kind of action, with its constitutive rules and conventions.

The problem which emerges is that there are two senses in which background may be taken as constitutive. There is first the weak sense in which it stabilises meaning, and secondly there is the strong sense of legislating what counts as a true or false assertion. The choice between one of these readings splits narrativists and it will provide the focus of a later discussion.

Once assertions are treated as performatives, issues of truth give way to issues of felicity. Although McClendon sometimes seems tempted by the prospect, he does not do away with the question of truth altogether, since one of the conditions for felicity is representative, or descriptive.[118]The question remains, however, whether this reorientation of theology and indeed knowledge towards its background conditions leads with necessity to what McClendon calls 'hard perspectivism.'[119] If truth becomes a matter of felicity and felicity is parasitic upon performing the *right* sorts of actions and having the *right* practical knowledge and wisdom, this would seem to imply that meanings and truths are local and only available to members of the same community. The following critical questions therefore seems inevitable: does the return of theology to practice not involve a renewed danger of ideological distortion? If setting determines meaning, conditions for

---

[115] McClendon and Smith, *Understanding*, pp. 49-59.

[116] McClendon and Smith, *Understanding*, p. 63.

[117] James Wm. McClendon, Jr., *Ethics: Systematic Theology I*, (Nashville: Abingdon, 1990), p. 335.

[118] McClendon and Smith, *Understanding*, p. 59.

[119] McClendon and Smith, *Understanding*, p. 78.

truth and the strategies of legitimation, there is very little room left for truly subversive readings and actions.

There cannot be a straightforward and definitive answer to this question. But the question itself should make us attentive with respect to what 'local' is supposed to mean and to how 'practice' is conceived. As it will emerge from the whole discussion, there is a fallacious way of conceiving locality, practices, meanings as being on the whole fixed. If theology is to return to such a notion of practice, it may be argued that it is an altogether unfortunate and undesirable return. McClendon himself is very much aware of the danger of ideological distortion and manipulation. He is also aware of the whole debate which perhaps forcefully opposed Habermas to Gadamer. The latter's optimistic construal of tradition as enabling meaning naturally lead to hard discussions about the extent to which tradition dominates selves. The notion of practice carries the same difficulty. But, if we cannot escape the entanglements of practices, how may we, so to speak, step outside of them in order to critically examine them? McClendon's solution is to propose a practice which contains within itself its own corrective: the practice of Bible reading.[120] But this suggestion is deeply flawed, unless a further clarification of just how connected knowledge is to practice, because McClendon seems to forget some of his most important insights. He supposes that Scripture is 'objectively *there*, a given.'[121] However, it may be replied, if practices go all the way down, and this is the thrust of any holist epistemology, the possibility of establishing what is given is foreclosed. Why should one suppose that Scripture, or rather Scripture reading should escape the practical conventions which govern its meaning, and indeed its very recognition as *Scripture*? What one 'recognises' to be *there* is always given as part of another *theory*, embedded within another *practice*.

With Stanley Hauerwas, such scruples about what is objectively there and ideological distortion are not really the issue. In *A Community of Character*,[122] he laments the emphasis on the Bible as revelation, considering it to be detrimental to understanding the role of the church in using the Bible.[123] The confusion of Bible with revelation leads to the wrong belief that anybody can grasp its meaning. One of his central claims is about the necessity of ecclesial practices for the correct understanding of the Bible. He understands community in institutional terms: 'a community is a group of

---

[120] Recognising the risk of ideological distortion, McClendon explicitly refuses to ground doctrine upon any other practice such as worship, preaching, etc. *Doctrine: Systematic Theology II*, (Nashville: Abingdon, 1994), pp. 34,35.

[121] McClendon, *Doctrine*, p. 41 (his emphasis).

[122] Stanley Hauerwas, *A Community of Character: Towards a Constructive Christian Social Ethic*, (Notre Dame: University of Notre Dame Press, 1981).

[123] Hauerwas, *Community*, p. 59.

persons who share a history and whose common set of interpretations about that history provide the basis for common actions.'[124]

It must be said that the presence of a historical element here is significant, for it opens the possibility for critical revision of the conventions and rules of community, just as MacIntyre's diachronic notion of setting provides for a critical stance with regard to tradition. For Hauerwas in particular, the historical perception of setting brings out the fact that the church is itself constituted by Scripture. It is this formative force of the texts which is absent in Fish.[125] The anti-formalist road is a one-way journey for Fish. He does not even consider the possibility of a dialectical and mutually constructive relationship between text and community. It is therefore surprising that Hauerwas does not challenge him on this account, although it may have to do with the fact that Fish is not concerned with religious texts as such. But it is after all Fish's hermeneutics that illuminates for him biblical interpretation.[126] A mere spatial description of setting runs the danger of losing sight of the constitutive character of foundational texts, which is more likely to be recognised on a diachronic model. Scripture is in our case the *summum bonum*, arguments about which extend through time and coalesce into several traditions. Yet, speaking about the Pope, Hauerwas writes:

> Consider why Stanley Fish and Pope John Paul II are on the same side when it comes to the politics of interpretation. Both men assume that the text, and in this case the text of Scripture, can be interpreted only in the context of an 'interpretative community.' For John Paul II (and all the apostles before him in the tradition) the community necessary for the reading of Scripture is the Roman Catholic Church, which includes the Office of the Magisterium.[127]

The common factor is overemphasised to the neglect of the differences. It is not that Hauerwas is ignorant of the difference and its significance. Ironically, he objects to David Kelsey for not having done justice to the scriptural shaping of community.[128] In fact Kelsey *is* aware of this aspect: 'God uses the texts to transform men's lives (...) Part of what it means to call the community church is that certain uses of Scripture in which God is said to make himself present, are essential to the preservation and shaping of their

---

[124] Hauerwas, *Community*, p. 60.

[125] Thiselton, Walhout and Lundin, *Promise*, p. 158. Thiselton points out a similar difference between the Fishean understanding of interpretive community – orphaned from the classical heritage – and Catholic views of the *magisterium*. This is significant in view of Hauerwas' positive comparison between the same concepts.

[126] See his essay, 'Stanley Fish, the Pope and the Bible', in *Unleashing the Scriptures*, pp. 19-28.

[127] Hauerwas, *Unleashing*, p. 21.

[128] Hauerwas, *Community*, p. 65.

self-identity.'[129] Then the question which emerges is whether this double recognition, that the interpretive community constructs the meaning of Scripture, and that the Scripture constitutes, challenges and shapes the Christian community, does not entail an unresolvable contradiction? For Kelsey, the very authority of Scripture is not an intrinsic function of the text itself, but a result of communitarian attitudes and recognition. The scriptural texts are separated from secular ones not by their nature or content, but by the nature of their interpretation.

The problem is especially poignant with Hauerwas, who proceeds on the basis of this social construction of biblical hermeneutics to a quasi-rhetorical understanding of Christian theological discourse. If all interpretations are political, there is nothing to ground interpretation other than the political will of the group. The tragic connection between knowledge and will, between interpretation and political preference cannot be avoided. Writing about McClendon, Hauerwas mistakenly identifies the essence of his theological proposal in *Doctrine* as rhetorical. He takes the grounding of theology in practice as being rhetorical in that there is no room for criticism.[130] One could accept this conclusion should there be only one understanding of setting. Yet, as we have seen in connection to Gadamer and MacIntyre, the critical possibilities are not simply written off by a strong notion of setting.

The argument so far points to a basic tension between seriousness and rhetoric within postliberalism. Hauerwas problematises the distinction between texts and their interpretations, in view of the fact that there is no disinterested access to the text prior to interpretation and prior to the political anticipations of the community. There is no dead space separating a text from its interpretation. However, from this correct observation it cannot easily be inferred that the content which the community supplies cannot be challenged in view of later interactions with the text. The ontological force of that politically prescribed meaning depends, as Kögler has argued, on a misconception of linguistic holism. There is no reason, he urges, why an interpreter should not be able to make those assumptions explicit, in the aftermath of interpretation and gain a second naiveté of the text and indeed of his own assumptions.

Hans Frei's work clearly illustrates the tension between seriousness and rhetoric. There are two distinguishable stages of his theological position, which parallel Fish's own successive stances. He first prefers a strong formalistic emphasis on the scriptural text, especially on its narrative quality.

---

[129] David Kelsey, *The Uses of Scripture in Recent Theology*, (Philadelphia: Fortress, 1975), pp. 93ff.

[130] Stanley Hauerwas, 'Reading James McClendon Takes Practice: Lessons in the Craft of Theology', in Stanley Hauerwas, *Wilderness Wanderings: Probing Twentieth Century Theology and Philosophy*, (Boulder: Westview, 1997), pp. 172-3.

Then he takes a step back from this recognition and relativises the qualities of the text to the attitudes of the community. Gerard Loughlin believes that the second stage represents Frei's answer to criticism of the notion of a world-absorbing-text. [131] In his *The Eclipse of Biblical Narrative*[132], under the influence of Auerbach's work on figuration, Frei sets forth a view not dissimilar to the New Critical absolute prioritisation of the text. He will himself notice the similarities in a later text:

> Both [my view and the New criticism] claim that the text is a normative and pure 'meaning' world of its own which, quite apart from any factual reference it may have, and apart from its author's intention or it's reader's reception, stands on its own within the authority of self-evident intelligibility.[133]

The emphasis falls on the 'formal stylistic devices' and on the 'literary body of the text'. One must understand, if we are to listen to Loughlin's caution, that Frei's hermeneutics of the literal sense is not simply a regional application of the theory of the New Criticism, but an understanding of the way in which Scripture has always been read in the church. So the *sensus literalis* is not an instance of a general rule, but a 'case specific way of reading.'[134] Kathryn Tanner suggests that the plain sense is not to be identified with an *immanent* sense of the text, but as a function of communal sense.[135]

This means that for Frei too there is no scriptural interpretation apart from a series of strategic political choices. Scripture is not available apart from a communal sense of how one should relate to it. What appear to be immanent features of the text are only the result of a trained perception. Decisions in interpretation are (minimally) aided and (maximally) prompted by the rules implicit in the practices which embed scripture use. Frei identifies three such rules in the Christian community: first, the literal reading must not deny the literal ascription to Jesus of all that is associated

---

[131] Gerard Loughlin, 'Using Scripture: Community and Letterality', in J. Davies, G. Harvey and W. G. E. Watson, eds., *Words Remembered, Texts Renewed. Essays in Honour of John F. A. Sawyer*, Journal for the Study of the Old Testament Supplement Series vol. 195, (Sheffield: Sheffield Academic Press, 1995), esp. pp. 332-334.

[132] Hans W. Frei, *The Eclipse of Biblical Narrative: A Study in Eighteenth and Nineteenth Century Hermeneutics*, (New Haven and London: Yale University Press, 1974).

[133] Hans Frei, 'The "Literal Reading" of Biblical Narrative in the Christian Tradition: Does it Stretch or Will It Break?' in Hans Frei, *Theology and Narrative: Selected Essays*, ed. by George Hunsinger and William C. Placher, (New York and Oxford: Oxford University Press, 1993), p. 140.

[134] Loughlin, 'Using Scripture', p. 333.

[135] Kathryn E. Tanner, 'Theology and the Plain Sense', in G. Green, ed., *Scriptural Authority and Narrative Interpretation*, (Philadelphia: Fortress, 1987).

with him in the stories in which he plays a part; secondly, no Christian reading may deny the unity of the Bible; finally, all readings which in principle do not contradict the first two rules are allowed.[136]

Scripture is thus only given in the context of a social practice with certain rules. McClendon defines a practice as 'a complex series of human actions involving definite practitioners who by these means and in accordance with these rules together seek the intended end.'[137] While he follows MacIntyre in discerning the positive value of the concept, he expresses reservations about the corruptibility of practice and seeks, as we shall see, to complement his narrative ontology with a critical epistemology of a narrative kind.

Rules are constitutive of the identity of a given practice. This means that once a practice is enacted, everyone involved understands that a series of conventions and rules are in effect. Such decisions are essential for the meaning of the elements of a given practice. It is precisely these rules and conventions which, according to Wittgenstein and to speech-act theorists, maintain the stability of meaning.[138] On the language-game model, we learn the meaning of words by learning a ruled way of using them. In Nancey Murphy's opinion, this is one of the more promising aspects of the pragmatic reorientation.[139] She believes that such rules and conventions keep relativism in check, at least within one community. This is where postliberals such as Murphy are over-enthusiastic about the merits of conventionalism.[140] She draws positive parallels between the work of her late husband, McClendon and that of Fish. While the early Fish is read as an ally of deconstruction, the later Fish is taken as an ally of McClendon and Austin. Speech-acts, for McClendon, initiate or refer to already existing conventions within practices. Murphy rightly believes that such conventions help stabilise meaning, but she wrongly associates this with Fish's interpretive communities. Deconstruction, she writes, has made the mistake of overlooking the conventional nature of language thus having done away with the concept of literary meaning.[141] But,

---

[136] Frei, 'Literal Reading', pp. 144f.

[137] McClendon, *Doctrine*, p. 28.

[138] Cf. Kevin J. Vanhoozer, *Is There a Meaning in this Text? The Bible, the Reader and the Morality of Literary Knowledge*, (Grand Rapids: Zondervan, 1998), pp. 245-6: 'a convention is a rule that says a particular action counts as such and such in the appropriate circumstances.'

[139] Nancey Murphy, 'Textual Relativism, Philosophy of Language and the Baptist Vision', in S. Hauerwas, N. Murphy, M. Nation, eds., *Theology Without Foundations: Religious Practice and the Future of Theological Truth*, (Nashville: Abingdon, 1994).

[140] As my argument will show, it is seriously problematic to anchor a theory of meaning on convention.

[141] Cf. also Vanhoozer's argument in *Is There a Meaning*, pp. 201-366.

if the texts' ability to perform a definite speech act depends upon the existence of a community with shared convictions and proper dispositions, then textual stability is in large measure a function not of theories of interpretation, but of how interpretive communities choose to live.[142]

What this suggestion misses is that Fish can only be associated with McClendon if one overlooks the former's notion of dead space. Murphy reads McClendon as offering a theological application of interpretive communities. The question of how to reach adequate interpretation is a question which already presupposes that suspended moment in which we hesitate between interpretations. But the whole point of Fish's position is that there is no such pre-interpretative moment in which a hermeneutical decision is deliberated. According to McClendon, as Murphy reads him, the community must strive to share interpretive strategies with the author and the original readers.[143] We must, as it were, enter the world of the Bible an join in the practices of the first community of believers.[144] Only thus can she read McClendon as guaranteeing the stability of meaning and even access to the intention of the author and the reference of the work: 'conventions enable the reader or listener to reach correct understanding of the writer's or speaker's intention and of the intended reference.'[145] If interpretation is indeed constrained by communal practices, then indeed all that one has to do in order to get the 'right' interpretation is to emulate the practices of the community which generated the text. Here, in a revised Baptist version of interpretive community, the stability of meaning returns with a vengeance. In the enthusiasm of the alliance, Murphy tends to forget one important factor. Fish never intended the community to act as a conscious deposit of conventions, of which the interpreter makes use in order to ascertain the right meaning. This would entail a return to the text itself: we have the text, now we have to figure out an interpretation. But for Fish the text is already interpreted. Finally, Murphy forgets that Fish never intended to prescribe interpretation, to give suggestions as to how it might best be carried out. His sole intention was to describe what goes on in all interpretation. His distinct notion that theory is uninteresting, that it has no consequences, means that interpretation *carries on regardless* of what conscious decisions we might make.

---

[142] Murphy, 'Textual Relativism', p. 270.

[143] Murphy, 'Textual Relativism', p. 264.

[144] Murphy, 'Textual Relativism', p. 266.

[145] Murphy, 'Textual Relativism', p. 256.

Initial Critique

As the argument unfolds, the notion of setting will be revised following suggestions from Kathryn Tanner, Michel de Certeau, Donald Davidson, and indeed others. The positive proposals must, however, await some extensive discussion of ontology and the problem of reference and, as a result, they will gradually emerge throughout the conversation. Some problems associated with MacIntyre and Fish need however to be pointed out at this time.

There is a clear intention in MacIntyre to endorse both a tradition-constitutive account of knowledge as well as the possibility to make a rational choice between traditions. It is only natural, then, that critics have seized upon the opportunity to challenge his proposals. It has to be granted that his use of notions like 'empathetic conceptual imagination,'[146] tolerance, openness to pluralism, suggests both that his critique of liberalism does not preclude him from employing specifically liberal concepts[147] and that inter-traditional understanding and conceptual choices are real options. A number of critics have suggested that he thereby does not sufficiently recognise just how serious is the determination of traditions to insulate themselves from criticism.[148] Some, such as Ian Markham, have even gone as far as to suggest that he may be employing a 'liberalised' notion of tradition. We remember having rehearsed a similar aspect of the problem with respect to Gadamer's critique of historicism, especially Dilthey. History, it may indeed be argued, and implicitly tradition – as the historically transmitted body of enquiry – are not simply present as recoverable objects in the past, but they mark our very being, they constitute the very way we understand the present and, even more importantly, they at least partly determine the very way we recover tradition and history.

But the question is whether *jouissance* should really characterise our reaction in the face of this 'tragedy'. Is the alternative version of setting, that proposed by Fish, to name but one example, more compelling? His idea of background is dominated by spatial metaphors: community is the fictional and imaginary point given by the intersection of interpretive forces, strategies and conventions. There is very little thought at all given to how this community was formed and what exactly gave it its present shape. Of

---

[146] Jennifer A. Herdt, 'Alasdair MacIntyre's 'Rationality of Traditions' and tradition-transcendental standards of justification', *Journal of Religion* 78 (1998), 524-46, p. 530.

[147] Jean Porter, 'Openness and Moral Constraint: Moral Reflection as tradition-guided inquiry in Alasdair MacIntyre's recent works', *Journal of Religion* 73 (1993), 514-536, p. 516.

[148] Ian Markham, 'Faith and reason: reflections on MacIntyre's tradition constituted enquiry', *Religious Studies* 27 (1991), 259-267, p. 262.

course, Fish would concede that interpretive communities have their own history. But he will not endow this temporality with the ontological force it has in Gadamer's hermeneutics, for example. While temporality suggests a certain continuity of inquiry between tradition and its *summum bonum*, for Fish the *sole* source of meaning is the interpretive community. In doing this, he presents us with an undesirable either/ or.[149] We are either the impotent subjects of an overpowering community/ society/ tradition, or we are autonomous agents standing unhindered by any constraints. Fish does indeed suggest that there is no need for such a radical choice,[150] but all his corrections do not gather enough force to point an alternative. Fish so privileges the interpretive community that agency is transferred from interpreter to community.[151] This results in an 'equally repressive objectivity'[152] which gives a hasty solution to a complex issue.[153]

Yet, by failing to preserve the excitement of an unresolved tension (between text and community) and by employing a 'wilful' community, i.e., one that makes interpretive decisions all by itself, Fish is bound to face a potentially decisive contradiction. If there is no distinction between text and interpretation, then interpretive decisions are not the result of interactions with a readily available text. Hermeneutical decisions are legislated by the community itself. Yet the empirical fact of a multitude of rival and apparently incommensurable interpretations within a single community poses a problem for the image of a unified and determined community.[154] The problem may also be framed alternatively: must one assume that those who interpret the text in a 'deviant' way are still members of the same community?

Much like MacIntyre, Fish is forced to give his own account of change. This is also the debate about textual realism: if there is no un-interpreted text, then interpretation cannot validate its choices by recourse to an objective source. There is nothing given out there, which may validate or falsify a given interpretation, for textual facts already presuppose a previous reading. For Fish this means that hermeneutical propriety is a political matter.

---

[149] Cf. also Terry Eagleton, 'The estate agent: review of Stanley Fish, *The Trouble with Principle*, Cambridge, Mass. and London: Harvard University Press, 1991', *London Review of Books*, 2 March 2000, 22/5.

[150] Fish, *Doing*, p. 441.

[151] Kathleen McCormick, 'Swimming upstream with Fish', *The Journal of Aesthetics and Art Criticism*, 44 (1985), 67-76, p. 71; S. Rendall, 'Fish vs. Fiss', *Diacritics*, 12 (1982), 49-56, p. 54; Scott C. Saye, 'The wild and crooked tree: Barth, Fish and interpretive communities', *Modern Theology* 12 (1996), 435-458, p. 438.

[152] McCormick, 'Swimming', p. 75.

[153] McCormick, 'Swimming', p. 70.

[154] Wesley A. Kort, *Bound to Differ: The Dynamics of Theological Discourse*, (University Park: Pennsylvania State University Press, 1992), pp. 24-25, 136.

Such a perceived relativism led to a debate with another legal philosopher, Ronald Dworkin. Fish's opening salvos are contained in two important essays: 'Working on the chain gang: interpretation in law and literature', and 'Change'. The debate is focused around the issue of whether one could give any interpretation to any text, hence relativism. Dworkin takes the example of an Agatha Christie mystery novel, which, he argues, cannot be read as a philosophical novel.[155] A text, he goes on to say, will not yield to any sort of interpretation without strain or distortion. For Fish, on the other hand, what we take as facts are already functions of assumptions we hold and of interpretations we have already given, so to speak, in the background. Textual facts are not properties of the texts, but objectifications of our attitudes towards them. The interpretations which are appropriate to a text are not given in the sub-structure of the text itself, but are legislated by the community. It has to be recognised that the notion of setting implicit here is more akin to Markham's than to MacIntyre's. Reading an Agatha Christie mystery novel as a philosophical text is indeed possible, not because the text itself allows it, but only if the community is 'geared up' for such a reading. However, the examples could be radicalised: could one for example interpret such a mystery novel as a musical script, or as instructions to play a soccer game?

Fish is resolute in his refusal to locate any interpretive force in the text itself. Yet in doing so, he places an enormous hermeneutical burden on the community. The question of what guides interpretation now becomes the question 'what determines a community's reading strategies to change?' Fish's precise answer to this question remains unclear, perhaps due to the inherent difficulty of ascribing such an importance to community. He could be taken to assert that any community may change to such an extent that the most unpredictable readings would be possible. Or, he might say that 'impossible' readings would simply not count as interpretations of this or that text. But this would be Dworkin's point. What could count against a given interpretation as being *of* that text, if not something at least having to do with the text, and not with the reading strategy?

The issue is perhaps clarified, or at least better focused, by the second of Fish's essays. In 'Change' Fish ridicules the naïve belief that change comes from outside the community. For anything to be recognised as significant (for change), it must comply with what the community has designated as possibly significant. MacIntyre seems unfortunately oblivious to this fact, as Markham and Milbank point out. In a strong sense, then, for something for the outside to change the inside, it must already have become internal to do so.[156] We obviously remain under the spell of spatial metaphors here as well. Nonetheless, the point is that the boundaries between outside and in-

---

[155] Fish, *Doing*, pp. 95ff.
[156] Fish, *Doing*, p. 147.

side need to be redrawn from the inside if a credible account of change is to be given.[157] Communities change not as a direct result of their interaction with their subject matter, which is in a sense external. In removing any external sources from the process of change, Fish runs the danger of making the very concept of community and interpretation meaningless. If there is nothing that may count as a bad interpretation, the very notion of interpreting *this text* is meaningless. Furthermore, if a community changes with no respect to its subject matter, but by arbitrary chance (since apparently this is the only remaining option), is it still a coherent notion? What exactly is it that holds this community together, apart from its own politics? What is the point of politics? As Paul Noble asks, how does one know of which community one is a member of?[158] Not only do such questions problematise Fishean solutions to the problem of the tension between text and community in interpretation, but they also raise serious doubts about the very coherence of the notion of community, at least as traditionally conceived, in a spatial fashion. Can the boundaries of one community be drawn with such precision and discrimination between inside and outside?

To sum up our critique of Fish, I have argued that he places too great a burden on a theoretical notion which eventually breaks down under the weight. The more fluid notion of community to which he arrives through his meditation on change is appropriate, but unable to support agency the way Fish may wish. Concurrently, his account appears ultimately too theoretical in that its preference for easy one-sided answers instead of complex solutions blinds it to another account of the sources of meaning which refuses its abandonment to either text or community. This brings us to the end of the first phase of the argument. Although any choice of beginning is fraught with subjectivism, I have followed Radical Orthodoxy's suggestion that the origins of modernity have to be sought much earlier than Descartes, perhaps going as far back as Scotus. Milbank and others have gone on to argue that with Scotus lie the origins of the modern concept of mind, the space where knowledge mirrors nature. The idea of mirroring and of representation will reappear as the argument progresses. Modernity may be read as originating in the Scotist desire for univocal knowledge and language, subject to the neutral hierarchy of Being. Yet the mind was itself unable to satisfy modern expectations. A Christian modernity, in Vico and Hamann, recognised the inherent nihilism in the modern quest for autonomy. In turn they proclaimed a return to tradition and community as the setting without which knowledge is 'broken'. They unmasked the philosophical purgation

---

[157] Fish, *Doing*, p. 148

[158] Paul Noble, 'Hermeneutics and postmodernism: can we have a radical reader-response theory? Part II', *Religious Studies* 31 (1995), 1-22. Fish's answer backfires when invoking an unmediated act: the mystical nod of recognition. cf. Fish, *Is There a Text?*, p. 173.

of knowledge as ironically mythic. It appears that the modern anxiety of constraint was nothing but a case of 'scratching where it does not itch.'[159] It did not itch because the erection of a Being independent of God, which resulted in the usurpation of reality from the Creator, was arbitrary. Theology, now liberated from a suspicious Enlightenment, no longer needs to satisfy externally imposed criteria of certainty and meaningfulness. On the contrary, it can and it should carry out its own business without restraint, within the epistemic safety of the Christian community. It can postulate its own being, or go beyond being, it can describe its own understanding of the relationship between finite and infinite. In more positive terms, theology assumes the project of reasserting the *will* to divine knowledge. It does not deny, as modernity does, that will is involved with knowledge, but it rejects the attempt to liberate knowledge from will, as concealing another political intention. Instead it reasserts the will to be schooled in the virtues of Christian community, whose creative practices (it believes) mediate transcendence.

For all my admiration towards the project of postliberalism and of Radical Orthodoxy, there are important difficulties in rejecting modernity and Enlightenment *tout court*. Once a strong and fixed notion of setting (community and tradition) has been adopted, there is no negotiation between the claims of this community, between its specific will, and the claims of other communities. An equally repressive community is inaugurated. The church imposes its own interpretation on the scriptural texts, on Jesus, on reality itself, without any mediation of other rival claims. Christians interpret the Jewish *tanakh* as 'Old' Testament, its unique individuals as figures whose fulfilment is Christ. An omnipotent Christian community violently reads the rest of reality. Nazis murder Jews in the moral haven of their own ethical community. There is no human requirement as such, no universally human duty other than the duty to faithfully adhere. Belonging begins to excuse violence and manipulation. Should this disenchant us of the attraction of tradition and community? Only if one does not accept that community and tradition continually redefine themselves in dialogue with other traditions. This conversation presupposes neither foundationalist arguments, nor rhetorical manipulation, but constructive and disclosive transparency. The next chapter discloses an early Christian understanding of inter-communitarian rationality through the concept of figuration. Milbank's agenda involves the return of knowledge to the will: the will to participate in God by partaking of the divine historical performances. This involves a re-symbolisation of epistemology: to understand particulars one must grasp

---

[159] Richard Rorty, 'Habermas and Lyotard on Postmodernity', in Richard Bernstein, ed., *Habermas and Modernity*, (Cambridge: MIT Press, 1985), p. 164.

them as participating in the divine, as being created. Their identity is narratively rendered by the Christian stories. Yet for Milbank this mediation is allegorical. Particulars run the danger of losing their own identity in their assumption into the Christian narrative. Early Christian accounts of figuration together with their modern employment in the work of Hans Frei, David Dawson, Erich Auerbach and others, suggests otherwise: identity need not be lost by baptism into the Christian community. This in turn has important implications for rationality.

Chapter Two

Hermeneutics

Realistic Narratives: Frei's Early Hermeneutics

If the previous argument is correct, postliberalism hesitates between two
different descriptions of the setting of knowledge. This chapter investigates
the postliberal understanding of scriptural hermeneutics in light of what
was said above about tradition and community. I shall argue that just as a
well determined notion of setting breaks down under its own weight, so will
a purely intra-textual approach to Scripture. Our readings are no more stable than the traditions which inform them. The way into this debate is given
by a discussion of Frei's early hermeneutical emphasis on the notion of *realistic narrative* and then his latter orientation towards literal sense and performance.

Hans Frei's early conception of the hermeneutical task is shaped under
the influence of New Criticism. As his writing career went on, however, his
initial formalism gave way to a socially pragmatic attitude to the construction of meaning and the norm of interpretation. The disintegration of objectivist approaches in the work of a series of philosophers[1] and theologians
has been taken to mean that foundationalism inevitably leads towards nihilism. In order to understand why Frei's later solution is not as helpful as
some suggest, the reasons why he abandoned the earlier emphasis must first
be explored.

It is a known fact that a large part of the Biblical material which the
Church takes as foundational is in story form. Although by no means the
first theologian with a sense of the primacy of narrative in the Bible, Hans
Frei has certainly been one of those responsible for a renaissance of interest
in this category. This is how Gerard Loughlin introduces Frei's work in his
discussion of narrative theology:

> Long before it was fashionable to be non-foundational, Hans Frei (1922-
> 1988) has learnt from Karl Barth (1886-1968) that Christian faith rests
> not upon universal reason or human self-consciousness, but is sustained
> through and as commitment to a story. The story is not supported by
> anything else, by another story, theory or argument. The story is simply

---

[1] One may point some notable figures here: Ludwig Wittgenstein, Martin Heidegger,
Stanley Fish, Hans Frei, Don Cupitt and others.

told, and faith is a certain way of telling it, a way of living and embody-
ing it; a habit of the heart. But it is not the way of modern theology,
whether liberal or evangelical.[2]

The considerable appeal of 'story' to the contemporary mind can be
traced back to its association with discourses which generally bracket the
notion of truth.[3] What becomes primary in a postliberal theology is the assumption of the priority of the Christian story itself. For Loughlin, whose
theological position embraces postliberals and Radical Orthodoxy, the assumption of the Christian setting is absolute. The possibility of stepping
outside it in order to ground its grammar is denied. There is no reading of
the Christian texts and indeed no rendering of the identity of Jesus Christ
except through the grammar of Christian practice. Last chapter suggested
the possibility of grounding, or at least being critical towards one's own
tradition without this involving stepping outside it. It also pointed out the
incoherence involved in arguing for a hegemonic setting which rules all
internal tactical moves.

To say with Loughlin that the Christian story rests on nothing else may
be interpreted in different ways, depending on what one means by story.
For example, if story refers to one of the parables of Jesus and which is
standing on its own, one may indeed conclude that there is nothing behind
it. On the other hand, if the story was intended to refer beyond itself, then
its retelling is not for the sake of the story, but the end of a process that
connects an author, a series of events, texts and their performative retelling.
Stories, we shall argue, are communicative acts and as such cannot be isolated from a larger setting, involving extra-textual factors as well. The initial intuitions about certain postliberal tendencies may still prove correct:
there is a drive to clearly distinguish between *inside* and *outside*, between
what is in the tradition and what doesn't belong to it, between what is *intra-
textual* and what is *extra-textual*. The means through which such a desire
for clear boundaries is fulfilled are textual entities. Traditions are considered unitary and texts are treated as closed units. But this strategy has historically given way to an increasing recognition of the futility of such de-
limitations. The apparently closed systems deconstructed themselves as
mere projections of communitarian attitudes.

In fact, the history of modern philosophy and theology may arguably be
put in terms of *receding realisms*. At first, to take one Christological example, Jesus was thought to be readily accessible to knowledge (ontological
realism), before, that is, one understood that there were only textual traces
of his person. However, these traces were themselves clearly legible (tex-

---

[2] Loughlin, *Telling God's Story*, p. 33.
[3] Garrett Green, "'The Bible as...'": Fictional narrative and scriptural truth', in
Garrett Green, ed., *Scriptural Authority and Narrative Interpretation*, p. 80.

tual realism). Then, the texts themselves begun to decompose under the penetrating gaze of the reader (reader response), whose interpretation in turn concealed the influence of community and tradition (realism of culture). The constant factor is that while realism retreats, it always manages to keep something visible, objective, representable. The desire to contain the person, the text, the reader, but also the community, is futile. As I shall argue, there are two possible responses to this cycle: the nihilist solution that there are no solutions and the journey to truth is an endless wandering and pilgrimage, or the more positive response, that nihilism itself cannot be seriously maintained and that in the face of such a recession one may find solace in the power of dialogue and the human conversation.

The progression shown by the work of Hans Frei illustrates the recession of realism from the text to the interpretive community. Frei's initial contribution to the theological discussion has been immensely important. He pointed out a specific textual feature of the Gospel stories, namely that they are best described by the category of realistic narratives. If one is to correctly interpret these stories, one must take into account their realistic narrative character. There are, however, difficulties in recovering the concept of realistic narratives, as the history of modern exegesis and apologetics reveals. Frei notes that although in the Eighteenth and Nineteenth centuries many writers had been aware of the realistic nature of the Biblical stories, these features were simply ignored for lack of an adequate method and analytical tools to exploit them. It was only with the advance of modern literary techniques of realistic writing and interpretation that the semantic potential of these features could best be brought to light.

Three major assumptions underpinned the pre-critical understanding of the Bible.[4] First, if the Bible was read literally, it was supposed that it *referred* to actual historical events. Secondly, if the Bible was to be read as one whole story depicting one single world, some way had to be found to read divergent passages in such a way as not to cripple the basic unity of the story. This lead to the employment of figural reading.[5] Finally, there was the conviction that the biblical world was the real world and that its story subsumes all other stories about the world, past and present. The biblical story extends to encompass any present or future reader.

Together with the advent of historical criticism it was precisely these assumptions that ensured the destruction of the pre-critical stance. Since the reality of the historical events *represented* in the scriptural accounts came under increasing scrutiny, the stories themselves appeared as second-rate, pre-scientific fictions. In order to restore their primacy and importance, their link with reality had to be mended. Such was the indissoluble link

---

[4] Frei, *Eclipse*, pp. 2-3.

[5] Cf. Loughlin's beautiful metaphor of the Bible as an 'omnivorous book', *Telling God's Story*, p. 37.

between their story-quality and their historical-representative-quality that if one suffered, as their historical character did, the whole notion was in danger of collapse. However, this state of affairs has made the Bible's primacy parasitic upon its historical credibility. In Frei's opinion, this mechanism of the recovery of the historical link rested on a fundamental methodological mistake: the confusion between the meaning and the truth of the story. Thus, on the one hand, conservatives attempted to 'prove' the truth of the story, with no regard to this very story's literary characteristics, in other words, without caring much about the story itself. This betrays a confusion between literal meaning and ostensive reference. They thought the story will be saved once the history is saved. Liberals, on the other hand, gave up the truth of the story altogether and reinterpreted its meaning as referring to existential moods and states. This diagnosis helps Frei to notice a common presupposition of both liberals and conservatives, namely that the meaning of the Bible stories lies elsewhere than inside the story, whether in historical or in existential reference. The unfortunate upshot of this situation is that the realistic or history-like character of the narratives was lost.

As a direct result methods of interpretation were applied which did not do justice to the *nature* of these texts. It is clear, then, that Frei's early strategy was to 'discover' a certain textual quality and to draw the appropriate hermeneutical conclusions from it. It is a formalist strategy, akin to New Criticism. This textually realist preference implied a suspicion about theoretical constructs in that theory was perceived as doing away with the particularity of the text. Although Frei was relentlessly calling attention to the danger of theoretical intrusion, he was too subtle a theologian to believe he can get away without theory. Instead, the theologian must strive to keep his or her theoretical apparatus to a minimum in order to allow the text to speak for itself.

The category of realistic narrative is described by Frei in as few theoretical terms as he can. He prefers to contrast it to that of myth. The confusion of literal meaning with ostensive reference led to the subordination of the meaning of the story to a neutral account of what really happened. Hence the liberal confusion between the biblical stories and myth. The point of myth lies outside the narrative structure of its story. Myths are secondary, they mediate a more basic truth, which is usually some aspect of the human drama of existence, or perhaps the relationship between the human and divine worlds. They are about the personification of abstract entities such as truth, depth, and so on.[6] Conversely, the biblical stories are about an unsubstitutable individual, Jesus Christ. Whereas mythical characters efface themselves before the higher truth which they represent, in the gospels the human figure of Jesus bestows identity upon the saviour and cosmic figure

---

[6] Hans Frei, *The Identity of Jesus Christ: The Hermeneutical Bases of Dogmatic Theology*, (Philadelphia: Fortress, 1975), pp. 54f.

of Christ.[7] The substance of the story, its emplotment, its material content are not arbitrary means towards the more important aim of depicting a universal human truth: 'each event in the story – passion, death and resurrection – has the sort of uniqueness, integrity, and finality one finds in lifelike reports, fictional or real, in contrast to mythical stories.'[8]

The key to understanding realistic narratives is to look no further than the story itself: 'what they are about and how they make sense are functions of the depiction or narrative rendering of the events constituting them.'[9] This is perhaps the most distinctive mark of Frei's conception of realistic narrative. In other words, meaning has nothing to do with ostensive reference, but it is a function of the text itself. By being so preoccupied with the priority of the biblical world, Frei runs the danger of advocating a self-enclosed world in which the texts refer to nothing but themselves. Gary Comstock, among others, voices this somewhat presumptuous criticism. He accuses Frei of making the narratives refer only to themselves.[10] He in fact oversimplifies and radicalises Frei's understanding of the relation between narratives and reality. Although it is not unfair to say that Frei has given plenty of reasons for such a mis-interpretation, the issue must be seen in the context of his astute refusal to identify meaning with some event in external history, standing independently of the texts themselves.

Frei ponders the irony of the hermeneutical situation in the Eighteenth and Nineteenth centuries. Although all across the spectrum, the narratives were being interpreted in light of the external world of historical fact or ideal reference to some essential characteristic of humanity, the realistic features of the stories were never entirely lost from sight.[11] Commentators were aware of the narrative nature of such stories[12] but for various reasons they were unable to disentangle themselves from their historicist assumptions. In the absence of a method, their understanding was doomed to remain limited to the notion of historical reference. Meaning came to be detached from the stories and located externally to it. Hence every time the feature was noticed, it was confused with historical truth, or reference.[13] However, Frei is by no means accusing past exegetes of ignorance or even stupidity. In fact he acknowledges the fact that the realistic nature of narra-

---

[7] Frei, *Identity*, p. 59.

[8] Frei, *Identity*, p. 57.

[9] Frei, *Identity*, p. 13.

[10] Gary Comstock, 'Truth or meaning: Ricoeur versus Frei on Biblical narrative', *Journal of the American Academy of Religion* 55 (1987), 687-717. See Ken Surin's critique of Comstock, *The Turnings of Darkness and Light: Essays in Philosophical and Systematic Theology*, (Cambridge: Cambridge University Press, 1989).

[11] Frei, *Eclipse*, p. 8.

[12] Frei, *Eclipse*, p. 15.

[13] Frei, *Eclispe*, p. 11.

tives invites questions about their historical reliability, especially in connection to the resurrection accounts.

The situation scrutinised by Frei betrays a dichotomy between letter and spirit. The assumption is that the meaning of a text somehow supervenes upon its graphic form. On the one hand there is the literary flow of the text, but on the other there is a realm where meanings take shape. What happens intra-textually, however, refers to that transcendental realm, which – importantly – is in no way influenced by the more mundane and graphic domain. It may thus be pointed out that there is a profoundly moral aspect to Frei's hermeneutical project. This concerns a certain duty to safeguard the text from the external meanings which would otherwise do violence to its body. Allegorical interpretations are vehemently rejected by Frei for the precise reason that they impose alien meanings to texts and because it presupposes a realm of meaning independent from the conflict of signs and human practices. Under such a regime, the text becomes a transparent medium which occasions the manifestation of these meanings. In itself it contributes minimally to those meanings, save calling them into action. It is for this reason that Frei takes issue with a certain kind of hermeneutical theory which locates the meaning of the text in the world the text projects between itself and the interpreter (Ricoeur). From this perspective, a paradoxical complicity is uncovered: between Scotist univocity and allegorical meanings. Both depict a realm of spirit untainted by matter. For Scotus true knowledge rests on a double assumption: that the forms of Being are universally given and that human signs can access them in the process of representation. Yet the will involved here was unmasked as arbitrary, the hierarchy of genera as cultural and politically negotiated. The arbiter of all truth and knowledge proves to be an accidental human scheme which regulates epistemic content. Scotist will, for all its pretence, is arbitrary and violent. Allegory is parasitic upon the illusion of independent meanings.

To return meanings to texts, the spirit to the body and content to form is therefore no exercise in academic fancy.[14] The moral intensity of the present discussion derives from the historical abuses to which such dualisms have been accomplices. In his seminal book on figural reading, John David Dawson recounts the story of the Nazi persecution of Jews. Just as in Adolph Eichmann's case, what is most instructive from a moral point of view is the justification given to actions undertaken by individuals against fellow human beings. In Eichmann's case, one notices the secular understanding of the absolute duty to obey the law, regardless of its content and moral implications. This duty derives simply from the law's being authoritative at a given time and in a certain place. But this is the very doctrine of legal

---

[14] For a survey of the literature on the relation between ethics and hermeneutics, see Charles H. Cosgrove, *Appealing to Scripture in Moral Debate: Five Hermeneutical Rules*, (Grand Rapids: Wm. B. Eerdmans, 2002), esp. chapter 5 (pp. 154-180).

positivism, as we saw with Vico. There is thus a questionableness about an authority which rests on no other legitimisation than its local and political status. I do not mean to suggest that there is a direct and necessary connection between legal positivism and anti-Semitism. But it cannot be denied that legal positivist doctrines were successfully employed by the Nazi propaganda machine.

Bishop Fulhaber, on the other hand, was a Roman Catholic cardinal archbishop and professor of Old Testament Scripture at the University of Strasbourg. During the later 1930's the dominant anti-Semitic attitude in Nazi Germany was thought to licence an attitude of disregard for the Jewish Scriptures as well. Bishop Fulhaber rejected such a position by giving a super-sessionist explanation of the identity of the Jewish people. He argues that the Old Testament are really the Scriptures of the Christians rather than of the Jews, for it is the Christians who have understood and appropriated their 'spiritual' meaning. Such Scriptures, being inspired by the Holy Spirit, can only be interpreted by the members of the community of the Spirit. What is interesting, writes Dawson, was that

> His dispute with anti-Semitic 'German Christians' fuelled not by their anti-Semitism but by their disparagement of the Old Testament, highlights the radical difference between guaranteeing the continued existence of Jews and defending the continued Christian validity of the Old Testament: *to save the text, some are prepared to sacrifice the people.*[15]

Once a rift was introduced between the spiritual meaning of a text, the socio-historical conditions which define it may easily be discarded. The spiritual interpretation performed by Christians can easily dispose with the people who originated the Old Testament, about whom and to whom it was written and indeed whose practices are centred around it. It appears that the very discussion of the interpretive community receives a moral orientation: which is the community most entitled to use a certain text? Moreover, what are the connections between communities which claim to interpret a certain text? Do not Christian interpretations of the Old Testament run the danger of supplying external meanings to a basically Jewish text? What may count as an external interpretation anyway? These turn out to be deeply ethical questions, concerning the relation between the particularity of a text, as a product of a community, and the universality of meanings ascribed to it.

To return to Frei: 'What [the narratives] are about and how they make sense is a function of the depiction or narrative rendering of the events constituting them, including their being rendered, at least partially, by the device of chronological sequence.'[16] A realistic narrative holds subject and

---

[15] Dawson, *Christian Figural Reading and the Fashioning of Identity*, (Berkeley, Los Angeles and London, University of California Press, 2002), p. 2.

[16] Frei, *Eclipse*, p. 13.

social setting together, while 'characters and external circumstances' fitly render each other.[17] It appears that for Frei realism is a literary *genre* which preserves particularity. In literary realism, meaning does not escape textuality.

The principal inspiration for his particular brand of realism comes from Erich Auerbach. In fact the ethical issues which gradually emerge as central to the present discussion also formed the focus of Auerbach's attention. Being exiled from Germany as a Jew in 1935, he places the violence of the Holocaust in the perspective of the larger European intellectual culture. He concludes that the denial of the historical being of the Jewish people could only amount to a betrayal of European and Christian identity. He argues that *secular* European identity (literary, political, social) derives from a specifically Christian mode of representing reality. The manner of such a representation is such that the identity of the particulars is left intact and preserved, although they are seen as small parts of a divine utterance. Fulhaber's arguments can only be called Christian at the cost of disregarding a respectable and ancient tradition of Christian figural reading. Furthermore, this tradition lies at the very heart of European civilisation.

Auerbach's opponents, people such as Fulhaber, Eichmann and Christians or non-Christians who undertake to drain the Old Testament of its Jewishness can only do so by wresting meaning away from the bodies of texts and giving it an existence of its own. In response, Auerbach wishes to eliminate 'spirit' and 'meaning' as free-floating concepts.[18] He redefines both of them as relational and abstract entities not having an identity of their own. They can only be described relationally. For Auerbach, the very existence of independent 'spirit' and 'meaning' constitutes a threat to the reality of historical events and people. It is on the background of this awareness (and wariness) that he describes what he is looking for. In Dawson's words: 'Auerbach's guiding question in the entire chapter is whether one can find in the ancient world representations of reality that do not reduce the complexity of human history to static, formal categories of ancient ethics and rhetoric, but instead do justice to the deep "historical forces" that underlie the lives of ordinary people and generate significant social and cultural transformation.'[19]

Christian figural realism is such a model for the representation of reality and it contained three elements: the two events or people which are figurally related, the relation between them and the interpretive act which discerns this relation. Auerbach's genius was to suggest that such an interpre-

---

[17] Frei, *Eclipse*, p. 13.

[18] Dawson, *Figural Reading*, p. 94.

[19] Dawson, *Figural Reading*, p. 97.

tation does not correlate an event or a person with a meaning.[20] Instead, a figural relation discovers the unique identity of distinct events or people which are part of an extended divine utterance in history. His suspicion of the tendencies of meaning and spirit to hijack texts prompts him to propose that the only spiritual aspect of the whole figural process consists in the act of understanding.[21] The upshot is that figural interpretation does not detract from the identity of the events correlated. The figure is not *aufgehebt* in the fulfilment. Joshua, for example, retains his own identity despite being a figure of Jesus. Because of such an ability to preserve textual and historical identity, Christian figural realism is the literary method best suited for the preservation of historical identity. The historical identity of the figure is not denied, for figuration does not add its own meaning to it, but simply discovers a divinely intended connection. Hence the spiritual character of figuration consists in recognising what is already the case.[22]

The threat of an independent meaning arises for Auerbach precisely at the point of Jesus' resurrection. 'Here meaning becomes the hermeneutical significance of spirit, and spirit comes to be disengaged from Jesus and transferred to his disciples.'[23] Yet at the very moment where meaning and spirit threaten to evacuate the text of matter, the gospels give such a realistic description that bodiliness and textuality are saved. For Auerbach, realism illustrates the conviction that persons receive their identity through their engagement with the contingent circumstances of life and the greater historic forces that move them. The classicists, despite their attention to detail, failed to grasp the real complexity of social events, the tragic sense of the literary characters who are caught up in life. Vico's perspectivism[24] is reincarnated in Auerbach's attention to the specificity of individual societies and times. The gospels exhibit the same awareness to complexity. Rather than loading their characters with pre-existing meaning, they provide a literary representation of reality in which 'the deep subsurface layers, which were static for the observers of classical antiquity, began to move.'[25] The symbiosis between history and letter achieves fullness in Auerbach's refusal to deny historical forces their due. There is nothing behind these forces to move figural reading, such as spirit. He illustrates this conviction

---

[20] Auerbach, *Mimesis: The Representation of Reality in Western Literature*, trans. by Willard R. Trask, (Princeton: Princeton University Press, 1953), pp. 73, 555; Frei, *Eclipse*, pp. 28-29.

[21] Dawson, *Figural Reading*, p. 92.

[22] Dawson, *Figural Reading*, p. 92; Auerbach, 'Figura', p. 32.

[23] Dawson, *Figural Reading*, p. 97.

[24] Claus Uhlig, 'Auerbach's "hidden" (?) theory of history' in Seth Lehrer, ed., *Literary History and the Challenge of Philology: The Legacy of Erich Auerbach*, (Stanford: Stanford University Press, 1996), p. 37.

[25] Auerbach, *Mimesis*, p. 45.

by giving a liberal exegesis of Peter's account of the resurrection.[26] The event of the resurrection is for Auerbach not a real life event in Jesus' life, but in Peter's. The spirit is only deceivingly heralded by the resurrection, when it is in fact a characteristic of Peter's response to the Jesus event. The insignificance of Peter and his denial become keys to understanding him as a tragic figure. It is precisely in his weakness, that he was able to grasp his own significance in the larger scheme of things. The gospels themselves arise from this sense of the tragic. Precisely in making the resurrection Peter's own, Auerbach is able to argue that Peter's own identity is intensified. There is no spiritual realm to threaten the bodily identity of both Jesus and Peter, as his follower. In Jesus' complete *kenosis* lie the seeds for the preservation of humanity.

We can now see where this argument is going. Auerbach thinks he has found a tradition central to European intellectual identity which envisages an inclusion in a body of believers which would not entail the negation of one's identity. Peter is able to follow Jesus not by having his personality denied in the act of following, but precisely by being more himself. Discipleship does not involve loss of identity. Furthermore, for Auerbach, this tradition can only be maintained by rejecting all forms of allegory and spiritual readings. Unfortunately, however, he takes this to involve an ontological rejection of a realm of the spirit beyond historical forces. History is everything to Auerbach, the flux of its forces being the guarantee of freedom in its realm. If this is the case, then allegorical readings such as Fulhaber's no longer qualify as Christian, and indeed as European.

Through this hermeneutical shift from Jesus to Peter, where the text is recalibrated around the latter, Auerbach suggests that the gospels figurally extend the story of Jesus. Not only are Joshua and Peter figures of Jesus, but so are the faithful readers of these stories. Dawson writes, 'We gravitate to Peter precisely because of a weakness he shares with us, from which he nevertheless derives the highest force, which we too might share. But like Peter, we discover such strength in weakness only when, turning away from purely personal concerns, we discern how we have become part of the larger historical forces that embrace our otherwise insignificant destinies.'[27] Auerbachian realism, therefore, presupposes a singular concentration on historical forces and events. The realm of the transcendent tends to disrupt it and is therefore marginalised. Auerbach thinks he can preserve the reality of the figure only by reducing the resurrection to a merely psychological event, thus collapsing the possibility of spirit into matter.

There is a certain anti-metaphysical bias here, tributary to the same modernist worldview which I have been rejecting. God and the realm of the transcendent can seem incompatible with human identity and dignity only

---

[26] Auerbach, *Mimesis*, ch. 2.
[27] Dawson, *Figural Reading*, p. 99.

as long as they both share in the same Being. To achieve true identity, one must first abolish God. Only for Auerbach this abolition is a divinely enacted act.[28] Jesus fully spends himself on the cross. Yet, as Dawson argues, by denying the historical resurrection Auerbach thereby forecloses the possibility of a peaceful and mutually supportive co-habitation of spirit and body, whereby Jesus' historical identity is not denied but precisely enriched by his resurrection from the dead, as Frei will later argue.

Although Auerbach believes to have located the true essence of the resurrection in Peter's response to Jesus, which thereby constitutes the possibility of our becoming figures of Jesus as well, the temptation to return text to spirit still remains. The only way out of the temptation of the spiritual and the figurative (as opposed to the figural) is a full *kenosis* of meaning into fully realised and concrete imagery. This can only be, Auerbach maintains, the achievement of poetic art, not of interpretation. This process does in fact take place in Dante's figural work and then through the history of European secular realism. What Dante achieves is again an intensification of the figure through an imagination of its extra-historical fulfilment. If the figural interpreters of the Bible preserved the historical identity and complexity of their characters despite their receiving fulfilment in Jesus, and if Dante's characters receive their identity as a consequence of their having extra-historical fulfilment,[29] later secular realists 'were able to portray fictional but historical realistic figures without the aid of any extra-historical fulfilment at all.'[30] Secular realism, from Boccaccio to Virginia Woolf, has learned from Christian figural realism to endow the contingent and the mundane with all the grandeur and dignity of spiritual life.

It is precisely the realistic techniques of the New Testament writers and of Christian interpreters in antiquity (starting especially with Tertullian) which left their imprint on European culture. Auerbach further argues that without such a figural reading, which displayed the continued significance of the Jewish Bible, European culture would never have been so influenced by it.[31] Crucially, however, figural reading ensured that such universal scope of the Jewish scriptures did not entail the effacement of the Jewish nation.

Auerbach's realism, unfortunately inevitably leads towards secularity. Transcendence and ontological difference are perceived enemies of the preservation of identity. In this case a very serious question arises here, which is also the literary counterpart to Milbank's persistent warnings: is

---

[28] See Gianni Vattimo, 'History of salvation, history of interpretation', in Niels Gronkjaer, *The Return of God: Theological Perspectives in Contemporary Philosophy*, (Odense: Odense University Press, 1998).

[29] Dawson, *Figural Reading*, p. 104.

[30] Dawson, *Figural Reading*, p. 105.

[31] Dawson, *Figural Reading*, p. 109, Auerbach, 'Figura', p. 52.

such an identity-preserving realism sustainable in the absence of a specifically Christian ontology?[32] Dawson wonders whether Auerbach's perhaps
idiosyncratic denial of the reality of the resurrection will ultimately not
backfire. Will not Milbank's ontology of peace and difference be better
suited for the preservation of the body? Auerbach does not seem to find
much value in the suggestion that a fulfilled Joshua (Jesus) is qualitatively
different from a fulfilled Virgil (in Dante). Nor does he seem to remember
the lesson taught by Fulhaber, that biblical figures could easily be turned in
the other direction: if one has Jesus as Joshua's fulfilment, does one still
need to keep Joshua?[33] This implies that every realism conceals an ontology,[34] a prior understanding of the self, or of the relationship between body
and spirit, for instance. A legitimate worry emerges that in order to salvage
identity, one may need not simply a literary style, but an ontology. As I will
show, this is precisely what Milbank demands, yet his ontology can only be
assumed rhetorically, for reasons of literary taste. This means that the worry
simply shifts to a different level.

There are, as could be intuited, important differences between Auerbach
and Frei, despite the congeniality of their projects. Francis Watson points
out that for Auerbach realism is the opposite of classicism, whose main
figures are heroes untouched by the force of the events around them, relentlessly carrying out their purpose and fate.[35] Realistic narrative is a so-
cio-political concept, as we saw, standing for serious representation of
problems, conflicts and indeed the identity of ordinary people. Realism,
especially secular realism, ensures that individuality is salvaged and that the
worth of ordinary life is discovered. Although no doubt Frei would sub-
scribe to such a political agenda, his concern is not so much with ordinary
people, but it is a more formalist one. Dawson writes that 'Frei is less concerned than Auerbach was to preserve the historical reality of figure and
fulfilment; instead, his primary goal is to preserve the authority of the Bible
to resist the subjective meanings of individual readers or their traditional
interpretations, for the sake of preserving its capacity to render the identity
of Christ and, hence, the identity of God.'[36] Auerbach's collating of letter
and history and his conception of texts as moved by historical forces makes

---

[32] Milbank, *Theology and Social Theory*, pp. 382-9.

[33] Dawson, *Figural Reading*, pp. 105-106.

[34] It is not difficult to see how Auerbach's realism could be shown to contain an ontology. His notions of 'destiny' and 'fate' are not without ideological import, cf. Uhlig,
p. 40. Auerbach also participated in the widespread hegelianisation of Vico. Hence the
Vichian conection is itself not free of metaphysical preference, cf. Timothy Bahti, 'Vico,
Auerbach amd literary history', *Philological Quarterly* 60 (1981), 239-255, p. 242.

[35] Francis Watson, *Text, Church and World: Biblical Interpretation in Theological
Perspective*, (Edinburgh: T&T Clark, 1994), p. 27.

[36] Dawson, *Figural Reading*, p. 141.

his realism to be more about reality that Frei's. This will eventually lead to a disjunction in Frei, one to be explored later on, between the literary identity of Jesus and his historical and personal existence. The problem is in fact one about the relation between the world of the text and the world of the readers, or the real world.

To be sure, Frei is also aware of the different emphasis. There is a dissimilarity between the realism of the novel and that of the Bible. In Frei's opinion, Nineteenth century realism 'was not simply a literary movement but a broad apprehension of the world and man's place in it.'[37] He seems to agree with our hypothesis that every realism, no matter how self-effacing before the subject-matter itself, conceals a theoretical view about the world. The very adoption of a literary doctrine commits one to making certain decisions about the fit between words and the world. The same is true for Frei: his adoption of the category of realistic narrative committed him to a certain understanding of the reference of the Biblical texts.

Frei's version of realism is coloured by his concern to guard against interpretive *laissez faire*. The meaning of the text is closely connected, almost to the point of complete confusion, with its textual form. For all its similarity to New Criticism, this doctrine, argues Frei, is in fact a consequence of the Chalcedonian reading of the literary narratives themselves. Since Jesus' humanity and divinity cohere inseparably yet unconfusedly in the same person, the narratives themselves insofar as they are realistic stories, do not permit a separation of meaning from their narrative shape. Admittedly, this analogy from Christology to the relation between letter and meaning stretches the imagination to some extent.

If Frei is less historically inclined than Auerbach, he is more 'spiritually minded.' He rejects Auerbach's description of essential Christian identity, which should not be sought in the 'spiritual' reaction of Peter and the disciples to Jesus' death, but in the narrative rendering of Jesus' life, death *and resurrection*. The crucial significance of the narrative rendering of Jesus' life is hard to miss. Frei does not locate Christian identity in the history of Jesus as such, but precisely in the narrative rendering of his life, death and resurrection. In departing from Auerbach's liberal notion of Christianity, Frei will avoid the sort of secularism that the former unwittingly makes possible. For example, Harvey Cox, in his influential and brilliant book, *The Secular City* builds upon this further separation of body from Spirit, of the letteral[38] from the spiritual. By reducing spirit to the reactions provoked by Jesus, a second order term,[39] Auerbach allows 'spirit to become little more than a symbol of the disciples' spiritual experience of the risen Je-

---

[37] Frei, *Eclipse*, pp. 136-7.

[38] Loughlin's term, *Telling God's Story*, p. 123.

[39] See chapter V for the significance of the distinction between orders of language for postliberal theology.

sus.'[40] Yet this very symbolism entails the arbitrariness of the textual content itself. Essential Christian identity could have easily received a different expression, other than that conveyed through the resurrection pericopes. Ironically, the very attempt to preserve textual and graphic singularity has led Auerbach back towards allegory: the resurrection as allegory of the disciples' existential transformation.[41]

Apparently supersessionist and fascist distinctions are still possible, even in the wake of Auerbach: 'The God of the Gospel is the one who wills freedom and responsibility, who points towards the future in hope. The law, on the other hand, includes any cultural phenomenon which holds men in immaturity, in captivity to convention and tradition,' writes Harvey Cox, making transparent a series of modern prejudices about tradition, and about the distinction between freedom and law.[42]The diremption of letter and spirit is maintained in this version of secularism. Yet in making such judgements, Cox authenticates the divorce between body and spirit. Although his later formulations polish somewhat the abruptness of his earlier statements, the general preference for the unrestrained freedom from law remains. In such secularism, identity can only be given in utter isolation from constraints.

Frei has no such typically modern prejudices against the positivity of the Gospels. Their material content and textual form should not be evaded in a fateful search for spiritual meanings. He places spirit securely at the heart of identity. Whereas Auerbach restricts the domain of the spiritual to the second-order *response* of the disciples, thus returning figuration to allegory and ensuring that future secular realisms are not fee from such allegorical lapses, Frei 'enhances Auerbach's relational or non-substantial conception of spiritual understanding by restating it as a negative rule.'[43] Frei writes: 'The pattern of meaning glimpsed in an historical event, or within two or more occasions figurally and thus meaningfully related, cannot be stated apart from the depiction or narration of the occasion(s). The occurrence character and the theme or teleological pattern of a historical or history-like narrative belong together.'[44]

The realistic or history-like character of the Bible is discovered on the basis of its structural features, at least in the first part of Frei's career. Realistic narrative assumes the functions of a genre, one very similar to a historical account: 'In all these characteristics: inseparability of subject matter from its description, literal rather than symbolic quality of human subject

---

[40] Dawson, *Figural Reading*, p. 142.

[41] As indeed Rudolf Bultmann elaborated.

[42] Harvey Cox, *The Secular City: Secularisation and Urbanisation in Theological Perspective*, (London: Penguin, 1968), p. 47.

[43] Dawson, *Figural Reading*, p. 153.

[44] Frei, *Eclipse*, p. 34.

and his social context, mutual rendering of character, circumstance and their interaction – a realistic narrative is like an historical account.'[45] Content and meaning are inseparably tied to form and narrative rendering. Thus, the meaning of the stories is not in the connection that obtains between the world of the text and that of the reader.[46] The gospels' realistic depictions, mingling of styles, force of circumstance and other features include the texts within a certain genre, that of realistic story. The confusion and category mistake of the preceding centuries was due to the neglect of such features of the text and the confusion of stories with histories. The Bible was treated as a historical document, whose meaning lies in the historical events of the past. Instead, Frei argues, one should recover a sense of the inseparability of form and content and treat the Scriptural documents as ends in themselves.

I shall argue that, on the contrary, the ostensive interest arose, in part, following he correction identification of what the gospels were about. However, following Frei, the ostensive interest should have been ruled by the texts themselves and not by neutral historiography. Frei has located the gospels within the category of realistic narrative. This situating was made on the basis of perceived textual elements. Several questions must be raised with respect to this procedure. The argument will include several movements: first, it will be argued that the category of realistic narrative is not a genre and cannot function as such in biblical hermeneutics. Secondly, its importance and relevance is a function of the context in which it is employed: historical or fictional; and finally, one cannot decide as to the most appropriate context by an appeal to structural and intra-textual features alone. The distinction between history and fiction, it will be argued, is not given wholly intra-textually, but should include extra-textual considerations as well. Such problems derive from the specific theory of meaning which Frei assumes and which I shall critique with the aid of Donald Davidson's philosophy. However, such discussions will have to be postponed for now.

A formal category such as 'realistic narrative' cannot be expected to bear the weight of interpretation all by itself. The desire to keep everything intra-textual derives from Frei's insistence that the singularity of the Christian scriptures is lost when read in light of external criteria of meaning and truth.[47] The gospels provide their own criteria for meaning and reference.

[45] Frei, *Eclipse*, p. 14.

[46] Cf. for example Scholes' and Kellog's definition of narrative meaning. Robert Scholes and Robert Kellog, *The Nature of Narrative*, (New York: Oxford University Press, 1996), p. 82.

[47] Charles Wood also finds more neutral reasons for adopting the 'principle of intra-textuality' in 'the more general features of language learning and conceptual growth' (Charles Wood, 'Hermeneutics and the authority of Scripture', in Green, ed., *Scriptural Authority*, p. 17).

This strategic move, however, backfires when theoretical categories are covertly imported back into hermeneutics. The earlier Frei believed one could have stable and autonomous texts. Walter Ong and Werner Kelber suggest that this naiveté was facilitated by a textual, written culture within which 'the technologizing, objectivizing impact of printing had reached a high point.'[48] Realism does indeed sponsor different ontologies, and Kelber sensibly points out that the formalist adoption of the category of narrative was not free from cultural assumptions. In fact, it assumed the colouring of the Eighteenth, Nineteenth and Twentieth centuries realistic novels in Anglo-American, French and Russian literature.[49]

The overloading of the concept could only fail since neither the category of narrative, nor that of realism are in themselves sufficient textual indicators.[50] As Meir Sternberg argues, more specificity is needed in order to make the category workable in interpretation. If realistic narrative is to have an explanatory value, it must neither be two narrow, as to render its application to a multitude of texts impossible, nor too wide as to allow for unrealistic genre variation. In Sternberg's opinion, Frei's category is too wide: 'generally speaking, realism or history likeness never has a bearing in its own right on meaning and interpretation because it signifies one thing in a historiographical and another in a fictional context.'[51]

Frei too hastily projects the concept of realistic narrative on the stories of the Bible and assumes that the proper context is a fictional one. The adoption of a fictional context, as his intra-textual procedure demands, is based on literary features. Until recently, the Bible's accounts were thought to be historical and thus was behind a certain ontological shift: 'all across the theological spectrum the great reversal has taken place; interpretation was a matter of fitting the biblical story into another world with another story, rather than incorporating the world into the biblical story.'[52] As I shall point out, the concept of world absorption is central for Frei and it provides the key to understanding the relationship between fiction and history that he has in mind. In order to undo this fateful ontological reversal, one had to refigure theological methodology so that external stories become figures of he biblical story itself. Secondly, one had to understand that the point of the

---

[48] Werner Kelber, 'Gospel narrative and critical theory', *Biblical Interpretation Bulletin*, 18 (1988), 130-136, p. 132.

[49] Kelber, 'Gospel narrative', p. 132.

[50] Daniel Beaumont, 'The modality of narrative: a critique of some recent views of narrative in theology', *Journal of the American Academy of Religion*, 65 (1997), 125-139, p. 127. J. P. Stern, *On Realism*, (London: Routledge and Kegan Paul, 1973), pp. 31, 156.

[51] Meir Sternberg, *The Poetics of Biblical Narrative: Ideological Literature and the Drama of Reading*, (Bloomington: Indiana University Press, 1985), p. 82.

[52] Frei, *Identity*, p. 130.

biblical story resides in the story itself, not outside it. For Frei this means that the Gospels could not be interpreted in light of historiographical canons. He hesitates to treat the gospel accounts as history because, contrary to modern history writing, they depict intention, inner thoughts and monologues, things which only an author of fiction could claim access to. These are therefore textual pointers to the fictive nature of the accounts.

However, one must ask, echoing Sternberg, does 'bad' historiography make fiction? Frei's procedure is that of distinguishing fiction from history on purely intra-textual grounds. The category of realistic narrative is discovered by a simple reading of the text. This leads Sternberg to point out three separate confusions made by Frei: first, he confuses history telling, which relates to the *truth claim* of the discourse, and historicity, which means the *truth value* and which has nothing to do with meaning or interpretation. The point is that there is a distinction between the intention of the author and the results of the writing, or the probable success of what he or she set out to do. Whether felicity attaches to a speech act is very much connected to the intention of the author.[53] Secondly, continues Sternberg, Frei confuses both with history-likeness. The category of history-likeness is not self-explanatory in the absence of a specific context. Both history and certain types of fiction are history like. Finally, there is the confusion betwenn the truth claims of history-like and historical narrative, whose variance is important for the meaning of those texts since it establishes the presence or absence of fictional license: 'And what is this if not a variance in genre and generic convention?'[54]

The difficulty of distinguishing history from fiction by attending to the text alone derives from the assumption that texts mean differently in a fictional and in a historical context. One cannot therefore derive the context from the meaning, for the meaning itself depends on such a context. A distinction can be made between an illocution and the meaning of the locution. The question is whether one could derive the nature of the illocutionary act from the meaning of the story. Should this be possible, then, as Searle argues, we cannot possibly imagine an illocutionary act of fiction for that would imply that words do not have their normal meaning in a work of fiction. The fiction writer only pretends to assert something. This is a pseudo-speech-act, parasitic upon serious discourse.[55] A set of extra-textual, non-semantic conventions break the usual assertorical connection between

---

[53] So McClendon and Smith, *Understanding*, pp. 59-63.

[54] Sternberg, *Poetics*, p. 82.

[55] Kendall L. Walton, *Mimesis: On the Foundation of the Representational Arts*, (Cambridge, Mass. and London: Harvard University Press, 1990), p. 75.

words and world.[56] Searle does indeed point in the right direction, although his solution may not be the happiest one.[57] There are no textual pointers[58] in the direction of fiction and interpretation cannot restrict itself to observing semantics. Context is always involved with a text.[59] As Thiselton has argued, following the speech act theory of Searle and Wolterstorff, the force of the narratives differs according to extra-linguistic, behavioural commitments.[60] The happy functioning of texts depends on events occurring behind them, which become institutional or behavioural pointers. This will involve a major shift in perspective, from an aesthetic treatment of texts as artefacts, as closed units of meaning (Walton, formalism, Frei) to a pragmatic-poetic discernment of the holistic process which involves texts from their composition[61] to their reception.

---

[56] John Searle, *Expression and Meaning: Studies in the Theory of Speech Acts*, (Cambridge: Cambridge University Press, 1979), p. 66; John Searle, 'The logical status of fictional discourse', *New Literary History*, 1975, p. 6.

[57] Walton objects that illocutionary aspects are irrelevant to the meaning of fiction: 'the action of fiction making does not have a place in the institution of fiction similar to that which illocutionary actions have in ordinary conversation' (p. 87). This has echoes in Ricoeur, Derrida and Frei ('Theology and the interpretation of narrative', in Frei, *Theology and Narrative*, p. 102). For Walton, fiction is determined by its serving as a prop in games of imagination. He extends the concept of fiction to non-authored texts (pictures, accidentally generated texts), whose textuality he dubiously takes for granted. Yet, while fiction making is not so central to its institutional interpretation, it is essential for what enters the so-called institution of literary fiction. The latter accepts or rejects a text regardless of whether it serves as a prop for imagination, solely on the basis of its being authorially identified as fiction.

[58] Searle, *Expression*, p. 68.

[59] For example, Sternberg, *Poetics*, pp. 11, 12, argues that every text presupposes a grammar which is external to the text, yet indispensable for its meaning. The same goes for metaphors, their meaningfulness depends on the reader being able to draw extra-textual connections. Also see Davidson's point that 'grammatical mood and illocutionary force, no matter how closely related, cannot be related simply by convention' (Davidson, 'Communication and convention', in *Inquiries into Truth and Interpretation*, (Oxford: Clarendon, 1984), p. 270).

[60] This account will be reinforced with Davidson's holistic theory of the interdependence of truth and meaning. See below, chapter 4. cf. also Peter Lamarque's distinction between surface-semantic properties and intention or use: 'The property of being a work of art is not reducible to any set of surface or semantic properties of language, but it is at least partly and essentially to do with intention and use' (Peter Lamarque, *Fictional Points of View*, (Ithaca and London: Cornell University Press, 1996), p. 25). cf. also R. M. Gale, 'The fictive use of language,' *Philosophy* 46 (1971), 324-339.

[61] Sternberg has been instrumental in calling attention to the poetics of narrative, *Poetics*, pp. 14, 36.

Searle dismisses the illocutionary act of fiction on the basis of his 'determination principle' which states that the meaning of the sentence determines the illocutionary act. Yet, as Gregory Currie points out, the same statement may be used to make different illocutionary acts. Take for example the proposition 'You are going to the concert' (intentionally left without any punctuation which might denote intention). The locution could be used to make an assertion ('*You* are going to the concert.'), ask a question ('You *are* going to the concert [, aren't you?].'), or give a command ('You are going to the concert [or else...]!'). Secondly, Searle's own theory is contradicting his determination principle: 'What Searle is saying is that the same sentence with the same meaning can occur in nonfiction as the result of the illocutionary act of assertion, and again in fiction as the result of an act which is not an illocutionary act at all. So the sentence meaning does not determine the illocutionary act performed.'[62] The solution offered by Currie is to take the writer of fiction not as pretending to assert something, but as inviting us to pretend or engage in games of make-believe. In this case as well, the author of fiction relies on the awareness of the audience that they are presented with a fiction.[63]

Another variant of the speech-act approach to basically the same effect is Nicholas Wolterstorff's. What makes a work fiction is a certain kind of authorial stance.[64] The mere existence of a thing – sentence, picture, a semaphore, a flag, or indeed an action – will not do.[65] By distinguishing between cause generation and count generation, Wolterstorff effectively ties meaning to the actions of the author who count-generates. Cause-generated things may be interpreted without respect to whatever actions

---

[62] Gregory Currie, 'What is fiction?', *Journal of Aesthetics and Art Criticism*, 63 (1985), 385-392, p. 386.

[63] The debate seems to be revolving around very different notions of meaning. For speech-act theorists meaning involves not only a textual property, but the significance of what the author is doing *in writing a text*. For Frei and the formalists meaning is restricted textually. The diversity of events attaching to the text (composition, reception, response, reference) although legitimate concerns, have no bearing on meaning. Jeffrey Stout forcefully argues that the whole debate around meaning is fuelled by contradictory definitions of meaning and that we would be better off by simply doing away with the notion. Instead one may concentrate on the variety of legitimate interpretive interests (Jeffrey Stout, 'What is the meaning of a text?', *New Literary History*, 14 (1982), 1-12. For a theological application of his suggestions, see Stephen Fowl, *Engaging Scripture: A Model for Theological Interpretation*, (Oxford: Blackwell, 1998), esp. pp. 56-61.

[64] Cf. also Thiselton's 'purposive directedness': Anthony C. Thiselton, *New Horizons in Hermeneutics: The Theory and Practice of Transforming Biblical Reading*, (Grand Rapids: Zondervan, 1992), pp. 13, 45, 50, but esp. 297, 558-562.

[65] Nicholas Wolterstorff, *Works and Worlds of Art*, (Oxford: Clarendon, 1990), p. 221.

brought them into being. In fact they do not require interpretation, except insofar they are parts of a semiotic structure. Count-generated things, on the contrary, have their very being in their originating event. Thus the essence of fiction lies in the mood-stance taken up by the author.[66] It is not the propositional content that makes a work of art fiction. Rather, 'What makes him a fictioneer nonetheless is that he nothing affirmeth, but something presenteth.'[67] What this means for our discussion is that Frei's deduction of the fictive nature of the gospels on the basic of their internal features is unwarranted. The absence (perceived or actual) of *truth value* in the gospel accounts is not definitive of fiction, nor does it detract anything from its *historical claim*.

The Gospels as History

Francis Watson voices our concern so far: it seems that Frei has employed constricting theoretical concepts such as fiction and history and forced the gospels into an either/or situation. These categories, however, are too rigid and do not take account of recent work on the interlacing of history and fiction.[68]

However, to say that Frei simply dismisses the historical claim of the gospels is to operate the same sort of dualistic categories as Gary Comstock, when he accuses Frei of choosing meaning instead of reference. Although Frei appears to unreservedly embrace the fictive status of the gospels, writing that we are fortunate that the gospel stories are more nearly fictional rather than historical,[69] historical questions do accrue eventually. The narrative rendering of Jesus' identity is more authentic in a fictive story

---

[66] Wolterstorff, *Works*, p. 234.

[67] Wolterstorff, *Works*, p. 234. Fiction, Wolterstorff argues, is distinguished by the fact that it presents something to our imagination.

[68] Francis Watson, *Text and Truth: Redefining Biblical Theology*, (Edinburgh: T&T Clark, 1997), p. 56; Paul Ricoeur, *Time and Narrative*, 3 volumes, trans. by Kathleen McLaughlin and David Pellauer, (Chicago: University of Chicago Press,1984-1988), esp. vol. 1; Paul Ricoeur, 'Toward a narrative theology', in Paul Ricoeur, *Figuring the Sacred: Religion, Narrative and Imagination*, trans. David Pellauer, ed. by Mark I. Wallace, (Minneapolis: Fortress Press, 1995), writes that one should neither use a concept of story that eludes the dialectic between story and history, nor a concept of history which doesn't take into account this 'variable curve of relationships between history and story' (pp. 244f). Stephen Prickett also comments that 'However different the biblical author's notions of history may have been from our own, we have no reason to suppose that they did not believe that they were relating 'fact', and not 'fact-likeness' in Frei's sense' (Prickett, *Words and the Word: Language, Poetics and Biblical Interpretation*, (Cambridge: Cambridge University Press, 1986), pp. 77f.).

[69] Frei, *Identity*, p. 145.

than in an historical account, in the accepted sense of these categories. The stories help believers identify Jesus Christ as well as grafting their own stories unto his. In preferring a narrative rather than an historical or scientific explanation of identity, Frei follows the trend we have traced back as early as Vico. The story's ability to mediate particularity enables it to be such a good negotiator of identity. Ricoeur too writes about the narrative ability to configure time, rendering it liveable and personal. In the same vein, J. P. Stern places realistic narratives at a *middle distance* between reader and reality.[70] It is a middle distance in that reality is described using imaginatively creative concepts and instruments, which are not as such derived from it.

The construction of fictions is an inevitable part of out coping with the world. Their metaphorical nature resides in the fact that in order to deal with the multitude of 'facts', we need concepts that perform a reductive function. This is the point of fiction for Hans Vaihinger, namely to provide us with manageable concepts in order to sort reality out: 'fiction means in the first place, an activity of *fingere*, that is to say, of constructing, forming, giving shape, elaborating, presenting, artistically fashioning; conceiving, thinking, imagining, assuming, planning, devising, inventing.'[71] The parallels with Vico could hardly be more obvious: making is already involved with knowing, with discovery. The point being argued by an increasing number of influential authors is that one need not be suspicious of elements of making and creation in works whose interest is knowledge and truth. To continue with Vaihinger, however, fiction is arbitrarily derived from reality; it disappears in the course of history or through the operation of logic; finally, it is self-aware of its fictiveness.[72] He contrasts fiction with hypothesis, which is oriented towards reality and demands verification, while fiction only demands justification in terms of its use. Interestingly, Vaihinger writes 'How easily the fiction can transform itself into an hypothesis can be seen by the fact that the audience and the reader are not able to maintain the psychical tension of the *as if* indefinitely.'[73]

As if quoting Vaihinger, Frei comments that 'If a novel-like account is about a person who is assumed to have lived, the question of the factuality is virtually bound to arise for psychological if no other reasons, either at

---

[70] Stern, *On Realism*, pp. 113ff; David Ford, *Barth and God's Story: Biblical Narrative and the Theological Method of Karl Barth in the 'Church Dogmatics'*, (Frankfurt am Meine and Berne: Verlag Peter Lang, 1981), p. 195.

[71] Hans Vaihinger, *The Philosophy of 'As If': A System of the Theoretical, Practical and Religions Fictions of Mankind*, trans. by C. K. Ogden, (London: Routledge and Kegan Paul, 1965), p. 82.

[72] Vaihinger, *As If*, pp. 97-99.

[73] Vaihinger, *As If*, p. 83. For a critique of Vaihinger, cf. Green, '"The Bible As..."', pp. 87ff.

specific points, or over the whole stretch of the account.'[74] One such point is the passion-resurrection sequence, where Jesus is narratively 'most fully historical at this point in the narrative, if by "historical" we mean that he is regarded as an un-substitutable individual in his own right.'[75] It is where Christ is most fully himself, and not at all points in the narratives, that the fact question arises: 'the question of factuality is bound to arise precisely at the point where his individuality is most sharply asserted and etched.'[76]

For Vaihinger, a fiction turns into a hypothesis because of a break in the extra-textual conventions which provide the context within which the work subsists. For Frei there are no such conventions other than their possible graphic embodiment in the text. Speech act theory derives fiction from external conventions which point to an original authorial stance, be it that of pretending, inviting readers to pretend, or presenting. Frei does not deny that the authors have written purposefully:

> It is, of course, that every author – including the authors of the synoptic gospels – writes from some governing convictions and with some theme or intention in mind, even if it be no more than the telling of a good tale. Obviously the gospel writers wanted to do much more than that. But we cannot with certainty tell their convictions and intentions apart from the narrative text.[77]

It might be supposed that he rehearses the modern argument against authorial intention. My position, however, is not based on a depth hermeneutics that recovers authorial mental states which are very much private. On the contrary, it assumes the existence of social and hence very public conventions,[78] which fulfil the role of institutional pointers. It is ironic that Frei ends up removing the text – as autonomous artefact – from the traditional history of interpretation, which includes such institutional conventions.

Should historical questions arise, they can only proceed from and on the basis of the text.[79] Indeed, they do arise precisely at the moment when the description achieves such a quality of life-likeness that factual issues not only arise, but are actually forced: 'the passion-resurrection account tends to force the question of the factuality because the claim is involved as part of the very identity that is described as enacted and manifest in the story-

---

[74] Frei, *Identity*, p. 141.

[75] Frei, *Theology and Narrative*, p. 76.

[76] Frei, *Theology and Narrative*, p. 83.

[77] Frei, *Identity*, p. 47.

[78] Cf. Vanhoozer, *Is There a Meaning?*, pp. 245-6, 348.

[79] William Placher, *Narratives of a Vulnerable God: Christ, Theology and Scripture*, (Louisville: Westminster John Knox, 1992), p. 97.

event sequence.'[80] At this point, fictional description merges with factual claim, for to know *who* the narratively painted Christ is means to know *that* he is.[81] Story overflows into reality, following its own logic. To understand the identity of Christ is to understand that he exists and lives in the present.[82] The transition is from a fictional point of view to the real world. But does this not involve an irreconcilable contradiction? On the one hand Frei insists that the gospels are fictional, while on the other he appears to be making strong ontological claims on a literary basis. If one takes the fictive nature of the stories to imply no involvement with reality, then the contradiction remains.[83] Yet there is every indication that the gospels, although fictive, are not unrelated to the 'real' world. For Frei, 'the narrated world is the real world and not a linguistic launching pad to language-transcending reality, whether ideal essence or self-contained empirical occurrence... the reality is given linguistically, it is linguistic for us.'[84] Resonances with Vico, Hamann, and Milbank are hard to miss here: we only have reality under a linguistic description. The textual boundaries of the biblical world are the real boundaries of the only 'real' world we know.

To understand this postliberal claim is to understand that no dualism may obtain between biblical meaning and historical reference, between Jesus' literary identity and his historical person. Reference is textually regulated by the grammar of the Scriptures, and with the later Frei, of the Christian tradition. Frei's project is an Anselmian one,[85] of the elucidation of the conditions and grammar of Christian faith. It is not a literary argument for the resurrection. The biblical world is simply assumed as being the normative measure of reality for the Christian.

This may confirm our previous suspicion that the assumption of a tradition ineluctably leads towards fideism, in the absence of any historical (or external) adjudication of the truth of the gospels. Should the locality of the Christian story simply be assumed and ascribed primacy over all other discourses? To a superficial reader this may indeed be the consequence. But this is where the discussion of figuration becomes relevant to issues of fideism. Having one's story absorbed by the biblical narrative need not mean an allegorical superseding of one's identity. The tradition of figural reading extends from biblical exegesis to a method of approach to extra-biblical

---

[80] Frei, *Identity*, p. 146.

[81] Frei, *Identity*, p. 145.

[82] This is the only hermeneutical direction recommended by Frei: from his textual identity to a doctrinal or existential description of his presence today, *Identity*, pp. 1-11.

[83] William Placher, 'Gospel ends: plurality and ambiguity in biblical narrative', *Modern Theology* 10 (1994), 143-163, and *Narratives of a Vulnerable God*, pp. 94ff.

[84] Frei, *Theology and Narrative*, p. 104.

[85] Kevin Vanhoozer, *Biblical Narrative in the Philosophy of Paul Ricoeur: A Study of Hermeneutics and Theology*, (Cambridge: Cambridge University Press, 1990), p. 160.

realities. A figural participation in God's story does not *necessarily* involve losing one's identity in a fideist and unreflected assimilation. On the contrary, the very idea of figuration reflects on that of world absorption in order to invite authentic dialogue and preservation of particularity. The fact that for the Christians the scriptures render not only Jesus' and God' identities but also the identities of extra-scriptural realities does not necessarily lead to a sectarian attitude of superiority. On the demonstration of this point rests my claim that there is a tradition-constituted preservation of uniqueness and ontology of peaceful difference.

Interpretation and Law

Emerging from the debates around tradition, community and interpretation is a moral spectre of questions having to do with personal identity, violence and manipulation. The self-sufficient world of the Biblical narratives purports to re-narrate reality for us, thus raising fears of insularity and irrationality. Although this danger is built into the claims of the Christian story, it is not its necessary outcome. Christian figural reading provides us with an account of how participation in the divinely enacted narratives does not sublate particularity, but actually intensifies it.

The previous discussion has touched upon the difficult relation between setting and agency. The discovery of the importance of human *artificium* by Vico prepared the way for an understanding of the habituated nature of all knowledge. Knowing assumes the existence of a context of human creations – which the later Vico increasingly associates with signs[86] – without which it would be rendered impossible. Here we have the abandonment of the original, as the absent cause. Human creations are not of secondary importance. They are indispensable in the mediation of truth. It is the setting, as the symbolic order constructed through human creations and signification, which conditions agency. The present discussion continues with Gadamer's suggestion that law provides the best example of interpretation. He argues that there can be no distinction between meaning and application. Again we witness realism taking another step back, from the text towards the setting which conditions its exegesis. For Vico too, language is first law, it violently 'manages' reality, postponing realism. Yet there is no textually un-mediated way to that reality. This linguistic pragmatism is adapted theologically by George Lindbeck who views religion as a language through which we perceive reality. The unmistakable tendency in postliberal circles is to assume a dualism between religious scheme and experiential content and to forego a dialectical negotiation between reality and this scheme through which we perceive it, or the setting. Language, constructed not as definitions but as use, imposes itself upon it, rendering it

---

[86] Milbank, *The Religious Dimension*, vol. 2, p. 4.

unreachable. Just as we have law only under the influence of its historical applications, so we only have God, Scriptures and reality only under their practical linguistic formalisation in religion.

It is well known that Gadamer capitalises on the Heideggerian heritage in the field of hermeneutics. His decision to make subjectivity central to meaning results in making application inherent to understanding. Understanding is no longer simply *discovery*, as the reader always brings his own symbolic horizon into the conversation. It presupposes the fusion of horizons. Hence the task of application cannot really be separated from that of application or use. The inevitable background of interpretation is a shared practice and social action which makes possible the disclosure of something.[87] The model of legal hermeneutics illuminates the relationship between understanding and application. The classical statement of the relation distinguished between *subtilitas intelligendi* (understanding), *subtilitas explicandi* (interpretation) and *subtilitas applicandi* (application – added by Pietism). Traditionally, Gadamer observes, there has existed a close kinship between the first two, to the exclusion of the third element.[88] Legal and theological hermeneutics, both dealing in application, were thus further inhibited, since both incorporated a basic tension between the fixed text and the sense which resulted by application to the concrete situation: 'A law does not exist in order to be understood historically, but to be concretised in its legal validity by being interpreted. Similarly the Gospel does not exist in order to be understood as a merely historical document, but to be taken in such a way that exercises its saving effect.'[89] Gadamer's claim involves two important elements. First, it is a claim made on behalf of a regional hermeneutics (legal and theological). It is therefore not immediately clear if it has a bearing on general hermeneutics, that is, if *all* understanding is application. Secondly, it is based on literary considerations, i.e., it is derived from the discovery of certain features of the text or behind the text. Gadamer implies that a proper understanding of the text needs to take into consideration the type of claim it makes. Considering the relationship between these regional instances and literary hermeneutics as such, or philological interpretation, Gadamer finds no real difference in this respect. He discerns a tension between understanding what a text means and understanding how it comes to be applied to a specific situation. The two tasks, the discovery of sense and the creation of sense in application, are not different: 'Our thesis is that historical hermeneutics too has a task of application to perform, because it too serves applicable meaning, in that it explicitly and consciously bridges the temporal distance that separates the interpreter from the text and

---

[87] Kögler, *The Power of Dialogue*, p. 88.
[88] Gadamer, *Truth and Method*, p. 308.
[89] Gadamer, *Truth and Method*, p. 309.

overcomes the alienation of meaning that the text has undergone.'[90] This development is significant since understanding and application increasingly seem to be mutually involved in one another. Understanding means that the reader has already concretised the sense of the text with respect to his own symbolic horizon, which is to say that the text has already been applied to his situation. To understand is already to appropriate.

Kathryn Tanner astutely points out that this pragmatic turn towards use does not issue in a neglect of the formal characteristics of texts. Although meaning is gradually being relocated in the space between interpreter and text, 'this relational account... does not eschew entirely, however, explanation in terms of the text's own properties.'[91]

Each interpreter, when approaching a text, is conditioned and constrained by a history of textual effects, that is by a history of application. Such a history involves a sedimentation of meaning, or what Gadamer calls history of effects. Each new textual use contributes something to the meaning of the text in view of the fact that it concretises the text for a given situation, audience, reader. Legal hermeneutics is an instance of such a process. After a laborious argument, Gadamer concludes that the task of the legal historian is not different from the task of the jurist or the normative interpreter. Both readings involve understanding the law according to its possible applications. The jurist, on the one hand, understands the law from the perspective of the case at hand. The legal historian, on the other, without being restricted to a particular case, 'seeks to determine the meaning of the law by constructing the whole range of its applications.'[92] The historian's is not a straightforwardly reconstructive enterprise, but a creatively interpretive one.[93] The upshot is that the distinction between meaning and application is eroded in favour of a pragmatist reorientation of hermeneutics. The reality of the law recedes before the practices which constitute its setting. The new applications will enter the history of effects as *precedents*. It is at this point that Gadamer's proposal is most problematic, for he goes on to say that the application adds new meaning to the law.[94] Meaning is sedimented through application: the content of law (and text) is creatively altered in the wake of its new applications. This is a radical proposal since it would seem that it effectively does away with the objectivity of the text. We remember Frei's earlier objections to this specifically 'hermeneutical' bias: the particularity of the textual sense is lost and its meaning is located

---

[90] Gadamer, *Truth and Method*, p. 311.

[91] Kathryn Tanner, 'Scripture as popular text', *Modern Theology* 14 (1988), 279-298, p. 283.

[92] Gadamer, *Truth and Method*, p. 325.

[93] See similar accounts of the task of historiography by Ricoeur, Hayden White, Arthur Danto.

[94] Gadamer, *Truth and Method*, pp. 330ff.

extra-textually. The text now seems to have become the absent cause of a complex of actions on the part of the interpreter, not an ontological entity in itself. The issue receives an even more relativistic twist when Gadamer writes that 'the judge cannot let himself be bound by what, say, an account of parliamentary proceedings tells him about the intentions of those who first passed the law. Rather, he has to take account of the change in circumstances and hence define afresh the normative function of the law.'[95] Authorial intention is not important when seeking the relevant application of law. Since the law, or the classic is a text with potentially infinite applications, the task of the interpreter is to fit it to ever new circumstances. This requires a certain amount of creativity and imagination. The question is whether by departing from a textual realism and from authorial intention Gadamer opens himself to the charge of relativism.

Kenneth Abraham reminds us that legislatures are corporate authors and do not necessarily speak with a unified intention.[96] Anyone at minimally familiar with parliamentary proceedings realises the common sense of such a reminder. Indeed, laws cannot envisage all contingencies. However, Gadamer avoids the relativist trap by making it clear that this does not give complete creative license to the jurist. The interpretation of the judge is not an 'arbitrary revision' for 'to understand and to interpret means to discover and recognise a valid meaning.'[97] This suggests that Gadamer's pragmatism is crucially tempered by an emphasis on the initiative of the text. Again Tanner gets it right: 'the text is somehow still in control of its own reception by way of its internal amplitude.'[98] The sedimentation of meaning in the history of effects is not an arbitrary imposition of meaning on top of the text, giving rise to the danger that an accumulation of corrupt practices might eventually obscure the truth of the text. Rather, it is the text itself, in virtue of its being a *classic* that demands following:

> We can, then, distinguish what is truly common to all forms of hermeneutics: the meaning to be understood is concretised and fully realised only in interpretation, but the interpretive activity considers itself wholly bound by the meaning of the text. Neither jurist nor theologian regards the work of application as making free with the text.[99]

---

[95] Gadamer, *Truth and Method*, p. 327.

[96] Kenneth S. Abraham, 'Statutory interpretation and literary theory: some common concerns of an unlikely pair', in Sanford Levinson and Steven Mailloux, eds. *Interpreting Law and Literature: A Hermeneutic Reader*, (Evanston: Northwestern University Press, 1988), p. 121.

[97] Gadamer, *Truth and Method*, p. 328.

[98] Tanner, 'Scripture as Popular Text', p. 284.

[99] Gadamer, *Truth and Method*, p. 332.

Jean Grondin calls attention to an ambiguity in Gadamer's hermeneutics at this point. While insisting that application is not the same in each case, it is also loosely defined as the connection between my world and the world of the text.[100] It is doubtful whether the Pietists would have considered this an application. In taking the example of a command, it is clear that Gadamer does not have in mind the same sort of application that is a postliberal emphasis. To understand a command is to apply it to one's situation. This does not mean that disobedience to the order is identical to misunderstanding it. Quite the contrary: it is precisely because one understood what the order entails for one's world that one has refused to obey it. Gadamer thus contributes an interesting insight here: one does not necessarily have to be part of a practice in order to understand its concepts. We shall return to this issue in our discussion of Frei's later notions of literal sense. Distinguishing between *imagined application* and *actual application* (being part of a practice and acquiring a skill),[101] one may say that it is only the former which is essential to understanding.[102]

It is true that Gadamer universalises the presence of application in all forms of human understanding. Application does not entail an original moment in which one has understood and a subsequent one in which one has applied. However, this sedimentation of meaning is not applicable to theological hermeneutics. As we have already pointed out, the context of Gadamer's argument is legal hermeneutics. It is the very nature of law that its applications add meaning to it. It is in this specifically local hermeneutics that new applications *add* meaning to law. Gadamer does not propose a theory of meaning, but an elucidation of what is the case in a specific hermeneutical context. He is providing us with an intra-textual, in this case intra-legal, description. He does something very similar to what the later Frei does and for two distinct reasons.

The first is a literary-legal consideration: laws are made with the knowledge that they are incomplete and that they need actualisation for specific circumstances. In civil law[103] there is a methodological distinction between general law and special law. General laws are addressed to all citizens of a country, while special laws apply only to certain categories of people. One

---

[100] Jean Grondin, 'Hermeneutics and relativism', in Kathleen Wright, ed., *Festivals of Interpretation: Essays on Hans-Georg Gadamer's Work*, (Albany: State University of New York Press, 1990), p. 315.

[101] This distinction is unfortunately not made explicit by Gadamer, who consequently becomes vulnerable to accusations of subservience to tradition.

[102] What this means in the long run, at least from the perspective of Gadamerian hermeneutics, is that members of different traditions may indeed understand one another, although being part of one tradition may provide one with a greater semantic depth of its own concepts.

[103] The legal system of mostly francophone countries such as France, Romania etc.

of the functions of the special laws is to provide the specificity and applicability of general laws by specifying rules for their application to particular categories of people. But on a more ideological level, there is the principle that no law is able to provide for all its possible applications. Hence the creative task is required by the law's very nature. One may also safely say that it was the very intention of the law makers that the content would be modified together with new applications.

The second reason is an institutional one: in the legal profession there are certain rules for arbitration and for the interpretation of laws, one of which is the principle of precedent. The judge is given this power in common law to supplement the law in virtue of future references to the precedent he will have established. Yet Gadamer makes it quite clear that this is an institutionally derived and arbitrary rule. It does not necessarily have an equivalent in all discovery and application of meaning. *Therefore the fact that all future applications of one given law in specific circumstances will add something to the content of the law is not deduced from a general philosophy of language, or theory of meaning.* If application does not universally add content to texts, laws, events etc., it is universally present in all understanding. What is not clear for Gadamer is in which cases other than the legal ones does application add meaning. Quite clearly, not in theological hermeneutics: 'Unlike a legal verdict, preaching is not a creative supplement to the text it is interpreting. Hence the Gospel *acquires no new content* in being preached that could be compared with the power of the judge's verdict to supplement the law.'[104] As in the case of law, the rules for the interaction of meaning and application are given locally and should not be fixed at a general theoretical level. In the case of theological hermeneutics the two considerations are these: a) the Gospel makes it quite clear that it is unique and not to be altered. It is the sufficient word of God and all proclamation, that is application, should submit to it. Furthermore, all proclamation is fallible, whereas the Word is infallible. b) The institutional rules governing meaning and application do not have a theological equivalent to the doctrine of strict precedent, or *stare decisis*. In a terminology with which we shall become more familiar later, there is an *ad hoc* correlation between meaning and application, a local determination of the relation.[105]

Summing up, Gadamer denies that one can validly distinguish between the two moments of application and understanding. Theoretical projects

---

[104] Gadamer, p. 330. (My emphasis).

[105] Even in the legal profession there is a dissimilarity in the function of precedent in *common* as opposed to *civil law*. Civil law holds the centrality of statutes and laws and does not have a doctrine of strict precedent. The judge is not constrained by the previous applications of law. In common law, where statutes are less important, *stare decisis* establishes a textual foundation and constraint for future decisions. In this context the sedimentation of legal meaning is most transparent.

such as Emilio Betti's,[106] which classify hermeneutics along three lines: cognitive, representational and normative, fail to see the point of all understanding, namely that it forges a relation between the textual world and my world. One cannot separate the cognitive from the representational and both from normative interpretation. My reading, however, shows that the pragmatic considerations are still, at least formally, under textual constraint. Neither judge nor jurist, neither preacher nor theologian may do away with the text.

Since Gadamer himself is not among the primary influences on narrative theologians, a more immediately relevant discussion is in American legal studies. Although theoretically Gadamer does privilege the prevenience of the text, methodologically speaking he remains vulnerable, as Kögler shows. If understanding is an event, it is not clear how its results could be made critically available to the agent. The moment of understanding is not separated from that of application by a deliberative time. One does not consciously 'take time' to understand a text, with the danger that consciousness will retain no critical control over the understanding one reaches.[107] The interpreter or judge is already immersed in the practices and contexts which shape any text. Is it not then legitimate to say that the judge has his decision made up for him? The discussion about the extent to which the judge is constrained and the extent to which he is free to do away with the text is part of the American legal scene.

One American legal debate is on the issue of whether judges have the right to create new meanings for the law. Ronald Dworkin's views on this matter sparked an interesting exchange with Stanley Fish. In his 'How Law

---

[106] For Gadamer's discussion of Betti, see *Truth and Method*, pp. 309-310; 'Hermeneutics and historicism' [supplement to *Truth and Method*]. Betti's views are explained in *Teoria Generale dell'interpretazione* (2 vols., Milan, 1955), a partial translation of which can be found Emilio Betti, *Teoria Generale dell'interpretazione*, translated by Susan Noakes, *Modern Language Studies* 12 (1982), 34-43; see also Joseph Bleicher, *Contemporary Hermeneutics: Hermeneutics As Method, Philosophy and Critique,* (London: Routledge, 1990).

[107] A more useful account may be found in Ricoeur's notion of second naiveté, which involves neither a total submission to the text, nor its violent schematisation by critical theoretical categories. cf. Ricoeur, *Time and Narrative*, vol. 1: pp. 77-81; vol. 3: chap. 7; Paul Ricoeur, *Symbolism of Evil,* trans. Emerson Buchanan, (Boston: Beacon Press, 1969), p. 349. For an excellent analysis cf. Mark I. Wallace, *The Second Naiveté: Barth, Ricoeur, and the New Yale Theology.* Studies in American Biblical Hermeneutics vol. 6. (Macon: Mercer University Press, 1990), *passim*; Dan R. Stiver, *Theology After Ricoeur: New Directions in Hermeneutical Theology*, (Louisville: Westminster John Knox Press, 2001), pp. 56-78.

is Like Literature'[108] and in *Law's Empire*[109], Dworkin compares the process
of judicial decision making with the writing of a 'chain novel' in literature.
In the chain novel, a group of novelists undertake the writing of a novel
seriatim:[110]

> Each novelist in the chain interprets the chapters he has been given in or-
> der to write a new chapter, which is then added to what the next novelist
> receives, and so on. Each has the job of writing his chapter so as to make
> the novel being constructed the best it can be, and the complexity of this
> task models the complexity of deciding a hard case under law as integ-
> rity.[111]

In this case interpretation is a matter of looking at what has gone on before,
at the way in which previous authors have constructed the subject-matter
and deciding how to best continue the enterprise. The governing rule, according to Dworkin, is *to make the object the best it can be*.[112]

Dworkin is concerned with the prescriptive aspect of the case: judges
and authors must[113] interpret in such a manner as to continue the enterprise
and make it the best it can be. This implies an active consciousness, rather
than interpretive passivity. For Fish, however, it betrays a fundamental misunderstanding:

> The force of the account in other words depends on the possibility of
> judges comporting themselves in ways other than the 'chain-enterprise'
> way. What would it mean for a judge to strike out in a new direction?
> Dworkin doesn't tell us, but presumably it would mean deciding a case in
> such a way as to have no relationship with the history of the previous de-
> cisions.[114]

There are, Fish argues, certain practices in the community which constrain
the judge to make certain decisions and not others. He also believes that
Dworkin misunderstands the actual position and possibilities of the writers
of a chain-novel. Dworkin would argue that the first writer is the least constrained and has the greatest freedom of all. There is no text before him to
be interpreted, nothing binds him to some objective foundation on which he
has to build. But the further you go down the chain, the more constrained

---

[108] To be found in his *A Matter of Principle*, (Cambridge, Mass.: Harvard University
Press, 1985).

[109] (Cambridge, Mass.: Harvard University Press, 1986).

[110] Dworkin, *Law's Empire*, pp. 229ff.

[111] Dworkin, *Law's Empire*, p. 229.

[112] Dworkin, *Law's Empire*, p. 53.

[113] Dworkin, Ronald, 'Law as interpretation', *Texas Law Review* 60 (1982), p. 543.

[114] Fish, 'Working on the Chain Gang: Interpretation in Law and Literature', in *Doing What Comes Naturally*, pp. 92-93.

authors you will find. Fish strongly disagrees with this. The first author is himself constrained by the range of what counts as a start to a novel in the language game of the profession.[115] In such a case, the *performance* of a given judge is constrained by the *competence* of his interpretive community. At any given time there are only a number of options open. This is Fish's solution to the tension between freedom and constraint. Fundamentally, this differs from Gadamer's emphasis: it is not the text which constrains the interpreter but the specific grammar of the practice and such a grammar cannot be eluded. The very notion of a judge who would go against the previous history of precedents and give a ruling which does not take this effective history into account is a practical impossibility, 'since any decision, to be recognised as a decision by a judge, would have to be made in recognisably judicial terms.'[116] If a judge would give a decision based on, say, the fact that it is raining outside, such a statement would not count as a judicial decision. What Fish is saying is quite commonsensical: there are given rules within a community which restrict the range of possible actions. Dissent and harmony can only be recognised as such and can only exist in a ruled context.

If Fish were to stop here he would have had the merit of supplying us with a theory of the regional application of meaning rules. But of course, he doesn't. In the process the very notion of the text is erased. To say that rules constrain interpretation is not to say that they do not change. Dworkin raises the issue of an interpreter who gives a philosophical reading of an Agatha Christie detective novel.[117] He argues that such a reading could only change the text of the novel. Fish begs to differ, for it is not the text which does or doesn't allow one to read it in a certain way. It is in fact the rules of the community that constrain interpretation. He is decidedly on the way to doing away with the text on this point.

One may ask what is the relationship between texts and the communal rules for reading them. Only when rules themselves are not connected to the text as such that one discovers the spectre of Fishean relativism. Together with other legal interpreters, Fish suggests that such a communal grammar cannot be legitimated by appeal to the texts.[118] But rules change, precedents are overturned and a consensus about which rules may be applied in which case cannot be taken for granted. Fish assumes that it is not a matter of dispute which rules to apply in order to decide whether a decision is appropriate. Rules are taken to function univocally and to constrain univocally. Realism has receded from the level of the text to the level of the communitarian grammar, which is taken as absolute and stable, transparent to every-

---

[115] Fish, *Doing What Comes Naturally*, p. 89.

[116] Fish, *Doing*, p. 93.

[117] See Fish's response in *Doing What Comes Naturally*, pp. 95ff.

[118] See for example K. S. Abraham, 'Statutory interpretation', p. 127.

one. The irony[119] is, of course, that he does not project textuality on the rules themselves. In the process of shifting the focus from texts to rules for their interpretation, he misses the fact that rules themselves are objects of interpretation and textual in nature.

A conflict of interpretative interests emerges: on the one hand, the text of the law (or the precedent) as a source of constraint, on the other rules of interpretation, legal and political grammar. Just as for Vico there is no reality without human creative making, taking the form of signs, art, language, there is no law without its poetic application to specific disputes. Reality, whether texts, events, people, God, is constantly deferred and textually mediated. Both Fish and Abraham want to force us into an either-or choice. Either we revert to a textual realism or even formalism, or we assume the pragmatic construction of texts and their reduction to a variety of literary interests. Both Ken Abraham[120] and David C. Hoy[121] point out that textualist arguments in the form of literary considerations deconstruct into pragmatist ones: from 'this is how the text is' to 'this is how we use it.' The same transition is made by Frei and to his later work will form the focus of our next section.

The Later Frei

In philosophical hermeneutics as well as in jurisprudence it has become increasingly difficult to separate text from interpretation and to maintain the distance between the moment of understanding and the moment of application. Reality is mediated through a complex web of signs, practices, social conventions, in short by textuality. Similarly, law effaces itself before precedent, its application to particular cases. There is no obvious reason why theology should not suffer the same fate: God is present only through the creative linguistic mediations of a religion. Liturgies, songs of worship, prayer, churchly practices and activities delimit the symbolic setting which makes God intelligible. Language, law and religion conspire to account for the absence of reality. The loss of the text results in the inability to differentiate between good and bad applications of the text. Preoccupation with

---

[119] It is ironic since he reminds Owen Fiss of this very textuality: Owen Fiss, 'Objectivity and interpretation', in Sanford Levinson and Steven Mailloux, eds., *Interpreting Law and Literature: A Hermeneutic Reader*, (Evanston: Northwestern University Press, 1988), esp. p. 233 on 'disciplining rules'; and Fish's reply, Fish vs. Fiss, in Levinson and Mailloux, eds. *Interpreting*, pp. 252ff.

[120] K. S. Abraham, 'Statutory interpretation', p. 122.

[121] David Couzens Hoy, 'Interpreting the law: hermeneutical and post-structuralist perspectives', in Sanford Levinson and Steven Mailloux, eds., *Interpreting Law and Literature: A Hermeneutic Reader*, (Evanston: Northwestern University Press, 1988), p. 321.

the text gradually gave way to a pragmatics of the textual communities and their hermeneutical grammars.

For Charles Wood, the test of understanding is the ability to use the text in significant ways.[122] As Stout and Fowl point out, accounts of meaning must make room for the more fruitful and descriptive accounts of use[123]. The relocation of the sign from semiotics to pragmatics means that its meaning derives from its use. It follows that 'understanding a text may not be a single thing at all.'[124] Hermeneutics is reduced to a more moderate role of describing which understanding is appropriate to which use.[125] This is indeed a far cry from the textually realist identification of literary features of the text and the consequent choice of reading strategy. Meaning is embedded in use. It follows that understanding is not a phenomenon, a mere event as for Gadamer, but an ability[126], a skill, following from the immersion in the practices of a community.

Stanley Hauerwas argues that texts themselves only emerge as a consequence of interpretive uses and that 'therefore we cannot ask how we ought to interpret the text because we then assume that the text exists prior to such interpretive strategies. We must acknowledge that interpretive strategies are already at work in shaping our reading, and hence our conception of what a text is.'[127] Questions of 'ought' and 'should' are effectively displaced. In Tanner's rendering, 'reasons end (and begin) ... with the consideration of behavioural habits (broadly constructed), with "this is what we do!"'[128] Under the influence of Lindbeck's pragmatism, Frei abandoned his earlier attempt to tie literal sense to a formal textual feature. Instead he understood the literal sense to be that which emerged out of the traditional ecclesial use of Scriptures. Frei became increasingly reluctant to base his hermeneutics on a literary theory which might be eventually superseded by other theories. He took Lindbeck's point that 'the proper way to determine what God signified is by examining how the word operates in religion and thereby shapes reality and experience.'[129]

In an important essay, 'The "Literal Reading" of Biblical Narrative in the Christian Tradition: Does it Stretch or will it Break?', Frei argues that the viability of the literal sense follows not from some immanent textual shape,

---

[122] Charles M. Wood, *The Formation of Christian Understanding: An Essay in Theological Hermeneutics*, (Philadelphia: Westminster Press, 1981), p. 17.

[123] Wood, *Formation*, p. 23.

[124] Wood, *Formation*, p. 19.

[125] Wood, *Formation*, p. 22.

[126] Wood, *Formation*, p. 51.

[127] Hauerwas, *Unleashing the Scripture*, p. 20.

[128] Tanner, 'Theology and the Plain Sense', p. 62.

[129] George Lindbeck, *The Nature of Doctrine: Religion and Theology in a Postliberal Age*, London: SPCK, 1984, p. 147.

but from its fruitful use.[130] The meaning of the Gospels is not given apart from the community that employs them. The task of hermeneutics then is a descriptive one, to discover the rules for literal sense in a given community. The literal sense is simply the sense naturally emerging from the historical interpretations of the text. Tanner argues that it is the sense which after proper training in the skills of interpretation and life, comes as a second nature to the interpreter.[131] Literal reading or plain sense is not a feature of the text, but a function of a mode of reading texts, "a discursive object that emerges only out of the relations that hold among inter-constituent elements of a particular practice."[132]

In the previously mentioned text[133], Frei argues that the literal sense is not a general hermeneutical rule, but a case specific instance, belonging in the context of a socio-linguistic community. This amounts to "a lowering of our theoretical sights yet further to the level of mere description rather than explanation."[134] Several rules obtain for the functioning of the literal sense: the first one, which is also the most important, is that it must not deny the literal ascription of identity to the Jesus of the stories. Secondly, it must not deny either unity of the Old and New Testaments, or the congruence of that unity with the ascriptive literalism of the Gospels; finally, it should be able to make room for various other readings which do not contradict in principle the two rules allowed.

Other postliberals suggest a fourth rule: the literal sense is usually the sense intended by God. Charles Wood argues that the literal sense was "generally held to be the plain sense of the text, intended by God and comprehensible to the reader who, by participation in the community of faith is furnished with the *basic conventions* governing its understanding."[135] Kathryn Tanner also points out that if one is working with an indetermined text, such as she holds the Scriptures to be, one can still hold on to a view of the plain sense as the Godly intention. She suggests that in a deconstructive manner one should pay good attention to the gaps and the way in which the Godly intention is imperfectly enacted in both texts and history.[136] Concerned to relativise both text and its interpretations, she believes that the literal sense may impose a constricting pattern of meaning on the community, inhibiting its critical functions. Claiming that the literal sense is

---

[130] Frei, *Theology and Narrative*, p. 120.

[131] Tanner, 'Theology and the Plain Sense', p. 63; cf. Wood, *Formation,* p. 43.

[132] Tanner, 'Theology and Plain Sense', p. 63.

[133] Frei, 'Literal Reading', esp. pp. 144-6.

[134] Frei, 'Literal Reading', p. 144.

[135] Wood, *Formation*, pp. 39-40 (my italics). Notice the conventionalised understanding of setting. Community is the bearer of primarily conventions, rules for meaning.

[136] Tanner, 'Scripture', p. 290.

authorial intention, G. Loughlin still holds that it is not a property of the text, but a function of using the Bible as God would have the Church use it.[137] The best way to do this is by being conformed to the one whom Scripture depicts.

Tanner comments that although Frei goes a long way towards a pragmatic reconstruction of knowledge and hermeneutics, literary considerations still figure prominently in his later writings. Frei and his colleagues "relinquish the insistence on textual self-sufficiency, and reader passivity characteristic of New Criticism, while resisting to a perhaps much greater degree than David Tracy any relinquishing of unitary sense."[138] The text still creates its own world, even if now it is a community of fellow readers which insists to read in a certain way. Something similar may be said about Hauerwas: for all his insistence on the text as discursive object (a construct of various readings), he nonetheless finds the resolve to criticise Kelsey for failing to do justice to the ways in which Scripture morally shapes a community.[139]

One of Frei's most important claims in *The Identity of Jesus Christ* was that to know Christ is to have him present. Gary Comstock believes that this betrays a basic contradiction in the earlier Frei for it contrasts the self-sufficiency of the text (its ability to mediate its own meaning) with a self-involving interpretation, where a certain existential stance is required before the reader grasps the meaning. Contrary to Frei's emphasis this would mean that only a believer could understand the meaning of the Gospels. The later socially-pragmatic orientation suggests that being part of a practice is an indispensable aspect of understanding its internal concepts and texts. Members of different traditions are in such a case unable to enter into conversation with other adherents. The spectre of relativism reappears in a pragmatist ontology. Yet there are intra-textual resources for responding to the challenge of relativism.

Ronald Thiemann observes that for Frei "there is a sense in which the reader has already to be in the world of the text (i.e., to be in the possession of Christ) in order to be at all cognisant of the invitation to enter this world (i.e. to be a follower of Christ)."[140] Based on these considerations, Surin believes that intra-textualism needs some modification, especially in its notions of textuality. The earlier Frei, he opines, was too dominated by literary and formalistic tendencies, while towards the end of his career he did not fully take into account the force of readership. Normally this suggestion

---

[137] Loughlin, *Telling God's Story*, p. 133.

[138] Tanner, 'Scripture', p. 288. This is part of Tanner's more recent arguments against the unity of the Christian context.

[139] Hauerwas, *A Community of Character*, p. 65.

[140] Ronald F. Thiemann, *Revelation and Theology: The Gospel as Narrated Promise*, (Notre Dame: University of Notre Dame Press, 1984), p. 143.

may seem puzzling, for is not the pragmatist orientation precisely about how communities shape texts? Surin believes that to argue like Comstock that Frei violated the principle of textual autonomy by supporting the concurrence of the identity of Jesus in the text with the presence of Christ in the life of the believer, is to do Frei a disservice. A further possibility is open to Frei, based on a Russellian theory of reference which he in fact holds.[141] Russell helpfully distinguishes between *demonstrative identification* which involves knowledge by acquaintance and *descriptive identification*, which involves knowledge by description. Each competent epistemic agent must furthermore posses a *discriminating knowledge* (G. R. Evans' term). In order to be able to think about an object at all, one must first be in a position to distinguish that object from other objects. This requires discriminating knowledge. Surin writes: "the subject must be able to distinguish the object of his knowledge from all other things. It is possible to have a fully coherent idea about a particular object *a* though there is nothing to be identified by the idea in question."[142] The non-Christian may understand what the Gospels mean. An agent who is not part of the practice of Christian discipleship, for example, may well understand the meaning and the point of the Gospels. But such an understanding will only present her with formal questions. She would have a discriminating knowledge of the following kind: "Jesus died, was resurrected and is present now (and this I do not believe)." On the other hand, participating in a given practice provides a certain *semantic depth*. A member of a practice may have a more intimate and authentic knowledge of the subject matter than the outsider, without, importantly, them meaning different things. Sabina Lovibond described the phenomenon of semantic depth with reference to Mark Platts:

> We start ... with a minimal, schematic understanding of the meaning of a moral term, such as might be captured in a dictionary definition; then, by exploring those aspects of life which moral terms pick out, we can enrich our understanding of those terms without it being the case that we ever come to mean something different by 'courage' (for example) from what we meant at an earlier stage in the exploratory process.[143]

Learning correct judgements, therefore, means learning a particular mode of behaviour. In the case of the literal sense, understanding the plain sense means adopting the relevant behaviour. Right understanding of the subject matter is conditioned by entering those practical structures in which the Scripture is used. Surin also writes that *progress* in theological reflection is "a concomitant of participation in a range of social practices mediated by

---

[141] Surin, *The Turnings*, pp. 208ff.

[142] Surin, *The Turnings*, p. 209.

[143] Sabina Lovibond, *Realism and Imagination in Ethics*, (Oxford: Blackwell, 1983), pp. 31-32.

the Christian semiotic system. Through such participation the Christian comes to know how to make "correct judgements" in the doctrinal realm."[144] Hauerwas adds that "Scripture can be rightly interpreted only within the practices of a body of people constituted by the unity found in the Eucharist."[145] What is apparently held in common by all these authors is that the social and pragmatic conditions of knowledge do not isolate meaning to specific communities. An in-depth discussion of meaning will be the focus of later chapters. If I may anticipate it, meanings can only be treated as incommensurable if they are taken as stable and determinate mental entities in the first place. But this conception of meaning has long been abandoned in the wake of Wittgenstein, but more especially Davidson. Postliberalism, while quick to capitalise on some of these philosophical insights, has been rather slow to follow them to their consequences.

Concluding Reflections

We shall conclude our discussion thus far by drawing some perhaps unobvious connections in our discussion. Vico establishes making as an integral part of knowledge, thus anticipating the Kantian schematisation of epistemology. God, Jesus, the Scriptures cannot be known independently of the performative community of faith. The liturgy of the Church, its prayers, its traditions and practices consolidate the matrix which provides these objects with meaning. In a sense, the postliberal doctrine of world absorption applies universally to all founding texts, for placed within an interpretive community they condition all other perception. In Christian theology reference becomes a matter of internal description of faith. There is no way around the textual metaphorical mediation of reality. Textuality is a necessary detour, sometimes transformed into an indefinitely prolonged exile.

It follows that Scotist univocity can no longer be seriously maintained. The Being to which agents allegedly had access decomposes as a political construct which differs according to culture. Kant who strives to keep concepts free from cultural contamination proves to be but "the great delayer".[146] The loss of univocity coincides with the demise of foundationalism and the regression of realism. Frei's earlier insistence on the formal category of realistic narrative naively assumed the existence of categories independently of a communal will. The next natural step was to evacuate the text into the reading community and to identify it with a multitude of uses. This is also a denial of the necessity of ontology for interpretation, other than Milbank's rhetorically marketed ontology[147]. Ontology and the-

---

[144] Surin, *The Turnings,* pp. 213f.

[145] Hauerwas, *Unleashing,* p. 23.

[146] George Grant's phrase, quoted by Milbank, *Theology and Social Theory,* p. 279.

[147] Cf. discussion in next chapter.

ory do violence to the text, substituting free-floating meanings for the corporeal text. This provides the rationale for Frei's insistence to keep everything intra-textual. The direction of Christology is from Jesus' textual identity to his presence. However, Frei's naïve belief that the boundaries of texts can be enforced becomes the naivety of the later Frei that the borders and identity of a given community can be policed, which is an overconfident supposition. Frei denies that there is any intrinsic need for the text to dialogue with external discourses such as, primarily, critical history. It is the biblical world and then the Christian social setting which has priority over all discourses.

We have reality only under the grammar of religion. But how can we be sure that this religion is appropriate for the use of these particular texts? Why should the Christian Church be the appropriate symbolic context for the interpretation of the Jewish Scriptures? An unapologetic assumption of the Christian practice must face questions about its moral right to interpret some texts. Is not the Christian reading of the Old Testament a violent imposition of form upon a particular content? Does not the interpretive *scheme* manipulate the received *content* once such a distinction has been allowed?

For strong textualists such as Milbank, Loughlin, and even Lindbeck there can be no question of any grammatical legitimation. The inaugurating object of a practice can only be retrieved as the cause of such a practice. The present way of doing things, Tanner's 'this is what we do' infects any archaeological enterprise. Milbank takes his inspiration from Michel de Certeau, who writes: "Insofar as it is inaugural, an event cannot be grasped in objective knowledge."[148] In a similar way to Auerbach, de Certeau suggests that "the writings of the first believers express not the event itself, but that which the event made possible for them."[149] For both Milbank and de Certeau the primary event and the founding texts cannot be disentangled from our second order attitudes, sedimented as a history and society of practices, religious, moral, social.

There are apparently two ontological extremes, to which correspond two interpretive extremes. Duns Scotus inaugurates foundationalism by attempting to ground knowledge in privileged representations. Theology desires to attain a univocal language of God, with no room for equivocity. On the other hand, Milbank, Loughlin, et. al. suggest that we must simply trust the performances which mediate our knowledge.[150] Since there is no getting

---

[148] Michel de Certeau, 'How is Christianity Thinkable Today?' in Graham Ward, *The Postmodern God: A Theological Reader*, (Oxford: Blackwell, 1997), p. 144.

[149] de Certeau, 'How is Christianity Thinkable Today?', p. 144.

[150] See the debate around 'performance interpretation': Stephen Barton, 'New Testament Interpretation as Performance', *Scottish Journal of Theology* 179-208; Nicholas Lash, 'Performing the Scriptures' in Nicholas Lash, *Theology on the Way to Emmaus,*

behind them in order to legitimise these, they must be assumed in a rhetorical manner. Ultimately, however, there is a fundamental similarity between
the univocal and the equivocal: both presuppose the existence of meanings
which float free of signifiers.

On the hermeneutical plane, univocity becomes literalism. The texts
themselves mediate their own meaning, without any help from the reader.
There are also obvious differences between the two: Frei's literalism, for
example, insists that there is no meaning outside the texts, whereas Scotus
grounds knowledge precisely by connecting it to pre-existing forms. But
both are foundationalist in the sense that both claim access to such privileged information: univocity claims to know Being, while literalism/ formalism claims to know meaning. Allegory, on the other hand, is the hermeneutical counter-part of equivocity in the sense that the various allegorical
readings cannot be legitimated by anything other than social practices. The
texts' meaning is located in an external domain, whether existential experiences (Ricoeur, Gadamer), or in its performative repetition (Milbank).
Furthermore, the text itself is not recoverable from beneath the sedimented
layers of communal meaning. While formalism permits no ontology, allegory believes that there can be no non-ontological reading, without however the possibility to legitimise that ontology.

Milbank and Radical Orthodoxy's plea is that we simply trust the appearances without attempting to ground them in reality itself. While the
proposal that we cannot escape schematic mediation is correct and that in a
sense all knowledge and language is equivocal, Milbank's theory of analogy is hardly distinguishable from mere equivocity. In terms of hermeneutics this amounts to an allegorical reading of the text which re-locates
meaning in the creative community without any critical dialectical mediation with the text itself. Is there not an inherent danger in allowing the
meaning of Scripture to be located in a second-order ascription? It appears
that Feuerbach's ghost again looms large over the whole project.

There are two assumptions that I shall try to undermine: first, Frei assumes that ontology is necessarily violent to the text and that the universe
of Scripture and of faith is well preserved from external interference. Secondly, Milbank assumes that since there can be no objective retrieval of
reality we must simply assume the schematic ordering in a rhetorical fashion. Again, this is based on a rigid, fixed notion of setting. For Milbank
there can be no middle way between univocity and equivocity for both as-

---

(London: SCM Press, 1986); Wolterstorff, *Divine Discourse*; Shannon Craigo-Snell,
'Command performance: rethinking performance interpretation in the context of *Divine
Discourse*', *Modern Theology* 16 (2000), 475ff, esp. p. 488. Frances Young, *The Art of
Performance: Towards a Theology of Holy Scripture*, (London: Darton, Longman and
Todd, 1990); Rowan Williams, 'The literal sense of Scripture', *Modern Theology*, 7
(1991), 121-134.

sume the opposition between the bodily and the spiritual; and there can be no mediation between the formalist and the allegorical because of the absolute opposition between the literal and the non-literal. The importance of figural reading resides in its denial of any absolute opposition between matter and spirit, or between the literal and the spiritual.

For Frei the self-referentiality of the biblical text is the literary equivalent of the dogma of the incarnate Son of God.[151] In Jesus the divine Word is united, although not confused, with the bodily person. A philosophical method such as hermeneutics completely misses the point because it does not understand that the world rendered by the Bible is not a revealed world, but a constituted world. Restorative or second naiveté hermeneutics equates meaning with possible truth, which is to be decided independently of the stories themselves, by appeal to anthropology, art, history etc. The direction of interpretation is from the world to the text. Should the narratives prove untruthful, their meaning can be rescued for it does not belong to the text, but to a domain of metaphorical reference.[152] However, as Frei points out, the resurrected spiritual Christ is the same with the pre-Easter embodied person of Jesus of Nazareth. The Auerbachian conception of Christian identity is relocated in the narratively rendered Christ, whose identity we receive. The prevalent concern here has been to safeguard Jesus' identity from subjective interpretation. The continuity between the literal and the spiritual is the strongest in the passion and resurrection narratives: precisely at the moment when God's action becomes the dominant narrative force, Jesus' identity emerges as most intense, at the moment of total submission to the father. The unity of Jesus' person mends the diremption between the spiritual and the material and between the literal and the non-literal. The discovery of a spiritual dimension of interpretation did not reduce the graphic aspect of the sign to a mere vehicle of spiritual meaning. Unlike allegorising, figuration "did not empty the Old Testament or post-biblical personages and events of their own reality and therefore they constituted a powerful means for imaginatively incorporating all being into a Christ-centred world."[153] Typology, unlike allegory and hermeneutics, does not make the biblical text into a metaphor for extra-Scriptural realities, but sees those realities as potential figures of Christ.[154]

Figuration, then, is a discerning of the structural pattern between events and people otherwise unrelated, but in fact part of the larger plan of God for

---

[151] Frei, 'Literal Reading', p. 142.

[152] Frei, 'Literal Reading', p. 139.

[153] Lindbeck, *The Nature of Doctrine*, pp. 117f.

[154] Lindbeck exemplifies this approach: 'the cross should not be viewed as a figurative representation of suffering, nor the messianic kingdom as a symbol for hope in the future, rather, suffering should be cruciform, and hopes for the future messianic.' (*Nature of Doctrine*, p. 118).

the world. The figure is left intact, for both figure and fulfilment are related to a greater ratio: the divine plan. Importantly, Israel is not superseded by the Church, and the Christian reading of the Old Testament is not a reading against Jewish exegesis. As Lindbeck masterfully shows, both Israel and the Church are types of Christ.[155] What this implies for Frei is that Christian identity is not accomplished by the sublation of previous identity and their replacement with a set of Christian convictions. Figuration entails the re-working of the notion of identity along other lines than sameness. Equality, writes Dawson, "is thereby constituted by a mutual ''identifying with,'' rather than a ''becoming the same as.'''"[156]

Surin implies that Frei and postliberal theology have not yet realised the ontological importance of these claims. The critical point, he writes, is that of the entry of the person into the Christian world. Surin's conviction is that the entry does not leave the narrative world unchanged, fixed and stable. Surin, Tanner and Rowan Williams suggest a rethinking of the textuality of intra-textual theology. The reification of setting, to the point where it is al-ienated from the individual agents translates into what Williams calls a 'ter-ritorial cast of images'. The inside is sharply distinguished from the outside. It is wrong, however, to imply that the entry of the person into the narrative is either a smooth transition,[157] or that it leaves the narrative world un-changed. Perhaps due to the Barthian influence narrative theology has little interest in subjectivity and its influence upon textuality.[158] The text, sug-gests Surin, must be seen as a "succession of actions on the understanding of the interpreter."[159] Again, in Surin's case, the text seems to give way to use, for all his calls for a truly dialectical understanding of text and reader-ship.[160] The important factor is that since the identity of the figure is re-tained, textuality has to be radically reconceived. This irruption of new subjectivity in the Church challenges the unified story of the Church and its practices. The tendency of the practices to monopolise the stories is thus corrected. A second correction offered by Surin is the "sub-textual" event of Christ who challenges our stories and our practices, as absent cause. Yet if this is to be more than a mystical meditation, some methodological de-

---

[155] George Lindbeck, 'The story-shaped Church: critical exegesis and theological in-terpretation', in Garrett Green ed., *Scriptural Authority and Narrative Interpretation*, (Philadelphia: Fortress Press, 1987), p. 43.

[156] Dawson, *Figural Reading*, pp. 175f.

[157] George Stroup re-interprets Gadamer's 'fusion of horizons' as 'collision of hori-zons.'

[158] Surin, *Turnings*, p. 216.

[159] Surin, *Turnings*, p. 216.

[160] Surin, *Turnings*, p. 216.

limitation for this dialectic between Jesus – texts – church must be provided.

It appears, then, that the reified nature of the setting can no longer be maintained. The very notion of figuration, which enforces the Christian claim to absorb the world, at the same time subjects the Christian discourse to external dialogue by preserving the identity of what was absorbed. It unfolds that there can be no sharp demarcation between scheme and content, but this is an issue which will receive more attention later on. Frei himself, towards the end of his career, understood the necessity to open up the Christian world to external discourses in an *ad hoc* process of legitimation.

Chapter Three

Ontology

Postliberal theology takes seriously the hermeneutical imperative that 'any sort of knowledge is bound to a tradition and that it therefore never sees things as they "really" are. All forms of knowledge are ...closer to forms of "making" than ... "finding"... and therefore comprise a continuum with creative enterprises in general.'[1] The perception that the *pathos* of knowledge is pregnant with a feeling of being in the world, that a thing becomes an object of knowledge by acquiring its place in a symbolic horizon, is decisive for a *poietic* account of knowledge.[2] Contemporary society, with its consumerist outlook is indeed a very fertile ground for this new 'rhetorical' understanding of Christian discourse.[3] The ever more pressing enquiry is whether we should accept that 'reason is able to recognise itself only in that which it itself (inter-subjectively or conventionally) produces, but will no longer be able to recognise any reality that lacks the element of construction?'[4]

The above example of post-metaphysical thinking suggests that the cardinal condition for knowledge is that it should be epistemic. That is, it must cohere with a conceptual scheme in order for it to be knowledge. Yet if all knowledge is ultimately *poiesis* how is legitimation possible other than through the preference of the audience or by the force of the consolidated conventions? The denial of un-mediated access to reality makes any attempt to dialectically justify a paradigm or a description by reference to what is real illusory. The ontology of postliberal theology is therefore in need of some scrutiny.

At this stage of the argument we shall point out that the rigidity and conventionalised nature of the setting make reference a matter of meaning, not

---

[1] Warnke, *Gadamer*, p. 141.

[2] I am using the term 'poiesis' in the general sense of creative making, as opposed to 'pathos,' namely being acted upon, suffering. I am drawing on Reinhard Hütter's use of the terms in *Suffering Divine Things: Theology as Church Practice*, (Grand Rapids: Eerdmans, 2000), esp. pp. 29-34.

[3] Cf. Anthony C. Thiselton, 'Signs of the times: towards a theology for the year 2000 or a grammar of grace, truth and eschatology in contexts of so-called postmodernity', in David Fergusson and Marcel Sarot eds., *The Future as God's Gift: Explorations in Christian Eschatology*, (Edinburgh: T. and T. Clark, 2000), pp. 9-40.

[4] Hütter, *Suffering*, p. 23.

of access to a non-linguistic object. But since settings are conventionalised patterns of meaning, self-contained worlds, the possibility of inter-communitarian dialogue is methodologically frustrated.

Cultural Linguisticism: Formal Considerations

Remember Kathryn Tanner's commentary on the persistence of traces of formalism in the later stages of Frei's oeuvre. She concludes that although Frei moves toward a pragmatic rethinking of epistemology, some of the older formalist habits – such as the conception of a unitary text, the implied ability to access its immanent features and the proposal of a single literal sense – still remain with him. That this is problematic is suggested by the methodological shift that he undergoes under George Lindbeck's influence. In Lindbeck's pragmatist interpretation, the object of knowledge submerges and is no longer available as a brute fact. To that extent any argument about a description cannot rest on our having access to the object of description.

George Lindbeck, in his *The Nature of Doctrine* advances a model of cultural linguisticism which is in contrast to both cognitive propositional-ism and experiential expressivism. His main concern, as Hütter rightly points out, is not to ride the wave of latest intellectual fashion, but actually to provide a more useful model for ecumenical dialogue.[5] He is attempting to construct a model that makes sense of a specific church practice: the practice of ecumenical agreement, the character of which other models have been unable to properly account for.

Cognitive-propositionalists understand truth claims after the manner of a naïve realism in which statements and words refer to reality in a direct way. Church doctrines are propositions about objective states of affairs[6], so re-ligions are schemes descriptive of reality and 'commensurate with truth.' This model is most clearly associated with realism, or rather what we should call, following Searle, epistemological realism.[7] The vehicle of this realism is a correspondence theory of truth. However, the theory is plagued by serious problems and it no longer seems a viable understanding of the way in which language and mind work.

Such a theory of truth finds it difficult to articulate what it means that a description corresponds to a fact. Quite obviously, a description is of a dif-ferent substance than a fact, most of the times anyway and therefore any relationship between them is bound to imply both similarity and difference.

---

[5] Hütter, *Suffering*, pp. 41-42.

[6] Lindbeck, *Doctrine*, p. 16.

[7] John Searle, *The Construction of Social Reality*, (London: Penguin, 1995), pp. 151-152. He makes the distinction between 'external realism' and 'ontological objectivity'. We might call epistemological realism the view that knowledge is true if and only if our descriptions correspond to reality.

The traditional way of solving the dilemma is to postulate the existence of forms which are somehow correlated with atomic facts. The task of knowledge is to correlate statements with those forms. This seems to have solved the problem of the difference in substance between statements and facts, but it begs the question about the correlation of forms to facts themselves, thus merely postponing the issue.

The special character of the mind, according to the cognitivist picture, resides in its ability to receive universal forms[8]. As Richard Rorty comments, the history of Western philosophy and especially epistemology has been dominated by an accidental choice of ocular metaphors[9]. The mind becomes that very special space where forms are transacted and the universal is thus negotiated. We shall return to Rorty in the next chapters, for his contribution to the present discussion is immense: he argues that both realism and idealism rely on the notion of mind as either receptivity of forms (Aristotle), or combination between receptivity and spontaneity (Kant), as the locus of privileged representations. To do away with 'the mind' is to make both ontological options appear unnecessary.

The second problem attached to the theory of correspondence is knowing when a particular description in fact corresponds. Verification is conditional upon postulating a non-inferential access to the facts in which we can verify our descriptions independently of them. But the very status of this non-inferential access is questionable. One argument holds that it does not even have the status of knowledge, i.e., it is non-epistemic. The cognitive-propositional model seems to boil down to a postulation of this non-epistemic representation. As opposed to this realism where truth is available non-epistemically, apart from our warrants and verification, anti-realism suggests – in one of its more respectable versions – that truth is nothing other than warranted assertability.[10] It is synonymous with what one is being justified in asserting at a given time under specific conditions.

Without implying that Lindbeck does not share these objections, they are not the reasons for which he refutes cognitivism. The model implies that in an ecumenical debate there can only be one loser and a winner. Doctrines are true once and for all, 'thus, on this view, doctrinal reconciliation without capitulation is impossible because there is no significant sense in which the meaning of a doctrine can change while remaining the same.'[11] Lindbeck may be read in two different ways: either ecumenical agreement must take place even if this means that a cognitive propositional model must be relinquished since it ties doctrines too closely with truth, or that the sheer existence of such agreement as a practice must be explained and this mani-

---

[8] Rorty, *Philosophy*, p. 40.

[9] Rorty, *Philosophy*, pp. 7, 38, *passim*.

[10] See especially Michael Dummett.

[11] Lindbeck, *Doctrine*, pp. 16f.

festly cannot be done by the propositional model. On the first interpretation, Lindbeck raises ecumenical agreement above the quest for truth. This is the least likely of the two readings and the reasons for this will become clear as we progress in our reading of Lindbeck. We shall then discover that he is not simply re-instating a model of warranted assertability which will drive ecumenical dialogue as an end in itself.

According to the experiential-expressivist model, doctrines are just metaphors for pre-conceptual religious experiences. They are 'noninformative and nondiscursive symbols of inner feelings, attitudes, or existential orientations.'[12] This model presupposes that the religious experiences have a logical and chronological priority and that language re-presents them symbolically. Both propositional and expressive models presuppose a level of pure receptivity, the existence of a 'given', although the received content is mediated differently. Symbols are arbitrary and they always differ from culture to culture, from religion to religion. Differences in religion therefore become surface differences in the choice of vocabulary. The model is exemplary of the turn to the subject in modern philosophy. Whereas the propositional model is governed by the objective reality it seeks to depict, the expressivists take their cue from the Kantian schematisation of knowledge. Insofar as knowledge is unable to grasp the thing in itself, it must restrict itself to descriptions of our fundamental emotions summoned by the encounter.

Again we may notice the regress of realism: it is assumed that while knowledge cannot portray reality as it is in itself, it can nonetheless more or less objectively portray our attitudes and reactions, our resonance to it. A causal model under which reality first impacts us at a non-epistemological and non-linguistic level, followed by a correct description of our attitudes, still prevails. Hütter nicely surprises the tension between the descriptive and the non-descriptive:

> This model understands theology either as being purely descriptive (second-order language) insofar as it coherently presents and interprets a given group's expressions of faith, or as being radically poietic-constructive insofar as it brings religious experience to immediate expression (first-order language) with the aid of metaphorical constructions and in so doing interprets it.[13]

Since realistic tactics seem to survive even in the most radical linguistic idealist strategies, it is important to point out that some description of either reality, or our attunement to it is still attempted even under non-discursive restrictions.

---

[12] Lindbeck, *Doctrine,* p. 16.

[13] Hütter, *Suffering*, p. 44.

The experiential expressive model cannot do justice to ecumenism either, because doctrines, being non-discursive, are not crucial for religious agreement or disagreement. They are not constituted by what happens on the surface level of 'symbolic objectifications', but by what is going on at the underlying level of religious sentiment.[14]

What is needed, in Lindbeck's opinion, is to maximise the strengths of both paradigms. The answer seems to lie in understanding religions as resembling languages and semiotic systems. Religions thus become idioms, cultures for the 'construing of reality and the living of life.'[15] It follows that doctrines are neither descriptive of objective states of affair, nor symbolisations of a pre-existing and pre-conceptual religious experience. Doctrines are rules governing a semiotic system which makes possible both the experience of reality and the symbolisation of religious experiences.

A religion is according to Lindbeck a *verbum externum*,[16] in that it makes experience possible. Cognitive propositionalism wrongly assumes that we have reality in a direct intuition and that we can use our descriptions correspondingly. This is what Rorty calls the invention of the mind as the Mirror of nature and the existence of a Mind's Eye.[17] Experiential expressivism, alternatively, is guilty of the same sort of directness in that it accepts a level of pre-linguistic awareness. According to Lindbeck, cultural linguisticism 'reverses the relation of the inner and the outer. Instead of deriving external features of a religion from inner experience, it is the inner experiences which are viewed as derivative.'[18] Reality is therefore given only within an already existing narrative.

Religions function similarly to a Kantian *a priori*, with the exception that such *a priori* are not given universally to all human beings. It is not the subject that forms religion, but the religious code which constructs the subject. Lindbeck has adopted the Wittgensteinian logic which tries to steer a middle way between both naïve realism and idealism. Indeed, the cultural linguistic model was drafted mainly under the influence of Wittgenstein and Clifford Geertz. For the former, the choice between empiricism[19] and idealism is a false one[20] since we are already in the context of a practice when we ask such questions. Forms of life already embed languages and

---

[14] Lindbeck, *Doctrine*, p. 17.

[15] Lindbeck, *Doctrine*, pp. 18, 32. Notice the similarity to Vico's views on the linguistic nature of religion.

[16] Lindbeck, *Doctrine*, p. 34.

[17] Rorty, *Philosophy*, pp. 38-39.

[18] Lindbeck, *Doctrine*, p. 34.

[19] Wittgenstein sometimes calls empiricism that which now is commonly called naïve realism.

[20] 'Not empiricism, yet realism in philosophy, that is the hardest thing.' (Wittgenstein, *Remarks on the Foundations of Mathematics*, VI, sect. 23).

when we speak a language we can only do so meaningfully on the backdrop of certain activities.[21]

Some of the main Lindbeckian insights are borrowed from Wittgenstein. Reality is available only under a scheme, a form of life, a set of practices which condition what may be experienced. The second model introduces a dead space between having the initial religious experience and giving it a symbolic presentation. The cultural linguistic type already fills any such space with communal conventions and rules which help pre-determine the content of that experience. This is the tendency of post-metaphysical thinking: something may be experienced only if the scheme is adequate to it. If a given form of life does not contain a certain grammatical possibility for a given experience, such an experience will never occur. However, Lindbeck does not conceive the relationship between scheme and experience in a uni-directional way. Rather, both scheme and experience determine each other: 'it is simplistic to say (as I earlier did) merely that religions produce experiences, for the causality is reciprocal. Patterns of experience alien to a given religion can profoundly influence it.'[22] This statement is crucial, for it opens the possibility for a way out of the solipsistic understanding of the scheme-content relation. Wittgenstein himself may be taken as advancing such a solipsistic method, as Fergus Kerr argues:

> A non-realistic form of subjectivist idealism, deriving from the anti-realist interpretation of Wittgenstein's writings on mathematics, is thus drafted into the service of a version of Christianity according to which it is, like mathematics and art and everything else, entirely subject to the will of its human creators.[23]

Later I shall have a go at this interpretation of Wittgenstein. There may indeed be language games where the rules are arbitrary, and the linguistic metaphors give the theory extra plausibility. Yet Lindbeck, at least formally, stipulates that religion by itself will only serve as the scheme under which given experiences are possible. Furthermore, he also argues that there might be experiences which are not pre-figured in a given code.

The scheme is thus necessary, but does not exhaust experience. It underdetermines it. Lindbeck adds that 'the richer our expressive or linguistic system, the more subtle, varied and differentiated can be our experience.'[24] Hütter nicely sums it up: 'Experience is thus a *poiesis* that is always *pathically* grounded.'[25] These are hints that the ontological commitments of

---

[21] See extended discussion of Wittgenstein, Rorty, Davidson in next chapter.

[22] Lindbeck, *Doctrine*, p. 33.

[23] Kerr, *Theology After Wittgenstein*, p. 129.

[24] Lindbeck, *Doctrine,* p. 37.

[25] Hütter, *Suffering*, p. 48 (my emphasis).

[26] Lindbeck, *Doctrine,* p. 47.

Lindbeck do not allow him to abandon all traces of realism in favour of a cultural linguistic idealism. The functionalism of theologians such as Kelsey and Hauerwas leaves the impression that postliberal theology is steadily moving towards non-realism. The object of knowledge appears to us only as trace, as re-constructed by our prior decisions, or by the decisions that the 'socially-linguistic matrix' made for us. Even the formal priority awarded to the text or to God is frustrated by the logically prior theological moves. Furthermore, such moves cannot be legitimated with respect to the sacred texts or God, since their perception always presupposes those moves. This is, however, to follow very literally Wittgenstein's argument that grammatical conventions cannot be justified by the description of objects. In fact, the Wittgensteinian position is that rules are not arbitrary in all cases, and their precision can be decided, although only in an *ad hoc* fashion.

The question is *how may an experience challenge a scheme if that experience is perceptible only from within such a scheme?* This is a very formal consideration, to be followed by a material, positively Christian one: *how may the prevenient action of God become significant for theology within a cultural linguistic ontology?* The suspicion is that a belief in God's prevenience (the fact that theology is an answer to an ontologically prior action of God) may be theologically inconsequential where the very construal of such prevenience follows a theological decision which is arbitrary. The challenge for Lindbeck's postliberalism is to articulate the mechanics by which the object of knowledge, although only available in schematised description, may nevertheless have an active role in the formation of knowledge. After all appearances, anchoring knowledge in a pre-existing context of practice renders obsolete all talk about perception scratching the surface of reality.

The rationale behind Lindbeck's proposals is to find an ecumenically appropriate model. In cultural linguisticism, religions may be compared according to what he calls 'categorial adequacy.' If in the propositional cognitive model, descriptions are true because they univocally correspond,[26] while the experiential model makes truth a matter of symbolic efficacy[27], namely how effectively they communicate the experience of the divine, in cultural linguisticism truth is a function of our concepts being adequate to what is 'ultimately Real.' Religions are schemes for the perception of reality. As such they are either adequate or inadequate *tools* for dealing with the divine reality and its activity in the world.

Adequate categories are those which can be made to apply to what is taken to be real, and which therefore make possible, though they do not guarantee, propositional, practical and symbolic truth. A religion that is

---

[27] Lindbeck, *Doctrine*, p. 47.

thought of as having such categories can be said to be 'categorially true.'[28]

Truth is therefore no longer a function of statements applying to facts in their own power, since the latter are simply unavailable. A different understanding of the relationship between statements and facts needs to be worked out. As it has been pointed out, religions are different vocabularies for construing reality. The criterion of truth must then be related to this function. Critics of Lindbeck have argued that this makes truth a matter of arbitrariness, that no ontological truth claims are therefore possible and that doctrine is purely functional. Yet there have also been more charitable readings. McClendon suggests that it is indeed possible to read Lindbeck as denying any reference to an extra-linguistic Being. But there is also a 'less extreme' way of interpreting him:

> On this view he is not denying that Christian doctrines refer to God above and the world outside, but is (strongly) urging that what Christians have to say about God and the world cannot be meaningfully separated from the network of rules and meanings that constitute Christian teaching.[29]

Let us allow Lindbeck himself to clarify the issue. He believes that we need to distinguish between two senses of 'truth': the intra-systematic and the ontological.[30] Intra-systematic truth is the truth of coherence, while ontological truth is the truth of correspondence. Another rather lengthier quote might help:

> For epistemological realists, intrasystematic truth or falsity is fundamental in the sense that it is a necessary though not sufficient condition for the second kind of truth: that of ontological correspondence. A statement, in other words, cannot be ontologically true unless it is intrasystematically true, but intrasystematic truth is quite possible without ontological truth. An intrasystematically true statement is ontologically false – or, more accurately meaningless – if it is part of a system that lacks the concepts or categories to refer to the relevant realities, but it is ontologically true if it is part of a system that is itself categorially true (adequate).[31]

Lindbeck's proposal makes better sense once another distinction is introduced: between first-order and second-order theological statements. First order statements are practices, beliefs, propositions that make up the religious system. To use Lindbeck's cartographic analogy, they construct the map which may be more or less adequate to the geographical terrain.[32] Sec-

---

[28] Lindbeck, *Doctrine*, p. 48.

[29] McClendon, *Ethics: Systematic Theology I*, p. 31.

[30] I am now referring to the (in)famous discussion of *Christus est Dominus*, pp. 64ff.

[31] Lindbeck, *Doctrine,* pp. 64f.

[32] Lindbeck, *Doctrine,* pp. 51-52.

ond-order statements are propositions that we utter by using the map, i.e., that London is due south, two hundred miles from here. That second-order statement, writes Lindbeck, is correct intra-systematically if it coheres with other beliefs, practices and forms of life that constitute the code. But such local and intra-systematic truth need not imply ontological truth. Rather, the first order statements that make up the scheme are either adequate, and thus they make possible either true or false propositions, or it is inadequate, resulting in its internal statements being meaningless.

Lindbeck's achievement was to provide a model in which intra-systematically true statements may nonetheless be ontologically false. He relocates the truth of correspondence at the level of first-order statements.[33] A religion may be seen as a gigantic proposition which may be adequate or inadequate to reality:

> There is, these comments assume, a sense in which truth as correspondence can retain its significance even for a religion whose truth is primarily categorial rather than propositional. A religion thought of as comparable to a cultural system, as a set of language games correlated with a form of life, may as a whole correspond or not correspond to God's being and will. As actually lived, a religion may be pictured as a single gigantic proposition. It is a true proposition to the extent that its objectivities are interiorised and exercised by groups and individuals in such a way as to conform them in some measure in the various dimensions of their existence to the ultimate reality and goodness that lies at the heart of things. It is a false proposition to the extent that this does not happen.[34]

However, the categorial adequacy of the scheme, or the religion, is only established in the eschaton. The reified and conventionalised nature of the scheme shows itself in its ability to be either true or false. The apparent lack of this-worldly verification prompts Sue Patterson to spot strong similarities with theistic realism.[35] Lindbeck comes close to a theistic realism by implying a truth outside our verification and outside the possibilities of our schematising faculty. She goes on to add that Lindbeck is quite ambiguous with respect to ontological truth-claims: 'for it seems that he is regarding Christian truths are either needing justification from beyond, or (confusedly) as non-ontological (although propositional) truths.[36]

To summarise, religions are schemes that colour our view of reality. As such they are judged according to how adequate they are to it. Our second order doctrinal statements are ontologically true if they are coherently cor-

---

[33] Lindbeck, *Doctrine,* p. 51.

[34] Lindbeck, *Doctrine,* p. 51.

[35] Sue Patterson, *Realist Christian Theology in a Postmodern Age,* Cambridge Studies in Christian Doctrine, (Cambridge: Cambridge University Press, 1999), p. 37.

[36] Patterson, *Realist Christian Theology,* p. 37.

related with the rest of the web of beliefs, practices, etc. on the one hand, *and if* that code is categorially true. It is only within such a religious system and through the particular grammar of the system, that reference takes place.[37]

If religions are systems that make possible the experience of reality and of God and if the way in which the object is given is always conditioned by the first order statements, then how is it possible that two different traditions may meaningfully agree or disagree? Lindbeck does envisage the chance that two religions are incommensurable, rendering all dialogue dead. But how do we know, for example, that Lutherans, Catholics and Jews refer to the same God? If reference is conditional upon an already existing practice, with its sedimented meanings, and such a faith, with 'its doctrines, cosmic stories or myths, and ethical directives are integrally related to the rituals it practices, the sentiments or experiences it evokes, the action it recommends, and the institutional forms it develops,'[38] and if all these differ, how can we ensure that reference is maintained across the divides?

Lindbeck never tackles the problem of reference in particular, but there are hints to the sort of theory suited for his views. He understands the relation between scheme and experience, at least formally, in a dialectical manner. The condition for knowledge is that both poles of the relationship, both the knower and the known are present in the process.[39] Ken Surin makes the same point in his discussion of realism:

> signification requires the dialectical tension between subject and object to be maintained, and it is doubtful whether proponents of the correspondence theory of truth have at their disposal the theoretical resources needed to hold this dialectic in place – theirs *is* a semantics; and seman-

---

[37] Cf. Hilary Putnam's discussion in *The Many Faces of Realism: The Paul Carus Lectures*, (LaSalle: Open Court, 1987), pp. 8ff, 31ff.

[38] Lindbeck, *Doctrine*, p. 33.

[39] Jameson writes: 'Thus, to insist on either of the two inseparable yet incommensurable dimensions of the symbolic act without the other: to over-emphasise the active way in which the text reorganizes its subtext (in order, presumably, to reach the triumphant conclusion that the "referent" does not exist); or on the other hand to stress the imaginary status of the symbolic act so completely as to reify its social ground, now no longer understood as a subtext but merely as some inert given that the text passively or fantasmatically "reflects" – to overstress either of these functions of the symbolic act at the expense of the other is surely to produce sheer ideology, whether it be, as in the first alternative, the ideology of structuralism, or in the second, that of vulgar materialism.' (*The Political Unconscious*, p. 82).

tics, unlike semiotics, does not in principle allow the (socially-instituted) subject a fundamental role in the appropriation of meaning.[40]

Initial descriptions of the subject-matter are provided by the first-order propositions of the code. Its vocabulary and grammar make possible the presentation of the object. Since legitimation is indefinitely postponed, the knowledge which is available within a scheme is not definitive. If reference is dependent on correct description, it is very difficult to see how any proposition, for any sort of *episteme* refers. At first blush, then, Lindbeck appears to promote a meaning based theory of reference. That would explain the suggestion that second-order propositional statements from religious schemes which are inadequate to the ultimately real are simply meaningless. Reference is, like meaning, a function of the statements employed. It is textually governed. It is propositions that either have reference or fail to refer. Since adequacy can only be eschatologically determined, it is impossible to say that any statement is ontologically meaningless. All evaluations can be made from within a cultural code, where reality is pre-given and from within which judgements about adequacy are made. But such judgements do not have any ontological value.

The predicament of Lindbeck's ontology is that he has tied reference to meaning and ontological meaningfulness, which, like truth and falsity, is available only at the end of days. The upshot is that Lindbeck cannot secure reference and dialogue. There is no common referent or subject-matter across traditions, or at least we cannot know it. Instead, other religions or religious denominations may actually refer to radically different entities. This thesis is related to an understanding of the absoluteness of Christianity according to which there can only be one categorially adequate religion.[41] He writes,

> To hold that a particular language is the only one that has the words and concepts that can authentically speak of the ground of being, the goal of history, and the true humanity (for Christians believe they cannot genuinely speak of these apart from telling and retelling the biblical story) is not at all the same as denying that other religions have resources for speaking truths and referring to realities, even highly important truths and realities, of which Christianity as yet knows nothing about and by which it could be greatly enriched.[42]

But to assert this is to take with one hand what was given with the other. While Lindbeck builds his method with the explicit purpose of making

---

[40] Surin, *Turnings*, pp. 50f.

[41] From this it follows that 'adequacy' should be read as 'correspondence' rather than 'practical usefulness'- which may have helped Lindbeck avoid contradiction.

[42] Lindbeck, *Doctrine*, p. 61; cf. Surin's analysis, *Turnings*, p.171.

sense of the ecumenical understanding, the above statements seem to render the whole attempt useless.

This is an empiricist account of reference. In the opinion of Richard Boyd, such an account is deeply flawed, for although it may be mistaken for a theory of reference, it is blatantly non-realist and non-referential, since in it extensions are largely fixed by arbitrary and empirically un-revisable definitional conventions.[43] As we shall see, it is the same problem that plagues Kuhn's model of theoretical change. It is not at all clear how new discoveries can be seen as advances in knowledge if they imply what he calls a conversion to a new paradigm with new meanings, in fact a new world. If reference is derivative of meaning, it is lost along the journey from one paradigm to another, or through conceptual change. Such difficulties with the theory of reference have caused philosophers like Putnam, Kripke and Donellan to revise it. What was needed was a theory that would permit reference to take place across theories. As such it could no longer be a reference tied to meaning, for that changes. The new, 'causal theory of reference'[44] understands reference as being not a property of statements, but of people. People, not statements, refer. Reference can take place by what Kripke and Donellan call 'dubbing' or 'baptism': a name designates whatever is causally linked to it in an appropriate way, which does not require speakers to associate an identifying description of the bearer with the name. Such fixing of reference by dubbing can take place when the subject has either perceived or described the object. What this ensures is that changes in definition, while affecting meaning, do not affect reference. Consequently, new theories can be seen as advances in knowledge by their ascription to the same object which is identified non-semantically or causally. According to Soskice, what the new causal theory provides is a way of access to reality in a realist key.[45] It ensures that words can still refer to reality while our descriptions of reality are still provisional or even plain wrong.

The *new causal theory*, on the other hand, is not without its problems. Readers may be struck by the innocence with which Kripke and Donellan suggest that we can perceive before naming. This is obviously not the way in which they phrase their remarks, but the upshot is that the theory avoids the difficult issue of the linguistic nature of perception itself. It first needs

---

[43] Janet Martin Soskice, *Metaphor and Religious Language,* (Oxford: Clarendon, 1985), p. 126.

[44] Cf. Saul Kripke, *Naming and Necessity,* (Oxford: Blackwell, 1980); Hilary Putnam, *Reason, Truth and History,* (Cambridge: Cambridge University Press, 1981); J.M. Soskice, 'Theological realism' in W.J. Abraham, S.W. Holzer, *The Rationality of Religious Belief: Essays in Honour of Basil Mitchell,* (Oxford: Clarendon, 1987) and *Metaphor and Religious Language.*

[45] For a critique of Soskice's account of reference, cf. Michael Durrant, 'Reference and critical realism', *Modern Theology,* 5 (1989), 133-143.

to explain why there can be a perception before dubbing in the first place, which does not submit to rule following and is thus not already social. Jerold Katz argues that if the traditional theory of reference erred in implying that meaning determines reference, the causal theory makes the opposite error of assuming that all criteria for the application of a name to a thing are grounded in extra-linguistic matters of fact – concepts about empirical science, information about baptismal ceremonies, and so on.[46] This model does not allow degrees of reference. A theory or description does not refer better or worse than another theory. It is simply people who refer and whose acts of reference employ better or worse descriptions of the objects. Quite clearly such a theory does believe in access to reality, without requiring that the ensuing descriptions themselves are correct. It's difficulty is that it assumes an initial stage where description plays no role in definition. If we have, as this theory seems to assume, access to our objects before the actual description, the contesting descriptions can be reconciled by such a non-descriptive access. However, thinking Wittgensteinian will mean that 'the canonical description of sensory input thus falls within the scope of Wittgenstein's considerations on rule-following, which would make the correctness of a perceptual judgement a function of human linguistic practice and not of fidelity to the supposed hard data of individual awareness.'[47] To sum up, the causal theory makes the connection between reference and meaning too loose.

> As Katz points out, the word 'witch' up to a certain time 'was used to refer to ugly, frightening women – and never to refer to women with supernatural powers acquired in a pact with the devil – yet the referent of 'witch' is not ugly, frightening women'. When we came to disbelieve in witches, we did not say 'witch' really means ugly frightening women just because the term had consistently been used to refer to such; instead we say witches do not exist. The meaning of 'witch' remains much the same as it always was and when we have a witch in a fairy story, we do not have simply an ugly frightening woman, but a woman with sinister supernatural powers.[48]

What is needed, therefore, is a combination of these theories which Soskice believes can be made once one observes together with Katz that both classical and causal theories failed to make the distinction between the referent of an expression in the language and the referent of an expression or use of an expression in context.[49] At the level of language, meaning does determine reference, but at the level of use in context, all sorts of factors deter-

---

[46] Soskice, *Metaphor,* p. 129.

[47] Lovibond, *Realism,* p. 38.

[48] Soskice, *Metaphor,* p. 130.

[49] Soskice, *Metaphor,* pp. 130-131.

mine it. Therefore 'what seems to occur in scientific language is an accommodation between the fixed senses and denotations of terms in the language, and the more flexible referential uses to which they are put in inves-
tigative procedures.'[50] Soskice's main concern is to elucidate how reference
can take place across theories, and this is what concerns us in relation to
Lindbeck as well. According to this synthesis between the causal and the
classical theories, terms are introduced in a debate with their acquired fixed
senses within a language. But such meanings are not strongly connected to
reference, so that new experiences can alter the meaning while retaining the
reference. The original sense of the term may be altered, or it may be decided that it simply fails to refer. Yet such initial and fixed descriptions are
important in guiding access, while nonetheless remaining secondary to the
pragmatics of discovery.[51]

Dialogue can take place only where meaningful disagreement or agreement is possible. A condition for such debate is therefore at least the possibility that two or more traditions, while having rival schemes of description
nonetheless employ those schemes in the search of a common object. Lindbeck's dialectical understanding of the relationship between scheme and
experience ensures at least theoretically that experience is not reduced to
the description already made available in the scheme and as such can guide
further investigation. But this is at a more formal level. At the material level
the question still remains whether encounter with the object may revise the
scheme itself. Unfortunately, by relegating the decision about the categorial
adequacy of a scheme to the eschaton and thus suspending all further legitimation, Lindbeck seems reluctant to allow major modifications of sense
in light of further investigation. The theoretical requirement that experience
should not be exhausted by the semiotic code is thus hindered by the practical resignation in the face of the legitimising task. It is therefore unclear
how such a model, in the absence of a more *optimistic* legitimising strategy,
could provide a model for ecumenical dialogue.

World Absorption and God's Prevenience: Material Considerations

Any model presupposes a fundamental tension between form and content. It
is therefore imperative that an awareness of this fact lead to the right pre-
cautions against the abuse of the model. Being a model and nothing else, its
appropriateness must be provisional and contextually dependent. According
to Hütter the limit of the cultural linguistic model is reached precisely at the
point where ethnology as a methodological requirement gives way to creative description.[52]

---

[50] Soskice, *Metaphor,* pp. 130f.
[51] Soskice, *Metaphor,* p. 131.
[52] Cf. Hütter, *Suffering*, p. 60

If the cultural linguistic model stipulates Geertzian thick description as the only strategy available to the theologian, when one comes to the specific requirements of the texts of such intra-textual theology, one realises that they involve much more than just description. The description of Christian practice can only take place if it is an appropriate description from within that practice. We are reminded here of Mark Platts' concept of semantic depth[53] and how definitions and sense can be improved by actually engaging in the afferent practice. This is similar to what Lindbeck has in mind when he implies that, contrary to the ethnologist the theologian must be 'inside' the practices:

> There is indeed no more demanding exercise of the inventive and imaginative powers than to explore how a language, culture, or religion may be employed to give meaning to new domains of thought, reality, and action. Theological description can be a highly constructive enterprise.[54]

Theology, therefore, is not simply empirical description of simple facts about the practices of the church. Rather such practices must be imagined in the whole nexus of relationships and implications that they engage in. Furthermore, intra-textual description is not merely interpretation of reality according to some code, but according to a literally textual code, the holy writ. The specific horizon within which all interpretation and action must take place is the canon of the Holy Scriptures. Testing the faithfulness of religions means to some extent testing 'the degree to which their descriptions correspond to the semiotic universe paradigmatically encoded in holy writ.'[55]

What is involved in this model is quite remarkable and most important. A failure to understand the moves Lindbeck is making will inevitably lead to asking the wrong questions of his proposal, especially to wrong questions about his notion of truth. *The logic of his understanding of the relationship between subject, reality, and God is not that of metaphor but that of typology.* Metaphorical logic requires that a given scheme is provisionally useful in giving us access to reality but eventually will be supplanted by better metaphors and concepts. The workings of typology are different, as we have seen in the last chapter.

> Typology does not make scriptural contents into metaphors for extra-scriptural realities, but the other way around. It does not suggest, as is often said in our day, that believers find their stories in the Bible, but rather that they make the story of the Bible their story. The cross is not to be viewed as a figurative representation of suffering nor the messianic kingdom as a symbol for hope in the future; rather, suffering should be cruci-

---

[53] Cf. the discussion in my previous chapter; also Lovibond, *Realism*, p. 33.

[54] Lindbeck, *Doctrine,* p. 115.

[55] Lindbeck, *Doctrine*, p. 116.

form, and hopes for the future messianic. More generally stated, it is the religion instantiated in Scripture which defines being, truth, goodness, and beauty, and the figures (or type or anti-types) of the scriptural ones. Intra-textual theology re-describes reality within the scriptural framework rather than translating Scripture into extra-scriptural categories. It is the text, so to speak, which absorbs the world, rather than he world the text.[56]

I have chosen to reproduce this quote at length for it signifies a properly theological shift in the relevant questions. Here reference is no longer a question of finding extra-scriptural realities to which our concepts or our scheme refer or is adequate to. *Rather reference becomes internal for there is no externality to this world.* The world of the Scripture is all-encompassing and herein lies the creative nature of the theological enterprise. To describe such a world stretches the imagination and the creative interpretation of the world in light of Scripture, not the other way around. Reference becomes meaning in a world textually rendered by Scripture. Therefore, questions of truth which are asked with the old metaphysical assumptions are simply meaningless, for there is no outside to this world. Typology therefore reverses the process of correspondence. It is no longer our statements that need to correspond to a world, or to God out there. Rather it is a matter of us being conformed to the being and will of God as given in the Scriptures. Bruce Marshall makes the same point when suggesting that it is primarily persons who are true rather than statements.[57] Figural reason implies that it is subjects as well as reality which are types or anti-types of scriptural realities, hence truth is already a practical activity. This is consonant with Putnam's argument that it is people who are the bearers of meaning and who refer, not statements or sentences.[58] It follows that 'realist explanation, in a nutshell, is not that language mirrors the world, but that speakers mirror the world, i.e., their environment in the sense of constructing a symbolic presentation of that environment.'[59] What emerges out of Marshall's and Lindbeck's arguments is that *to ask the question of truth under a metaphysical key is to misunderstand the logic of Scripture.*

The previous discussion of truth has shown that the ontological truth of second order doctrinal statements depends on the adequacy of the scheme

---

[56] Lindbeck, *Doctrine,* p. 118.

[57] B. D. Marshall, 'We shall Bear the Image of the Man of Heaven: Theology and the Concept of Truth', *Modern Theology* 11 (1995), p. 111.

[58] According to Soskice, this realism 'emphasises rather than conceals contextuality by emphasising that descriptive language, while dealing with immediate experience, will be language embedded in certain traditions of investigation and conviction.' ('Theological Realism', p. 114.)

[59] Putnam, quoted in Soskice, 'Theological realism', p. 118.

to reality. But the intra-textual Scriptural logic suggests that the adequacy of the scheme is a matter of whether it enables people to 'bear the image of the man from heaven'. This is not a formal requirement for adequacy, but a material, positive and Christian one. Hütter makes the same point: noticing that Lindbeck's formal theory of truth does not stipulate to what does the 'praxis of faith'[60] correspond, the scriptural logic suggests that 'the performance of the praxis of the Christian faith corresponds to the essence of God insofar as it becomes transparent for the performance of God's salvific action.'[61] This means that the Christian scheme is categorially adequate when it allows the salvific action of God to be carried out through it. *But this refocuses the locus of truth not on the action of people alone, but on the action of people insofar as it is conformed to God's action.* Here Hütter's *pathically poietic* activity is more clearly evident. Truth does indeed involve the construction of a human scheme, the creative application of that scheme to human activity and knowledge, but it also implies much more than that. In Marshall's words,

> the truth of sentences about the triune God (like 'Jesus is risen') depends primarily on the action of the triune God, and that action is chiefly to make us images of the Son, then the correspondence between persons in which this likeness consists will itself belong to the truth conditions for these sentences. They will be true only if they are the linguistic means by which, when held true, the triune God brings about our correspondence to Jesus Christ, crucified and risen.[62]

Admittedly this is quite a considerable achievement, namely to have moved from an affirmation of local and intra-systematic truth only, to an affirmation of ontological truth in light of extra-linguistic factors[63] (God's action). But this brings us to another material consideration, that of the prevenient action of God. Is the talk about such a prevenient action of God coherent within a system which understands truth internally? If the formal understanding of cultural linguisticism stipulated an understanding of truth local to the system, yet dependent on its categorial adequacy, material considerations pointed out the Scriptural demands for God's active agency for any ontological truth to be possible.

---

[60] In other words my scheme, which includes practices, beliefs, stories etc.

[61] Hütter, *Suffering*, p. 55.

[62] Marshall, 'We shall bear the image', p. 111.

[63] I may be wrong in calling God's involvement extra-linguistic, for there is nothing external to the scheme. But then it becomes difficult to understand how something internal to a scheme can validate it, while itself being in no need for validation.

It is a traditional aspect of the self-understanding of theology that it is meaningful only as an act of obedience to the grace of God.[64] In this sense, it is always a response to something more primordial, not just chronologically, but (onto-)logically as well. Barth's understanding of this relationship between theology and the self-disclosure of God, together with the ability of faith to grasp such a discovery, is part and parcel of what is distinctively Christian about theology. Yet the present cultural linguistic context raises serious questions about the way in which such a prevenient action of God can still be functional. The tension between *poiesis* and *pathos* in theology, between construction and discovery which all too often tends to be resolved by subsuming finding under making leaves precious little room for a logical priority of God. We have seen how both Lindbeck and Marshall's theory of truth leads to a possible recovery of the action of God in the process of justification. But how is that action possibly discerned from within the web of our beliefs, stories, practices and forms of life? Is such a theological model not haunted by the Feuerbachian sin of projection?[65] Is not God's action a mere mirroring of a logically prior imagination?[66] And if it is an antecedent imagination which prompts a reading as if 'God acted first', are we simply not 'playing Bible land?'[67] The seriousness behind such re-constructions must be assessed, lest they be little more than games with arbitrary rules. The difficult task is that of articulating an understanding of the prevenient action of God which the positive logic of Christian belief calls for, from within a cultural linguistic framework. In Lash's words, 'the narrative that declares our hope to be "received" and not "invented" is itself an interpretative and in that sense a "constructive" enterprise.'[68] Understanding the Christian truth as textual runs the danger of confusing our constructions of

---

[64] See especially Karl Barth, *Church Dogmatics*, vol. 1/1. Translated by G. W. Bromiley, edited by G. W. Bromiley and T. F. Torrance, (Edinburgh: T. and T. Clark, 1975), pp. 4, 22: 'Dogmatics must always be undertaken as an act of penitence and obedience. But this is possible only as it trusts in the uncontrollable presence of its ontic and noetic basis, in the revelation of God promised to the church, and in the power of faith apprehending the promise.'

[65] Lash argues that 'a form of Christian faith which had surrendered all attempt to speak of our perception of meaning, our apprehension of hope, as fundamentally "given" in revelation would have surrendered without a struggle to Feuerbach's perceptive but partial critique.' (*Theology on the Way to Emmaus*, p. 97).

[66] Cf. Green, *Theology, Hermeneutics, and Imagination* for a recovery of the concept of imagination for theology. However, the next chapter will expose some of the dangers associated with that proposal.

[67] Terrence F. Tilley, 'Incommensurability, intratextuality, and fideism', *Modern Theology* 5 (1989), 87-117, p. 98.

[68] Lash, *Theology,* p. 97.

the Real, with the being of what we are trying to conceptualise.[69] Apparently this is a danger not easily avoided by the cultural linguisticism of Lindbeck. If there is no outside to this world, under the Christian description, then we risk what Surin warns against, namely confusing the sign with the reality signified. The same danger haunts the project of Ronald Thiemann.

In his 1985 book, *Revelation and Theology: The Gospel as Narrated Promise*[70], Thiemann establishes himself as yet another theologian working in narrative key, with a project of recovering the prevenient action of God after the demise of foundationalism. He is concerned that the modern attempts to revive a concept of the prevenient action of God, and of theology as a response to revelation, have been plagued by a reliance on a non-inferential understanding of knowledge. The great challenge facing such attempts is to show how 'God's prior reality is both prior and in relation to human concepts.'[71] One of the main interlocutors of Thiemann is T. F. Torrance and his attempt to work out a realist understanding of theology as a response to God's prior action. Thiemann faults Torrance for accepting the inter-locking of mind and reality at the level of general knowledge, while refusing such a relation at the level of divine revelation. Torrance quite comfortably accepts that in human knowledge the mind plays an active role. However, when it comes to theology, the specificity of its object means that God cannot be coerced into a scheme. For Thiemann this suggests that Torrance works with an equivocal concept of knowledge: 'If Torrance consistently denies that human subjectivity has a reciprocal effect on the divine object, then either he must deny theology's rationality or he must use the terms *knowledge* and *rationality* equivocally.'[72] Thiemann grants that Torrance attempts to salvage his own position from inconsis-

---

[69] Surin, *Turnings*, p. 220: 'But the "reality" of the Second Person of the Trinity is not exhausted by the "reality" of Jesus of Nazareth. In this differentiation between the divine logos and the "historical" Jesus we are confronted by that which is inherently "sub-textual". The "historical" Jesus is "real" but his is what Fredric Jameson has called "the reality of the *appearance*", an "appearance" which is necessarily textualised. By contrast, the divine Logos, insofar as its "reality" is not exhausted by Jesus of Nazareth, is the Real, that is the essentially un-representable and non-narrative "absent cause" (F. Jameson, 'The political unconscious', p. 82), known only through its "effect", that is, Jesus of Nazareth. The Real, because it is inherently "sub-textual" is able to resist all human formulations and eludes the grasp of all our discourses. The Real – the Second Person of the Trinity – is thus able to be the fathomless source of disruptive significations which "interrupt" our unredeemed condition, and which are in consequence the source of our hope.'

[70] (Notre Dame, Indiana: University of Notre Dame Press, 1985).

[71] Thiemann, *Revelation*, p. 5.

[72] Thiemann, *Revelation*, p. 38.

tency by arguing that revelation does not deny subjectivity but reforms it to correspond to revelation's essential structure.[73] Such an attempt relies on the possibility of intuition, Thiemann assumes, and as such it is deemed to failure. That is, like all modern attempts, it tries to defend God's prevenience by confusing rational justification with causal explanation.[74] For Thiemann, however, such causal explanation is out of the picture since one simply cannot leave one's scheme behind and gain a direct access to reality.

It must be pointed out however, that Thiemann's accusations of Torrance are unconvincing. They rely on what Marshall calls a bad reason to give up realism, that is, its non-epistemic character.[75] The non-epistemic argument charges that realism is wrong because it cannot possibly justify its conclusions, it cannot verify them. And according to Dummett, to say that something is true without being able to supply reasons is meaningless.[76] However, as we have seen, Torrance is not arguing that the knowledge conferred in revelation does not conform to any scheme. Rather he merely points out that God somehow makes that scheme able to receive revelation. This is a translation of Barth's claim that revelation needs nothing for it to become actual, no *Anknüpfungspunkt* of any sort. And to some extent it is also part of the better material insights of the cultural linguisticism of Lindbeck, Marshall and Surin. It is God's action which ultimately makes the scheme as a whole adequate to Him. Yet Thiemann can only complain about the modern fallacy of granting human agency in normal knowledge but asserting human passivity in divine knowledge.[77] In all fairness, Torrance is no narrative theologian, but to charge him with the sort of naïve non-inferential foundationalism, is to dismiss his brilliance too hastily. If Thiemann is right, the surprising consequence is that 'as long as prevenience is defended by a conception of God's causal and thus epistemological priority, God's grace will have a merely extrinsic relation to human life.'[78] The reason for this is that under such a model grace would be relegated to the moment of crisis where the sphere of supra-human knowledge is instantiated.[79]

Where to go from here then? Thiemann analyses two alternative models, Gordon Kaufmann's Kantian model and the functionalism of thinkers like

---

[73] Thiemann, *Revelation*, p. 38.

[74] Thiemann, *Revelation*, p. 43.

[75] Marshall, 'We shall bear the image', pp. 93 ff. That is not to say that Marshall hasn't got any good reasons to give up realism, especially in light of D. Davidson's work.

[76] Lovibond, *Realism*, p. 26.

[77] Thiemann, *Revelation*, p. 48.

[78] Thiemann, *Revelation*, p. 48.

[79] This in itself is suspect of throwing the baby out with the baby water, for it need not be assumed that under this realist model God's grace need be restricted to the moment of *Krisis*.

Hauerwas, Wood and Kelsey. We are concerned with the second variety only. The promise of the functionalist approach to the authority of God and Scripture is that it allows for a diversity of uses of the objects. Whereas foundational epistemologies struggled to find a single use, deriving from a univocal description of the thing, functionalism can accommodate both normativity and diversity.[80] In functionalism, authority cannot be defined as a quality of the text, but rather as a quality of our reading.[81] It is thus parasitic upon logically prior decisions to regard something as authoritative. Kelsey's understanding of the authority and unity of the Scriptures betrays the same commitment to a logically prior *discrimen*. A discrimen is a configuration of criteria which allow a theologian to read the Scripture according to a heuristic image. The same could be said about Wood's and McClendon's insistence on the literal sense. McClendon, for example, argues that 'we can make full sense of biblical narrative only when we see its implied narrator not as the human author, but as the very God of whom Scripture speaks.'[82] That is, theologians formally decide to regard the Scripture as God's word, or to regard God as the initiator of human-divine dialogue and draw material conclusions from this.

However, according to Thiemann, it is not clear that functionalism can preserve the doctrine of God's prevenience since it can quite easily depict the process of identity formation of the Church without explicit reference to God. Stephen Sykes points out that Hauerwas' account of Scriptural authority is left intact and coherent even if God's action is left entirely out of the picture.[83] In other words, what the principle materially affirms, the method formally makes redundant. *While the Christian understanding of prevenience takes God to be the supreme authority in matters of faith, the formal methodological requirement is that such an authority needs first of all to be established by a decision of theological imagination.*[84] Thiemann would quite gladly accept functionalism if such a decision would be grounded in something else than communal authority. Appeal to decision is not inherently arbitrary for Thiemann, but, when challenged, the refusal to bring arguments in support of the decision may appear to be arbitrary.[85] Functionalism thus constrains prevenience in two ways: first, it subordinates theology as a response to grace to theology as imaginative use of the

---

[80] Thiemann, *Revelation*, p. 60.

[81] Cf. also Wesley A. Kort, *Story, Text and Scripture*, p. 7: the sacredness of Scripture does not reside in any inherent characteristic, but is a quality of reading.

[82] McClendon, *Systematic Theology*, vol. 1, pp. 40-41. This is an un-Wittgensteinian move, as Thiemann also points out with respect to Kelsey and Wood (Thiemann, p. 65).

[83] Article in *Modern Theology*, before Greg Jones' reply.

[84] Thiemann, p. 62, 63, 65. cf. also N. Lash, 'Ideology, metaphor and analogy', in Nicholas Lash, *Theology on the Way to Emmaus*, p. 97.

[85] Thiemann, *Revelation*, p. 65.

text to form Christian identity. And secondly, it accommodates prevenience through its emphasis on decision. 'But the grounding of the belief in God's prevenience in decision runs counter to the very intention of the belief itself.'[86]

Thus far we agree with Thiemann's analysis of functionalism. It raises very pertinent questions about the rehabilitation of imagination for theology. Formally, imagination is indeed a lucrative concept and it plays very well into the hands of the expressivist renaissance of epistemology after the rediscovery of the tradition of Herder, Hamann and Vico. Yet when material issues are considered, imagination and the logic of 'as if' comes in conflict with the ontological vehemence of Christian talk. Thiemann's solution to this muddle is a model of retrospective justification. For our discussion, however, it is important to say that such imaginative decisions need to be grounded, at least provisionally. A non-inferential causal justification is out of the question, as we have seen, hence Thiemann will advance a model of justification which betrays a theory of justification as coherence according to which God is not a causal agent external to the narrative.[87] Beliefs cannot be justified by reference to some intuition of reality, believes Thiemann. Yet the conclusion he draws from this basically correct premise is that they can only be justified with reference to other beliefs. He offers what he calls a holist model of justification.[88]

Lindbeck, Schemes, and Content

A recurring critique accuses Lindbeck of giving a very confused account of ontology. Sue Patterson discerns in *The Nature of Doctrine* both theistic realist and pragmatic-linguistic orientations.[89] His cultural-linguistic model employs both propositionalist notions of truth in the absence of verification and variants of warranted assertability. It may be argued that this is a muddled attempt to reconcile realism with non-realism when in fact both options are the results of an arbitrary philosophical choice, which also influenced theology. We have already hinted at the argument that nihilism and skepticism were in fact the direct consequences of the theological move to erect the edifice of a Being univocal to both the finite and the infinite. The Scotist unease about equivocity ironically issued in nihilism. Scotus' assumption that the forms of Being actually described the finite and infinite

---

[86] Thiemann, *Revelation*, p. 68. cf. Barth's argument that no reasons could be adduced for revelation for if ever such reasons were produced, they would constitute a logically prior ground upon which even revelation would be derivative. I do not have the reference yet.

[87] Thiemann, *Revelation*, p. 81.

[88] Thiemann, *Revelation*, pp. 72ff, see the discussion in next chapter.

[89] Patterson, *Realist Christian Theology in a Postmodern Age*, p. 37.

objects begged the question. It was only a matter of time before a historicist account of culture will take the place of a foundationalist metaphysics. The deconstruction of Being carried out by Schopenhauer, Nietzsche and more recently Derrida, to name only some of the major figures, is the inevitable consequence of what Milbank calls a theological heresy. Milbank's is but one genealogy of modernity, coloured by a strong theological (and Christian bias). It is not incompatible in its diagnosis, however, with Rorty's archaeology of modern epistemology in *Philosophy and the Mirror of Nature*. The story of modern philosophy has been dominated by a series of ocular metaphors, whose election was entirely arbitrary. The mind, the Eye of the mind, representation, perception, all these determined a certain foundationalist trajectory of epistemology. There was a certain anxiety of constraint, that knowledge should be conditioned by something prior to it, that it should either behold the forms of Being, or become one with them.[90] What Rorty calls the invention of the mind, is the positing of a non-spatial entity where the forms of Being could be contemplated by the 'eye of the mind.' The visual metaphors of perception and representation become the instruments and the arbiters of knowledge.[91] Current forms of skepticism and irrationalism are the heirs of the Augustinian-Aristotelian choice of tropes, and its consolidation in Cartesian certainty. The Cartesian anxiety, the desire for foundations is destined to bear the 'bastard' offspring of nihilism. The mechanism by which skepticism arises is an arbitrary positing taken as a necessary, natural objectivity. For Rorty this was the concept of Mind and the family of notions it encapsulates: representation, perception, etc. For Milbank it was the construction of a secular city, on the same plane of Being with God. What is revealing for our project is that the invention of the mind as the locus of a causal and hence epistemic relation between agent and world has continued to dominate philosophy even its 'cultural-linguistic' variants.

If Rorty's recounting of the history of epistemology is to be persuasive, he must show that major figures such as Kant, are counter-intuitively prisoners to the same set of metaphors. Just as Alliez recognises in Kant the last Scotist, Rorty denounces the Kantian dualism between receptivity and spontaneity. Although Kant moves in the direction of a knowledge not modelled on perception, it is only a half-way progress[92]: he is still under the cartesian spell in his attempt to phrase an answer to the question of how to get from the inside to the outside. Rorty forcefully objects to the Kantian and Lockean confusion between causation and justification. Only through a confusion between elements of knowledge and physiological conditions can

---

[90] Rorty, *Philosophy and the Mirror of Nature*, chapter I, sections 4, 5.

[91] Cf. also Nancey Murphy, 'Illuminating skepticism', Unpublished paper read at the conference *Illuminations: Reason, Revelation and Science*. Oxford, July 2002.

[92] Rorty, *Philosophy*, p. 147.

any idea be described as an impression.[93] The immediate problem with
Kant's 'revolution' is that it still kept in sight that which the mind apparently only organises. The task of post-Kantian philosophy was consequently that of illuminating the contribution of our own minds to the recep-
tive process. Kant does not even for a moment consider the double contradiction involved here: first, could any one after having read Kant still argue
that the Mind is presented with a diversity if we are never conscious of un-
synthesized intuitions?[94] Second, how is it that the forms of sensibility
themselves can become the object of introspection?: 'Kant was never trou-
bled by the question of how we could have apodictic knowledge of these
"constituting activities," for Cartesian privileged access was supposed to
take care of that.'[95] Realism, or direct access retreats with Kant from the
things in themselves to the direct knowledge of the mind's contribution to
knowledge. The *poiesis* which Kant schematically introduces is still realis-
tically known: we have better access to the made, to the objects framed
with our own contribution, just as Vico foresaw. It would exert an undeniable attraction were it not for the realisation that 'knowledge of necessary
truths about the made ("constituted") objects is more intelligible than about
found objects [, a realisation which] depends upon the Cartesian assumption
that we have privileged access to the activity of making.'[96]

Predictably, with hind-sight, post-Kantian philosophy could not protect
the mind's receptivity from linguistic infection for too long. The traditional
problems of epistemology were believed to come within the purview of the
philosophy of language. Instead of asking how does mind connect to the
world, philosophy thought it had to investigate first the meaning of language and then how language hooks unto the world.

The linguistic reformulation of Kantian doctrine stipulates that 'every
statement contained our contribution (in the form of meanings of the component terms) as well as the world's (in the form of facts of sense-
perception).'[97] *To cut a long story short, linguistic philosophy presupposed
that meanings are fixed whereas truth had to be established.* What Kant did
in the name of epistemology, namely to interpose the schematised *a priori*
forms between the agent and the world, thus grounding knowledge in them,
linguistic philosophy did by taking meanings for granted and seeking to
establish their relationship to the world. On this model knowledge was
modelled as an architectonic structure, whose foundations lie in the so-
called protocol statements, or statements of observation. It is these state-

---

[93] Rorty, *Philosophy*, p. 143.

[94] Rorty, *Philosophy*, pp. 154-5.

[95] Rorty, *Philosophy*, pp. 137-8.

[96] Rorty, *Philosophy*, p. 155.

[97] Rorty, *Philosophy*, pp. 258-9.

ments which connect to the world and upon their foundation is erected the whole edifice of knowledge.

Truth is arrived at through meaning. The supposition was that the meaning of the words and the statements could be established quite apart from the investigation into their truth. This strategy has also dominated theology, as Bruce Marshall shows. It is no longer the mind which anchors all thinking, but language, or the theory of meaning.[98] The theological assumption is that 'inner experiences or emotions can have determinative content without depending on having specific beliefs.'[99] This specific linguistic turn continues the separation of meaning from beliefs, from truths. The result has been getting 'the relation between experience and beliefs backwards.'[100] Modern theology, following Schleiermacher, all too easily distinguishes between experience and its conceptual interpretation. Both propositionalist and experiential models exhibit the same problematic aspect. Belief is built on meaning, just as reference is.

Lindbeck tries to combine the insights of both propositionalism and expressivism into cultural-linguisticism. He maintains the absolute distinction between experience and beliefs, where beliefs form the scheme which conditions what we experience. This is where his project takes a wrong turn, for it adopts both realist and anti-realist elements, without rejecting their common assumptions. The holist philosophy of Rorty, Quine, Davidson and Wittgenstein unmasks the arbitrary choice of mental and ocular metaphors which led philosophy in a foundationalist direction. Rorty speaks of the time when 'something which seemed much like idealism began to become respectable.'[101] This is the notion that language through its conventionalised patterns of meaning interposes itself between the knower and the world. The task of the knower therefore becomes that of making visible those patterns of meaning which inevitably condition perception. Quine's and Feyerabend's work, however, removed the innocent claim that one could know meanings of statements independently of convictions about their truth.[102] Beliefs conspired to account for the meaning of utterances.[103]

---

[98] Cf. Michael Dummett: 'the theory of meaning, which is the search for such a model, is the foundation of all philosophy, and not epistemology, as Descartes misled us into believing.' Rorty, *Philosophy*, p. 262.

[99] Bruce D. Marshall, *Trinity and Truth*, Cambridge Studies in Christian Doctrine, (Cambridge: Cambridge University Press, 2000), p. 73.

[100] Marshall, *Trinity*, p. 76.

[101] Rorty, *Philosophy*, p. 275.

[102] Cf. W. V. Quine, 'The two dogmas of empiricism' in W. V. Quine, *From a Logical Point of View*, (Cambridge, Mass. and London: Harvard University Press, 1964); Rorty, *Philosophy*, 268ff.

Observation statements could no longer assume the primordiality and directness they enjoyed in foundationalism, for their meaning now depended on the rest of the web of beliefs. Hence meanings were seen as shifting together with new beliefs. The reaction to the relativistic horror of these proposals is aptly narrated by Rorty:

> The response of many philosophers [...] was to grant that meanings *could* shift as a result of new discoveries – that the permanent neutral framework of meanings within which rational enquiry could be conducted was not so permanent as had been thought. But, they said, there must be such a thing as a 'rational' and principled change of meaning, and it is now our task, as the guardians and explicators of the rationality natural to natural scientists, to explain what principles are involved.[104]

Hence the notion that sameness of meaning, objectivity, and truth are relativised to a conceptual scheme. Which would not be troublesome as long as there were criteria for knowing when and why it was rational to change the scheme. But, as Rorty says, this remnant of certainty and objectivity was only briefly tempting, for schemes could not be changed according to any rational criteria. Shifts in conceptual schemes became nothing more than shifts in especially central beliefs. The reason for this is simple: there can be no confusion between causation and justification, of between intuition and beliefs. As Bruce Marshall comments, since we cannot swear our intuitions to truth, we would be better of without them, and rest justification squarely on other beliefs. Conceptual change becomes rational, at the very best, only *retrospectively*, through a historical reconstruction of the relevant change in the belief system.

The irony of this is that it does not necessarily imply relativism, as I shall try to argue. Rorty writes: 'Once schemes became temporary, the scheme-content distinction itself was in danger, and with it the Kantian notion of philosophy as made possible by our prior knowledge of our own contribution to inquiry (the schematic, formal element – e.g., "language").'[105] What Rorty denies is the interposing of a special thing such as 'mind' or 'language' between us and world, such that the task of philosophy is to clarify its contribution to our knowledge, thus grounding it. *The notion that reality is 'mediated' to us by some such scheme, be it Kant's schematism, or the linguistic complex of meanings, has unnecessarily grasped the imagination of philosophy.* We would be much better off, argue the philosophers of holism, to conceive the unity of agent and world without epistemic or linguis-

---

[103] Cf. next chapter's discussion of Davidson's theory of meaning as empirical. Since meanings and beliefs are inextricably bound together, the recovery of meaning is not a transcendentalist enterprise, but a thoroughly empirical one.

[104] Rorty, *Philosophy,* p. 271.

[105] Rorty, *Philosophy,* pp. 272f.

tic intermediaries. Meaning is undisociable from beliefs, facts from meanings.

This turns the tables on reference, truth as well as a host of other issues.[106] The theory of reference, for Rorty and Davidson, is the result of the confusion of sustaining the hierarchy and dualism of meaning and truth. As we saw with Frege, reference describes something like language reaching down to the world in virtue of the meanings of words and then propositions. It builds on pre-existing meanings of statements and words. But if we give up the idea that such statements have meanings which are fixed independently of our adjudicating their truth, then the very notion of reference as something mysterious and which needs explanation needs to go as well[107]. The result is that reference cannot be taken to be parasitic upon meanings, or upon schemes which 'organise' reality, perception, our intuitions etc. Meanings, as Davidson suggests, return to the field of empirical data, they are discovered along with the beliefs that accompany them. Reference begins to seem like an 'all or nothing affair'[108], since it is people who refer, by using language to cope with the world, and not statements, or words.

Now we are in a better position to examine Lindbeck's confusion resulting from the adoption of the scheme-content distinction. The cultural-linguistic model theoretically assumes a dialectical relationship between cultural scheme and experience, but it has great practical difficulty to maintain that tension. The model tends to bias towards the scheme side, without at the same time renouncing talk of an experience 'out there' which is shaped by the scheme. Knowledge is correct if the scheme as such is adequate to ultimate reality. There may be other, incommensurable schemes which 'divide' reality differently. Lindbeck confusedly says that only one of these schemes is ultimately appropriate for the description of reality.

Cultural-linguistic reference is a matter of statements and vocabulary allowing certain ontological moves. The assumption of a scheme-content dichotomy is apparent at this point as well. Truth and reference are not basic notions, but parasitic upon pre-existing, though culturally conditioned meanings. They are not specified 'directly in world-involving terms.' Lindbeck all too easily takes the meaning of the religious scheme to be fixed, while the truth of the adherents utterances needs to be decided by reference to those very meta-narrative meanings. The 'language' in 'cultural-linguistic' stands for a conventionalised, static, fixed structure of signs, not for an ability which may be better described as a force field, in which justificatory and referential energy is equally distributed and which does not

---

[106] Our use of Rorty and Davidson does not endorse all of their positive conclusions, but more especially their criticism of the priority of mind and language and the notion that knowledge is grounded by illuminating human creativity.

[107] Rorty, *Philosophy,* pp. 274, 276, 284-295.

[108] Rorty, *Philosophy,* p. 287.

'rest' on any privileged elements, rather than as an architectonic structure. The task of postliberal theology becomes that of describing the structure of the scheme, of laying bare its grammar, so that correct ontological speech may be possible. Kant's epistemic direction from the inside to the outside is maintained: from the logically stable first order vocabulary and grammar of the religious scheme to the truth assertions of second-order statements about external reality.

Only by considering the meaning of the vocabulary to be fixed can Lindbeck suggest that there may be incommensurable schemes.[109] The next chapter will follow through the consequences of the dissolution of the scheme-content dualism for epistemic justification. Once the scheme-content distinction is jettisoned, one no longer investigates how something like 'language' or 'mind' hooks onto the world, thus giving either realist, or non-realist solutions. Lindbeck's takes language too seriously. He still attempts to give an account of how it connects to the world. His pendulum move between realism and non-realism is thus but a consequence of asking the wrong questions.

---

[109] Gadamer, *Truth and Method*, pp. 281, 306.

Chapter Four

Justification

Postliberal theology assumes the textual construction of knowledge. Truth claims and interpretation function in the context of a setting, which takes the form of tradition or of community. Owing to a number of factors, the notion of setting became dominated by spatial and territorial metaphors which describe it as a reified structure. Rather than construing language as an enabling ability, it mistakes it for a conventionalised structure of meanings and actions which sediment meaning. In other words, language, just like mind, becomes schematised and it helps set up a dualism between scheme and content. By interposing language between the self and world, the task of philosophy is to show precisely how language connects with the world. Realism and non-realism become the epistemological alternatives. There isn't the slightest interest in how people connect with language. Meanings are taken as readily available and the structure of the language is transparent to inquiry. Theology assumes the task of re-describing the language of religion which grounds all ontological claims.

Following directly from the reification of language and schemes, is an aesthetic understanding of justification. Since schemes are understood as spatial structures, as incommensurable ways of dividing the world, dialogue between them inevitably involves distortion and misunderstanding. Criteria for choice being internal to a given tradition, all dialogue between rival traditions is destined to be an exercise of the will to power. The moral imperative attaching to this study, if only marginally, points out the danger attaching to a certain understanding of what it means for knowledge to be local. Both universalist and, let us call it contextualist or localist, approaches to knowledge end up threatening the 'Other'. Universalist strategies posit an absolute ground from which all other discourses are to be judged. Localists, on the other hand, assume the absoluteness of their own local preferences, leaving no room for universal mediation and rational agreement. In the first instance manipulation and domination hide behind objective legitimation, while in a localist key, deference issues in neglect and presumption. Ironically, as Milbank's case testifies, contextualist strategies united with a vision of the superiority of Christianity themselves turn towards domination.

There is reason to hope that having a local conception of knowledge does not arrest change, healthy criticism and inter-communitarian rational agreement, as Christian figural reading promises. Furthermore, the dissolution of the scheme-content dichotomy engages philosophy and theology on a more fruitful path, away from the false alternative between foundational-ism/ realism and skepticism/ non-realism.

Problems with Justification

The textual setting of tradition and community plays a constitutive role in what counts as interpretation, even in what can be perceived. Reality is no longer transparent, ready to aid justification. There have been several mo-ments in the process of disenchantment with justification. W. V. O. Quine rejected the view that all meaningful discourse can be translated into lan-guage about immediate experience.[1] Words and sentences are too small units to be reducible to experience. Rather, it is the whole web of words and beliefs which 'faces the tribunal of sense experience.'[2] The upshot of this holist understanding of validation is that what he calls 'recalcitrant experi-ence' will be accommodated by the system according to pragmatic criteria, such as simplicity and conservatism. The consequence of all this for justifi-cation is that one can no longer contrast the discourse of science with the matter of nature in order to validate the former. Secondly, the way in which a system may react to recalcitrant experience is not provided by any algo-rithm, it cannot be decided before hand. One could easily imagine a system adjusting itself to such experience in many different, often contradictory ways. Quine provides us with an understanding of the process of knowl-edge and justification which involves a number of factors. Traditionally it has been assumed that philosophy, metaphysics, the sciences have acquired such a respected status precisely because of their self-critical ability. How-ever, such a distinction between 'true' knowledge and 'mere' opinion has been increasingly difficult to maintain.

Thomas Kuhn deploys a scientific-philosophical version of Quine's ho-lism. He contrasts an understanding of scientific progress with the notion of scientific paradigm. According to the positivist notion of science, knowl-edge advances through gradual accumulation of evidence and data, which all adds up to the epistemic archive. This model presupposes the transpar-ency of experience and what Rorty calls the commensurability of contribu-tions to a discourse.[3] Reference is thus immediately available in a neutral language which then can be compared to the language of the given scien-tific theory. Yet, just as Quine questioned this reductionistic dogma, Kuhn also radically challenges the 'democratic' availability of facts. Facts are

---

[1] For a discussion of Quine's importance for theology, cf. Nancey Murphy and James McClendon, 'Distinguishing modern and postmodern theologies', *Modern Theology* 5 (1989), 191-214, p. 200.

[2] Quine, *From a Logical Point of View*, p. 41.

[3] Rorty, *Philosophy*, p. 315.

only available under a description internal to the paradigm itself and not present in some neutral language. Each paradigm employs its own standards of justification, criteria of what counts as a good explanation, or what counts as a fact. Hence justification is arguably a circular process: the paradigm always already provides for what counts as a good theory.

The outcome of such arguments, *on a certain reading of Kuhn*, is that there is no rational debate between rival scientific paradigms. How was such an interpretation possible? One may easily blame it on the idiosyncrasy of any pendulum reaction: one usually goes too far in the opposite direction when virulently reacting to a view. What is more important, nonetheless, is that Kuhn's early language about holism was often in terms of metaphors which lead one to assume that he is a committed relativist. Talk of different worlds, conversion experiences and *gestalt* switches certainly excuse such an interpretation. Kuhn may have been speaking about the same hermeneutical circle that Rorty had in mind when he wrote that 'We will not be able to isolate basic elements except on the basis of a prior knowledge of the whole fabric within which these elements occur.'[4] Incommensurable paradigms will lead to different perceptions of the 'data,' to put it simply. Hence there can be no rational comparison between schemes. Yet what exactly does Kuhn mean by his incommensurability argument? Gerald Doppelt[5] has uncovered several strands of the argument, the arrangement of which is decisive for how one reads Kuhn's overall view on relativism. Paradigms are incommensurable because a) they do not speak the same scientific language; b) because they don't perceive or address the same observational data; c) because they are not concerned with the same questions and finally d) because they do not construe what counts as adequate explanation in the same way. If one understands Kuhn's incommensurability thesis as hanging on the incommensurability of meaning, then one can indeed read Kuhn as a relativist. For if one speaks about different meanings, then there is no way in which such meanings are reconcilable without significant loss. The necessary inference from this is that incommensurability entails incomparability. Doppelt goes to great pains to disassociate Kuhn from such a reading, as will be seen later on. Crucial for now is the post-positivist belief in the absence of any neutral observation language.

Donald Davidson's criticism of the scheme-content dualism also goes against the notion of incommensurability. Since we are not in possession of a neutral language, completely transparent and not culturally conditioned, it does not make sense to speak in such dualistic terms, argues Davidson. Even Quine, by hanging on to the notion of recalcitrant experience is guilty

---

[4] Rorty, *Philosophy*, p. 319.

[5] Gerald Doppelt, 'Kuhn's epistemological relativism: an interpretation and defense', *Inquiry* 21 (1978), 33-86.

of maintaining the illusion of a scheme organising a given content. What remains in Quine 'is the notion of a type of evidence or justification for belief which is not itself a belief and which reliably informs us, in the crucial basic cases, about the truth of belief.'[6]

Bruce D. Marshall[7] disentangles three aspects of the foundationalist strategy of justification. Firstly, foundationalism argues that with respect to at least some of the sentences we hold true, we have direct or immediate access to states of affairs, events or experiences in virtue of which those experiences are true (F1); secondly, that this direct access guarantees the truth of those sentences and so justifies us in, or serves as the, ultimate evidence for holding them true (F2). Finally, that the rest of our beliefs must be justified by establishing some suitable kind of warranting link with those which are directly tied to the world (and who thereby serve as the justificatory 'foundation' for the rest (F3). Davidson's argument is to the effect that F1 and F2 are untrue. There is no point in rehearsing the argument against realism here, but it amounts to a rejection of the dualism of scheme and content. Davidson is quite adamant that there are no epistemic intermediaries between us and the world. This is not to say that there are no causal mediators, but their epistemic function is quite undecidable, rendering them useless for epistemology. The search for such intermediaries, for stable foundations to our thought on which to erect the structure of the rest of our knowledge, is futile. Rorty calls it the desire for constraint, yet epistemology has died, and 'hermeneutics is an expression of the hope that the cultural space left by the demise of epistemology will not be filled.'[8] Davidson and Marshall argue that since we cannot be certain that such intermediaries do not mislead us, there is no point in employing them. This, then, is the coherentist approach to justification, which arguably is the strategy of narrative theology as well, with the exception of Milbank: only beliefs justify beliefs. For Marshall, the jettisoning of F1 and F2 means that one is free to take basic Christian convictions as foundational.[9]

To sum up, the problems associated with foundationalism and with justification have lead narrative theology and philosophy in general to an allegiance to a doctrine of incommensurability and an account of justification as coherence. The question which might be put now is: how does one understand incommensurability and will such an understanding allow for comparability, for a rational choice between theories and paradigms? Or are we left with merely proclaiming the superior coherence of our own paradigm, rhetorically established as it is, and believe that all questions of justification are rhetorical?

---

[6] Marshall, *Trinity*, p. 84.

[7] Marshall, *Trinity*, p.54.

[8] Rorty, *Philosophy*, p. 315.

[9] Marshall, *Trinity*, p. 82.

Our discussion will follow two lines of approach, one philosophical, the other theological. On the philosophical front we shall juxtapose the views of Kuhn, Davidson and MacIntyre. To cut a long story short, I distinguish between two versions of the incommensurability thesis[10]. According to the strong version, incommensurability entails different meanings and different conceptions of truth and standards of justification. Such a version makes comparison between different self-contained 'schemes' impossible. A weaker version will allow for the possibility of comparison, yet precisely how that comparison is possible is something to be decided *ad hoc*. I shall take Kuhn to be proposing the weaker version of incommensurability, allowing for comparability. MacIntyre rejects Davidson's refutation of incommensurability and insists on a holist account of paradigms and traditions. However, his commitment to realism will lead him to provide an account of rational justification which turns on the impossibility of translatability and on the need to learn a second first language. What will hopefully emerge out of this debate is a vindication of the notion of rational theory choice, between rhetoric and seriousness. On a theological front, the hermeneutical (in Rorty's sense) exuberance of theologians such as Milbank will have to give way to a 'good reasons' attitude towards theory choice and belief justification.

One last mention need be made here. It concerns the relationship between truth and meaning and it has been brought into sharp focus by Bruce Marshall. Foundationalism, believes Marshall, is often accompanied by an epistemic dependence thesis, according to which the primary criteria for deciding the truth of Christian or religious affirmations must be non-Christian, or external. The obvious bearer of such criteria is philosophy. Marshall convincingly argues that the assumption behind this thesis is that the meaning of the belief will remain unaffected by the strategies of justification, by the decision of whether it is true or not.[11] In essence, his argument, to which we shall return later on in much more detail, is that the meaning of a sentence, or a belief or doctrine, is its truth conditions. Notwithstanding the fact that this relies on a dubious understanding of the nature of meaning, which sometimes covertly re-employs the notion of ostensive reference, the upshot is that one can no longer test Christian beliefs in just any way and expect their meaning to remain the same. This brings to the fore the relationship between theological discourse and other discourses or meta-discourses, external to the Christian faith. Can Christianity operate at a level of sufficient self-description, or must it engage other semiotic codes as well? And if it must, according to what criteria? Or perhaps the

---

[10] cf. Robert Miner, 'Lakatos and MacIntyre on incommensurability and the rationality of theory choice' [online]. Available at:
http://www.bu.edu/wcp/papers/scie/sciemine.htm

[11] Marshall, *Trinity*, pp. 50, 90.

quest for criteria is itself pointless? Marshall will argue that one needs internal strategies of justification, which will preserve the original and fundamental meaning of Christian claims.

Richard Bernstein argues that Kuhn is actually closer to the 'good reasons' approach in ethics, rather than emotivism.[12] He takes issue with a
reading of Kuhn which depicts him as arguing that rational theory choice is
impossible. Kuhn does indeed argue that there is no algorithm, there are no
external standards that one can employ in a rational comparison between
traditions. We have seen that the demise of foundationalism was brought
about by a series of factors such as: the absence of a neutral observation
language, the unavailability of pure, immediate experience, the connection
between truth and meaning and so on. Yet to deny criteria for objective
justification is not necessarily to proclaim subjectivism and irrationalism.
On the contrary, the spectre of skepticism arises precisely where a foundationalist quest ended in disappointment. Kuhn, by defusing the Cartesian
anxiety for foundations and an a priori methodology for rational choice
does seem to have opened the way for relativism. This is also a major
strand of Kuhnian interpretation[13].The fallacy of such a reading is to propose a false alternative: either objective standards, or irrational and arbitrary norms (eg. by way of conversion or a gestalt switch). It is not difficult,
then, to realise the force of the return of rhetoric in philosophy and the human sciences especially, but in the natural ones as well. If there are no objective and external standards then there are no independent evaluations of
paradigms. All explanation and justification will have to be circular, presupposing the truth of the internal standards of evaluation.

The haste with which Fish introduces a dualism in order to end all dichotomies suggests that a certain anxiety is present in these post-critical
writings as well. If foundationalism suffered from the anxiety of closure,
seeking an argument that would constrain every rational self into accepting
the truth of the theory, then perhaps the Fishean anxiety is rather similar. It
attempts to decide before the actual debates that all debates are useless
since they are irrational and undecidable. Why should this anxiety be less
crippling than the foundationalist one? Where the Cartesians sought external foundations which they would then apply with minimal modification to
the particular debates, relativists are quite impatient to wait for the actual
debates before they label them as irrational. However, are we right in ex-
pecting some rational debate to be possible? Could it be that some debates
are settled on the background of mutual understanding and acceptance? We

---

[12] Richard J. Bernstein, *Beyond Objectivism and Relativism: Science, Hermeneutics
and Praxis*, (Oxford: Blackwell, 1983), p. 57

[13] Israel Scheffler, *Science and Subjectivity*, (Indianapolis: Bobbs-Merrill, 1967).

are not suggesting any ideal speech situation scenario, like Habermas,[14] but only that one delay the decision as to whether a dispute can be rationally resolved until the moment of the discussion itself. This is precisely what Fish is not doing. What he does is precisely what he visibly reacts against: doing theory. But doing theory means just predicting outcomes, legislating moves in a debate, imposing a general grid on the particular cases.

To say that Fish and indeed others have been infected with the disease they are trying to cure does not legitimise the disease. Foundationalism is not a desirable option. Nor does it mean that relativism is wrong in itself. Perhaps the crucial factor here is the willingness to approach actual debates and conflicts between paradigms. Kuhn's interest in revolutions and paradigm shifts in science is well known. The presence of revolutions in the history of science points out the fact that paradigms are not closed systems but that they do interact with one another. A concentration on the holist model of meaning and justification, without any glance at the way in which internal standards and meanings relate to external ones may be one reason why Fish and Feyerabend are relativists, while Kuhn and MacIntyre are not. But this still remains to be established. Kuhn has become rather weary of people mistaking him for an irrationalist. In his later writing he has insisted that he never intended his views on incommensurability to cast any doubt on the fact that paradigms are comparable. As Richard Bernstein observes, that is obscene, for the very reason behind his introduction of the notion of incommensurability to the debate was to aid in the comparison of paradigms.[15] What Kuhn is doing, in fact, is not to dispense with rationality but rather to point out its 'judgmental character.'[16]

In a 1977 text, 'Objectivity, Value Judgement and Theory Choice,' Kuhn argues that he was not in fact suggesting in the earlier writings that any choice between paradigms is irrational and arbitrary. On the contrary, he is proposing a shift from understanding such external criteria for choice as *rules* to an understanding of such criteria as *values*. One may say that Kuhn is accutely aware of the rhetorical purchase of any debate. But that is not to deny that choice is rational and is governed by rational factors. What distinguishes Kuhn from the relativists is that whereas the latter do not allow the specific case to decide on the possibility of rationality, Kuhn will use theory only in a heuristic fashion, to be modified by the particulars in question. To be precise, there are shared standards that guide any rational exchange and conflict. However, such standards do not function in a 'noise-free' context. Hence 'choice between theories depends not only on shared

---

[14] See Jürgen Habermas, 'On systematically distorted communication', *Inquiry* 13 (1970); Jürgen Habermas, 'Towards a theory of communicative competence', *Inquiry* 13 (1970).

[15] Bernstein, *Beyond Objectivism*, pp. 84-86; cf. Tilley. op. cit., p. 90.

[16] Bernstein, *Beyond*, p. 74.

criteria but also on idiosyncratic factors dependent on individual biography and personality.'[17] He lists five criteria which serve as values in theory choice: accuracy, consistency, scope, simplicity and fruitfulness. Yet Kuhn also understands that the way in which these standards are applied to the specific debate may differ from case to case and there may indeed be disagreements about the appropriate application. Hence there is a fundamental relationship between reasons and my judgement in favour of a paradigm. This is not an irrational model of science, but a shift in models of rationality, from a theoretical to a practical rationality; from a foundational to a contextual reason and from apodictic judgements informed by objective factors to warranted judgements guided by rational values.

Now it may be seen how this model of incommensurability aids comparability rather than denies it. First of all, it suggests that the older understanding of the cumulative nature of scientific work is not helpful for understanding the way in which paradigms conflict. Then, by drawing attention to idiosyncratic factors, it broadens the understanding of what is involved in the decision making process. To be sure, comparisons between rival paradigms are no longer as straightforward as in positivism. There is no longer a neutral paradigm, the mirror of nature for example, in relation to which one would judge the success of a paradigm. Kuhn also points out that the success of a given paradigm in relation to another has nothing to do with a better adequacy to reality or a close affinity with truth. Such judgements remain impossible for Kuhn.

Kuhn's is an *ad hoc* model for the rationality of theory choice. The superiority of one tradition over another can be decided rationally, yet the decision will always be rhetorically mediated. Yet the precise nature of this rhetorical mediation will have to become clearer as we go along. It will be delimited from Milbank's understanding of rhetorical mediation, for example. The main reason for this is a commitment to the view that not all relevant areas of rationality have been infected by subjectivism and difference. It also believes that perhaps difference is not so different as to render all understanding impossible, or all agreement forced.

There remains a problem with Kuhn's account of incommensurability. Doppelt has tried to isolate one strand of the incommensurability argument as being the pivotal one for Kuhn. Robert Miner has also distinguished between different versions of the theme and he also suggests that the proper Kuhnian version is not an incommensurability of meaning, but of standards of justification.[18] Bernstein[19] and Doppelt arrive at the same conclusion. On

---

[17] Thomas Kuhn, 'Objectivity, value judgement and theory choice', in Thomas Kuhn, *The Essential Tension: Selected Studies in Scientific Tradition and Change,* (Chicago and London: University of Chicago Press, 1977), p. 329.

[18] Miner, 'Lakatos and MacIntyre'.

[19] Bernstein, *Beyond,* p. 82.

Doppelt's reading, the incommensurability thesis turns on the difference in standards of evaluation and in perception of problems between two rival paradigms. The problem is aggravated when such standards are embedded in the very fabric of tradition to the point where their negation would amount to a significant change of identity for the given tradition or community. This reading of Kuhn is accurate to the extent that it makes better sense of Kuhn's notion of anomaly, to which readings pivoting around incommensurability of meaning could not do justice. For the present purposes it is also beneficial for our purposes for it allows for some overlap between traditions. Kuhn is quick to point out that there is never sufficient overlap in order to determine objectively the superiority of one tradition in favour of another.[20] Yet 'Kuhn clearly holds that there is an overlap of observational content and language between rival paradigms, one which essentially figures in the grounds on which some scientists transfer allegiance from the old to the new paradigm.'[21] There are good reasons for adhering to a paradigm, but such reasons are never compelling by themselves. Moreover, the strength of those reasons is relative to the paradigm itself. This explains why Kuhn still felt the need to speak in terms of a conversion and a Gestalt switch:

> If one accepts this Kuhnian view of the relativity of reasons (in particular their relative strength) to the standards internal to particular paradigms, then one can make sense of his emphasis on the element of 'conversion' in the revolutionary progress, without presenting it as a glorification of irrationalism.[22]

To sum up, Doppelt makes a distinction between an incommensurability which turns on the difference between standards of evaluation and problems, which I shall call weak incommensurability, and a strong version of incommensurability whose main pillar is difference of meanings. However, a look at the philosophy of Donald Davidson and especially his views on the relationship between truth and meaning will make that distinction very problematic. To anticipate, if one makes meaning dependent on truth and if the meaning of a belief are its truth conditions, then one can no longer resort to an incommensurability of standards of justification and hope that it will not amount to an incommensurability of meaning.

Where the foundationalist strategy attempts to grasp meanings prior to deciding about their truth, Davidson argues that belief and meaning are necessarily presupposed by each other in a holistic account. Meanings are

---

[20] Notice that Kuhn is guilty here of the same mistake of presumption in favour of is theory of difference before getting down to the particular case. cf. Doppelt, 'Kuhn's Relativism', p. 45.

[21] Doppelt, 'Kuhn's Relativism', p. 47.

[22] Doppelt, 'Kuhn's Relativism', p. 54.

not un-problematic and are themselves in need of elucidation, which for Davidson can only be an empirical matter. One cannot get at the meaning of the sentences uttered by a speaker by appealing to the beliefs he is holding or the intentions he has. To the extent to which the meaning of those beliefs themselves needs to be established,[23] they cannot serve as evidence for a theory of interpretation. According to Davidson, 'beliefs and meanings conspire to account for utterances.'[24] A theory of meaning has to avoid circularity, as much as possible, and invoke non-semantic factors for the determination of semantic meaning. For the same reason, standard theories of communication which invoke convention as the essence of language miss the point. Convention involves belief and intention and cannot serve as basis for understanding the specific meaning on a specific occasion. One cannot use thought in order to explain linguistic meaning, for it is itself linguistic.

Davidson attempts to focus the issue by using an idealised situation of interpretation, or what he calls radical interpretation. In such a situation there is no convention in place, therefore the interpreter cannot make use of any previous knowledge of the intentions or of the beliefs of the speaker, to say nothing about the meaning of words. It is quite obvious that this is the only situation imaginable in which a non-circular theory of interpretation can be constructed. In radical interpretation we do not have access to the thoughts, intentions, beliefs, or the vocabulary of the speaker. We must make do without these. The only thing on which we can build are the public dispositions and behaviour of the person in front of us. Yet for Davidson this is ideal, since it provides us with a non-semantic starting point. He suggests that what one must do is to *hold for truth, while testing for meaning*. He calls this the principle of charity, a notion taken over from Quine's work, who has applied it to more formal cases of communication such as those involving logic. However, Davidson applies it across the board, due to his conviction that radical interpretation permeates all cases of communication, and is not a special case only.

If belief and meaning form an indissoluble pair, then one would have to hold one stable while testing the other and this is precisely what Davidson attempts to do. Yet he must find those cases of belief where semantic content is minimal and the prime candidate for that is what Quine calls 'prompted assent:'

> What a sentence means depends partly on the external circumstances that cause it to win some degree of conviction; and partly on the relations,

---

[23] As opposed to the older model which presupposes that meaning to be already fixed, the task being that of discovering its truth.

[24] Davidson, 'Belief and the basis of meaning', in Donald Davidson, *Inquiries into Truth and Interpretation,* (Oxford: Clarendon, 1984), p. 142.

grammatical, logical or less, that the sentence has to other sentences held true with varying degrees of conviction. Since these relations are themselves translated directly into beliefs, it is easy to see how meaning depends on belief. Belief, however, depends equally on meaning, for the only access to the fine structure and individuation of beliefs is through the sentences speakers and interpreters of speakers use to express and describe beliefs. If we want to illuminate the nature of meaning and belief, therefore, we need to start with something that assumes neither. Quine's suggestion, which I shall essentially follow, is to take *prompted assent* as basic, the causal relation between assenting to a sentence and the cause of such assent.[25]

In practical terms, then, the interpreter should 'watch out' for the prompted assent of the speaker to certain events around him and while holding such assent to be true, to test the meaning of the ensuing sentences. For example, should a speaker in a circumstance in which it is snowing utter the words 'es schneit', and provided that he only holds it true when it snows, one would infer that the meaning of the sentence is closely related to his belief that it snows. Hence, 'behavioural or dispositional facts that can be described in ways that do not assume interpretations, but on which a theory of interpretation can be based, will necessarily be a vector of meaning and belief.'

The understanding of the close relationship between meaning and truth is pivotal to my argument, and consequently accusations levelled at Hans Frei for his confusion of truth with meaning, or for mistaking meaning for truth will have to be seen in a completely new light. Davidson does not see much promise in the use of convention for communication. Indeed, in the later writings he has come to speak in terms of prior theory and passing theory, which may be plausibly read as paralleling Soskice's concerns about both Russellian and causal theories of reference. What he means by this is that we all approach speech situations armed with a prior theory.[26] This will include specific beliefs that we have about the speaker(s), expectations, understandings of conventions and rules of grammar and so on. But this prior theory must make room for the exercise of radical interpretation. That is to say, one must allow convention and all previous expectations to be shaped and modified by the dispositional and behavioural facts associated with the utterances. In 'Communication and convention'[27] Davidson argues that convention is never enough in order to understand someone's speech. One could always construct anew a theory of interpretation in the absence of any

---

[25] Davidson, 'A coherence theory of truth and knowledge', in Davidson, *Inquiries*, p. 159.

[26] Soskice's *langue*.

[27] Davidson, 'Communication and convention', pp. 265ff.

convention or common language.[28] However, since this would be too time-consuming and impractical, one relies on convention on a day to day basis. But since convention-use is present this has obscured the fact that radical interpretation always takes place, conventions are always modified so that they would fit specific beliefs and intentions. A speaker may always provide adequate clues as to the meaning of his words.

The importance of these claims can hardly be overrated. If convention is not irreplaceable and can be supplemented, then we as speakers can experience a great degree of 'liberation' from the constraints of language. It means that there is in principle no un-translatable language. It also means that one cannot expect the conditions for the truth of a sentence to change while the meaning of that sentence will remain the same. For it is precisely those conditions of truth that conspire for the meaning of the associated utterance. At this point we can return to Doppelt's defence of Kuhn's incommensurability and understand how his belief that one can hold on to an incommensurability of standards and problems while denying an incommensurability of meaning is naïve. Such a strategy obscures one of the main insights of holism, the close relationship between meaning and truth.

Davidson's arguments for truth and meaning also go in the direction of showing that an account of incommensurability is unintelligible. Given the 'underlying methodology of interpretation'[29] it would be impossible for us to judge people as having completely different schemes from our own. The reason for this is that understanding meaning is parasitic upon largely holding other people's beliefs to be true. It is only on the basis of a tremendous amount of agreement that disagreement or agreement can take place. Davidson's arguments against incommensurability pivot around the question and possibility of translatability. In essence he argues that translatability requires commensurability. Given this basic assumption, namely that difference can only be recognised as such on the background of identity or similarity[30], Davidson argues that Kuhn, Feyerabend and other proponents

---

[28] Davidson, 'Communication and convention', p. 278

[29] Davidson, 'On the very idea of a conceptual scheme', in Davidson, *Inquiries*, p. 197.

[30] For a congenial argument, see Ruth Ronen, 'Incommensurability and representation', *Applied Semiotics/ Semiotique appliqué* (A Learned Journal of Literary Research on the World Wide Web. Une Revue internationale de recherche litteraire sur Internet no. 5: July/ juiller 1998, pp. 267-302. Ruth Ronen, 'Incommensurability and representation', *Applied Semiotics/ Semiotique appliqué (A Learned Journal of Literary Research on the World Wide Web. Une Revue internationale de recherche litteraire sur Internet*, 1998, 5 (July/ juiller), 267-302. Available at: http://www.tau.ac.il/~ronnen/documents/inc-rep.html

of radical difference in schemes are incoherent[31]. He marvels at the way in which, for all their theoretical allegiance to untranslatability and incommensurability, Whorf, Kuhn, Quine and Bergson are all able to translate this difference into one language:

> Whorf, wanting to demonstrate the Hopi incorporates a metaphysics so alien to ours that Hopi and English cannot, as he puts it, 'be calibrated', uses English to convey the contents of sample Hopi sentences. Kuhn is brilliant at saying what things were like before the revolution using – what else? – our post-revolutionary idiom. Quine gives us a feel for the 'pre-individuative phase in the evolution of our conceptual scheme', while Bergson tells us where we can go to get a view of a mountain undistorted by one or another provincial perspective.[32]

This reinforces my point that Kuhn and others are still doing theory. Their optimism remains strong as ever. Davidson's point is rather simple: if two schemes are incommensurable, how is it that we can talk about them, describe them and so on? Incommensurability, in his opinion, should entail un-translatability. But untranslatability implies that we cannot even count the respective 'noises' as being part of a language.[33] And this is his strategy in demolishing the radical difference in schemes: one cannot make any sense of the notion of *failure* in translation[34]. The only thing we *can* make sense of are *difficulties* in translation. But the basic point is that such failures can be perceived as failures of translation precisely because one assumes a great amount of understanding between the two languages. His point is that translation problems can only make sense if they are local enough,[35] whereas the notion of a language which cannot be translated at all is incoherent. For by what standards would we be entitled to take it as a language?

---

[31] R. Harvey Brown argues that Feyerabend and Kuhn fail to account for the continuity of intellectual traditions which is the pre-condition for the intelligibility of their own historical narratives. cf. R. Harvey Brown, *Society As Text: Essays on Rhetoric, Reason and Reality,* (Chicago and London: University of Chicago Press, 1987), p. 167.

[32] Davidson, 'On the very idea of a conceptual scheme', p. 184.

[33] Cf. Heidegger's point that perception is in terms of meaningful wholes. 'What we "first" hear is never noises or complexes of sounds, but the creaking wagon, the motorcycle. We hear the column on the march, the north wind, the woodpecker tapping, the fire cracking. It requires a very artificial and complicated frame of mind to "hear" a "pure noise."' (Martin Heidegger, *Being and Time,* translated by John Macquarrie and Edward Robinson, (Oxford: Blackwell, 1962), p. 207).

[34] Davidson, 'On the very idea', p. 186ff.

[35] Davidson, 'On the very idea', p. 192.

His attack on the dualism of scheme and content, what he calls the third dogma of empiricism[36] has focused on both sides of the dualism, as Bruce Marshall points out. By refuting the scheme side of the dualism, he has in fact refuted relativism. On the other hand, to deny content means to deny intermediaries between scheme and world, such as sensations. One is left, rather only with other beliefs, no matter what one calls them.

Davidson's account is not without its difficulties, however. The main problem has to do with his recourse to 'prompted assent.' While he is trying to do without semantic evidence for a meaning theory, his critics are not completely satisfied that a semantic element is not present in his account. Thus, Envine argues that semantic factors creep back into the procedure, since even the assent could be taken as a belief which itself needs to be interpreted.[37] J. E. Malpas further argues that it is difficult to start a theory of meaning from a non-semantic basis, precisely because of the holist nature of understanding:

> Interpreting a speaker as holding some unspecified belief true is surely dependent on other assessments of the speaker's beliefs and desires. Thus it would seem doubtful to suppose that we can find any place to begin our interpretative project which is unaffected by the holistic nature of interpretation. Insofar as he assumes that we can do just this, Davidson is surely mistaken.[38]

Davidson is surely wrong if he believes that he can thus escape the hermeneutic circle, that he can find an uncontaminated moment of pure reference and perception. Even the very act of discerning the prompted assent of a speaker is bound to other perceptive acts. One for example must postulate that the speaker so intends to assent to something, that the speaker so believes that something causes his assent, and so on. Perhaps the issue is resolved through Davidson's later emphasis on 'prior' and 'passing theory.' He may thus be interpreted *not as attempting to provide us with a pure starting point for an interpretation theory, but of providing a phenomenology of how convention communication (prior theory) can and must answer before the tribunal of the disposition and behaviour of the speaker.*

Apparently the earlier Davidson seemed to usher in a return of ostensive reference, not as a doctrine of reference, to be sure.[39] However, to rehearse one of Wittgenstein's arguments against ostensive reference, how does one know to what is the speaker pointing? In our case of radical interpretation, how does the interpreter know to what object or states of affairs does the

---

[36] Davidson, 'On the very idea', p. 189

[37] Simon Envine, *Donald Davidson*, (Cambridge: Polity, 1991), cf. sect. 5.3.

[38] J. E. Malpas, *Donald Davidson and the Mirror of Meaning: Holism, Truth, Interpretation,* (Cambridge: Cambridge University Press, 1992), p. 44.

[39] Rorty, I suspect, would call it philosophically or epistemologically uninteresting.

speaker assent? One would have to rely here on further specification, either in the form of already existing conventions, known by both parties, or in the form of further clues given by the speaker. However, if such clues may come only in the form of prompted assent, this gets us nowhere. The problem, therefore, for radical interpretation is that once it attempts to conceive itself in non-foundational terms (and it does so by attempting to escape circularity by ostensivity), it is left in complete epistemic darkness. A speaker always speaking in the circumstance of snow and uttering the words 'es schneit' may point to the fact that it snows, may point to the colour of the snow flakes, or he may point with amazement to the unique shapes of each flake, and so on. As with the fate of foundationalism, if Davidson intended his theory to provide us with a stable and solid starting point it will inevitably lead to relativism, for such stability will always elude us.

If Davidson and Kuhn disagree on the issue of incommensurability, MacIntyre disagrees with Kuhn on the notion that a conversion or a gestalt switch is needed in order to move from one tradition to another; and he disagrees with Davidson's argument that translatability requires and implies commensurability.

It is wrong to argue, as Kuhn did, that the proponents of competing paradigms will fail to make complete contact with each other's view points and that the transition from one paradigm to another requires a conversion experience. Such conclusions do not follow from his premises which do not contain the necessary premise for such an argument, namely that *every* relevant area of rationality is invaded by disagreement.[40] In fact, Kuhn's wholesale rejection of a paradigm amounts to a Cartesian rationality in which the whole of a tradition is questioned at once. However, not everything can be simultaneously doubted, argues MacIntyre.[41] By arguing along these lines, he wishes to keep more continuity between the old and new paradigms so that transition is not irrational or rhetorical, but rationally mediated.

Reading Kuhn in this way is not without its problems. MacIntyre believes that Kuhn's later 'recantations' did not go far enough towards undoing the damage. MacIntyre, on the present view, is wrong to read Kuhn as denying any relevant contact between traditions. The external standards of rationality that he enumerates, which will serve as values that inform theory choice, are such points of contact. At a formal level, therefore, almost all scientific paradigms will count them as goals of their respective endeavours. What Kuhn is denying in fact, is that they are by themselves sufficient in ensuring an objective transition. Perhaps the key concept here is 'objective.' Neither Kuhn nor MacIntyre deny that transitions are rational, yet they both deny they are objective in the sense of logically necessary. Yet

---

[40] MacIntyre, 'Epistemological crises', pp. 465-6.

[41] MacIntyre, 'Epistemological crises', p. 466.

while Kuhn allows for idiosyncratic factors which will make the interpretation of the criteria for theory choice incommensurable, MacIntyre does not.

It is important to remember that the background to MacIntyre's discussion is always a conversational, hence a rhetorical one. Charles Taylor significantly points out that the arguments presented are *transition arguments* and they go to make up comparative rather than absolute judgements or claims.

> A foundational argument to the effect that Y is the correct thesis shows its superiority over the X thesis only incidentally. That proof also shows Y's superiority over all rivals. It establishes an absolute, not just a comparative claim.[42]

Hence, MacIntyre is not arguing for the absolute truth of one theory over another, but only for the fact that this may be the best theory yet. This may be obscured by the fact that sometimes the conversational background is absent: 'the test for truth in the present, therefore, is always to summon up as many questions and as many objections of the greatest strength possible; what can be justifiably claimed as true is what has sufficiently withstood such dialectical questioning and framing of objections.'[43] One may argue that this is a dialectical rather than a rhetorical mode of reasoning, opening his views to charges of a return to foundationalism and dialectics. This is one prong of Milbank's refutation of this account of justification, but as we shall see, it pivots around a false opposition established between rhetoric and dialectics.

The mechanism of justification is outlined by MacIntyre in his narrative of the epistemological crises. A tradition usually becomes aware of inconsistencies between the way it construes reality and what its beliefs and values are. Every tradition which is not considered to be a closed system is vulnerable to such moments of epistemic crisis. To this extent, any tradition may at one point encounter a rival tradition which is better able to make sense of what it takes to be reality in terms of its beliefs and thought structures. Epistemological crises are possible because all dialogue between traditions is driven by a common concern with what they take to be reality. Such crises are resolved by the construction of a new narrative which enables the agent to understand both how he or she could intelligibly have held his or her original beliefs and how they could have been so misleading. The original narrative, thus, becomes a subject of the enlarged narrative.[44] Again, 'the criterion of a successful theory is that it enables us to understand precisely why its predecessors have to be rejected or modified

---

[42] Charles Taylor, 'Explanation and practical reason', in Charles Taylor, *Philosophical Arguments*, (Cambridge, Mass. and London: Harvard University Press, 1995), p. 54.

[43] MacIntyre, *Whose Justice?*, p. 358.

[44] MacIntyre, 'Epistemological crises', p. 455.

and also why without and before its illumination, past theory could have remained credible.'[45] In other words, 'to justify is to narrate how the argument has gone so far.'[46]

There are two discernible moments in this process, the relation of which is instructive for our verdict on MacIntyre. First there is the moment of dialectical and socratic questioning: to summon up as many and as good arguments as possible against the paradigm. If it withstands such rigorous questioning, we are assured of its superiority. Some may argue that this is the moment where one no longer is considering transition arguments but absolute ones. The second moment is historical: the narration of this process of dialectical legitimation. Holism teaches us that one can no longer separate reason and tradition, understanding reality and becoming involved in it. As Charles Taylor comments on the pre-modern *episteme*:

> The notion that explanation can be distinct from practical reason, that the attempt to grasp what the world is like can be made independently of the determination of how we should stand in it, that the goal of understanding cannot be uncoupled from our attunement to it, this makes no sense on the premodern understanding.[47]

To follow closely this mind-set, explanation and justification, as all operations of reason or mind, cannot be dissociated from our place in the world, from the practical engagement with reality. Perhaps Kuhn has observed this principle more closely than MacIntyre. The latter seems at times to dissociate the activity of thinking from the entanglements of practical life, maintaining the distinction between theoretical and practical reasoning. His accusations of cartesianism, directed against Kuhn's notion of conversion, backfire. While he is proclaiming that traditions have rhetorical starting points, these nonetheless ascend towards universality through this process of dialectical testing.[48]

The fact that traditions can and do engage with one another should not be obscured by the fact that they are partially incommensurable. While he takes Kuhn's theory to lead to a rejection of rational comparability, he understands incommensurability to allow for the possibility of precisely such a comparability. However, if our initial reading of Kuhn has some element of truth in it, it would then seem that Kuhn and MacIntyre are not that far apart. Michael Fuller believes he has discovered an inconsistency in MacIntyre's employment of both incommensurability and the notion of *sum-*

---

[45] MacIntyre, 'Epistemological crises', p. 460.

[46] MacIntyre, *Whose Justice?*, p. 8.

[47] Taylor, 'Explanation and practical Reason', p. 45.

[48] MacIntyre, *Whose Justice?*, p. 360.

mum bonum[49] as a notion common to traditions. Along the same lines, Herdt challenges his notion of 'empathetic conceptual imagination' as having a liberal origin. What is apparent is that all these objections spring from a difficulty of comprehending how one philosopher may at the same time hold on to an account of incommensurability and allow both for rational theory choice and external criteria of rationality. The distinction between criteria taken as rules and criteria taken as values that inform judgement is very instructive in bridging the gap between the rhetorical and the serious.

Furthermore, both Kuhn and MacIntyre provide strong accounts of how the tradition abandoned can rationally be deemed weaker and less true than the tradition in favour of which it was jettisoned. However, such standards are *ad hoc* and cannot be principled. Bernstein, reading Kuhn, comments that

> Nevertheless, in the course of the evolution of scientific development we can come to see the force of better practices and arguments and why certain historical practices and modes of argumentation are abandoned.[50]

The fact that no prior statement of criteria can decide in advance what will be the outcome of an intellectual dispute does not mean that there are no better or worse arguments in support of a theory. To reinforce this point: what is important is the relationship between those arguments and the final judgement.[51]

MacIntyre, on the other hand, argues that after a paradigm shift has been effected, the old beliefs are seen as inferior to the new ones.

> When the third stage of the development is reached, those members of the community who have accepted the beliefs of the tradition in their new form [...] become able to contrast their new beliefs with the old. Between those older beliefs and the world as they now understand it there is a radical discrepancy to be perceived. It is this lack of correspondence, between what the mind then judged and believed and reality as now perceived, classified and understood, which is ascribed when those earlier judgements and beliefs are called false. The original and most elementary version of the correspondence theory of truth is one in which it is applied retrospectively in the form of a correspondence theory of falsity.[52]

---

[49] Michael B. Fuller, *Making Sense of MacIntyre,* (Aldershot: Ashgate, 1998), cf. chapter 3.

[50] Bernstein, *Beyond*, p. 68

[51] One may still wonder, however, if this is not only a postponement of the theoretical reasons until the very moment of the debate.

[52] MacIntyre, *Whose Justice?*, p. 356.

Traditions, then, are comparable and a dissociation between 'better' and 'worse' arguments can be made. Taylor also argues that MacIntyre is able to justify the transition from one narrative to another by showing how one represents a gain in understanding over the other.[53] But that is only to be done in the idiom of the successful tradition and – even more importantly – according to criteria elucidated only *post hoc*. There are external standards of rationality, but their functioning only as values makes their decisiveness dependent on other factors as well, mainly having to do with the specificity of the context. Nonetheless, once these factors have become operational (at the end or during the debate), it makes sense convincingly to apply the external criteria.

This raises a further problem: if the winning tradition is able to narrate the failures of the older tradition, what remains of incommensurability? MacIntyre wants to retain continuity between traditions at all costs. What is at stake, as he sees it, is the very rationality of the switch. Hence, he is forced to provide this criterion for the winning tradition: that it is able 'to provide an explanation of just what it was which rendered the tradition, before it had acquired these new resources, sterile, incoherent or both.'[54] MacIntyre seems to imply that translation is certainly possible between two rival schemes. Or, when speaking about two traditions which have been united under the banner of a third narrative which solves the problems of both, a certain implication seems to follow. If two traditions are commensurable with a third, then the two traditions must be commensurable with each other. If MacIntyre requires the winning tradition to narrate the failures of the defeated one, can he still maintain that the two had been incommensurable? Davidson, we remember, expresses the same worry with respect to the relativists who are able to describe seemingly incommensurable narratives into one language. He then argues that translatability entails commensurability. This poses a serious problem for MacIntyre who is intent on keeping both incommensurability and an account of translatability.

Davidson, we have seen, objects to the incommensurability thesis on the grounds that if something is incommensurable it will not even count as a language. His arguments have sometimes been construed as contradicting MacIntyre's own project, by arguing that translatability entails commensurability. Yet MacIntyre wishes to dispel any sense in which what Davidson is saying contradicts his own project. Consequently he will try to argue that untranslatability allows commensurability, and that untranslatability is not an incoherent notion. Davidson argues that

> 'finding the common ground is not subsequent to understanding, but a condition of it. ... A creature that cannot in principle be understood in

---

[53] Taylor, 'Explanation and practical Reason', p. 42.

[54] MacIntyre, *Whose Justice?*, p. 362.

terms of our own beliefs, values and modes of communication is not a creature that may have thoughts radically different from our own: it is a creature without what we mean by thoughts' (*Expressing Evaluations*, Lawrence, 1984, p. 20).[55]

To this MacIntyre complains that Davidson does not explain how different difference has to be in order for it to be radical difference. The way he will proceed to respond to this argument is to clarify a distinction between understanding a different language by translation and understanding it by learning it as a second first language. The notion of learning a second first language is introduced into the discussion as the only possibility open for the translation of an incommensurable language. The holistic imprint is apparent at the point where the acquisition of a language involves the learning of a new mode of behaviour. Language is connected to belief in a way not unrelated to Davidson's explorations. The point of all this is that one cannot simply learn another language by adding a new grammar and phraseology to the first language. The fact that language is so closely tied in with a belief system as well as one's perception of the world and one's place in it and because such belief systems may be radically different and contradictory from each other makes translation into one's own language impossible. Yet how can one become aware of this if translation is impossible in the first place? MacIntyre is able to break the hermeneutic circle with the notion of the learning of a second first language. If Davidson attempted (not without difficulty) to break the hermeneutic circle of a semantic theory by non-semantic factors, MacIntyre will attempt to break the circle with the practice of learning another second first language.

Once one has mastered a second language one will become aware of the fact that some of its concepts are untranslatable into the original language: 'The characteristic mark of someone who has in either of these two ways acquired two first languages is to be able to recognise where and in what respects utterances in the one are untranslatable into the other.'[56] He purports to have shown how in the absence of translatability, one is still able to recognise incommensurability. Furthermore, the learning of a second first language is an indispensable requirement for all traditions that do not want to take their hegemony for granted:

> Only those whose tradition allows for its hegemony being put into question can have rational warrant for asserting such hegemony. And only those traditions whose adherents recognise the possibility of untranslatability into their own-language in use are able to reckon adequately with that possibility.[57]

---

[55] Quoted in MacIntyre, *Whose Justice?*, p. 371.

[56] MacIntyre, *Whose Justice?*, p. 375.

[57] MacIntyre, *Whose Justice?*, p. 388.

The ability to learn a second first language, then, is the condition for the justification of a given paradigm or for its flexibility in finding new ways to express itself. Although MacIntyre's arguments may have successfully answered the possible criticisms that use Davidson's views, two problems still remain.

If the holist nature of understanding and language as a doctrine is accompanied by a version of incommensurability, how is it that members of one tradition, speakers of one language infused with a belief system can so easily *pretend* to acquire the culture, belief system and semiotic code of a second first language? Ironically, these tactics of 'mask wearing' are strongly criticised by MacIntyre in his very own *Three Rival Versions of Moral Inquiry*.[58] Secondly, granted that his later argument against translatability holds, the second requirement for a successful new narrative: that it must narrate the failure of the older narrative, is rather difficult to fulfil for it amounts to a translation. Hence the dilemma: either MacIntyre rejects translatability, while retaining the ability to learn a second first language, but then the new victorious paradigm will not be able to narrate the failures of the older one, hence there will be no sense of continuity but a complete Gestalt switch. Or, he maintains translatability, but then the whole problem of incommensurability will disappear.

To sum up my philosophical argument so far: an understanding of Kuhn which relies too much on an incommensurability of meaning will not do sufficient justice to the way in which he understands theory choice to depend on rational factors as well. However, arguments that connect truth and justification to meaning raise doubts about any separation between an incommensurability of meaning and an incommensurability of standards of justification. If meaning depends on truth conditions, then once one changes the strategy of justification, one must expect the meaning to alter significantly as well. Finally, MacIntyre's vindication of rational choice both mis-reads Kuhn and continues to employ translation. However, what has gradually emerged in this prolonged discussion is that the centre of justification has shifted from an atomic model of correspondence: the pairing of one sentence with one piece of the world. Rather, the holist nature of understanding and knowledge have shifted the agenda to a model of justification by coherence. Yet it has proved a mistake to assume that such a model of coherence will not allow for comparison between different schemes and narratives. And, as Marshall argues, coherence does not mean taking a break from justification with respect to external criteria and ignorance of other traditions, especially when it comes to the Christian religion.

---

[58] Pp.32-58; 196-216. cf. also Fuller's comments to the same conclusion (Fuller, *Making Sense of MacIntyre*, p. 102).

Justification in Narrative Theology

The debate between MacIntyre and Davidson pointed out the relations between issues such as incommensurability, holism, translation and the ability
to learn another language. I have pointed out the difficulty with the notion
of moving between traditions and learning second first languages. In Milbank's opinion, entertaining other such cultures is like suggesting that 'one
holds the notion somehow in theatrical brackets, on a stage aside from
one's usual ruminations.'[59] The trouble with such a notion is not that it is
does not anchor the subject sufficiently to one tradition, but that it does so
too much. Both sides of the debate assume a unitary and stable mental subject. Consequently, when Davidson argues that one such subject must be
able to fit whatever new scheme he perceives into his beliefs and mental
states or not perceive it at all, he assumes a unitary mind. MacIntyre, on the
other hand, by suggesting that one set aside one's beliefs and learn another
culture projects the same type of mental subject. Milbank's philosophy of
radical difference leads him to suggest instead that one become another
person, that we are not wholly united individuals occupying a single 'holistic world.'[60] Hence,

> Davidson is wrong: the alternatives are not between finding English
> equivalents for American, and an incomprehension implying either inefa-
> ble otherness or else a failure of linguistic skill. Something else happens;
> I simply become American as well as English, or more American for a
> time, before reverting. As Feyerabend points out against Putnam, transla-
> tion is not the vital crux of the problem of relativism, because to negotiate
> the Other, one can bypass the moment of translation altogether – were
> this not so infants would never learn their native tongue.[61]

This is a vindication of MacIntyre's arguments for the learning of a second
first language. While Milbank appreciates MacIntyre's defence of a strong
version of incommensurability, he does so on a linguistic-idealist basis.[62] If
MacIntyre charges idealism with not being able to recognise real difference,
the only standpoint from which this could be done being critical realism,
Milbank points out two assumptions behind this view: firstly, that different
cultural discourses are all approximations of a common world, and secondly, that the acknowledgement of cultural change will keep pace with the
observations of new features of reality. Herein lies the rub, in Milbank's
opinion: MacIntyre completely subordinates the telling of different stories

---

[59] Milbank, *Theology and Social Theory*, p. 341.

[60] Milbank, *Theology and Social Theory*, p. 341.

[61] Milbank, *Theology and Social Theory*, p. 341.

[62] Milbank, *Theology and Social Theory*, p. 343. He is nevertheless wrong in suggesting that MacIntyre works with a thesis of incommensurability of meaning. Cf. Robert Miner, 'Lakatos and MacIntyre'.

about reality, with their cultural conditioning and specific practices, to the rational and dialectical adjudication of their truth.

Conversely, Milbank's linguistic idealism suggests that there is a close connection between spirit and matter, between argument and the contingencies with which it is involved. For this reason he can reply to Davidson and Putnam that the absence of a scheme separable from content will not lead to a unitary world, but instead to a plurality of worlds, discontinuous as well as continuous.[63] This is also the reason behind the rejection of any hermeneutics of restoration, such as Ricoeur's for example, which try to recover a depth of the text, on a spiritual level. There is nothing beyond the syntax of the text, no meaning or essence that needs to be recovered.[64] All that there is left for interpretation to do is to experiment with new arrangements of the text, in other words to re-narrate. The notion of narration replaces both explanation and understanding by proposing a single mode which takes account of the interconnectedness of spirit and matter.[65]

MacIntyre's problem, then, is to have succumbed to the dialectical and metaphysical lure. His is a genuinely Hegelian moment, despite all denials, through the discovery of a dialectical essence in the midst of narrative and historically contingent shifts.[66] For MacIntyre dialectics takes over from narrative at the moment where one has to make a theory choice[67]. We have seen how he understands the rational shift from one tradition to the other to be informed by considerations of the ability of one tradition to better make sense of so-called reality. The criteria which determine such a switch, argues MacIntyre, are internal to the original tradition and not external to it. Yet does such a methodology make sense on a holist background? Milbank believes that if the criteria for rationality within one tradition are in full force, then there is a 'questionableness about every switch of tradition which escapes dialectical adjudication.'[68] The standards for rationality within the original tradition will never prompt the switch by themselves. Hence there has been no narrative victory, but only a narration of a dialectical triumph of the new paradigm. Needless to say that this triumph cannot make sense, as MacIntyre wishes it would, due to the better ability of the new paradigm to explain reality. Milbank replaces better explanation with the fact that the theory was able to 'provide models more easily buildable,

---

[63] Milbank, *Theology and Social Theory*, p. 342.

[64] Milbank, *Theology and Social Theory*, pp. 263ff.

[65] Milbank, *Theology and Social Theory*, pp. 263-268.

[66] Milbank, *Theology and Social Theory*, p. 344.

[67] The use of the procedure of falsification, comments Milbank, commits MacIntyre to a view of the exact repeatability of the experiment, which is an escape from the narrative contingencies of space and time. (*Theology and Social Theory*, p. 345.)

[68] Milbank, *Theology and Social Theory*, p. 346.

repeatable and operable in human practice.[69] But crucially, the victory of the new tradition involved a moment of *rhetorical persuasion*, not accountable for in dialectical terms alone:

> The encounter of these diverse reasons cannot be contained and mediated by dialectical conversation alone; at the limits of disagreement it will take the form of a clash of rhetorics, of voices addressing diverse assemblies. And decisive shifts within traditions, or from one tradition to another, have to be interpreted as essentially 'rhetorical victories'. In a rhetorical perspective, narrative really ceases to be a mere appendage, because here the story of the development of a tradition – for example in the case of Christianity, a story of preachings, journeyings, miracles, martyrdoms, intrigues, sins and warfare – really is the argument for the tradition (…) and not just the story of arguments containing a certain X (…) lying outside the story.[70]

The divergence cannot be clearer. While Milbank is proclaiming a return to a rhetorical mode of reasoning, he fears that MacIntyre works with a deficient notion of rhetoric, one associated with individualism and a lack of concern for truth.[71] This obscures the fact that MacIntyre's entire discussion has been in the dialogical context, while dialectics involves an appeal to 'clearly defined hierarchical classification.'[72] Furthermore, if C. Taylor's arguments have some strength, MacIntyre employs transitive arguments and his claims are not absolute but merely comparative.

Milbank's rhetorical stance situates him in a rising tide of theologians who find in rhetoric resources for the methodological elucidation of their own discourse. People such as David Klemm[73], Stephen H. Webb[74], Rebecca Chopp[75], David Cunningham, David Jasper[76] and others are among

---

[69] Milbank, *Theology and Social Theory*, p. 346.

[70] Milbank, *Theology and Social Theory*, p. 347.

[71] MacIntyre, *Whose Justice?*, pp. 55-6.

[72] Milbank, *The Religious Dimension*, I, p. 284.

[73] David Klemm, 'The rhetoric of theological argument', in J.S. Nelson, A. Megill and D. N. McCloskey, *The Rhetoric of the Human Sciences,* (Madison: University of Wisconsin Press, 1987); David Klemm, 'Toward a rhetoric of postmodern theology', *Journal of the American Academy of Religion* 55 (1987), 443-469.

[74] Stephen H. Webb, *Re-figuring Theology: The Rhetoric of Karl Barth,* (Albany: State University of New York Press, 1991).

[75] Rebecca Chopp, 'Theological persuasion: rhetoric, warrants and suffering', William Schweiker, ed., *Worldviews and Warrants: Plurality and Authority in Theology,* (Lanham: University Press of America, 1987).

[76] David Jasper, *Rhetoric, Power and Community: An Exercise in Reserve*, Studies in Religion and Literature, (Louisville: Westminster John Knox Press, 1993); 'From theol-

this group. Milbank's version of rhetorical theology originates in a theological reading of Hamann[77], Jacobi, Herder and Vico. These were all thinkers ahead of their time in that they anticipated some of the habits of postmodernity, cherished by Milbank too: the priority of existence over thought, the primacy of language, the ecstatic character of time, the historicity of reason, the dialogical principle, the suspension of the ethical and ontological difference.[78] Among other things, they argued that a separation of ontology from theology and revelation can only lead to nihilism. As such, nihilism is the necessary outcome of the modernism of Spinoza and Hegel. By contrast one would have to reaffirm the connection between the Christian narrative and beings. The reason behind this is that it is only in light of the divine revelation and only in light of the relation to the infinite that the real can be discerned. The failure of neo-orthodoxy, for all its preoccupation with the priority of God was neglecting to construct a specifically Christian epistemology.[79] Failing to define Being and knowledge theologically will again and of necessity lead back into nihilism. By arguing that a kind of faith is needed when recognising the real, these critics of the Enlightenment and Milbank in fact argue for the inseparability of narrative and reason: 'the rational gaze in space evaporates the real into phantoms, whereas to hold on to each reality we must regard it as an unfathomable "revelation."'[80] Milbank in effect argues that the only way in which the philosophy of Hamann, Jacobi and Vico can make sense is within a Trinitarian and incarnational ontology. However, such an ontology cannot be dialectically tested, it is always rhetorically mediated.

Drawing on Vico, Milbank argues that it is only the aesthetic valences of language which can bring about persuasion and conviction.[81] Justification is not something that will take place outside the context of conversation and

---

ogy to theological thinking: the development of critical thought and its consequences for theology', *Literature and theology,* 9 (1995), 293-305.

[77] Cf. Green, *Theology, Hermeneutics and Imagination.*

[78] Milbank, 'Knowledge: The Theological Critique of Philosophy in Hamann and Jacobi', in *Radical Orthodoxy,* p. 23.

[79] Since knowledge involves selection and will, it draws not on mere perception but on selective memory and prompting desire – *Radical Orthodoxy,* p. 28. Hence, even chains of reasonings are *only* 'aesthetically preferred patterns'.

[80] Milbank, *Radical Orthodoxy,* p. 25.

[81] This is unintelligible without the vision of the convertibility of the true with the made, or of knowledge with creation. The respective traditions of Vico, Hamann, Jacobi and Herded which emphasise the creativeness of knowledge serve as the background for Milbank's arguments.

in the absence of an audience.[82] It will always be justification for someone, for some specific public. Hence it will always be narratively embodied. This is the claim of the rhetorical resurgents: there are no universally convincing arguments, there are only arguments designed to persuade a given audience. And it is not just the arguments that do the convincing, but the whole story of their narration, ingredient in which are style, plot, metaphor, gaps in the text and other elements of form. Hence rhetoric recognises the internal relationship between language and argument. One does not first elucidate the arguments (*Inventio*), chose their most effective and logical ordering (*dispositio*) and only finally put them into language by using elements of style (*elocutio*). What Milbank realises following a detailed exegesis of Vico is that *elocutio* itself is integral to reason. During the Baroque degradation of rhetoric, *inventio* and *dispositio* have been hijacked by dialectics. It was only *elocutio* that remained in the strictly confined space of rhetoric. This in turn occasioned an aestheticism according to which *elocutio* was synonymous with mere ornamentation. However, Vico, by reuniting the three: *inventio*, *dispositio* and eloquence, brought *elocutio* under the scope of reason.

We can now observe, according to this classification why Milbank takes issue with MacIntyre. It is principally because MacIntyre tolerated the hijacking of *ars critica* by dialectics and left the *ars topica* for rhetoric. He merely perpetuates this state of affairs by electing to leave justification to dialectics and confine rhetoric to the role of reciting laudatory songs to the victor.

For Vico, the importance of rhetoric, or more specifically of elocutio is obvious in the work of persuasion that it must do. He invects against the rationalists (cartesians and Port-Royal logicians) of his day who wished to move straight from general principles to particular cases without any mediation. To this he opposes an understanding of persuasion which holds that dialectics can move the mind, but to move to action one needed something else. He preaches that 'the mind [mens] may need to be ensnared by those delicate nets of truth, but the soul [animus] cannot be turned and conquered except by more bodily means.'[83] And again, 'An ethics that seems true in the abstract but lacks the capacity to persuade, to affect the transformation of desire, is a self-discrediting ethics.'[84] It appears, then, that the reason why Vico employs *elocutio* and *ars topica* is because it has the ability to

---

[82] The fact that *After Virtue*, for example, appears both as history and as philosophy is not accidental. Miner suggests that critics who cannot decide to which category it belongs miss the point entirely (manuscript, p. 225).

[83] Robert Miner, 'Verum-factum and practical wisdom in the early writings of Giambattista Vico', *Journal of the History of Ideas* 59 (1998), 53-73, p. 62.

[84] Miner, 'Verum-factum', p. 62.

move from the universal to the particular[85], thus challenging the soul. David Cunningham also lists this rhetorical feature as one of the reasons for his rehabilitation of rhetoric. He lists three methodological reasons: a) because this would help Christian theology to emphasise its own incompleteness[86]; b) because rhetoric emphasises how argument can move audiences to both thought and action, a rhetorical approach to theology requires attention to concrete praxis; finally c) because it provides an excellent paradigm for the analysis of the categories of revelation, proclamation and hermeneutics.[87]

This is a very long cry from suggesting that because theology is rhetorical, or because justification should be rhetorical one ought not give any reasons for it[88], but merely persuade for reasons of literary taste.[89] Vico's combination of the *ars critica* with the *ars topica*, but especially his allocation of a more constitutive role to *elocutio* has certainly lead towards such a relativist conclusion. However, by rescuing *dispositio* and *inventio* from dialectics and setting them aside *elocutio* he has not abandoned reason for irrationality. Milbank argues that

---

[85] Cf. Gadamer on phronesis as directed towards the concrete situation and presupposing a direction of the will (*Truth and Method*, pp. 21f.). See also the narrative tradition of employing novels as tools for the learning of virtues (Stanley Hauerwas, *Dispatches from the Front: Theological Engagements with the Secular*, (Durham and London: Duke University Press, 1994), p. 53.) The connection between realistic literature, the loss of narrativity, and ethics still remains to be explored. Thus far only scant attention, often contradictory has been paid. Compare Brown, *Society as Text*, p. 149; Webb, *Re-figuring Theology*, pp. 150ff. who both argue that the birth of the novel coincided with a loss of rhetorical mediation, hence of narrative depth, with S. Hauerwas who believes that the very reading of the novel entails moral training (op. cit. p. 55.).

[86] See Don Compier's suggestion that the Christian doctrine of sin rules out the possibility of human knowledge more certain than that which persuasion may achieve (Don Compier, *What is Rhetorical Theology: Textual Practice and Public Discourse*, (Harrisburg, Pa.: Trinity Press International, 1999), p. 30). Such a pattern of argumentation - also encountered in others such as Sue Patterson – must however do better justice to the Pauline emphasis on both rhetoric and sound argument. cf. John D. Moores, *Wrestling with Rationality in Paul: Romans 1-8 in a New Perspective*, (Cambridge: Cambridge University Press, 1995), p. 42.

[87] David S. Cunningham, *Faithful Persuasion: In Aid of a Rhetoric of Christian Theology*, (Notre Dame: University of Notre Dame Press, 1991), p. 37.

[88] To be sure, Milbank also believes that not just any narration would do. In his essay on 'Knowledge' he further speaks about a literary judgement which is anguished, fearful and uncertain, but not merely arbitrary, if submitted to a *philologia crucis*. (p. 29) These remarks, however, lack any consistency for he does not specify how such narration or judgement can be other than arbitrary.

[89] See also Cunningham, *Faithful Persuasion*, p. 17.

Whereas the traditional art of persuasion as viewed from a philosophical, dialectical perspective supposed something given to be appealed to, such as commonly accepted norms of truth and justice, the use of 'acute' speech makes it possible for the orator to occasion in the minds of the jurors a modification of these norms prompted by the unique circumstances of the case in question.

Hence,

The mere 'aestheticism' of both the Baroque conceit and the classical category of elocutio, is now cancelled out in that elocutio – the most purely aesthetic, emotional and linguistic moment of rhetoric – becomes also the key rational and ethical moment.

This securely restores the connection between language and thought, between narrative and argumentation.[90] By failing to pay sufficient attention to the shift introduced by Vico and later by Hamann and his like-minded philosophers, MacIntyre too quickly dismisses rhetoric to his own disadvantage. To say that however, is not to say that Milbank is justified in making choice a matter of mere aesthetic preference. And in arguing this Vico is an ally. Robert Miner comments that Vico 'does not reduce truth to pragmatic adequacy'[91] and that he hesitates to choose in favour of either *ars topica* or *ars critica*.[92] In the search for truth, criticism no less than rhetoric was required.[93] One must not give in to the temptation of the extreme and

---

[90] Coupled with an understanding of incommensurability, it makes sense to say, following Walter J. Ong, that 'rhetoric fixed knowledge in agonistic structures' (quoted by Cunningham, p. 68). Also see Oliver Davies, 'Revelation and the politics of culture: a critical assessment of the theology of John Milbank', Laurence Paul Hemming, ed. *Radical Orthodoxy? A Catholic Enquiry*, (Aldershot: Ashgate, 2000), who argues that this understanding of rhetoric conflicts with his ontology of peace: 'incommensurability licenses a polemical and oppositional view of narrativity, setting the Christian story over and against other narratives' (p. 116).

[91] Miner, 'Verum-factum', p. 60. cf. Werner Stark, 'Giambattista Vico's Sociology of Knowledge', in Giorgio Tagliacozzo and Hayden V. White eds., *Giambattista Vico: An International Symposium*, (Baltimore: The Johns Hopkins Press, 1969), esp. pp. 305-306.

[92] Cf. Miner's manuscript: an ethical theory involves the articulation of goods first apprehended in the sensus communis and it may develop, extend or modify the knowledge acquired in the sensus communis (p. 225).

[93] Comprehension and quickness, believes Vico, cannot guarantee truth. Since therefore rhetoric leads to scepticism, a genuinely philosophic rhetoric must perceive the limitations of the *ars topica*. Milbank would strongly disagree with Miner's scepticism here for fear of a 'methodised' idea of rhetoric. The same fear is expressed by Jaspers, op.cit., and by McGee and Lyre in Michael Calvin McGee and John R. Lyre, 'What are nice folks like you doing in a place like this? Some entailments of treating knowledge

jump from a rejection of dialectics as the necessary and sufficient modality of justification to rhetoric as the sufficient heir. Miner again:

> Interpreters who take Vico to propose a 'topical philosophy' that excludes or subordinates the role of criticism tend to ignore the multiple passages in which Vico ascribes the attainment of truth to critica or iudicio.[94]

Although Miner accurately points out the difference between MacIntyre and Vico in their respective attitudes towards rhetoric, 'perhaps the most striking parallel between [them] is the desire to combine a type of historicism with a teleological ethics.'[95] Yet MacIntyre overlooks the alternative conception of rhetoric that aims at truth without collapsing thereby into Socratic dialectic. This is neither non-rational persuasion (Milbank), nor the mere ornamentation of previously acquired truth. Moreover, as O'Banion explains, speaking about the rhetoric of Quintilian, one should bear in mind the 'near interchangeability of what modernists tend to isolate: logical and narrational proof'[96]. Milbank, just as Fish, attempts to introduce a dichotomy to erase all dichotomies.[97] By too radically juxtaposing dialectics and rhetoric[98], he obscures an important strand in the rhetorical tradition which emphasises sound argument and the search for truth. As David Cunningham also observes, rhetoric was concerned with the summoning of as many credible arguments as possible (inventio and dispositio). Yet by rescuing these from dialectics one must not undress them of their original meaning which has to do with rationality, or else one hasn't rescued anything from

---

claims rhetorically', in J.S. Nelson, A. Megill and D. N. McCloskey eds., *The Rhetoric of the Human Sciences,* (Madison: University of Wisconsin Press, 1987), p. 396.

[94] Miner, 'Verum-factum', p. 61. Also cf. Vico's metaphor of 'dissection' : it serves to suggest that there is something to dissect. (Miner, 'Verum-factum', p. 65.) Although on our reading Vico is guilty of employing the scheme-content dualism, the point that creativity is not merely arbitrary is valid.

[95] Miner, unpublished manuscript on Vico, p. 225.

[96] John D. O'Banion, 'Narration and argumentation: Quintilian on narration as the heart of rhetorical thinking', *Rhetorica* 5 (1987), 325-351, p. 328.

[97] Cf. D. Hedley's otherwise misjudged article on Milbank's radical dichotomy between reason/ rhetoric, Christian story/ secular story and so on: 'Should divinity overcome metaphysics? Reflections on John Milbank's theology beyond secular reason and reflections of a Cambridge Platonist', *Journal of Religion* 80 (2000), 271-298, pp. 272, 275.

[98] Cf. A. C. Thiselton's argument to the same effect in Anthony C. Thiselton, *The First Epistle to the Corinthians,* (Grand Rapids: Wm. B. Eerdmans, 2001), p. 42.

dialectics. Milbank should have realised both the rhetorical element in dialectics and the dialectical element in rhetoric.[99]

If I may recapitulate the argument thus far: justification is construed by
contemporary philosophers such as Thomas Kuhn, Donald Davidson and
Alasdair MacIntyre as lacking the foundational access to an un-interpreted
world. For Davidson, even the contents of the sensations cannot serve as
foundations for knowledge, since it is not the sensations themselves which
can serve as epistemic causes, but the beliefs about these. Thomas Kuhn
and Alasdair MacIntyre are not worlds apart, as they have usually been understood, or as indeed they have sometimes portrayed each other. Rather
both share a sense in which theory choice can be rational, although the precise nature of that rationality is still disputed. It then follows that Milbank's
reading of both philosophies and of Davidson assumes too radical an opposition between dialectics and rhetoric.

It will be argued that postliberally speaking, the philosophical situation is
reflected in a renewed desire to treat basic Christian beliefs as epistemically
primary. The notion of world absorption that we have seen outlined in various narrative theologians implies that between the Christian discourse and
other philosophical discourses a relationship of asymmetry holds, such that
the Christian discourse will always receive primacy in the event of dialogue. Our discussion of incommensurability has shown that rational comparison between traditions is a possibility, but the specific ways in which
postliberal theology construes such a conversation still have to be discussed. The distinction between pure narrativists and impure narrativists, a
classification operated by a number of theologians such as Gary Comstock[100], Wentzel van Huysteen[101] and Edward T. Oakes[102] describes the
former as being oriented towards the meaning of the biblical narratives,[103]
while the latter stake a claim on their truth.[104] Impurists such as Ricoeur and
Tracy uncover a fundamental drive towards reference and truth within the
narrative itself. It stakes a claim on the reader, it describes a world and so

---

[99] The presence in the rhetorical tradition of the notion of 'flattery' suggests that persuasion must start from a common ground. That is to say that commensurability is not
denied by persuasion but is rather its very presupposition. cf. Cunningham, p. 48.

[100] Gary Comstock, 'Two types of narrative theology', *Journal of the American
Academy of Religion* 55 (1987), pp. 688ff.

[101] Wentzel van Huysteen, *Essays in Postfoundationalist Theology*, (Grand Rapids:
Wm. B. Eerdmans), 1997, p. 181.

[102] Edward T. Oakes, 'Apologetics and the pathos of narrative theology', *Journal of
Religion* 71 (1992), 37-58.

[103] He calls it the 'radical subjectivity of narrative meaning.'

[104] Cf. David Fergusson's portrayal of Lindbeck's confusion of use with truth: David
Fergusson, 'Meaning, truth and realism in Bultmann and Lindbeck', *Religious Studies*
26 (1990), 183-198, p. 197.

on. However, what this means is that there can be no fundamental opposition between the ontology of narrative and general ontology as such. The being disclosed in narrative is commensurate with Being as such. Hence theology will not shy away from engaging in an ontological project as such and making its claims responsible before the tribunal of a general theory of meaning and of truth. The virulence with which Milbank reacts to such a capitulation of theology before a putatively neutral discourse is understandable. However, the difference between the Christian cultural system, with its beliefs dictated by the plain sense of the Bible and revelation, on the one hand, and a general (what ever that means) philosophical system will make any such correlation very troublesome:

> Under the relentless pressure of the demand of general criteria to provide a systematic correlation, you do one of two things: either you provide an allegorical interpretation of the New Testament, in which the predicate exemplified by Jesus overpowers the ascriptive subject himself and then you return to Kant, as does David Tracy in *Blessed Rage for Order*, or your interpretation ends up having two meanings or referents at the same time, Jesus or some general experience, as Tracy does in a later book, *The Analogical Imagination*.[105]

What Frei implies is that by submitting the specificity of the Christian faith before a general theory of meaning, one will make the characteristics of Jesus dependant on such general meaning. Hence, for example, his activity of redemption, or his goodness will receive their content from a pre-determined notion of redemption or goodness. All specificity is lost in this model. What Frei proposes instead is that Christianity as a cultural system should not give up its claim of uniqueness, should not recant its positivity of the Gospel, but should rather itself try to absorb the world into the Scriptural universe. As we saw earlier with respect to Lindbeck, under such a model, it is the world which becomes a type of Christ and which is read in the light of the ascriptive primacy of Jesus Christ. Theologically this means that Christian concepts will not derive their meaning from external discourses, but rather they will inform the way in which those external concepts themselves are read. Hence what redemption in general means, or what love in general means will assume a secondary status with respect to how these predicates are illustrated by the Jesus of the Gospels.

The theological reservation, however, is that this unashamed assumption of self-sufficiency will lead to variants of fideism or anti-intellectualism, even to isolationism.[106] The three narrative theologians which I shall ex-

---

[105] Hans Frei, *Types of Christian Theology*, edited by George Hunsinger and William C. Placher, (New Haven: Yale University Press, 1992), p. 82.

[106] For example, Oakes wrongly believes that Barth and Frei reject all forms of apologetics. ('Apologetics and the Pathos of Narrative Theology', p. 48).

amine, all have a stake in this issue and they all provide us with examples
of either the promise or the peril of this narrative theological methodology.
The fundamental failure of those that distinguish radically between a preoccupation with questions of meaning alone or truth is that they do not take
into account of the connection between truth and meaning, as we have observed it. That is not to say that some narrativists which consider themselves to be purists, in the sense mentioned above, do not themselves fail to
notice the connection. To understand that questions of meaning can only be
discussed, on a non-question begging theory of interpretation, by relating
them to questions of justification means that a concentration on the meaning of the Gospels without an adequate attention to the truth of the Gospel,
more especially to the truth-claim of its writers, is incoherent. Furthermore,
it will lead one to conclude that a concentration on the coherence and the
internal meaning of the Christian semiotic system without any attempt to
correlate it with alien[107] claims to truth, such as those coming from philosophy, science, politics etc., is again incoherent. The promise of thinkers such
as Marshall and Frei is that they both outline the self-sufficiency of theology and the necessity of engagement with other fields as well. One cannot
argue along with Oakes that of all narrativists it is only Ricoeur that provides opportunities for the justification of the truth claims of Christianity. It
is not only from that perspective that apologetics can be done. Narrative
purists, if we are to indulge in this classification for the sake of simplicity
and distinction, also allow for apologetics and for testing truth claims. The
only provision is that such engagement will be only possible once the superiority of the Christian cultural system is assumed.

Ronald Thiemann, in *Revelation and Theology,*[108] provides a model of
theology as a purely descriptive activity. Following the recent trend he also
rejects foundationalism *tout court* and argues that the only possible justification is holist in nature. Such a model is concerned only with the internal
re-description of Christian claims and as such cannot be concerned with
either epistemology or apologetics, although on occasion it may engage
with both of these.[109] In the absence of any external reality unmediated by
the cultural code, justification can only involve testing the coherence of one
disputed belief against the web of accepted beliefs. We remember from the
previous chapters that Thiemann is dissatisfied with models which ground
authority and revelation either in some foundational intuition or in the mutual acceptance of the community. In either of these cases the very meaning
of authority is undermined, in the first by the erection of a more fundamental level (such as perhaps a general theory of intuition and sensory experience) and on the second, by the subjective dependence of such an

---

[107] Marshall's term for discourses external to Christianity.

[108] (Notre Dame: University of Notre Dame Press, 1985).

[109] Thiemann, *Revelation*, p. 74.

authority. What is needed, therefore, is a model of justification which would escape the predicament of foundationalism. Thiemann believes that holist justification provides just such a model. The obvious difficulty is in the case of a background belief which is itself in need of justification.[110] The procedure in that case is to show how the specifically Christian beliefs and the practices which accompany them presuppose the background belief. This would be a case of 'retrospective justification'.[111]

It is important to remember that Thiemann will not be content with just a very local justification, for that is the reason for which he dismisses the constructivist grounding of authority. In this case the argument is quite difficult to maintain. He constructs his model of holism on Quine's and Ullian's *The Web of Belief*. Yet Quine is the very philosopher who unmasked the two dogmas of empiricism, one of which being the distinction between synthetic and analytic truths. What Quine teaches us is that certain sentences can be called analytic and other synthetic not in virtue of some internal property, but in virtue of the grammar of the whole system. In other words, given a different arrangement of the system one would have a completely different registry of analytic and synthetic statements. This amounts to a severe criticism of any hierarchical system according to which some statements are more basic than others. Such foundational, pyramidal systems fail precisely because they mistake their internal logic for the logic of nature. But in our opinion, Thiemann does exactly that: he distinguishes between background beliefs, constitutive beliefs, un-constitutive beliefs, generally accepted beliefs and so on. In doing this he fails to see that such a structure is rhetorically mediated and can be changed at any time. Hence by bearing in mind Quine's own recommendations and his own desire to provide a more than just arbitrary justification, his project fails. Milbank would argue in response: coherence is not a good defence against nihilism. Thiemann should simply not look for a justification.

Such a retrospective justification is an *ad hoc* procedure, as Thiemann himself argues, since it proceeds from actuality, the *sensus communis*, not from generality.[112] One may say that it is a rhetorical procedure, for as Quintillian urges, rhetoric and persuasion should start from a level of agreement between orator and audience. Its starting point is not some universal linchpin, but the narrative contingencies of a story.

Bruce Marshall's ground-breaking book, *Trinity and Truth* is a very complex and complicated commentary on the relationship between truth, meaning, the doctrine of the Trinity and, not least, Donald Davidson. In essence, the relevance of his argument to our discussion is that by an intelligent combination of Davidsonian holism and the Christian world absorp-

---

[110] Thiemann, *Revelation*, p. 76.

[111] Thiemann, *Revelation*, p. 77.

[112] Thiemann, *Revelation*, p. 77.

tion, coherentism is described as by definition excluding fideism, anti-intellectualism or isolationism. His argument is long and complicated and we shall not deal with, for example, the relationship between the doctrine of the Trinity and truth, or the way in which the Holy Spirit has a stake in any understanding of truth.

Marshall reveals that one of the assumptions behind the foundationalist thesis was a thesis of epistemic dependence. The implication is that the adjudication of the truth claims of Christian beliefs would leave their truth unchanged. Marshall, following Frege and Davidson argues that such an understanding misses the point that to understand the meaning of a sentence or of a belief is to understand what would make it true, or what would falsify it. It would be helpful to bear in mind Davidson's arguments about the principles of radical interpretation. The consequence of this understanding is that Christian theology cannot afford to subject its own beliefs to the test of external sytems and criteria of judgement and hope that their meaning will remain unchanged. This has also been Frei's argument. And it is precisely this argument which has caused the misperception that narrative theologians are uninterested either in justification or in truth but only in meaning. Hans Frei for example argues that to use the category of factuality for Christ is to impose a foreign concept and that is to cause prejudice to the biblical text:

> Of course, they [type 4 theologians] say when you use that category, he was a fact rather than a fiction, but as the ascriptive subject of the portraits, it is his relation to God that identifies him, and are you seriously proposing that the relation is best specified under the interpretive category 'fact'? Surely not, unless you are ready to say that 'God' is a historical fact. The category 'factuality' is simply inadequate (not wrong) for the interpretation of this text.[113]

When narrativists such as Frei will be hard pressed to express their opinion in relation to theories of truth they will do so, but only hesitatingly, since it is their conviction that the way in which the truth of a discourse is assessed will have an effect on the meaning of that discourse.

If Christian claims are not to be subordinated to an alien system of truth or of standards of legitimation, nor are such claims to be submitted to the tribunal of sensory experience. In Davidson's and Marshall's opinion, even Quine is guilty of maintaining the scheme-content dualism by the suggestion that the statements about the external world will have to face the tribunal of sense experiences. In contrast to this, Marshall and Davidson propose that it is only beliefs which can justify beliefs. Since we cannot swear intermediaries to truth (the content of sense experience may deceive us), it is best to refuse such epistemic mediators and proceed merely on the basis of

---

[113] Frei, *Types*, p. 85.

belief. To say that the only justification possible is coherence is not to imply an understanding of truth as coherence.[114] Indeed, Marshall is quite correct in affirming that even the most coherent of systems, or what can be warranted as coherent with a body of beliefs need not be true. Such an understanding of justification in his opinion allows for any theoretical account of truth, be it Davidsonian, Tarskian, realist, idealist and so on.

Marshall further rejects the pragmatic thesis, sometimes associated with narrative theologians like Hauerwas or Metz, that successful practice helps to justify true belief. He points out a number of difficulties with this view, which cannot be discussed here. Thus it proves very difficult to decide what counts as successful practice; then it is even more difficult to decide which are those practices that a specific belief requires. As Paul Lauritzen concludes in his comparative study of Hauerwas' and Metz's narrative strategies, both imply that because Christians share a common story, they will also agree about the range of practices implied by that story. Yet they both fail to account for the diversity of practice and moral patterns derived from the same story.[115]

Instead of conceiving the relation between belief and practice at the level of truth, he conceives it at the level of meaning. Here we come upon an interesting aspect of Marshall's project. He borrows from Lindbeck the example of the crusader who upon seeing a Muslim cleric running away, charges in gallop toward him and with a loud cry, 'Christus est Dominus!,' raises his sword in order to split the skull of the infidel. Marshall's thesis is to the effect that the practice in which this person is engaging upon uttering those words will have a bearing on the meaning of the words themselves. By employing the theory of radical interpretation, where meaning is not assumed, but tested for while truth is assumed, Marshall argues that one has to pay attention to modes of behaviour and dispositions associated with the utterance of certain words. We have already described the methodology: look for what someone is expressing assent to, in this case 'Christus Dominus est', pair it with your belief about the circumstance which accompanies it and you will have the meaning. The obvious conclusion is that the crusader and St. Francis who would accompany this cry with acts of peaceful self-denial will be taken to mean very different things by it.

Yet there is a problem associated with any such theory of meaning as use, and the problem is that any theory will have to allow both for divergence of meaning, that is people who mean different things than they are

---

[114] Truth, for Davidson and Rorty, as well as some narrative theologians such as Hauerwas, attaches not to statements, but to persons. cf. Stanley Hauerwas, 'Why the truth demands truthfulness: an imperious engagement with Hartt', *Journal of the American Academy of Religion*, 52 (1984), 141-147.

[115] Paul Lauritzen, 'Is narrative really a panacea? The use of "narrative" in the work of Metz and Hauerwas', *Journal of Religion* 67 (1987), 322-339, p. 339.

expected to, and for sameness of meaning. Hence a theory which ties meaning exclusively to practice, due to the infinite plurality of such practices will never be able to account for the sameness of meaning and hence for the possibility of understanding. This is even more so in the absence of any use of convention, since as we have seen Davidson and Marshall following him reject convention as a key to meaning. The only possibility open for Marshall is to maximise the scope of practice. Consequently we find him speaking about the total practice, not just an isolated act. Davidson himself is constrained to make recourse to such a totality, yet one still wonders just how practical is such a theory of meaning. Unfortunately Marshall fails to tackle the issue at least in light of the distinction between prior and passing theory. Were he to do so, then he would be able to operate on the basis of a shared meaning and test for specific meaning in the particular case. What one means by using conventional words need not be limited to already determined meanings. One can expand on those by using metaphor, by giving clues as to how he intends meanings differently. The basic difficulty with such a method of interpretation is that in actual fact and in the absence of any knowledge of intentions (because those too are dependent on knowing meaning) it is very hard to decide which are the relevant practices. So the problem which Marshall pointed in relation to the relevance of practices for truth returns in the discussion of meaning. How is one to decide which practices are relevant for meaning? No satisfactory reason has been provided. To be sure he does understand that in some cases meaning is already secure: 'While we can surely test the truth of sentences of whose meaning we are already confident, our right to be confident in the meaning we have assigned to those sentences depends on our ability to find them false.'[116]

While intra-systematic truth can be decided through checking coherence, how is extra-systematic truth to be assessed? Marshall names the 'assimilative power'[117] of the Christian beliefs as the test of truth. Yet, since the meaning of alien claims which are to be assimilated cannot be decided apart from deciding whether they are true or not, and furthermore since it cannot be decided apart from ascribing as much truth as to maximise agreement, in Marshall's case *coherentism will block fideism by definition.* Theologically primary claims can be tested by verifying their assimilative power. From Lindbeck Marshall has learned that the logic of typology involves that the identity of the type is not to be denied by its inclusion under Christ. Identity is safeguarded in figuration. Hence if the world is to be a type of Christ and if theology will test its claims of world absorption, then alien claims (philosophical, sociological etc.) will have to be treated with utmost respect.

---

[116] Marshall, *Trinity*, p. 99.

[117] Marshall, *Trinity*, p. 147; cf. also Rowan Williams' 'generative power', in Rowan Williams, 'Trinity and revelation', *Modern Theology* 2 (1986), 197-212, p. 199.

Again the principle of charity leads the way out of the fideist trap: if we are to understand such claims, one must be ready to consider them true, even if in the process one's own primary claims will have to suffer. As MacIntyre has argued: any tradition's claim to allegiance should be based on the openness and risk that one day its claims will be invalidated by a rival tradition. The strategy of justification, or rather of falsification is again strikingly similar to MacIntyre's: our *own* epistemic priorities will require us to change established belief if given sufficient reason to.[118] If accepting novel and alien claims will lead to the jettisoning of primary claims, it follows that those claims did not have any assimilative power, i.e., they were untrue. As such, assimilative power can only discover falsity, not establish truth and here again one is reminded of MacIntyre's correspondence theory of falsity.[119]

To conclude: assimilative power rejects the thesis of an incommensurability of meaning. If, on the other hand, an incommensurability of standards of judgement would be possible, then assimilative power would be useless, for every system would pass its test, since it would contain within it vaccination against any rival.[120] But 'there is no chance that we can differ massively from them on what to count as good reasons, any more than we can differ massively on what to believe.'[121] This reflects on MacIntyre's own discussion, as interpreted by Marshall, to the effect that his notion of epistemological crises can only make sense if he gives up incommensurability of warrant. This confirms the initial suspicion that for a thinker that closely binds truth to meaning one would either have to tie incommensurability of warrant with incommensurability of meaning, or deny both altogether. One difference between Marshall and Milbank is that while Milbank dismisses coherence as a dead end precisely because he trusts the vision of incommensurability, Marshall on the other hand due to his denial of incommensurability, is able to provide a defence of coherence which is at the same time a refutation of fideism. Thiemann, while acknowledging the possibility that Christian discourse may encounter alien texts, nonetheless believes such encounters to be marginal to Christian identity.

Hans Frei has often insisted that the logic of belief is not the same with the logic of coming to believe. Crucially however, that is not to say that they are contrary, but merely independent. Narrative theologians are weary of submitting Christian claims to foreign arbitration courts, but this weariness does not come from a lack of preoccupation with truth or disregard for justification, much less from any chronic vulnerability to fideism. Rather,

---

[118] Marshall, *Trinity*, p. 144.

[119] Marshall, *Trinity*, pp. 149-50, MacIntyre, *Whose Justice, Which Rationality?*, pp. 356ff.

[120] Marshall, *Trinity*, pp. 160-3.

[121] Marshall, *Trinity*, p. 164.

this attitude springs from a legitimate concern with what are specifically Christian meanings and from a disenchantment with respect to putative universally applicable categories such as factuality, historicity, being and so on. But, and this is the thrust of the present chapter, that is not to say that engagement with such external criteria is ruled out. Instead of that, what Frei proposes is that to read the Bible without philosophy is impossible[122], to do theology without science and epistemology is again impossible. But what is imperative is that the concepts borrowed from those contexts acquire specific Christian valences and they are ruled by the Christian context. This goes hand in hand with a belief in commensurability of warrant, but also with an equally strong belief in the positivity of the Gospel. Although there will be a certain similarity between Christian concepts and general concepts derived from a theory of meaning, in the final analysis it is the ascriptive subject of Jesus who governs the predicates. Lastly, the *ad hoc* nature of such a correlation implies that there will be no master theory, no *prolegomena* to legislate the relations between theology and the external codes. [123]

Deciding to do philosophy and theology without the scheme content dualism means that we have abandoned the quest for unshakeable foundations. The attempt to ground grammar, or to secure reference, to point out the connection between mind, language and world, has given way to a nonfoundational justification based on a good reasons approach. For modernity the road towards an unequivocal knowledge and language goes through the elevation of mind to an intermediary position between agents and life. There was something special and at the same time mysterious about the mind, once it was understood to be composed of that extraordinary matter which allowed itself to be modelled according to the forms of being, or to become one with them. Univocal philosophy naively believes it has discovered the *ratio* which connected us with God and the rest of creation. Equivocation is banned from serious discourse. In comes the rational production of signs, the linear organisation of time, and the civic constitution of the *polis*. Modernity is therefore based on a mythic creative act, the creation of the mind, the positing of Being. In its Scotist beginnings, modernity lifts spirit, or mind, above its material, fleshly, textual conditions. Herein we have the roots of the violence associated with metaphysics: to suppose that a given hierarchy discovered by the mind and represented in language is the natural way of things, that the code 'found' in spirit actually unlocks the complexity of the body. In this version of modernity the body is managed by a spirit detached from and sovereign over it. Bishop Fulhauber was nothing but an heir of this mentality when he believed he could rescue

---

[122] Frei, *Types*, pp. 81, 85.

[123] Cf. also Will Werpehowski, 'Ad Hoc apologetics', *Journal of the American Academy of Religion* 66 (1986), 282-301, p. 287; Tilley, pp. 87-111, *passim*.

the text of the Old Testament while rejecting its people. The same mentality thrives in allegorical readings of the Scriptures and in the figurative techniques whereby the textual and historical reality of the figure is sublated in spiritual meaning. The predicament of modernity is thus one of negotiating the Other and identity.

One may hope that another, more radical modern vision, based as it is on the notions of creativity, textuality, tradition and rhetoric successfully navigates the road between the self and the other. A strand of modernity which we find in Vico, Hamann, Herder, Jacobi and indeed others,[124] resists the arbitrary imposition of a metaphysic and un-apologetically assumes the contingency of its own truth. Thus, spirit no longer blissfully levitates above matter, but is indelibly compromised with it. In some of its more contemporary versions, spirit becomes nothing other than the repetition of a performance. For Milbank there is no spirit outside matter. Hermeneutics consequently should not aim for the recovery of a textual 'essence', but merely rotate various permutations of the text. In this context there can be no question of a manipulative violence through the imposition of arbitrary order.

This is not to say that the only possible violence is metaphysical. There is a more subtle manipulation taking place in late modernity. We have already traced the possibility of such violence from Vico through legal positivism and on to anti-Semitism. It is the result of the intersection of two notions: the notion that there is no spirit outside matter – pure textuality – and the notion that texts are complete, that meanings are unproblematic. This is the coalition between textuality and territorial metaphors, between the quest for the singular identity through the rejection of extra-textual factors and a spatial cast of metaphors. The all-penetrating assumption is that meanings are fixed, that territories are clearly marked, that there are no disputed spaces. Another positivism takes shape in late modernity: the assumption of textual superiority. Coupled with a Christian notion of world absorption which makes 'gigantic claims'[125], it has the potential of turning into one of the more manipulating and difference-sublating philosophies. Yet, for Milbank, it carries the flag of a philosophy of alterity.[126]

---

[124] Gadamer, Ricoeur, Davidson, Wittgenstein, Gillian Rose.

[125] Milbank, *Theology and Social Theory*, p. 388.

[126] This is a very common criticism of Milbank: Lewis Ayres, 'Representation, theology and faith', *Modern Theology* 11 (1995), 23-46, p. 29; Ronald Spjuth, 'Redemption without actuality: A critical interrelation between Eberhard Jüngel's and John Milbank's ontological endeavours', *Modern Theology* 14 (1998), 505-522; Nicholas Lash, 'Not exactly politics, or power?' *Modern Theology* 8 (1992), 353-364, p. 358; Steven Shakespeare, 'The new romantics: a critique of Radical Orthodoxy', *Theology* 103 (2000), 163-177.

Both versions of modernity are in fact, I have argued, examples of preferring either scheme (textuality) or content (foundationalism). Modern
theology, in both its propositional-cognitive and its experiential-expressive
versions assumes the priority of the content, while postliberal theology
takes the scheme as primary.

Yet, if we are to follow Davidson's and Rorty's arguments against this
dualism, we should be careful to avoid both extremes.[127] From the perspective of justification, the postliberal tendency to consider transitions rhetorical must follow Bruce Marshall towards a good reasons approach to the
issue. As Rorty suggests, a holist approach is more like building bridges
between islands than like attempting to bring everyone to the same island.
The assumption that holism implies relativism owes much to the notion that
knowledge must first establish a 'skyhook' that would raise it above human
history, when in fact it only needs 'toeholds' within history.[128] Both Jeff
Stout with his idea of *bricolage*[129] and Stephen Toulmin[130] suggest that justification becomes less a question of anchoring knowledge securely in nature or in a representational mind, but a dialogical and rhetorical process.
Yet the dissolution of scheme-content and the return of knowledge and language to life involves a re-figuration of rhetoric as well, away from Milbank's pure aestheticism. Argument and rational dispute are still important,
criticism still a possibility. The holist and pragmatic suggestion, just as
Hans Frei had the wisdom to observe, is that 'we can understand more and
communicate better [...] than we'll ever be able to understand *how* we understand, or what the conditions of the possibility of our understanding [...]
might be.'[131] Knowledge and language, in other words, can be successful
(whatever that means) in the absence of a foundational linch-pin, or of a
causal explanation, which even if given would be philosophically inconsequential.

---

[127] A failure to renounce the dualism has led to confused attempts such as W. Werpehowski's. He enforces a rigid distinction between first and second orders of language
and between scheme and reality: the argument 'must show the way in which the scheme
makes better sense of features of reality' (p. 287).

[128] Richard Rorty, *Objectivity, Relativism and Truth*, (Cambridge and New York:
Cambridge University Press, 1991), pp. 14, 38, 216, 221.

[129] Jeffrey Stout, *Ethics After Babel: The Languages of Morals and Their Discontents*, (Boston: Beacon Press, 1988), pp. 74-77, 218, 240, 292.

[130] Stephen Toulmin, *Cosmopolis: The Hidden Agenda of Modernity*, (New York:
Free Press, 1990).

[131] Frei, *Types of Christian Theology*, p. 86.

Chapter Five

Doctrine

The Regulative View of Doctrine

I have already discussed Lindbeck's distinction between and criticism of the two models of doctrine, the cognitive-propositional and the expressive-experiential. The failure of these two models occurs on more than one front. The propositional model cannot account, for example, for new doctrines that are created by the community. This verdict is disputed, however, since more than one factor may be responsible for the reluctance of a propositional model of Christian doctrine to allow for new doctrines. In support of this it may be pointed out that the propositional model of doctrine does value the utter novelty of the Christian doctrines which were drafted as a result of new religious experiences. Thus the reluctance to accept novelty follows as a material implication from the content of the doctrines themselves, and not as a formal one from the theoretical model. This distinction will assume an important place later on when it will be argued that Lindbeck, as opposed to Frei, but more especially Barth, does not do sufficient justice to the material requirements of the Christian religion.

The two models above both presuppose the distinction between scheme and content. For the cognitivist, the function of a theological statement is to correctly represent a state of affairs obtaining in a realm outside that of language. For the experiential-expressivist, the task is that of symbolising an original and normative experience. Neither of these two views does full justice to the interdependence of scheme and content. Lindbeck correctly points out that experience is not available apart from an already existing frame of concepts, that is, apart from an already present and normative narrative[1]. However, in light of criticism of the dualism between scheme and content, it is apparent that Lindbeck merely reverses the hierarchy between the two[2]. Although he ambitiously wants his model to provide a more dialectical alternative, he ends up privileging the scheme side of the scheme-

---

[1] I use the term 'narrative' here in the sense of discursive and non-discursive constellation of practices and beliefs, and not in the literary sense of a story, or text.

[2] Cf. Stephen Stell, 'Hermeneutics in theology and theology of hermeneutics: beyond Lindbeck and Tracy', *Journal of the American Academy of Religion* 61 (1993), 679-702, 681.

content distinction. A further reason why Lindbeck deems it necessary to replace the two models is their ecumenical inefficiency. I need not rehearse the arguments, since they were already mentioned[3]. As Hütter comments, Lindbeck is able to free doctrine from the constraints of reference and truth and thus make it the object, not an obstacle for ecumenical consensus[4]. What was needed for an explanation of ecumenical agreement is a model that would account for the situations in which a confessional group comes to agreement *without denying* what they have previously believed.[5] The empirical starting point of his argument, then, is the fact that the parties of an ecumenical debate have not capitulated when they have reached an agreement. For Lindbeck this is a confirmation that the propositional model cannot do full justice to the complexity of the situation for it implies by necessity that one of the parties is right while the other is wrong. Nor can the second model be of more use, since it does not take seriously questions of diversity. It has to be pointed out that Lindbeck does not ask further questions about how one party may reach agreement without capitulation. He takes the absence of any declaration or of admission of capitulation at face value. In light of the critique of ideology[6] this is a very questionable assumption to make. He does not seek to justify it at all.

The task of the cultural linguistic model is to maximise the strengths of both paradigms. It is not entirely clear what line of reasoning leads Lindbeck to this model. One of two possibilities must be chosen: either he has reached the cultural linguistic model as a consequence of his investigation into the best models in social and anthropological sciences, or he has derived it from an understanding of the plain sense of the Bible, according to which the world of the Bible subsumes all reality within it. It is difficult to chose between – let us call them – the formal reason and the material reason. Nonetheless, Lindbeck seems to assume that the two reasons are commensurable. That is, following either one does not lead to any contradiction of the other one. Bearing in mind that his intention is primarily to aid the ecumenical discussion, it makes sense to suppose that he would chose a neutral model which would be readily accepted by the participants in the debate. He alludes to the theoretical work of Clifford Geertz,[7] to his successful techniques in the study of religion and proposes that we use the same philosophical model. Since no religious party has any special investment in it, it should best serve the ecumenical cause. The model, then, has to be a very formal and flexible one. Hütter argues that it is precisely be-

---

[3] Cf. chapter 3.

[4] Hütter, n.45, p. 216.

[5] Lindbeck, *Doctrine*, pp. 16-7.

[6] The assumption that all claims must be taken at face value has been decisively challenged by Foucault, Habermas and others.

[7] Lindbeck, *Doctrine*, p. 20, 27.

cause the model is so formal that it must be applicable everywhere[8]. Once again theological methodology turns prescriptive, as we have seen in the work of Kuhn, and other relativists. This is a remarkable difference from Frei's concerned attempts to keep the models and theories imported from philosophy as much as possible subordinated to the positivity of the Gospel.[9] The scheme, or religion becomes the linguistic horizon within which alone experiences are possible. Religion is the unsurpassable framework which makes possible, through its grammar and vocabulary the religious experience.[10]

The narrative of a religion now occupies the principal position in the tension between religion and experience. The tension perhaps is inevitable in any attempt to sort out confusion by way of an externally borrowed model. But in my opinion, Lindbeck eventually does little justice to the positive requirements of the Christian narrative as such.

All discourse takes place against the background of a linguistic practice. Theological discourse and religious experience always presuppose the existence of a sedimented linguistic pattern of meaning. It is a common place now to argue that discourse in general presupposes, springs from, builds on a prior engagement with the world. However, for Lindbeck, such a prior narrative completely fills the field of vision. There is no access beyond this lens, there is no getting around it or beyond it. The flow of life, with its conventional habits and rules accompanies any experience as its very condition of possibility. This is a radical claim to make, yet Lindbeck does not shy away from making it poignantly:

> There are numberless thoughts we cannot think, sentiments we cannot have, and realities we cannot perceive unless we learn to use the appropriate symbol systems. It seems, as the cases of Helen Keller and of supposed wolf children vividly illustrate, that unless we can acquire language of some kind, we cannot actualise our specifically human capacities for thought, action and feeling.[11]

What precedes theological discourse is a narrative web of activity, signs and signification. When it comes to theologically applying this formal model, Christian practice is the context in which theological reflection operates. Kathryn Tanner makes the same point: the existence of an already constituted and well defined Christian community of discourse exercises a

---

[8] Hütter, p. 47.

[9] Cf. Frei, *The Identity of Jesus Christ*, p. xv: 'therefore the amount of theory involved is minimal. There should be enough to elucidate what is actually being done in exegesis and no more.' Also see Frei, *Types of Christian Theology*, pp. 86-87.

[10] Lindbeck, *Doctrine*, pp. 35-36.

[11] Lindbeck, *The Nature of Doctrine*, p. 34.

determinative influence upon theoretical reflection.[12] But that is not the whole story: the web of practice does not only determine theological reflection, so that the later can 'take off' towards the heights of theological and religious truth. Tanner is quite adamant, as is Lindbeck that practice is the end point, not simply the starting point of reflection[13]. Theology is therefore constrained by religious practice. By being caught up in the prison house of practice, it does not have any other object of knowledge other than the practice itself.

Such an understanding of the relationship between theory and practice is generally pragmatist in origin. Tanner cites both C. S. Peirce[14] and N. Rescher[15] as sources for her perspective. Theory in this perspective is secondary to practice, in that it only has a place when the practice calls for it.[16] The practice may falter and inquiry will attempt to meet the problems that threaten a practice as an ongoing concern.[17] What this involves is a discourse setting in which the theoretical concepts employed are already determined by the historical narrative of that culture. Truth claims are determined by the conceptual vocabulary, whose meaning is fixed, and by the syntax or the inner logic.[18] Meaning is not, for postliberals, a concept to be recovered through a depth hermeneutics, or through a psycho-intuitive access to the intentions of the communicator. Rather, meaning is in such cases formalised as use, as previous performances. Thus to understand the meaning of a concept is to become skilled in its employment in actual life. All such previous performances contribute to the sedimentation of meaning, or what Jauss may call reception history[19] and what Gadamer calls effective

---

[12] Kathryn Tanner, *God and Creation in Christian Theology: Tyranny or Empowerment?* (Oxford: Blackwell, 1988), p. 15.

[13] Tanner, *God and Creation,* p. 15.

[14] For a somewhat technical analysis of the resources in the philosophy of C. S. Peirce, see Peter Ochs, *Peirce, Pragmatism and the Logic of Scripture*, (Cambridge: Cambridge University Press, 1998). Also see Peter Ochs, 'Rabbinic pragmatism', in Bruce D. Marshall, ed., *Theology and Dialogue: Essays in Conversation with George Lindbeck*, (Notre Dame: University of Notre Dame Press, 1990), and Nancy Levene and Peter Ochs, *Textual Reasonings: Jewish Philosophy and Text Study at the End of the Twentieth Century*, Radical Traditions. (London: SCM, 2002).

[15] Nicholas Rescher, *Methodological Pragmatism*, (New York: New York University Press, 1977).

[16] Other exponents of this version of pragmatism include MacIntyre, Kuhn and Feyerabend.

[17] Tanner, *God and Creation,* p. 16.

[18] Lindbeck, *Doctrine,* p. 35.

[19] Hans-Robert Jauss, *Towards an Aesthetic of Reception*, translated by Timothy Bahti, (Minneapolis: University of Minnesota Press, 1982).

history.[20] The agent becomes subject to a tradition which supplies him or her with the requisite tools for having the sort of experiences he is having. I have also noted the danger of a loss of agency implied in this model. Both Gadamer and Jauss tread carefully so as not unduly to reify tradition. However, a number of postliberal theologians are not as aware of the danger and become complacent in this loss of agency. Thus, Lindbeck and Tanner understand this tradition[21] as containing the meanings of concepts, as already identifying objects, and as conditioning the very possibility of any experience. Theologically speaking, the meaning of 'God' is given in the multiple layers of the sort of actions one is inclined to involve 'God' in. 'God' is already identified in a given tradition and one can only experience 'God' if one has already learned the sort of language that gives the grammar of the notion. The identification of God is not accomplished by the individual theologian, or by his theological statements, but by the whole form of life, through its sedimented meanings. What this amounts to is that the Christian theologian has nothing else to turn to except the network of signs, narratives, prayers and the liturgy of his own tradition. It is improper to speak of theological knowledge, since, to echo Nicholas Lash, theology doesn't add anything new to the idea of God as present in prayer, liturgy etc.[22] We may sum up this development by saying that what is taking place in narrative theology is a reification of language or, the reification of 'religion'.

If all we have is practice, then theology can no longer be conceived as description of objects outside this practice. Rather, as Lindbeck proposes, it can only take the shape of a thick description[23] of the actual practices of the church. This is consonant with Tanner's and Lash's suggestions that theology is parasitic upon practice. Here we have the theological counter-part of the hermeneutical shift from immanent meaning or textual meaning to active use or application. The case of a succession from understanding the right meaning to application, or from text to action, or from sermon to life is no longer intelligible. The tables have turned: one starts with application in order to get at the 'meaning', or one already applies the sermon before one gets it. Finally, one is already engaged in action before textual under-

---

[20] Gadamer, *Truth and Method*, pp. 300-307.

[21] In this context tradition, community, narrative, historical narrative, practice may be taken to mean basically the same thing: that practical horizon which conditions and constructs the 'idea.'

[22] Cf. Gale Z. Heide, 'The nascent noeticism of narrative theology: An Examination of the Relationship between Narrative and Metaphysics in Nicholas Lash', *Modern Theology*, 12 (1996), 459-481, p. 470.

[23] Clifford Geertz's notion.

standing is a possibility. In the case of religion, one already does ethics before one starts doing theology.[24]

Beginning to take shape here is a distinction of momentous importance:
between first order and second order language. All narrative theologians
adopt this distinction. Not only is it a distinction between two orders of language, but it gets dichotomised in the work of some. The distinction is not
meant to separate the passing and peremptory aspects of religion from the
constant and stable core at the bottom of it, indeed both of them are sufficiently unstable. The previous judgement depends on what sort of statements and actions are seen to be part of either order of language. Postliberal
theologians, to the best of my knowledge, have not proposed any clear
definition or clarification of the two levels of language. There are in fact
uncontested members of first order language as well as of the second type.
Part of the first order Christian language is the complex of prayers, acts of
worship, symbols, sacred texts and liturgy of one religion, what Higton[25]
calls the actual performances of one religion. This would be the outer aspect of religion, what Lindbeck calls the *verbum externum*. To say that this
is the outer shell of religion is not to say, as in experiential-expressivism
that the core of religion is something that can easily dispense with its external symbolic garments. It is precisely these cultural forms and manifesta-
tions that provide the very scheme which filters through the experience of
the sacred. The sacred can then be constructed as a function of these characteristics.

Second order language, conversely, is the principled reflection upon the
first order language, in other words, theology. For Milbank, who also employs this distinction, it is principled reflection upon the narratives and the
tradition which constitute the first order language of the Church.[26] Hans
Frei interprets the first order as comprising first-intentional addresses to
God, self-involving speech and actions, biblical confessions and exegesis,
while second order language contains language about God.[27]

The point which needs to be clarified is where does doctrine belong?
Some construe doctrine as belonging to the first order language, since it is
itself a performance.[28] Others, by understanding it as a reflection on Christian practice, place it firmly in the second category.[29] However, the sugges-

---

[24] This is the context of James McClendon's decision to start his Systematic Theology with Ethics, while Dogmatics comes in second.

[25] Mike Higton, 'Frei's Christology and Lindbeck's cultural linguistic theory', *Scottish Journal of Theology*, 50 (1997), 83-95, cf. p. 84.

[26] Milbank, *Theology and Social Theory*, p. 382ff. for his understanding of theology.

[27] Frei, *Types*, pp. 26, 43.

[28] Brad Kallenberg, 'Unstuck from Yale: theological method after Lindbeck', *Scottish Journal of Theology*, 50 (1997), 191-218, p. 195; Higton, p. 84.

[29] Lindbeck, *Doctrine,* p. 80; Milbank, *Theology and Social Theory*, p. 385.

tion has been made that what we take to be doctrines are not really doc-trines, but 'paradigmatic instantiations of doctrinal rules.'[30] Hence they too are a species of performance, belonging to the first group.[31] The distinction is very problematic indeed, for it seems that there are certain statements in the Christian form of life with a share of the characteristics belonging to either of the two groups. In fact it is not clear what determines whether a statement belongs to the first or the second group. Lindbeck, and following him almost all narrative theologians have confidently assumed that the dis-tinction raises no problems. It seems natural squarely to align the two or-ders with the pair of practice-theory. But should not the very fluidity and inherent instability of this distinction make us wonder whether it is able to accomplish what it set out to? This volatility is at least glimpsed by Lind-beck and Milbank when they both observe the transitions that take place between the two orders of discourse. Lindbeck notices, for example, how second order doctrinal claims appear as first order ones, while Milbank comments on how the 'idea' finds is way back into the narratives them-selves.[32] Yet they do not question the very distinction itself, in a way that we shall see Frei and Barth (implicitly) doing.

This is a hierarchical model where second level claims are subservient to first order language. Charles Wood's analogy of the map provides a good illustration. First order claims are the general claims made on behalf of the map to correctly represent the world. In narrative parlance, it is the claim of being adequate for our orientation in the terrain. The first order claims of religion either facilitate, or they do not facilitate our 'acquaintance with God'[33]. I have already discussed this issue in a previous chapter. Second level claims are not claims about the terrain as such, but claims about the map itself. They do not involve any propositions or descriptions of the world. In that sense, they are descriptive of the practices of the first order and not of anything outside it. This is the theological symptom of the reifi-cation of religion: theology, as second order talk, cannot speak about God, or about any extra-linguistic, or extra-religious realities, but can only de-scribe the actual features of religion. It is in this sense that Lash needs to be interpreted when he says that theology adds nothing new to the notion of God. The grammar of God has already been given in the religious sedi-

---

[30] Higton, 'Frei's Christology', p. 84.

[31] It seems that one needs to distinguish between three categories: doctrines, Doctrine and theology. One way to use this distinction is to say that doctrines are first-order in-stantiations, Doctrine is what lies beneath both second order and first order, and theol-ogy is the reflection upon both of these, belonging to second order.

[32] Milbank, *Theology and Social Theory*, 384.

[33] Lash's terminology. He is much more theological than the ecumenically-minded Lindbeck who speaks of a religion being adequate to the Ultimate reality, whatever that may be.

mentation of meaning in conventions attaching to liturgy, prayer, confession, bible reading and so on. Should the forms of our religion, in Wood's analogy – the map, prove adequate to the task of ensuring access to God, then our theological claims as well may have the property of being true. But the inherent contradiction here,[34] between the swearing of theology to descriptive duties alone and the claim that theology can also make truth claims, should the religion prove adequate, will have to be carefully discussed later on in this chapter. For now, let us note the hierarchy: second order claims are parasitic upon practice. Theology always starts with a practice which involves what Tanner calls 'unreflected habits of speech'[35] and theology's task is to step in when such a practice encounters contradictions and inconsistencies. The task of theology is to serve as the conscience of the practice, by elucidating its very conditions of possibility, in other words: by supplying its grammar. Thus first order language needs theological second order claims in order to function coherently and, perhaps most importantly, to safeguard its continuity. To paraphrase Kant, practice without theology is blind, while theology without practice is empty.

What then is the task of theology? What does it mean to supply the grammar of a practice? Tanner comments that the linguistic turn in philosophy means that statements about God become statements about God-talk.[36] Lindbeck also borrows the linguistic metaphor and argues that religion as a *verbum externum* is like a language which makes possible certain experiences.[37] Since we can distinguish in a language between its vocabulary and its grammar, we are told that the same distinction holds in religion as well. The vocabulary of a religion is its rites, stories, symbols, actions. The grammar of a religion, on the other hand, is the enduring core, what all of the above reflect. Church doctrines reflect not the lexicon, but the grammar of a religion.[38] To say that religion is understood like a language is also to say that it is linguistic. Tanner, for instance, argues that the grammar of a religion, its conditions of possibilities are themselves linguistic, unlike the transcendental conditions for the possibility of experience as Kant and modern philosophy discussed them.[39] And to say this is to effectively constrain the range of possible experience and belief to what has already been identified in the narratives of the tradition itself. Theology, as such, is nothing else but the elucidation of the grammar of a religion. Doctrines must then be understood as the rules which give that grammar.

---

[34] For a clear statement of the contradiction, see Hans Zorn, 'Grammar, doctrine, and practice', *The Journal of Religion*, 75 (1995), 509-520.

[35] Tanner, *God and Creation*, p. 14.

[36] Tanner, *God and Creation*, p. 13.

[37] Lindbeck, *Doctrine*, p. 34.

[38] Lindbeck, *Doctrine*, p. 81.

[39] Tanner, *God and Creation*, p. 26.

A significant influence for Lindbeck, besides that of Geertz, has been Wittgenstein.[40] It is him who first understood theology as grammar. His esoteric remarks on theology as grammar have been the focus of much theological and scholarly interest[41]. Realising that 'How words are understood is not told by words alone,'[42] Wittgenstein looks at the way in which the concept of God signifies. What he finds is that clues for the essence of any concept are not to be found primarily in that concept, but more specifically in the various ways in which it is used. How does a concept figure in the practices of one community, for example, is more important than the definition given to that concept by some expert authority. One has to investigate the various such uses of words, the sorts of activities that they are embedded in. How this connects with an understanding of meaning as use and application has already been pointed out. Perhaps the most quoted remark, often disputed, is that 'Grammar tells us what kind of object anything is. (Theology as grammar.)'[43] The first half of this remark reinforces the point that to get at the meaning of something one does not point towards the object in reality that the concept refers to. That would be misleading. Indeed, the whole thrust of Wittgenstein's later philosophy is an exercise in disabusing ourselves of the notion that the meaning of language is outside linguistic practice. Wittgenstein's intention was to carefully teach us to 'remember' the unity of language and life. To a certain extent, his philosophy may be interpreted as an anticipation of the Davidsonian deconstruction of the scheme-content dualism. Thus there is nothing behind or beyond what we do with a concept, the activities in which it finds itself. Such is the grammar of the concept. Philosophy becomes flat,[44] for there is no semantic depth, in the sense of a realm of meaning over and above language and practice. To learn a concept is to become skilled in its application, to learn to use it, to learn what is appropriate and what is not appropriate to do with

---

[40] Alan Keightley, *Wittgenstein, Grammar and God*, (London: Epworth, 1976), isolates three main sources for Wittgenstein's ideas on religious beliefs: a) his 'Remarks on Frazer's *Golden Bough*,' b) Lectures and Conversations on Aesthetics, Psychology and Religious Belief, and c) some isolated remarks in the *Philosophical Investigations* and *Zettel*.

[41] Theologians such as Peter Winch, Rush Rhees, Paul Holmer, D. Z. Phillips have consciously attempted to delineate a new theological method or rather self-understanding in light of the post-positivist philosophy of the later Wittgenstein. We shall not engage in their debate, with a few exceptions.

[42] Ludwig Wittgenstein, *Zettel*, translated by G. E. M. Anscombe, (Oxford: Blackwell, 1981), §144.

[43] Wittgenstein, *Philosophical Investigations*, § 373.

[44] Gordon P. Baker and P.M.S. Haker, *Wittgenstein: Rules, Grammar, Necessity*, (Oxford: Blackwell, 1985), p. 22.

it. It is to learn its grammar. This is the context in which one has to look at the second half of his remark.

If one is still lured by the older ostensive, Platonic definition of meaning, one would be tempted to assume that the meaning of 'God' is given by the referent of the term. That is, one would be tempted to treat the notion of God like a picture. Consequently, one would have to think about what this picture represents. But that is to obscure the fact that the way in which 'God' is used differs tremendously from the way in which, for example, 'aunt' is used. Wittgenstein asserts, without any argumentation however, that when believers use the word God they do not think of an object to which they refer, unlike what happens in the use of 'aunts.'[45] In the believer's use, the word depicts nothing at all, it does not serve as a picture.[46] A look at the grammar of our concept would point out that no prior identification of God is necessary before one uses 'God' in such speech acts such as 'God help us!', or 'God will provide' and so on. Consequently, God is not an object of our language, which we could then represent, or refer to. To talk about God is merely to talk about the variety of the terms' applications.

For Wittgenstein, as for the narrative theologians, God is a concept which we have relaxed into accepting[47]. It is embedded into our language. Thus theology has no work of retrieving anything from beyond language. Theology should be content with giving a thick description of the linguistic practices of the Christian community. This remark of Wittgenstein's can be read in two different ways. On the one hand one may read a lot in it and thinkers such as Phillips, Winch, Holmer argue that this means that theology can make no claims about God whatsoever. Or, one can exercise some reserve and we have examples of such an attitude in Keightley and Thiselton, who argue that one should not read too much into Wittgenstein's aphoristic remarks about theology as grammar. However, 'it seems reasonable to assume that Wittgenstein's correlation of grammar and essence implies that theology must be related to a living community which embodies the conventions and beliefs expressed by theology.'[48] No matter how one reads Wittgenstein, the sense of a tension within the postliberal camp, between a docile theology which aims at nothing else but at a sociology of Christian

---

[45] Wittgenstein writes: 'The word "God" is amongst the earliest learnt – pictures and catechisms etc. But not the same consequences as with pictures of aunts. I wasn't shown that which the picture pictured.' Ludwig Wittgenstein, 'Lectures on religious belief', in L. Wittgenstein, *Lectures and Conversations on Aesthetics, Psychology and Religious Belief*, edited by Cyril Barrett, (Oxford: Blackwell, 1966).

[46] For a rather uncritical discussion, see William H. Brenner, 'Theology as grammar', *The Southern Journal of Philosophy*, 34 (1996), 439-453, pp. 442-445, 449.

[47] Keightley, *Witgenstein*, p. 45.

[48] Thiselton, *The Two Horizons*, pp. 391ff.

practice and knowledge, and a more potent and incisive theological inquiry, remains quite acute.[49]

We may sum up what has been said thus far: since religion is a closed system[50] and there is no way of grounding, or legitimising the grammar of that religion[51], then talk about God can only take the form of non-identical repetition and redescription of the rules of the Christian 'game'. We shall now turn our attention to the specific way in which narrative theologians themselves understand theology as grammar. Two narrative theologians while all agreeing on the understanding of theology as grammar differ in their respective understanding of what this entails for the nature of doctrine. We shall analyse the perspective of Lindbeck and Frei on doctrine, grammar and rules respectively, pointing out the differences of emphasis between them and their significance for this project.

Lindbeck's ecumenical focus arguably requires him to find a core to the religion. Such a core could not be available aside from its performances, but it must allow for the possibility of a diverse array of performances. He locates this core in the grammar of religion, which be believes is the unchangeable, stable core of what a religion is. To get at the essence of religion, one must understand the rules according to which the practice of the *fideles* functions.[52] Hence the *positing of a normative performance of the core, that is, a community of skilled practitioners of a religion*. The grammar of the respective religion will be given by their doctrines, which are the rules which constitute that grammar.[53]

Doctrines, therefore, cannot describe an actual state of affairs which obtains independently of the forms of life of the community or religion. Instead they describe the rules for normative practice. The object of doctrines are not extra-linguistic objects, but the concepts which are embedded in the religion.[54] Doctrines, Lindbeck tells us, 'are communally authoritative

---

[49] To my knowledge, no analysis of the various aspects of such a tension has been attempted. This study suggests at least the possibility of such an investigation.

[50] I use 'closed' in the sense of there being no way around the linguistic practices of one religion.

[51] Keightley, *Wittgenstein*, p. 44.

[52] For the problems associated with what I shall call 'ecclesiological reduction' see Paul Rigby, 'The nature of doctrine and scientific progress', *Theological Studies*, 52 (1991), 669-688, pp. 677-8.

[53] If practices are all we have, than the locus for the distinctiveness of a community is within the practices themselves. Yet the possibility of errant practices and corrupt practitioners solicits a normative practice which Lindbeck identifies with the behaviour and attitudes of the *fideles*.

[54] The obvious assumption is a separation between meaning and truth: Lindbeck believes that one can get at the meaning of doctrines, rules, grammar independently of examining their truth.

teachings regarding beliefs that are considered essential to the identity or welfare of the group in question.'[55] Since a propositionalist account cannot do justice to the parasitic nature of doctrine, it needs to make room for a 'flat' account of doctrine. Hence, first order language differs from second order language in that it makes truth claims regarding extra-linguistic realities, whereas second-order language doesn't. To say that doctrines are rules does not mean that they do not involve propositions. But these propositions refer only to the practices themselves, to the forms of life and not to extra-linguistic or extra-human realities.[56] In other words, they make intra-systematic rather than ontological truth claims.

The *verbum externum* which constitutes the *pathos* under which theology is to be done is constituted by the first-intentional[57] uses of language, the forms of life which make experience possible. Such factors are of a practical, behavioural nature, they are the life within which theoretical reflection is inescapably placed. The assumption behind this is twofold: that this is a hierarchical system in which doctrine is always secondary to practical behaviour and its grammar.[58] This argument is reinforced by the fact that doctrine has no new identification to perform, no new knowledge to deliver other that to discover what the practice already implicitly contains. The second assumption is that the first order language can be defined in and of itself with relative ease. Countless times, both Lindbeck as well as Frei and Nicholas Lash speak about the reference which is ensured by the first level language quite independently of the second level. They speak with confidence of love of God, worship of God, being adequate in an existential sense to God and so on, as if such attitudes were at all possible in the absence of any propositional attitudes. There are sufficient reasons to doubt this assumption. On the other hand, this dichotomy between the two orders of discourse is perhaps essential to Lindbeck's ecumenical task. The orders must be kept distinct in order that two distinct *loci*, one for agreement, another for diversity may be found within religion, for ecumenical purposes. A confusion of the two would lead to grave problems for the ecumenical venture. Should the practical, performative level be invaded by propositional attitudes and grammar, it would then become apparent that difference and diversity permeates all levels of discourse. Furthermore, the Christian community would lose all sense of continuity and of a common narrative.

Thus, Lindbeck's is a prescriptive model legislating that doctrines are rules and nothing else. Doctrines are already encoded in the practical web of behaviour, with its own inner grammar. The grammar of a religion is, for

---

[55] Lindbeck, *Doctrine*, p. 74.

[56] Lindbeck, *Doctrine*, p. 80.

[57] Another term for first-order, self-involving statements.

[58] Lindbeck speaks in terms of a priority given to the code rather than the encoded. (p. 35.)

him, implicit and unchangeable, while the religion is understood in purely *pathic* terms[59]. That is to say, agents have no place in the formation of religion, the concepts are not critically mediated from religion down to the agents, but rather one 'learns to live with them' – quite literally.

We have had an opportunity to notice Frei's reserves towards theory. Paul Schwartzenbrunner argues that they are theological in motivation.[60] This seems to be a correct verdict, since in his opinion, theoretical devices, while indispensable to theological discourse, must nonetheless remain subject to the theological matter at hand. Such reticence helps Frei guard against prematurely expressing an opinion about what theological statements or doctrines can do. Such judgements are always to be made *ad hoc* and need not be prescribed in the manner that Lindbeck does. Higton comments on the methodological differences between Frei and Lindbeck and traces them down to the former's Christological focus, as opposed to Lindbeck's more formal and philosophical starting point.[61] On his analysis, Frei is not as dependent on a simplistic social theory, such as Geertz's[62]. He will not propose a general theory that declares formal second order rules to be the necessary form of the dogmatic pronouncements.[63] He will not wish to sharply distinguish between changeable first order enactments and the unchangeable second-order rules. That is not to say that he does not make such a distinction, but only that it is not as rigid as in the case of Lindbeck.

In his *Types of Christian Theology*, Frei distinguishes between different types of theology, according to the relationship between external description and internal description that they exhibit. Type 4, corresponding to the work of Karl Barth is the closest to the understanding of doctrine that Frei himself favours. It most accurately applies his understanding of the plain sense of Scripture.[64] Frei interprets Barth as not sharply distinguishing between first person address to God and talk or discourse about God.[65] Theological statements can take two forms for Barth: cognitive, where theology takes the form of dogmatic assertions, even though this use is not backed by

---

[59] Hütter's notion, *Suffering*, p. 52.

[60] Paul Schwarzenbrunner, 'The modesty of hermeneutics: the theological reserves of Hans Frei', *Modern Theology*, 8 (1992), 181-195, pp. 181-3.

[61] 'Where Lindbeck had a cultural linguistic theory, Frei had Christology', writes Higton ('Frei's Christology', p. 95). The same difference obtains, in Hunsinger's opinion, between Barth and Lindbeck: George Hunsinger, 'Truth as self-involving: Barth and Lindbeck on the cognitive and performative aspects of truth in theological discourse', *Journal of the American Academy of Religion*, 61 (1993), 41-56, p. 46.

[62] Higton, 'Frei's Christology', p. 86.

[63] Higton, 'Frei's Christology', p. 93.

[64] Frei, *Types Of Christian Theology*, p. 44.

[65] Frei, *Types Of Christian Theology*, p. 39.

a general theory of reference.[66] The second use is the regulative one, as self-involving statements.[67] The doctrine of justification by faith, for example, can function both as a description about how God saves, asserting something about an extra-linguistic reality; but it can also function in a regulative mode, as self-involving. Self-involving statements are those whose meaning and truth is unavailable apart from the attitude and behaviour accompanying the statement. The important difference in Barth's and Frei's theology from Lindbeck's cultural linguisticism is their reluctance to prescribe. They both refuse to give a 'super-rule' which would say which function should be used. This decision is entirely *ad hoc*, to be made in the particular theological situation[68]. Frei's discussion asks whether the texts of the Gospels should be taken in a referential or self-involving, i.e. regulative mode. The theological methodology of Barth, he comments, is consonant with the literal sense interpretation of Scripture.

We do not have the same loss of reference, or description in Frei. His earlier texts were easily predisposed to misunderstanding, since he was refusing to say that the Gospel stories accurately portrayed the historical Jesus. Now we can more clearly see, especially in light of his posthumously published comments on theory, that he simply refused to discuss the Gospel stories in terms of external notions like reference, historical correctness and so on. The reason for this has been double: on the one hand a hermeneutical refusal to locate meaning at any sub-textual level (reality, author's intention, communal reception), on the other an understanding of the need to allow the text to control our heuristic concepts.[69] Both requirements hold not only for the gospel stories but for theological statements as well. Their meaning must be found in their plain sense, and decision regarding the appropriate use, whether referential or regulative or both, is one that must be taken in light of the theological context itself, not in view of a prescriptive and external methodology.

As Frei notes, one cannot do without such methodological categories such as reference, truth and so on.[70] Conversely, Lindbeck understands doctrines to be devoid of any reference other than to the practices of the church, as their regulators:

> To say that doctrines are rules is not to deny that they involve propositions. The rules formulated by the linguist or the logician, for example, express propositional convictions about how language or thought actually work. These are, however, second-order rather than first-order proposi-

---

[66] Frei, *Types Of Christian Theology*, p. 41.

[67] Frei, *Types Of Christian Theology*, p. 42.

[68] Frei, *Types Of Christian Theology*, p. 43.

[69] Frei, *Types Of Christian Theology*, p. 81.

[70] Frei, *Types Of Christian Theology*, p. 41.

tions and affirm nothing about extra-linguistic or extra-human reality...
they make intra-systematic rather than ontological truth claims.[71]

Lindbeck adopts here what Frei calls a prescriptive stance[72] with regard to
the function of doctrines. Kallenberg rightly comments that Lindbeck
hasn't given up the language-world dichotomy.[73] Reflecting on the linguistic turn of philosophy it may be argued that it may lead discourse into two
directions. It may lead to a linguistic idealism of the sort adopted by Milbank, Lindbeck and so on which presupposes the reifcation of language.
Or, with the later Wittgenstein, Austin and Davidson, it may lead to a reaffirmation of the seamless unity of language and life. The second option
makes it difficult to affirm what language cannot do, or what thought cannot express, since it has already deconstructed the dualism of scheme and
content.[74] Frei is an illustration of a theologian who has gradually moved
closer to the second route. One cannot treat the incommensurability of
paradigms as absolute, nor can one drive a wedge between religion and life,
tradition and experience as Lindbeck does. Such a separation would render
religion utterly irrelevant to life. There is a certain sense, therefore, when
the meaning of religious concepts, or of religion in general depends on
something external to it.[75] This is suggested by the fact that to learn a concept, albeit a religious one, means learning to apply it in contexts other than
the original one. It means acquiring the skill and the intuitive knowledge of
appropriate uses outside religion. Bruce Marshall gives more coherence to
this notion, as we have observed. He interprets world absorption as requiring, in a Davidsonian fashion, that we treat that which is external and alien
as true in order to understand it. Therefore, far from promoting a sectarian
isolationism with its own esoteric meanings, Frei's understanding of religion and of world absorption builds on the unity between religion and life,
not on their dualism.

Hence, concepts such as reference, facticity, truth, meaning and so on,
while being defined internally in the religion, are nonetheless correlated in
an *ad hoc* fashion with their 'secular' counterparts. Reference is a necessary
notion for Frei. Commenting on his earlier writings on the referentiality of
the Gospels, he makes an important distinction between 'assertion as part of

---

[71] Lindbeck, *Doctrine*, p. 80.

[72] He comments on the prescriptive stance of both Phillips (p. 52) with regard to the
relation of outside/ inside; and Kelsey – who interprets Barth as reading the Gospels as
loosely organised non-fictional novel, when in fact Barth never adheres to a general
relation between literary exegesis and historical statement (p. 90).

[73] Kallenberg, 'Unstuck', p. 200.

[74] See for example the way Davidson uses this deconstruction to argue against incommensurability.

[75] Frei, *Types Of Christian Theology*, p. 53.

the narrative sense' – if the plain sense of the story has it that one of the figures of the story or the story as such refers – and assertion as a trans-hermeneutical judgement, whether the author's, the theologian's, or the reader's. The only acceptable employment of assertion, or one may say the same thing about 'reference' is in the former sense[76]. The Gospel stories may refer or not, but the way they do is not decided before-hand by a neutral philosophical theory. I would suggest that the failure of the so-called Wittgensteinian theologians is to apply such notions as the Wittgensteinian criticism of the picture theory to God without any regard for the positive theological requirements of the Christian stories and doctrines. Frei's more nuanced position helps him to affirm together with Lindbeck that the meaning of the stories and of the doctrines is given intra-textually, yet stress that intra-textuality does not involve non-cognitivism with regard to God.

The reasons for a denial of reference or propositions are various. We will enumerate but a few, starting with the reification of language and practice. For Lindbeck, if anything refers it is the practice, or the language as a whole. Thus statements within the practice can only be about the practice. Lash echoes the same argument when he suggests that theological language is language designed to enhance the practice's access to God.[77] For Lash it is the practice which 'touches down' ontologically. It is in other words either adequate or inadequate to God. The task of doctrine is that of best elucidating the conditions for the possibility and success of that practice, so that believers may be adequately related to God. The doctrine of the Trinity, for instance, is not a series of statements about God, but about how we should proceed in order to get acquainted to him. Stanley Hauerwas argues that to insist on first order language is not to imply that questions of truth do not matter. Instead it is a reminder that people, not sentences, make truthful claims.'[78] Reference is thus mediated by people, not sentences. Hauerwas, in fact, loses sight of what we have called the loss of agency in narrative theology. People cannot be the bearers of either truth or reference in this socially-constructivist scenario. Reference and truth have already been decided for them and they have merely 'relaxed into' accepting them.[79]

A second reason for the loss of reference is the neo-Wittgensteinian conviction that God is not an object to be talked about. Both Lindbeck and Paul Holmer make this point. Holmer argues, following Wittgenstein, that God

---

[76] Hans Frei, 'Historical reference and the gospels: a response to a critique of *The Identity of Jesus Christ*' [online]. Notes edited by Mike A. Higton from the Frei archives at Yale Library. Available at: http://www.library.yale.edu/div/freidoc3.htm [June 2001].

[77] Heide, 'Noeticism', p. 470.

[78] Hauerwas, *Wilderness Wanderings*, p. 145, speaking about Paul Holmer.

[79] Keightley, *Wittgenstein*, p. 45.

is not a name for an object, but rather a concept that arises out of the traditions, conventions and practices of a given spiritual community.[80] Theology's task is not description, but grammatological elucidation of the rules, it is a project of definition. Such a grammatical discourse, to follow Thiselton's argument about certain of Paul's concepts, does not give new and fresh information about a given object, but expands the horizons of the reader's understanding.[81] D. Z. Phillips distinguishes between a referential use of 'this is red' and a grammatical use of the same proposition.[82] The referential function is to point to an object in the world and associate that object with a description (redness), while the grammatological function is to define what redness is. Connected to this reluctance to talk about reference is a certain positive stance towards God: namely that it is not an object.

There are two possible sources of such a stance. One is Wittgensteinian: the way in which the notion 'God' is used makes it dissimilar to pictures. However, this analysis of use fails for it does not take into account, as we shall see, those referential uses of God, as for example 'Christ is God', or 'God was in Christ'. A second possibility is straightforwardly agnostic, or apophatic: it derives from a certain theology. It is in fact an elucidation of the rules of such a theology. No attempt is made, however, towards the legitimation of such a theology.

Summing up, we discern two orientations in narrative theology: first the prescriptive stance that doctrines only refer to practices, while it is the practices themselves which are either adequate to God or not (what being adequate means has never been explained). Here the tradition already prescribes experiences and creates the concepts which theology can only permute. Beliefs about God are therefore not falsifiable by anything we may say about the world, or about God as such, no observational knowledge of God being possible.[83] Theologians such as Lindbeck, Tanner, Holmer may be associated with these views. On the other hand one finds the theologically restrained interpretation of people like Frei and Marshall. These argue that whether theological statements refer or not is not something to be decided theoretically, but only *ad hoc*. Although reference is a notion to be described internally, it is nonetheless a necessary one. Such thinkers are more decidedly theological and Christological than their colleagues who are arguably more influenced by philosophical views.

---

[80] Paul Holmer, *The Grammar of Faith*, (San Francisco: Harper and Row, 1978), p. 185.

[81] Thiselton, *The Two Horizons*, p. 391.

[82] D. Z. Phillips, 'Lindbeck's audience', *Modern Theology*, 4 (1988), 133-154, p. 148.

[83] Thomas B. Ommen, 'Wittgensteinian fideism and theology', *Horizons*, 7 (1980), 183-204, p. 193.

What the thinkers of the first sort assume is that reference, or rather that ontological adequacy to God, the point where the practice as a whole touches the divine (or whichever) reality, is something available quite apart from any propositional stance.[84] Such a reference is dependant on being immersed into the practice and having acquired the skills of that religion which is categorially adequate to God. I am not contradicting what I have said in an earlier chapter about narrative theology as working with a description based theory of reference. Such description is accomplished at a meta-religious level and not at the level of propositional statements. But thinkers such as Kallenberg, McClendon and Marshall argue that successful performance is connected indissolubly with ontological truth. Kallenberg[85] argues that there are two possible ways of doing theology without falling into the temptations of modern thought. One is to follow Austin in saying that there is both a truth component as well as a 'happiness' component in any speech act. That is, one cannot dissociate the regulative function of doctrine from its representative dimension.[86] The other way is to argue with Wittgenstein for the seamless unity of life and language, thought.[87] The earlier McClendon takes the first route in arguing that every successful speech act needs to fulfil a representative or referential condition, it must make certain propositional truth claims – and be recognised as making them. Secondly, Marshall argues that successful performance depends on right propositional identification. We shall take these two perspectives into account as we revisit the question of the truth and meaning of doctrine.

The self-involving nature of theological statements[88] requires that their truth depends on the quality of a person's performance.[89] We have already engaged in the discussion about the crusader's cry, 'Christus Dominus est!' and will not rehearse the whole argument advanced by Lindbeck.[90] Since he understands truth to be attaching to forms of life rather than to propositions as such, it is only appropriate that the crusader's statement be validated in

---

[84] See also Marshall, 'Aquinas as postliberal theologian', pp. 360-361.

[85] Pp. 201-202.

[86] Cf. also Anthony C. Thiselton, 'Knowledge, myth and corporate memory', in *Believing in the Church: The Corporate Nature of Faith*. A Report by the Doctrine Commission of the Church of England, (London: SPCK, 1981), p. 71.

[87] Kallenberg attempts an argument along these lines. Talk about God becomes a possibility once he is conceived as a fact of the social world, and not above it or beyond. The argument is similar to Holmer's point about 'God' as concept. ('Unstuck', pp. 192, 202ff.)

[88] Cf. McClendon's suggestion against doctrines as discrete propositions. Instead they should be conceived as practices themselves (*Doctrine: Systematic Theology II*, p. 28.)

[89] We may call this *performance-related truth*.

[90] Cf. the discussion in and around p. 65 in *The Nature of Doctrine*.

the whole context of his behaviour. It is the form of life as such which possesses truth and clarifies meanings, rather than particular propositions. And since the meanings have already been fixed, what has to be decided is not the truth of this or that proposition, but the truth of the form of life as such. This would mean that there can be no talk about ontological truth whatsoever, attaching to isolated statements. However, Lindbeck seems to want it both ways. The fact that he speaks about ontological truth which has as its condition intra-systematic truth has made critics such as D. Z. Phillips to accuse him of inconsistencies.[91] According to Lindbeck, the cognitive truth of a religious utterance depends on how the utterance is employed within a correlative mode of life molded by such activities as prayer, worship, proclamation and service.[92] Intra-systematic truth, then, is a necessary though not sufficient condition for ontological truth. This is a consequence of the understanding that we relax into accepting concepts, that human agents do not partake in any active knowledge and active creation of concepts to fit new experiences. All that one needs in order to be a good practitioner is to adapt to the narratives of the church and learn to read the world and everything else through them.

Lindbeck's claim is that they are advancing a model of theological knowledge commensurable to Barth's confessionalism. In light of our discussion of reference in the preceding section, it may be safer to say that Lindbeck's understanding of the possibilities of theological knowledge resemble more the earlier Barth of the 1920's, rather than the Christologically-minded Barth of the *Church Dogmatics*. It is in fact theologians such as Frei, Marshall, Hütter and Hunsinger that better resemble the later Barth. While Lindbeck *et al.* stress the importance of human performance alone – the intra-systematic aspect of truth – for the ontological truth of statements, a proper Barthian understanding of the relationship between truth and behaviour would reveal certain differences.

Hunsinger and Hütter both argue that it is in fact the action of God on which the truth of the human theological speech acts depends. The former charges Lindbeck with not properly distinguishing between statements and speech acts, therefore tying the truth of statements to the successful performance of the form of life. One of the problems which this raises, as we pointed out above, was that it is difficult to connect the theological statement with the relevant form of life or behaviour. Hunsinger raises the same question: what is the total relevant context of action needed to judge the success or failure of a form of life?[93] A more important problem pertains to

---

[91] Phillips speaks about Lindbeck's inherently unstable position (*passim*). The former would do away with first order truth claims altogether ('Lindbeck's Audience', p. 146).

[92] Hunsinger, 'Truth as Self-Involving', p. 42.

[93] Hunsinger, 'Truth as Self-Involving' p. 43; cf. also Milbank's question about total practice: *Theology and Social Theory*, p. 382ff.

some theological circumstances which makes the two approaches very different. To argue that the truth of the statement depends in part on the success of the human form of life is to lose sight of the fact that it is God's involvement that guarantees the truth of the assertion, quite apart from the human effort to do so. Hunsinger's perhaps over-stretched conclusion is that we are in fact witnessing the difference between an account that stresses God's grace and an account that places undue stress on the human ability.[94] It is the epistemological equivalent to the debate between grace and nature.[95]

Hunsinger's argument is rather important at this juncture: what is needed for the evaluation of a statement, or a form of life is a paradigm case, a normative practice.[96] And such a normative practice is localised by Hunsinger as well as Barth, Marshall[97] and Hütter[98] in the action of God. This is a reaction against the anthropocentric expression of meaning and truth,[99] and a declaration that it is God's action, quite apart from the human effort, that guarantees the attachment of truth to statements. The importance of this argument becomes apparent, for it points out that in the absence of a normative context, in other words an ontology, interpreting action becomes impossible. *What is there to distinguish between correct and incorrect practice, if there is no propositional imagination of an ideal practice?* Gale Heide levels a similar criticism against Lash: if description of external realities is denied, what is to distinguish theology from a sociology or anthropology of religion?[100] I have called the imagination of a normative practice an ontology and this has to be clarified below. For Lindbeck the 'vehicle of correspondence', what Marshall calls 'truth bearer' is not divine activity, but human forms of life. It is precisely in the oblivion towards this central theological insight that Lindbeck's cultural linguistic model for doctrine betrays some of its more dubious sympathies.

---

[94] One would expect Lindbeck to introduce the Holy Spirit as that which ultimately makes the forms of life adequate to divine realities. Instead he construes the HS – the *verbum internum* – as that capacity for hearing and accepting the true religion. (*Doctrine*, p. 34.)

[95] At one point Lindbeck confesses to a certain 'tilt toward Rome': George Lindbeck, 'Confession and community: An Israel-like view of the church', *Christian Century* 107 (1990), 492-496, p. 494.

[96] Hunsinger, 'Truth as Self-Involving', p. 47. Charles Wood also draws attention to the need for normativeness : paying attention not only to how we speak but what to speak, in Charles Wood, 'The Nature of doctrine: religion and theology in a postliberal age: review article', *Religious Studies Review*, 11 (1985), 235-240, p. 240.

[97] Marshall, *Trinity*, pp. 246ff.

[98] Hütter, *Suffering*, p. 54.

[99] Hunsinger, *Suffering*, p. 47.

[100] Heide, 'Noeticism', p. 471.

Hunsinger is not alone in making such arguments. Reinhard Hütter as well as Bruce Marshall make a similar case. For Lindbeck, the claim that 'God is Three in One' is false when the pattern and form of life associated with it contradict the Christian pattern that affirms God's being and will. This position is true, counters Hütter, only if it is taken in the weak sense that the meaning of the theological speech act is given in part by the correlative form of life.[101] Marshall also points out that the truth of 'Jesus is risen' cannot be brought about except by the action of Jesus Himself. He includes a sophisticated theological adaptation of the Davidson-Tarski theory of truth[102] and he also argues that having a relation to Jesus involves a cognitive component.[103] For Marshall there can be no strict demarcation between first and second-order statements[104], for practice always involves a normative ontological context.

To sum up the argument so far: narrative theologians understand doctrine as grammar, as reflection upon the practices of the church. Such an understanding is by no means uniform, but the issues with which I have disagreed are the non-cognitive emphases, the lack of reference, and the dualism between first and second orders of language. In what follows I shall argue against the reification of language and consequently against the strict dualism between theory and practice. What will then emerge is a model of doctrine which may serve as both regulative and cognitive, with ontology as a necessary backdrop for any practice.

Against the Reification of Practice

Lindbeck's reification of practice has its origin in the linguistic and ontological turn in twentieth century philosophy. Evident in the work of such thinkers as Heidegger, Gadamer, Wittgenstein, Kuhn and so on, it adapts in various ways the Gadamerian insight that 'Being that can be understood is language'[105] For Heidegger this means that the experience of a new object or thought is always in the background of a prior involvement in the world which is linguistic in nature. Wittgensteinian language games stress the same idea of a prior linguistic activity determining meaning, while Kuhn adapts the insight epistemologically to argue for the connection between argument and context. For Lindbeck, the insight takes the form of a belief that theology is always internal to religion and subservient to it. Attaching to this perspective is a sharp distinction between what is 'inside' and what is 'outside' religion, or the specific language game. The same may be said

---

[101] Hütter, *Suffering*, p. 52.

[102] See chapter 5.

[103] Marshall, *Trinity,* p. 246.

[104] Or, if there can be, it would have no epistemological import.

[105] Gadamer, *Truth and Method*, p. 474, 475.

about D. Z. Phillips, as Frei points out.[106] Religion, just like incommensurable language games, creates its own world, with well distinguished boundaries and with a clear logic of its own. It is religion understood as language which dictates the realm of the possible. We have argued that this is reinforcing a dichotomous split between scheme and content. Stephen Stell is right to conclude that 'Whereas Lindbeck affirms a dialectical relation between experience and tradition, the dichotomous structure which he consistently imposes upon them hermeneutically constructs their actual interactions.'[107] George Hunsinger points out the same failure to maintain an authentic tension between language and world in terms of the way in which the scripture cannot influence the tradition:

> In this conception of the relationship between form of life and Scripture, although described in dialectical terms, is made logically to depend in some strong sense on human use. Just as the use of Scripture shapes the form of life, so also does the form of life shape the use of scripture, yet it is finally the form of life as a whole rather than scripture as such which is brought to mediate the correspondence between a normative theological utterance as rightly used and the ultimate divine reality.[108]

This polarity ensures the normativity of the practice, or of the language of religion with respect to what can be experienced within religion. Second order language will therefore assume a subservient role in relation to first order language. However, this hierarchy is logically dependent on the normativity of language. Therefore, if this normativity is questionable, the dualism will no longer hold. Doctrines are subservient to practice because, so the argument goes, there is nothing beyond practice that doctrines might refer to. The various reasons for such a thesis have already been pointed out. One must show, therefore, that while language is necessary for the experience of the world and of God, it need not be construed in such a way that those very experiences are already a *fait accompli*. It must be shown that there are extra-linguistic experiences, and that language does not preform thought.

The locus classicus for such a discussion, and I can only attempt to draw some pointers towards its resolution, is Gadamer's discussion of the universality of hermeneutics. Hans Herbert Kögler[109] points out that his remark to the effect that being that can be understood is language can be interpreted in three ways. On a platonic-realist reading, this is an assertion about the lin-

---

[106] *Types of Christian Theology*, p. 49. cf. Fergus Kerr, 'Frei's Types', *New Blackfriars*, 75 (1994), 184-193, for a review of Frei's book and a critique of his interpretation of D. Z. Phillips, esp. pp. 190ff.

[107] Stell, 'Hermeneutics', p. 681.

[108] Hunsinger, 'Truth as Self-Involving', p. 53.

[109] Kögler, *The Power of Dialogue*, pp. 60ff.

guisticality of being as such, that the very structure of being is linguistic. On a Kantian-epistemological interpretation, what is understandable or intelligible to us is accessible in no other way that through language. Both readings fail, for different reasons. What emerges instead is a Hegelian-idealist reading according to which language has already disclosed reality, because comprehending something as an object prior to its linguistic determination is as such impossible.[110] Thus, for Gadamer, subject and object can only be conceived as relations in language. Kögler's main complaint is that such a reading will not allow for anything completely novel to be comprehended. There will be no experience of alterity as such on a linguistic ontology such as Gadamer's.[111] Even if he accepts the presence of non-linguistic factors, such factors will work solely in support of the linguistic praxis.[112] One may wonder, however, if Kögler has grasped all that Gadamer was trying to assert. When hard-pressed, the latter would acknowledge that such a project as his does not mean that one cannot criticise the practices in question. He envisages the possibility of going beyond what is pre-given: 'the possibility of going beyond our conventions and beyond all those experiences that are schematised in advance opens up before us once we find ourselves, in our conversation with others, faced with opposed thinkers, with new critical tests, with new experiences.'[113] At least formally, then, Gadamer does allow and cherish the presence of real alterity. Kögler's critique then will refer not to the intention of Gadamer's arguments, but to their logical consequence. And the establishment of this logical consequence depends at least in part on a crude[114] understanding of language. Gadamer clarifies this point and it is worth reproducing his conclusion at length:

> To sum up, I would say that the misunderstanding in the question of the linguisticality of our understanding is really one about language – i.e., seeing language as a stock of words and phrases, of concepts, viewpoints and opinions. In fact language is the single word, whose virtuality opens for us the infinity of discourse, of speaking with one another, of the freedom of 'expressing oneself' and 'letting oneself be expressed.' Language is not its elaborated conventionalism, nor the burden of pre-schematization with which it loads us, but the generative and creative power to unceasingly make this whole once again fluent.[115]

---

[110] Kögler, *Power*, p. 66.
[111] Kögler, *Power, p.* 69.
[112] Kögler, *Power, p.* 64.
[113] Gadamer, *Truth and Method*, p. 546.
[114] Thiselton, 'Knowledge, myth and corporate memory', p. 51.
[115] Gadamer, *Truth and Method*, p. 549.

Regardless of whether Kögler's argument touches on the substance of what Gadamer argues, what the latter asserts in the passage above is important: namely, that first order language is not unsurpassable. We have interpreted Davidson as arguing essentially the same thing, namely that convention is not necessarily the only method of communication. It is indeed a common mistake to confuse language with its conventionalism,[116] as Gadamer warns us.[117] Davidson's arguments in terms of prior and passing theory suggest that while one may approach a situation of communication or discovery armed with facilitating conventions, such conventions can always be reformulated in terms of the novelty of what is experienced, or simply new beliefs.[118] Gadamer does not deny pre-linguistic, or extra-linguistic experiences.

The questionable assumption of theologians such as Lindbeck and Holmer is that ordinary language, or first order practices and statements are all right as they are.[119] Hence theology cannot seek to correct those linguistic practices with respect to extra-linguistic realities, for such realities are already prescribed within the language. It must simply assume a clarificatory role, subservient to the practice itself. The model of theoretical inquiry presupposed here is that of a practice whose goals of inquiry, strategies of justification and meanings are prescribed wholly internally. However, as I

---

[116] Though 'convention' may be taken as the last barrier against the indeterminacy of meaning, as for example Vanhoozer tends to do in *Is There a Meaning in This Text?*, too much weight can be attributed to it. To say that convention is not enough in securing understanding is to realise that there is no philosophical point to be made about the communitarian, social, conventional context of conversation. It is also to echo Davidson's remark that:

> It is easy to misconceive the role of society in language. Language is, to be sure, a social art. But it is an error to suppose we have seen deeply into the heart of linguistic communication when we have noticed how society bends linguistic habits to a public norm. What is conventional about language, if anything is, is that people tend to speak much as their neighbours do. But in indicating this element of the conventional, or of the conditioning process that makes speakers rough linguistic facsimilies of their friends and parents, we explain no more than the convergence; we throw no light on the essential nature of the skills that are thus made to converge. ('Communication and convention', p. 278).

[117] Philosophers of language who have emphasised the creativity of language instead of its formal aspect as convention are Davidson, Benedetto Croce, Eugenio Coseriu.

[118] D. Davidson argues, for example, that grammatical mood or illocutionary force cannot be related simply by convention ('Communication and convention', p. 270). Also see his principle of 'the autonomy of meaning' (p. 274).

[119] Cf. Ommen, 'Wittgensteinian Fideism', p. 194.

have argued with respect to Kuhn, this is not a correct understanding of what actually takes place in scientific argumentation.[120]

If one has been disenchanted of the superiority and un-surpassability of the practices of one tradition, the distinction between first and second order can no longer hold, except as weak and inconsequential. This will better explain those 'cases' in which the idea filters down back to the level of narrative. It will be the task of the next section to show that practical performance always presupposes an ontological and propositional horizon. Before we go on to those matters, some more clarifications regarding the separation of the two orders must be made.

Lindbeck hopes that this separation will be able to provide him with an account of both diversity as well as unity. The performances of the tradition are the variable factors, but the grammar of those performances, given by the doctrines which express the implicit rules, is the unifying common denominator. Lindbeck does not sufficiently answer D. Z. Phillips's concern that once one changes the performance, one also changes the grammar[121]. Phillips and Kallenberg[122] in fact argue that there is no grammar apart from its actual instantiation. There are no rules without a game.[123] It is therefore wrong to assume that one can have the same grammar regulating different performances. Furthermore, even if Lindbeck's arguments may hold, he cannot understand how it will no longer involve capitulation. Grammatical disagreements are also a possibility and a very real one. If Phillips were correct we would face the following problem: the unity which Lindbeck seeks will be impossible to establish, if theology is only grammar and if grammar is subservient to the practical performances. It is such an understanding that will lead to an uncontrollable relativism. However, if our argument holds, namely that doctrines are not simply a redescription of the practices of the church, the possibility opens up to maintain unity despite diversity in performance.

This has not been an argument to the effect that theology simply describes divine realities quite apart from the grammar of the practices of the church. That would be like saying that one could describe God in the absence of any language. I have simply tried to argue that doctrine's context is not restricted to those practices, but that through those practices it is able

---

[120] Cf. my chapter 6 and also Rigby, *passim*. Rigby building upon Larry Laudan's philosophy of science argues that there is nothing incommensurable about goals, tests and meanings.

[121] Phillips, 'Lindbeck's Audience', pp. 146, 150.

[122] Kallenberg, 'Unstuck', p. 199.

[123] Similarly, David Ford suspects that Frei has not paid sufficient attention to Bourdieu's objections to rules: David Ford, 'On being theologically hospitable to Jesus Christ: Hans Frei's achievement', *Journal of theological studies*, NS, 46 (1995), 532-546.

to talk meaningfully about divine realities.[124] By undermining the thesis of
the ubiquity of religion we have therefore cleared the way for the more
theological insight that theology is a faith activity whose conditions of truth
necessarily involve God's action. This has been our own injunction against
religion, in a Barthian fashion.

The question which remains to be answered is this: if theology need not
be merely redescription of performance, what is it positively?

Doctrine and Ontology

Edmund Schlink[125] lists four types of theological statements: prayer, doxology, witness and doctrine. Prayer and witness may be described as inter-
subjective, while doxology and doctrine as objective. Creeds originally
contained all of these forms, but they gradually allowed the doctrinal form
to dominate.[126] This testifies to the *cognitive content and intention of the
early doctrinal statements*. Should this evaluation be correct, then Lindbeck
would have to clarify one aspect of his account. He argues that doctrines
are best understood as rules. But if the theological community has historically interpreted doctrines as cognitive, his account must offer an explanation of how they could function as rules. Lindbeck's theology, therefore,
would have to provide a re-interpretation of historical accounts of doctrine.
This will sit uncomfortably with an understanding of the plain sense which
argues that the meaning of the biblical narrative is what it says and nothing
behind the text or in front of it. He could suggest that biblical hermeneutics
and general hermeneutics do not work according to the same set of rules.
The interpretation of the meaning of doctrinal statements, as propositions
which fall within the domain of general texts, does not work according to
the criteria of the plain sense. One must remember, however, that plain
sense interpretation does not derive from a set of immanent features of the
text, but from a ruled way of reading by the community of interpretation. If
that is so, one should also derive the rules governing the meaning of Christian doctrines not from their immanent features, but from what the community does with them. And one of the essential features of the historical reception of doctrines was their cognitive function. It must be pointed out that
what is disputed here is not the success or failure of their reference or description, but their intention to refer and describe.

---

[124] Cf. also Barr's arguments against Whorf in James Barr, *Semantics of Biblical
Language*, (London: SCM, 1983).

[125] Edmund Schlink, 'The study of dogmatic statements as an ecumenical problem',
in Edmund Schlink, *The Coming Christ and the Coming Church,* translated by G.
Overlach and D. B. Simmonds, (Edinburgh, 1967).

[126] Cf. also Vernon Neufeld, *Earliest Christian Confessions*, (Leiden: E. J. Brill,
1963).

Thus Lindbeck's re-interpretation of doctrines as rules comes danger-ously close to the work of revisionists. Theology is no longer flat here, but is transformed into a depth hermeneutics. I shall argue that Lindbeck, by not paying attention to the ontology presupposed and intended by doctrines, has failed in his work of thick description and in his phenomenology of the practice of doctrine. John Milbank's criticism of Lindbeck is very much to the point. His main contention is that Lindbeck does not correctly perceive the dynamics of narrative interpretation. Lindbeck works with a dualism between the narratives of the given religion and the culture of the agents. What must happen is that such narratives would take over the cultural fac-tors and reinterpret them.[127] The skills nourished in a religion, the practices of worship, its stories and prayers, the practical and what Milbank calls the 'syntagmatic' element is very much able to infinitely organise the cultural data.[128] *Religion is able to organise experience and absorb the world be-cause the integrity of the syntagmatic level is taken to be very much intact.* But Milbank is a subtler hermeneutical analyst than that. He understands that every syntagmatic deployment, every narrative performance presup-poses a paradigmatic imagination of a total context.[129] Milbank, with one stroke, has dismissed the entire notion of a naked practice, an un-interpreted performance. This is a very Kantian move. Intuitions without concepts are blind, argues Kant. In respect of its nature it is not Kantian at all, since for Kant the concepts, or pure forms are universally mediated, while for Mil-bank the paradigmatic moment is imposed by the imagination. It is rhetori-cally established.[130] Thus the dialectic of narrative always presupposes a propositional, cognitive moment, where an ontological setting is imagined, which would make any performance meaningful. Milbank thus refuses the Lindbeckian understanding of doctrines as regulators of practice.[131] Instead doctrine provides the paradigmatic or synchronic setting for the syntag-matic practice. This leads Milbank to speak about the Idea which grows out of the narrative and sometimes returns to it covertly.[132] The doctrine of the incarnation, for example, is not to be taken as a rule – governing, for exam-ple, our relations to one another and to Jesus – but as a genuine proposi-tional imagination of an ontological context. For Milbank this is a radically inventive moment, a point to which I shall return later, but his understand-ing of practice is certainly 'thicker' in this sense than Lindbeck's.

---

[127] Lindbeck, *Doctrine,* p. 84.

[128] Milbank, *Theology and Social Theory,* p. 386.

[129] Milbank, *Theology and Social Theory,* p. 383.

[130] He speaks about doctrine's 'inventive moment.' (Milbank, *Theology and Social Theory,* p. 384.)

[131] Milbank, *Theology and Social Theory,* p. 385.

[132] Milbank, *Theology and Social Theory,* p. 384.

One may further distinguish between a *movement*, an *action* and a *practice*. A movement is a physical occurrence which takes place, as for example my moving the left arm. An action, on the other hand, is distinguished from a simple movement by the intention it is enacting. The same act of moving the arm may be taken as a simple physical move as well as the action of waving to someone, saluting, lifting something and so on. What is important is that the action of doing something presupposes the intention behind it. Indeed in an inter-subjective context it may also presuppose the intention that my physical act be taken as an action, that it may count as a salute, as a wave and so on. A practice, on the other hand, presupposes both the physical aspect, as well as the intentional aspect, but it also assumes a larger setting. A practice includes an understanding of goals, of means, of rights and wrongs. Practices are complex actions which cannot be explained by mere reference to their physical actions, or to their intentional aspect.[133] For example, within the practice of architecture one needs to go beyond the description of the mechanical movement of the arm moving bricks and placing them on top of one another, but also beyond the intention of 'laying' bricks, or building a wall and so on. The practice of architecture also presupposes the larger ontological setting of goals, rules, propositional accounts of building methods and principles.[134] In the absence of reference to such goals, or to the values that accompany them, I submit, any description of the rest of the goings-on will not amount to a thick description of the phenomenon. Any intellectual discourse that contributes to our being in the city, that is, which is more than simply an individual and private rumination, must take into account a series of so-called extra-textual and even extra-linguistic factors, as Rowan Williams points out:

> What is here being affirmed against the general idiom of postmodernity is that what human beings do is characterised by the kind of difficulty that arises when the effects of action or decision are open to the judgement and interpretation not only of other finite agents as individuals or clusters of individuals, but what is discerned as the order or structure of a reality not determined by anyone's decision. To 'produce' or to engage in work that issues in the changing of the environment, material or conceptual or imaginative, is to accept conventions or standards, communicative and evaluative conventions, outside the power of the producing agent, if what is produced is to 'count' as a recognizable production, an entity capable

---

[133] Illustrative here is MacIntyre's discussion of behaviour, intention and setting (*After Virtue*, pp. 175, 206-208.)

[134] Amongst other things it also presupposes propositional attitudes about what is physically possible, or available materials and building techniques, philosophical notions of private and public space, of the environment and of the nature of the built environment.

of being described and discussed with reference to more than the producer's will in itself.[135]

Perhaps now one may better understand what Milbank argues: he aims to give a thick description[136] of what is actually going on in the interpretation of the Christian stories. Doctrines supply the ontological setting within which such narratives can be constituted as a practice. If our analogy is correct, in the absence of such ontology, the narratives of one religion could not be distinguished from the narratives of another. All such religious narratives would remain unintelligible moves made by intelligible people. Stuart Brown also argues that what one needs is a bare minimum of assertions about states of affairs. There must be at least one claim which can only be of a matter of fact character, namely the claim that God exists.[137] One may wonder what status would such a doctrine have for Lindbeck?

I hope we have done away with the naïve supposition that one could speak of practice without theory. A practical performance which is not accompanied by a propositional explanation is meaningless, or at least subject to varied and contradictory interpretations.

This argument also reflects on Lindbeck's attempt to tie the ontological truth of doctrines to their intra-systematic coherence with some practice. What practice, I asked, is the appropriate context for such decisions? If practice itself is blind without ontology, one needs an ontology in order to test the truth of doctrines. What Lindbeck, Tanner and Lash seem to believe is that practice can provide us with access to God, either through its being adequate to the Ultimate Being, or to God and so on. Marshall, on the other hand, argues that successful performance depends on holding true certain true propositions. Authentic performance is dependant on correct identification and correct identification depends on holding certain true beliefs:

> To have knowledge of Jesus is to have a certain relation to him, but many other relations to Jesus depend on having knowledge of him, and in that sense have a cognitive component: loving, worshipping, following, and so forth.[138]

As the previous discussion of reference pointed out, it is perhaps wrong to dissociate strongly between a theory of reference which makes it dependant

---

[135] Rowan Williams, 'Between politics and metaphysics: reflections in the wake of Gillian Rose', *Modern Theology*, 11 (1995), 3-22, p. 8.

[136] See Gilbert Ryle's notion of thick description, also taken over by Geertz, in 'Thinking and Reflecting and The Thinking of Thoughts' in Gilbert Ryle, *Collected Papers,* Volume 2, Collected Essays, 1929-1968, (London: Hutchinson, 1971). Also of interest here is N. Wolterstorff's notion of 'count-generation' (*Divine Discourse*, 45, 54, 76-94).

[137] Stuart Brown, *Do Religious Claims Make Sense?*, (London: SCM, 1969), p. 152.

[138] Marshall, *Trinity*, p. 246.

on right description and one where description is not important. What emerged out of our discussion is that both description is necessary for right identification, but that description itself may be modified in the course of interaction with the object. The theory of reference which underlies narrative theology may be called a *performance-related reference*. Namely, if our theological statements are combined with authentic performance of those dispositions most central to the Christian forms of life, and provided that the vocabulary of Christianity is adequate to the Ultimate reality which is God, then theological statements may be said to refer. Marshall's objection to this is that having a right practical relationship to Jesus, or performing successfully depends on holding certain true beliefs. We grant that Marshall is correct only if he does not require that all description must be correct in order for reference to be successful. For example, I may be referring to Jesus while believing that he was risen on the fourth day. Therefore he should clarify his account so that only certain beliefs, necessary for the right identification of Jesus, must be held (discriminatory beliefs). One such central belief is the belief that he was resurrected. The belief that he was resurrected on the third or fourth day may be of little consequence for the purposes of identification. Having clarified this, what Marshall contributes to my larger argument is that there is a cognitive aspect to all performative actions. Lindbeck and Tanner, then, are wrong to drive so sharp a wedge between regulative and cognitive, performative and propositional. In fact it is the performative which depends on the propositional.

James McClendon makes the same point when discussing confession and other such speech acts. The conditions for the felicity of speech acts include a representative dimension, namely that the 'speaker describes or represents the relevant states of affairs with sufficient exactness to make it possible for him to take up that stance and display it.'[139] The pitfalls associated with taking the context of behaviour to be integral to the truth of the theological statement can be avoided if one simply takes the context of behaviour to bear on the meaning of the theological statement as a speech act. This is Hunsinger's position. McClendon may be too optimistic to think that Lindbeck can also be read in this 'soft' way. He argues that Lindbeck may be read to say not that doctrines have no cognitive aspect, but that such content cannot be meaningfully separated from the network of practices, rules and meanings that constitute Christian teaching.[140] Doctrines are not simply rules, then. Narrative theology may be classified in terms of its understanding of doctrines: Lindbeck and Tanner argue prescriptively that doctrines are rules alone, subservient to practice, with no cognitive content[141].

---

[139] McClendon and Smith, *Understanding Religious Convictions*, p. 66.

[140] McClendon, *Doctrine*, p. 31.

[141] We have noted Lindbeck's confusion here: no cognitive value yet making ontological truth claims through the first order speech.

Frei, on the contrary, argues that doctrines may be taken as both descriptive and regulative, but one must not provide a theory for distinguishing between the two. McClendon, on the other hand, provides such a super-rule by his use of speech act theory: doctrines are both regulative as well as cognitive.

Perhaps one of the more obvious difficulties of Lindbeck's model is its philosophical inclination, to the detriment of paying attention to specific Christian requirements. Such an inclination prompted him to transform his theological methodology into a prescriptive system, in sharp contrast to Frei and Barth. On the other hand, his omission of the believer's intention behind the articulation and employment of doctrines inflicts a grave prejudice to any thick description.[142] Ironically, failure to observe the believer's intentions does not mesh with a philosophical understanding of rule. Baker and Hacker in their discussion of Wittgenstein have distilled a number of principles according to which rules function. Any rule must be expressed; it must be possible to follow or to violate a rule; rules are creatures of the will[143] (namely they are not naturally given); rules provide standards for correctness and guides to action; finally, rules must be more or less transparent to participants in a rule-governed activity.[144] It is this final condition which is not fulfilled on a material level. Christians themselves have historically taken doctrines to have a cognitive value, instead of a regulative one. In order to save coherence, Lindbeck's project must turn to a reinterpretation of the history of theological doctrine, which in turn violates the principle of the plain sense readings.

Another area where the philosophical preference has taken the place of careful description of the positivity of Christian doctrine has been in the area of knowledge of God. A philosophical agnosticism dominates the vision of how and whether God could be known. Yet neither Wittgenstein, nor Lindbeck pay sufficient attention to the theological belief in the knowability of God through Christ. It is this insight too which transformed the whole of Barth's project. What then are we to make of statements such as 'God is not an object for knowledge' when in fact there is a strong Christian sense in which he is precisely so in the person of Christ? Furthermore, the truth of our theological statements about this Christ and his God are not made true or false by our right performance, but by God's action and being.

Finally, the same reading of the Christian religion in philosophical terms is evident in Lindbeck's understanding of having a religion as in learning a certain language. To be a Christian, in this theology, is to have learned the

---

[142] Cf. MacIntyre, *After Virtue*, p. 206.

[143] Cf. also Hütter's point that Lindbeck does not understand that agents take active part in the making, sustaining, and preservation of tradition (p. 47.) Instead, he speaks about a *poietic pathos*.

[144] Baker and Haker, *Wittgenstein: Rules, Grammar, Necessity*, pp. 62-63.

language of the Christian stories, the liturgy, the right practices which are those practised by the well-versed in the given religion. Yet, if one wanted to understand what is involved in being a Christian from the point of view of those very narratives, one would arrive at a very different picture. For to be a Christian is not a matter of performance, but precisely of ontology: of some state of affairs which obtains between God and the human person. Here to be a Christian, to be religious in this sense, is not to learn a specific language, which amounts to Kierkegaard's 'second-hand faith.'[145] One may be very successful in learning the language of Christianity, and indeed of any other religion, without being a true Christian. One may mimic the signs of Christianity, yet not be a Christian. From the point of view of the Christian narratives, being a Christian does not speak so much about the person who becomes, but about the God who saves. Lindbeck's theology exhibits a failure to come to terms with specific material insights of the Christian gospel.

Conclusions

We may now pause and review the argument so far. It has not been a simple one. It tended to take off towards politics, ethics, sociology, literary theory, even jurisprudence. At best this centrifugal drive reveals the centrality of the subject to the larger field of the human sciences; at worst it is a proof of the undecidability of modern authority. Which discourse occupies the privileged position of the arbiter of truth? This inter-textuality has been both the pathos of this book, as well as one of its arguments. The different, perhaps sometimes conflicting lines of inquiry have one common thread running through each: the reification of the setting of knowledge, or the scheme which conditions it.

Both modern and post-modern approaches develop such a dualism. Only for modernity the scheme becomes universal through the Scotist indistinctiveness of Being. Even God conforms to it. The benefit is the inauguration of a culture of univocal language and rational mastery of the world. Which, of course, was nothing but an illusion. But the damage had already been done: something interposes itself between world and humanity, or God and humankind. Soon most of the intellectual resources of humanity are spent investigating this mysterious entity, which some call mind. But whether in modernity, or in the present age, the scheme-generating mind still regulates contingency.

If we may be permitted another escapade into foreign territories, the illustration of urban architecture may help. Eric Alliez traces the development of the city to the ultimately Scotist erection of rational Being which triggered a shift from a rural mode of human community to an urban one.

---

[145] Thiselton, 'Corporate memory', p. 60.

Cities become dominated by a rational order, stretched across a linear and de-sacralized time. Post-modern cities, on the other hand, have abandoned the rational efficiency of modern planning and are driving towards ever greater fragmentation. Yet crucially *this very fragmentation remains representable*. One may still cast one's gaze upon it, describe it, catalogue it. For all the talk about incommensurability and difference, the schemes and the unique individuals still remain transparent. Realism recedes from God, to the world, to mind, to language, to practices and so on. But what everyone takes for granted is our ability to know all these things, to represent them. And the reason given is authentically Vichian: they are made. Should we then not entertain the following question: Are not post-modern schemes just as constricting as their modern versions, only on a smaller scale? Do they not conceal the multitude of practices, choices, moves, significations, which cannot be accounted for by the scheme itself? Or, to quote Michel de Certeau, do we not transform 'the city's complexity into readability' and freeze 'its opaque mobility into a crystal-clear text[?] Can the vast texturology beneath our gaze be anything but a representation? An optical artefact?'[146] This has been my argument all along: to represent the scheme is to reify it. It is to entertain the dubious illusion that it can be represented independently of the actions of agents, of the ongoing activity of sustaining and indeed changing it, and also independently of ascertaining its truth. To put it more shortly, it is to separate its meaning from its truth.

Postmodern theology reifies the scheme. Postliberal theology reifies tradition, community, the practices which make up the first-order vocabulary of religion.[147] Their meaning is available prior to any legitimation of their truth. The un-doing of the scheme-content dualism means that theology and knowledge in general can proceed directly in world-involving terms, to echo Davidson. Furthermore, propositional talk about the world is the necessary condition for the meaningfulness of our practices. The assumption that practices are meaningful in and of themselves is mistaken. Theologically speaking there can be no strict separation between first and second order language. This means that ontology returns in the discourse of theology, whatever the differences in re-appropriation.[148]

What remains of the fear voiced by Levinas and others that ontology is necessarily violent? Such is the entrenched character of this assumption that Auerbach's only alternative to the destruction of identity was the relegation of spirit to the second-order reaction of the disciples. Following the placing

---

[146] Graham Ward, ed., *The Certeau Reader*, (Oxford: Blackwell, 2000), p. 102.

[147] Cf. Rusty Reno's verdict that Radical Orthodoxy has an allergy to the particular: 'The Radical Orthodoxy Project', *First Things*, 100 (2000), 37-44.

[148] Sensing that disaffecting ontology may produce irreparable damage to the narratives themselves, Hauerwas re-asserts the necessity of a practically and narratively mediated ontology ('Why the truth demands truthfulness?', p. 144).

of humankind and God along the same spectrum of Being, one's identity could only be conceived in a confrontational manner. Human freedom could only come at the expense of God's omnipotence, or through God's *kenosis*. Spirit becomes nothing but the metaphorical and allegorical expression of basic human attributes. Milbank himself is an accomplice to this upheaval by his conception of spirit as performance, completely submerged in textuality. An empty secular realism, developed from Dante's figural tapestry into Virginia Woolf's realism becomes the prime means for the description of human identity. However, what Auerbach and Milbank fail to discover is a non-violent relation between body and spirit in the resurrected Jesus[149], engendering the possibility of a peaceful ontology whose connection to textuality heeds to more than aesthetic and rhetorical requirements. Auerbach understands the preservation of identity through the banishing of transcendence and ontology, while Milbank defends difference by a rhetorically mediated ontology of original peace and plenitude. The problem attaching to Milbank's arbitrary ontology is double: it fails to distinguish a third alternative beyond foundationalism and aesthetic rhetoric, which the previous chapter outlined as a good-reasons approach to justification. Secondly, it conceals a further violence, precisely where it effaces dialogue and conversation and replaces them with the arbitrary imposition of a rhetorical stance. Spirit is connected to matter in a purely rhetorical fashion in Milbank. Both Auerbach and Milbank fail to question the modern locus of identity: the inter-textual world of performance, literature, music, art which may be described as peremptory, mythic, oniric. As Dawson writes, they both fail to envisage the possibility of a transformation of personal identity through engagement with a real, ontologically transforming world of divine activity.[150]

I have attempted to recover the possibility of ontology, yet in a different, non-foundational key. To discover facts about the world does not mean to find an anchor for the certainty of knowledge. That particular metaphysical anxiety has already been aleviated. But through the very disappearance of such intermediaries the objects of knowledge can once again assume a prominent place and guide our inquiry. Significantly Davidson, Dworkin and MacIntyre speak in terms of allowing the subject matter itself to dictate reasons.[151] Had the idea of an intermediary language not been dispensed with, we might have said this is a realist account of knowledge. But, as Rorty says, 'we no longer have dialectical room to state an issue concerning "how language hooks unto the world" between the "realist" and the "ideal-

---

[149] Cf. chapter 2 above.

[150] Dawson sees this transformative account of identity to be represented in Origen's work. pp. 194-206.

[151] Cf. Ronald Dworkin, 'Objectivity and truth: you'd better believe it,' *Philosophy and Public Affairs*, 25/2 (1996).

ist."'[152] The surprising result is that holism does not invite relativism, but precisely a good reasons approach and the recovery of the identity of the objects themselves. Davidson's principle of charity, Dworkin's determination to 'make the text the best it can be'[153] and MacIntyre's notion of the learning of a second first language all strike in a common direction.

---

[152] Rorty, *Philosophy and the Mirror of Nature*, p. 265.
[153] Dworkin, *Law's Empire*, p. 53.

Chapter Six

Christology

We have been looking at various aspects of the postliberal stance on theological knowledge. The story of narrative theology has not been completely straightforward, as tensions within the movement were brought to light. The reasons for disagreement were various, but should not overshadow the accomplishments of postliberalism. Such accomplishments range from the narrative return to the canonical texts of Scripture, to a realisation of the inter-penetration between rationality and life-world, to a recognition of the place of the Church in legitimising belief and interpreting Scripture. Were one to name a single success of postliberal theology, which would rank chiefly among all the others, one would probably be inclined to name its concern for particularity. In rejecting the dogmas of modernism and of liberalism, as well as in its healthy reaction to conservatism,[1] postliberalism poses a serious challenge to all attempts to bring the story of the Gospel and the positivity of the Christian religion under the domination of some universally-available totalising discourse.

The Christian convictions about the person of Jesus Christ form an interesting test case for the success of the postliberal defence of particularity. It is fitting that the argument should close with a look at postliberal interpretations of Christ, given the intuition that prompted this study. The main question that has been guiding it has been whether it is possible to reconcile the twin emphases of a narrative theology: on the one hand, a determination to allow all reality (culture, history, science) to be read Scripturally, that is the belief in the world-absorption power of the Scriptures; on the other hand a philosophically-derived skepticism with regard to knowledge and language. To put it simply: how can one read reality Scripturally and theologically, if the vision of God and Scripture is frustrated by the perceived deficiencies of knowledge? The investigation has brought us to this point, following various engagements with postliberal hermeneutics, ontology, rhetoric and theological method. The final question that remains to be asked is this: can the narratively rendered Christ still authoritatively address a postliberal community?

---

[1] I also have in mind a less healthy reaction, chiefly its rejection of the possibility of propositional knowledge of God, as opposed to a rejection of a propositional theory of truth. See Stephen Williams, 'Lindbeck's regulative Christology', *Modern Theology* 4 (1988), 172-184, p. 181.

Given the concern for Scriptural absorption it is not surprising that postliberal theologians also have a special interest in Christology. Hans Frei has in fact blurred the line between hermeneutics and Christology by seeing the former as a direct consequence of the latter. Bruce Marshall has contributed a very concise book on the respective Christologies of Barth, Rahner and Aquinas. Ronald Thiemann has also written on the narrative description of the identity of Jesus Christ. Among the other narrative theologians we have considered, James McClendon has naturally included a chapter on 'Narrative Christology' in his systematic magnum opus; Lindbeck's short but decisively influential section on the grammatical reinterpretation of Chalcedon, Kathryn Tanner's lectures on Jesus, Humanity and God; not least, Milbank brings Christ into his radical orthodoxy readings, as well as Loughlin, Ken Surin and indeed others. Clearly then, the choice for this doctrine as a test case is a little more than arbitrary. It is demanded by the frequent engagement with Jesus' identity that takes place in postliberal circles.

Christology in Conflict: Rival Christological Methods

Bruce Marshall's concise book, *Christology in Conflict*[2] is a study of the question 'which theoretical method best describes Jesus' identity?' The respective Christologies of Rahner and Barth are taken as examples of two rival ways of doing Christology. The theological differences between the two theologians are a common place, but it is in their shared assumptions about the importance of the particularity of Jesus Christ and in their desire to preserve this particularity that they generate an interesting debate. Marshall concludes that among the two, it is Barth who is best able to retain the particularity of the Saviour, due to his methodological choices. What transpires here is *the postliberal conviction that it is only in a narrative description that particular identity can be made accessible.* Ontological descriptions are not able to do justice to the particular. Identity cannot be conveyed by the use of metaphysical categories, but only rhetorically, by telling someone's story, since it is only in the story the un-substitutable identity is presented.

Marshall points out that Rahner fails according to his own criteria, since both Rahner and Barth share a commitment to Jesus' particularity. However, the difference is that Rahner wants to make that particularity accessi-

---

[2] Bruce Marshall, *Christology in Conflict: The Identity of a Saviour in Rahner and Barth*, (Oxford: Blackwell, 1987). For a critical discussion, see James Buckley, 'Adjudicating conflicting Christologies', *Philosophy and Theology*, 6 (1991), 117-135.

ble in terms of the universal meaningfulness of the concept of an 'absolute saviour'[3]. Marshall summarises Rahner's argument:

1. The absolute saviour is *heilsbedeutsam*[4] (method)
2. Jesus Christ is the absolute saviour (presupposition)
3. Jesus Christ is *heilsbedeutsam* (goal).[5]

For Rahner, essential to the intelligibility of the Gospel is that the redeeming significance ascribed to Jesus (in the Scriptures and the Christian convictions) be displayed in a transcendental argument which translates it in universal concepts. However, for Marshall, to read Christ's particularity in terms of a universal language of 'absolute saviour' is only to affirm a vague or positive individuality rather than a particular one.[6] The result is that Rahner's argument cannot fulfil these requirements without sacrificing the particularity of Jesus that he also emphasises. This boils down to the fact that Jesus Christ conceived as *heilsbedeutsam* can only be taken as a vague individual, where the specific features which are otherwise central for his identity would not matter. What Marshall and many postliberals object to is the Kantian anxiety that unless the Christian concepts and convictions are translated into universal categories of reason, they are meaningless and ineffective. Kant argues:

> In the appearance of the God-man, it is not that in him which strikes the senses and can be known through experience, but rather the archetype, lying in our reason, that we attribute to him (since, so far as his example can be known, he is found to conform thereto), which is really the object of saving faith.[7]

Marshall will be arguing in *Trinity and Truth* that the whole strategy of rendering Christian meanings in terms of external ones betrays their essence. By then he will have worked out his Davidsonian account of how truth relates to meaning, which will allow him to safeguard the positivity of Christian meanings.

One of Rahner's mistakes is to have defined what is 'meaningful for salvation' before actually engaging with Jesus Christ. He thus provides us with a counter-example to Frei's strategy of the ascription of meaning. For Frei, it is the particular person of Jesus Christ that gives meaning to the concepts ascribed to him. Titles such as 'Son of Man', or 'Son of God', are

---

[3] Marshall, *Christology*, p. 33-42.
[4] Marshall's German term for 'meaningful for salvation'.
[5] Marshall, *Christology*, p. 32.
[6] Marshall, *Christology*, p. 45.
[7] Immanuel Kant, *Religion Within the Limits of Reason Alone*, translated by T. Greene and H. Hudson, (New York, 1960), p. 110; see discussion in Marshall, *Christology*, p. 104.

being 'baptised' into the particular identity of Jesus Christ. For Rahner, on the other hand, the basis on which he will thus proceed is an independently acquired definition of what an absolute saviour is, what redemption means. Hence, concludes Marshall,

> It seems as though there is no coherent way to honour both (1) the con-
> viction that only Jesus Christ as a particular person can be the unique re-
> deemer; and (2) the methodological assumption that the ideas of redemp-
> tion and a redeemer are only credible, meaningful and intelligible for us
> as, or on the basis of, general criteria or patterns.[8]

It must be admitted that one advantage of Rahner's collage of the particularity of Jesus the Saviour and a descriptive metaphysics, or rather a transcendental ontology, is that it at least attempts to place the answer that Jesus is within a context of human questions. The danger run by the first way, exemplified by Barth, among others, is that Jesus provides an answer to a question no one may ask.[9] Marshall unnecessarily assumes that the marriage between narrative and ontology is despotic, a case of ontology completely taking over particularity. The argument is that where there is a translation of the particularity of Jesus in terms of universal concepts, particularity is effaced by ontology.

Rahner's failure leads Marshall to Barth, in the search for a 'different strategy or method of answering the question "how can Jesus Christ be *heilsbedeutsam*?", and thus a different strategy for defining "that which is significant for salvation" in a meaningful and intelligible way.'[10] Barth suffers from no Kantian anxiety. In fact he gives heed to Kierkegaard in affirming the positivity of Christian revelation. Theology is for him a purely intra-textual matter. Barth is the theological counterpart of one who, like Burke, would say: there are no facts, nor rationality apart from the acts and practices of people. Barth's is the position of the lawmaker who moves strictly within the boundaries set by precedent and tradition.[11] Hence theological legitimation is always intra-textual. Theological faithfulness is then for Barth a matter of following the particular Scriptural descriptions. In terms of Christology and Marshall's conclusions about Rahner,

> the significance for salvation of any concept or explanation of what Jesus
> Christ is (such as 'the absolute saviour') depends upon its predication of
> and reference to this particular subject. The criterion for that which is

---

[8] Marshall, Christology, p. 105.

[9] Marshall, *Christology*, p. 146.

[10] Marshall, *Christology*, p. 106.

[11] We shall return to the connection between law, rhetoric, rationality and personal identity.

heilsbedeutsam is therefore its conformity and applicability to the particular life of Jesus Christ.[12]

I want to draw attention to a specifically postliberal preference, or assumption. That is the belief, never quite explicitly defended, that there is a solid link between narratives and the presentation of particularity, such that a philosophical discourse made up of universal concepts is not able to present that which instead flourishes in a narrative. There is indeed a growing consensus that the identity of a human person is the story of his life[13], but the link between particularity and narrativity still has to be legitimised.

It might be argued that Barth's supposed preference for intra-textuality is not a philosophically-derived decision, but a consequence of the close reading of the narratives themselves. The need to remain inside these narratives in order to best understand them, derives from a specific belief in the lack of a 'single universal subjective condition'. In other words, there is no common language between God and the world, so that what Christians say about God must first be translated in language universally intelligible. Barth believes that there is no direct fit between the human subjective aspirations, which strive to be persuasive to anyone who understands them, and a unique redeemer.[14] Barth is in fact adamant that revelation is its own ground and to proceed otherwise would be to *de facto* relinquish its priority. Stanley Hauerwas argues along the same lines for his preference for intra-textuality. It is not that Scripture does not make statements about reality and the world which, since being about an object common to both believer and unbeliever, should be understood in universal vocabulary. But such statements are never dissociated from a view of the world and reality as tainted by sin[15] and thus unable to be grasped without a re-positioning of the self vis-à-vis God:

> That the Gospels have such a [reality intending] character or that they involve 'foundational metaphysics beliefs,' I have never sought to deny or avoid. Rather, my concern has been to insist, along the lines suggested by Wesley, that the kind of truth entailed by the Gospels, the kind of demands placed on reality, cannot be separated from the way the story of God we claim as revealed in Jesus' life, death, and resurrection forces a re-positioning of the self vis-à-vis reality.[16]

As I have argued in a prior chapter, this theological conviction about the need for salvation in order to understand the claims of the Gospel is to be dissociated from Lindbeck's philosophically informed belief in the incom-

---

[12] Marshall, *Christology*, p. 118.

[13] See for example MacIntyre, *After Virtue*, pp. 204-225.

[14] Marshall, *Christology*, p. 148.

[15] Hauerwas, 'Why the Truth Demands Truthfulness', p. 143.

[16] Hauerwas, 'Why the Truth Demands Truthfulness', p. 142.

mensurability of schemes. What I have also argued, and will return to later, is that the difference this re-positioning makes is not as radical as Hauerwas and others would like to believe. Rather, it involves a progress towards a deeper meaning, commensurable to the intelligibility discovered before and 'outside' the community, as it were, but semantically deeper, improved, or as Telford Work would call it, 'intensified.' This will be of vital importance for the rationality of our textually discovered beliefs and for their connection to ontology.

It must be asked, however, whether this rejection of a common ground between insiders and outsiders does not make Jesus' message incomprehensible to the larger humanity? There is an undeniable loss involved in the choice for intra-textuality, yet Barth seems to think that it is preferable to that which the second way involves.[17]

Barth's intra-textuality does not prevent him from making mistakes, in Marshall's perception. Although for Barth the particularity of Jesus is given by an exegesis of the stories the Gospels tell about him, he also proceeds to give a description of the reality implied in such gospel accounts. Admittedly this starts from a description of what it means to say that Jesus' history is God's own. Barth then moves from a textual exegesis to an ontological description of what is involved in those Scriptural claims. It is not the claim that only by recognising God as the subject of Jesus' history that seems suspicious to narrative theologians such as Marshall. Indeed, the same claim has been made by McClendon, among others: 'Jesus is not identified merely as one of God's children (itself a glorious destiny) but is re-identified, resurrected, as the *unique sharer of God's own identity: for us, by his resurrection, the whole story of Jesus is God's own story.*'[18] The problem, according to Marshall, is that 'Barth's account of the conviction that God is the ultimate subject of Jesus' history or particular identity ... relies heavily upon the explicative and clarifying force of an ontological description.'[19] Marshall is concerned that an ontological level of identification takes off from the narrative and becomes independent from it, when it is only supposed to elaborate the meaning of the text.

There is thus an incoherence in the first way itself, to the extent that one is tempted to proceed from a description of textual meaning to an independent and genetically-causal account of reality. Such an ontological description is one which is (a) supposed to be true, in the sense that it obtains in reality and (b) uses concepts which can be applied although perhaps not in a univocal sense, to realities other than the one described.[20] Marshall does not deny the possibility of such ontological description, then, but is

---

[17] Marshall, *Christology*, pp. 147-9.

[18] McClendon, *Doctrine*, p. 148.

[19] Marshall, *Christology*, p. 175.

[20] Marshall, *Christology*, p. 193, n. 21.

not convinced of the propriety of the amount of work which it supposedly does for Barth. In response, he turns to Aquinas whose ontology is grammatical rather than descriptively metaphysical.

For Aquinas, the function of ontological description is to 'save' the *modus loquendi* of Scripture, to render an account of reality governed by the way in which Scripture speaks about Jesus Christ.[21] What governs theology, as in Barth, is the scriptural speech-mode. Marshall's contention, however, is that Barth is much more realist than Thomas, the latter being more aware of the intricate relation between language and reality. He points to a distinction in St. Thomas between the definition of truth and the criterion of truth[22]. Although truth for Aquinas is correspondence to reality, the criterion for truth is not the assessment of claims at the tribunal of reality, given by independent ontological descriptions, but their relative conformity to the *modus loquendi* of Scripture.[23] Ontological description cannot give an account of the union between Jesus' history and God's, because of the deficiency of human language about God. So, for example, both scriptural statements and ontological descriptions of the concept of *homoousion*, to which we shall return, are true if they correspond to reality. But the criterion of the correspondence is not given by an ontological description, but by conformity to Scripture's *modus loquendi*. In other words, Marshall argues that Barth should have distinguished 'saving the modus loquendi of Scripture from giving a description of reality.'[24] The absence of such a distinction (between grammar and ontological description) makes him oblivious to the danger that such a description may assert itself over the intra-textual task.

This is a subtle and dense argument. Credit should be given to Marshall for his brilliant receptivity to the nuances of the problem and their implications. But I want to express one reservation. One wonders whether Marshall can seriously argue that one can read intra-textually without any ontology. Can grammar be distinguished so sharply from ontology? Secondly, Marshall has not properly established why precisely must Barth's ontological description be considered detrimental to the grammar of the *modus loquendi*. His whole argument pivots on the dualism between narrative, which is best suited to render particularity through grammatology and ontological description, which for some reason scatters the unique into universality. I grant that Barth should distinguish his descriptive metaphysics from the clarification of the texts, but that is not to say that he is to dispense with it altogether.

---

[21] Marshall, *Christology*, p. 179.

[22] Marshall, *Christology*, p. 180.

[23] Marshall, *Christology*, p. 180. Also see Marshall's earlier article, 'Aquinas as postliberal theologian', esp. pp. 370ff.

[24] Marshall, *Christology*, p. 198, n. 58.

A further problem arises when one discriminates between those who try to understand the meaning of Jesus as Saviour intra-textually from those who do it extra-textually. The coherence of such a procedure depends on the ability to sustain the diremption between inside and outside in a very strict way, which is questionable. One is reminded at this point of Rowan Williams's reservations about the spatial metaphors in postliberal theology, or about Stanley Hauerwas' suggestion that the border between the world and the church runs through the middle of each of us.[25]

Hans Frei's Narrative Rendering of Identity

The above debate serves as a good introduction to the issues most central to a narrative Christology. This is concerned with finding the most appropriate discourse which would display Jesus' and God's identity and preserve their particularity. It understands universal discourses, by which we mean those discourses which make use of universal categories, such as metaphysics and philosophy, to pose a threat to particularity. The relationship between internal and external in Christian description has already been intimated in a discussion of Frei's *Types of Christian Theology*. It became apparent that in contrast with other postliberal thinkers, most notably Lindbeck and Tanner, Frei follows Barth and Schleiermacher in allowing the correlation between external and internal. Such correlation is not according to any rule that would give priority to either one of these poles, but in an *ad hoc* fashion.

What Frei does in the *Types* is apparently different from his earlier comments on theory. Both in his *Eclipse of Biblical Narrative* and in *The Identity of Jesus Christ*, Frei's position is very close to the view Marshall is expounding. He steers clear of any universal categories and there is no talk of even correlating them in an *ad hoc* fashion with particular Christian meanings. Where Marshall believes that one should start from the intra-textual identification of Jesus and not with prior elucidations of the meaning of certain concepts which would then be applied to Jesus, Frei offers that we start not from Jesus' presence, but from his identity. What Frei means by presence is the way in which the person of Christ may be understood to be related to contemporary human beings. It is in fact a short-hand term for any prior philosophical construction of what Jesus might mean, one which would draw on various factors, such as, in the case of Rahner, a transcendental method of deduction. Christ's presence is then the image of Christ in human understanding, arrived at independently of careful engagement with the Christian texts which, as we shall see alone represent his identity. Theologians who start with presence, as we have seen Marshall argue, suffer from the anxiety of making Christian meanings correlatable with trans-Christian categories or independent descriptions of reality. Pan-

---

[25] Unpublished Firth Lectures, Nottingham, July 2002.

nenberg, for example, attempts to place Jesus in a pre-existing framework of meaning, which is the context apocalyptic expectations, while Rahner understands Jesus in terms of what is meaningful for salvation. He writes:

> The governing conviction of this essay is that in Jesus Christ identity and presence are so completely one that they are given to us together. We cannot know *who* he is without having him present. But I also want to suggest that if we begin with the often nagging and worrisome questions of *how* Christ is present to us and *how* we can believe in his presence, we shall get nowhere at all. It is far more important and fruitful to ask first, *Who* is Jesus Christ?[26]

Frei is here rehearsing a position that is now closely identified with postliberal theology: that there must be a strong distinction between questions of what one believes and how one comes to believe. It has been unawareness of such a distinction that has, in Marshall's opinion, made Rahner commit to unnecessary and detrimental arguments. The desire to make Christ intelligible to the present generation and to external listeners and discourses is indeed commendable, argues Frei. But one must not confuse it, nor give it priority over the task of elucidating Christian meanings. The latter project is a purely descriptive matter, claiming no neutral discourse which accesses reality and which can without pain of distortion be translated into external talk. Apologetics transforms into an *ad hoc* affair in postliberalism and Dogmatics alone, as opposed to fundamental theology, is given the task of Christian re-description. To ask first how can Christ be present is to engage in a conversation which lacks the meaning of Christ and his identity. Such meaning will be supplied by providing either an independent metaphysic, or a transcendental argument about an Absolute Saviour, or a Kantian reduction to what is given in reason or experience. Following such assignments of meaning, the final move from presence (thus established) to identity, cannot in any way shape or fashion lead to the particular being of Jesus Christ, that Christians adore.

The sense of a sharp distinction between insiders and outsiders is intensified when Frei speaks about 'the gulf between believer and nonbeliever.'[27] In Frei and in postliberalism this translates into the doctrine of incommensurability according to which meanings are entirely given intra-textually. That is, a person must first become part of a social community, or, as with Hauerwas, a person must first become a disciple, in order to understand Christian meanings. Christologically this means that there are no shared subjective dispositions which would allow a common ground between believer and non-believer.

---

[26] Frei, *The Identity*, p. 4.

[27] Frei, *The Identity*, p. 33.

Frei speaks with some frustration about those anxious to have it both ways: hold on to the particularity of the Gospel as well as make that Gospel translatable in universal language. He has in mind

> those Christian theologians who have adopted this general theory for regional hermeneutical application to the New Testament. They have been motivated by a desire on the one hand to claim the unsurpassability of the New Testament narratives' ascriptive reference to Jesus, so that they do not become exoteric or carnal shadows, in principle surpassable by a later and fuller spiritual 'reference' or 'disclosure', but on the other they deny that this unsurpassability involves the invidious distinction between insiders and outsiders to the truth. So they try to maintain that Jesus is the irreducible ascriptive subject of the New Testament narratives, while at the same time they make general religious experience (or something like it) the referent of these stories.[28]

Although especially with biblical scholars in mind, it is not a secret that he also directs such criticism to 'hermeneutical' theologians who have been under the influence of Paul Ricoeur, such as David Tracy. Frei's major complaint against this special theology is that it makes the meaning of the text subordinate to the experience of understanding that the text generates in the reader. Ricoeur's concept of 'split reference' occasions a moment of disclosure in which the reader understands herself in the world projected by the text. It is then this self-understanding that guides her further engagement with the text. Not surprisingly then, the text is evacuated of meaning, while its centre of gravity is placed outside it, in the existential experience it produces in the reader. In Frei's opinion this is tantamount to the complete loss of the text and of the particularity of the message, as it is emptied into the subjective world.

The limits this imposes on the sort of move from identity to presence that Frei wishes to make are plain. He presents them:

> It seems that *any* kind of ascription of 'meaning' to a personal subject within the narrative world is highly tenuous, if not simply dissolved, under this hermeneutical governance. The clearly and irreducibly personal focus in this scheme is constituted not by the meaning of the narrative but by the interpreter – that is, the understanding to which 'meaning' is related. What narratives present (whether or not literally) is not in the first place ascriptive selves that are the subjects of their predicates, not even really the self expressive, centred consciousness or transcendental ego, but the 'mode-of-being-in-the-world' which these selves exemplify and which is 're-presented' by being 'disclosed' to 'understanding.'[29]

---

[28] Frei, 'The Literal Reading of Biblical Narrative', p. 129-130.
[29] Frei, 'The Literal Reading', p. 127.

The text becomes transparent, not to a reality behind it, but to the consciousness of the interpreter. Frei is right to say that this type of reading is closer to allegory that to the literal sense and that in fact it does away with the text. It remains to be seen, however, whether Frei's alternative methodology is able to steer clear of its own associated dangers. Ricoeur, Frei rightly counsels, runs the danger of turning the text into an illusory self-projection.[30] The Christological move from presence to identity is plagued by a similar condition: projecting our best concepts, however well intentioned and highly regarded, may only lead back to a deified humanity rather than a particular human being which is also divine. Frei's Christology, as in fact the rest of postliberal Christologies, serve as reminders that the highest Christologies may in fact be mere anthropologies with a wrong subject.

All the more urgent it is then to return to the text. But such a return must avoid both the pitfalls of the eighteenth century focus on the world behind the text, as well as the contemporary judgement that texts are oriented towards present self-understanding, although transcending it ontologically.

I am trying to convey something of a crucial omission in Frei, which will also form an important part of our positive proposal. His essay on the literal reading is known to have something of a confessional value, in fact like almost all of his work, in that it admits to having been too fascinated early on with the possibility of New Criticism to carry on his programme of retaining the particular identity of Jesus Christ through a type of formalist exegesis. In this essay Frei changes his initial position: he is no longer willing to hang his preference for the literal sense on any theory. Instead, he turns to pragmatics and argues that the literal sense reading should be adopted because it simply represents what the church has always been doing. It is important that in the first, formalist phase, Frei operated with what amounts to a clear disjunction between text and reading and forcefully argued against importing theory to judge the text, as we shall see. So formalism involved by necessity a purity of reading. In moving from formalism to functionalism, however, Frei *does not explicitly modify his initial position on the purity of reading*. This has important consequences for his and the rest of postliberal understanding of criticism. For in his slide from formalism to functionalism Frei is tacitly admitting that there can be no presuppositionless reading of the book. If such a reading were possible, he would have argued from the book that such and such is the case. But he opens the Pandora's box by leaving the church's interpretation of the Bible unchallenged. I wish to argue precisely for such a transparency of the reading theory with regard to the text, and this crucially involves its provisionality. Formalism furnished Frei with the illusion that he was reading without the-

---

[30] This criticism finds support in Kevin J. Vanhoozer, *Biblical Narrative in the Philosophy of Paul Ricoeur: A Study in Hermeneutics and Theology*, (Cambridge: Cambridge University Press, 1990), p. 156, but not in Stiver, *Theology After Ricoeur*, p. 201.

ory. Functionalism, without criticism, contributes the illusion that the theory in use is the appropriate one. By not leaving enough distance between the church and the text, the move to functionalism seems to have robbed postliberalism of tools for ideology criticism. I shall now analyse in turn the formalist and the functionalist Frei.

Frei's Christology is grounded on the text, the whole text and nothing but the text. Or so he wishes. His strong conviction is that the right Christological direction is from textually mediated identity to the presence of Christ. I shall only be discussing certain aspects of Frei's Christology, as they bear on our theme of the relation between the particular and the universal.

The Gospels are realistic narratives, and their nature and problems associated with this description have already been discussed. Their function is that of rendering the identity of Jesus Christ. Like Barth, Frei affirms that we cannot side-step these texts and construct the identity of Jesus on an independent basis. These texts are all we have. Together with his conviction that the meaning of the texts lies nowhere else but in the text, this makes up for a strong case that Christology is simply a matter of working out the *logic* of the Scriptural narratives. In these Gospels, and for the Christian, the identification of Jesus has already taken place. As we argued, this poses various conflicts for the theologian, and this chapter will only intensify the sense of these problems. The Christian first order language, Lindbeck's vocabulary, identifies God and Jesus. The rest of the Christian statements and doctrines are merely second-order moves within the universe generated by the Scriptural statements. Postliberalism has accepted the narration of the world from the perspective of Scriptures. There is therefore no independent reading of the world which might bypass the narrative texts themselves. According to Milbank and the radical orthodox theologians, all such putatively objectivist readings of reality end up in nihilism. There is no reading that does not proceed by faith. Together with narrative theologians, remarks such as these have worked a great deal toward relieving the Kantian anxiety of theology. If all is narrative and there is nothing beyond textual mediation, then Christian theology can confidently concentrate on the theological matters themselves. There might be more than enough speculation here, but it is not too far-stretched a supposition that thinkers such as Frei, Lindbeck, Tanner and others, have had enough of the relegation of theology to endless debates about method. One is here reminded of the change of atmosphere occasioned by Barth's *Romans* and its call to an end to pointless talk about method.

The present study is in fact both a recognition of the accomplishment of narrative theology, as well as a warning that there is a fine line between narrative sanity on the one hand, and the pitfalls of narrative frenzy or narrative amnesia on the other hand. These matters will be discussed below, but for now it serves to remind us of our guiding inquiry: although narratives are necessary for particularity, at what point does particularity itself end up in nihilism?

Given this intra-textualism, doctrinal truth is a matter of intra-systematic coherence first of all. Although Lindbeck distinguishes and accepts both intra-systematic truth and ontological truth, it is the former that is the criterion of truth for theological statements, to use Marshall's terminology. Ontological truth is something to be decided only in the eschaton.[31] All theology has to work on are the first-order narratives. It is these narratives which are doing the identifying job and not an independent ontology.

The complaint addressed to Ricoeur that he reads the text in the light of the extra-textual ontology that the text creates is also evident here. Texts do not uniformly serve as mere channels through which some content is delivered. Allegory, not literal sense, is the procedure that brings that result, and we have already seen what Frei thinks of allegory. It is apparent, if one were to grant the argument of John David Dawson that the reasons for Frei's choice here are as much theoretical as specifically Christological. We have here the first glimpse of a hermeneutical circle that is at the basis of Frei's Christology. We are able to grasp the identity of Jesus Christ by paying close attention to the literal sense of the gospels, which alone conveys that identity. But the very reason that text conveys the identity is because of a prior belief in the Chalcedonian explanation of the two natures. So Frei has to already assume that Christ is of the same substance with God in order for that literal reading – which will supposedly lead him to that affirmation – to be possible. This circularity, in contrast to other discourses, where it would pose a serious problem, does not seem to bother postliberal theologians too much. The anxiety of beginning[32] is not a given with postliberals, who quite candidly assume the circularity of their own projects[33], as tasks of re-description. To follow Dawson's argument:

> Frei's conception of the literal sense bears some resemblance to the way American New Critics insisted that poetic meanings were so textually embedded that paraphrase was impossible, but is more profoundly related to the way Christian theologians, following the Creed of Chalcedon, insist that Jesus' divine and human natures cohere inseparably yet unconfusedly in a single person.[34] [...] Frei holds onto the tension of the Chalcedonian rules that govern his own construal of the biblical text. The text does not

---

[31] Dirk-Martin Grube calls this 'critique immunising' in 'Realism, Foundationalism and Constructivism: A Philosopher's Bermuda Triangle?', *Neue Zeitschrift für Systematische Theologie und Religionsphilosophie*, 40 (1998), 107-126, pp. 109-110.

[32] See Gillian Rose, *The Broken Middle: Out of Our Ancient Society*, (Oxford: Blackwell, 1992).

[33] See McClendon, *Doctrine*, pp. 239-40.

[34] Dawson, *Figural Reading*, p. 144.

deliver God to its reader, as though it were a mere channel through which God might be conveyed. On the contrary, the text that renders the identity of Jesus, like (although not identical to) the logos incarnate in Jesus, just *is*, says Frei, the linguistic presence of God.[35]

This strategy, Dawson further argues, is part of Frei's constant concern to preserve an identity-in-distinction between letter and spirit. What the texts convey is not some message behind the text and accessible without this particular text, as Ricoeur's allegorical readings may be taken to imply. Rather, the text is integral to the meaning itself. The connection between this understanding of the literal sense and the Christological analogy will be further analysed below, together with a reading of Telford Work's *Scripture in the Economy of Salvation*, which attempts precisely such a resuscitation of the Christological analogy for the Bible.

How do the realistic narratives of the Bible convey the identity of Jesus? Frei is aware of the need for some formal categories in order to clarify the meaning of the gospels. However, he does not wish to load such categories with too much content before actually getting down to textual matters. Instead he prefers to leave them as formal as possible. The categories of self-manifestation and intention-action are meant to be as formal as possible and their job is none-other than to mediate the text. At this point one has to wonder whether Frei is able to save the purity of his reading, despite the necessity of using some theoretical concepts.

'A person's identity is the self-referral, or ascription to him, of his physical and personal states, properties, characteristics and actions.'[36] Frei has little patience with theories of the human person which locate a substantial centre, or with those views according to which a person is little more than an allegory of some ideal. A person, writes Frei, 'is not merely illustrated, he is *constituted* by his particular intentional act at any given point in his life.'[37] This is a holistic anthropology in that it refuses reductionistic approaches to human personality. It is also, however, a distinctly *modern* perspective. For Frei does not simply argue that the person is nothing other than or beyond his intentional acts, but also the person is that which holds everything together, the one who integrates the story: 'Identity occurs at the point of the integration of the self by itself.'[38] It is still the self who 'presides' over what is happening to him and who integrates the contingencies encountered. However modern a take on personality this seems, Frei considers these tools for understanding identity to be similar to those used by the New Testament writers themselves:

---

[35] Dawson, *Figural Reading*, pp. 165-166.
[36] Frei, *The Identity*, p. 38.
[37] Frei, *The Identity*, p. 44.
[38] Frei, *The Identity*, p. 40.

First, it is assumed that both the New Testament writers and we ourselves hold in common some of the same sorts of description of human identity and, furthermore, that the identity of Jesus which the New Testament discloses – along with the clue it gives to the identities of other human beings – is of vital importance within the New Testament itself.[39]

In his refusal of any explanatory approach, which would isolate one characteristic[40] of the story in light of which to explain all others, Frei is therefore committed to upholding the unity of the story in its rendering of the identity of Jesus Christ. 'A person is what and who he is just by the way he holds all these things together and orders them; and to tell how he does that, all we can do is refer to the same qualities and the way they are ordered.'[41] But are we not falling into the trap of allowing a technical description to dictate the content of the New Testament? Not if we only use such tools in order to allow the structure of the text itself to come to light. In the final analysis, it is their actual success in practice which will legitimise the use of such tools. Immediately one may wonder how is such a success to be ascertained in the absence of the very tools which need legitimation, but Frei doesn't really consider this issue. He takes such tools as 'organising patterns,'[42] which allow us to understand the very structure of the text. Frei is indeed aware that such intellectual instruments have a habit of taking over the text, yet his confidence that this does not happen in his own technical description is surprising.

Nonetheless, it is the identity of Jesus which the Gospels set out to depict.[43] Jesus' identity is, according to the method described above, given at the place where he is most fully himself, namely in the passion-resurrection sequence[44]. Frei's analysis is a brilliant piece of what he calls aesthetic interpretation[45]. We are in a fortunate position to be left with a fictional rather than a historical account of his life, for this affords us a better insight into his identity.[46] And this identity is not given by any adoption of this human being by some archetypal person who bestows identity on him. Such is the

---

[39] Frei, *The Identity*, p. 46.

[40] Frei, *The Identity*, p. 42.

[41] Frei, *The Identity*, p. 41.

[42] Frei, *The Identity*, p. 46.

[43] One question which remains to be answered is, should the main intention of Gospels not be that of depicting the identity of Jesus, but as Milbank argues, for example, of the community, would this technical description of identity still hold? The question is in fact about the relation between such tools and the authorial intention behind the narratives.

[44] Frei, *The Identity*, p. 49ff.

[45] Frei, *Theology and Narrative*, p. 40.

[46] See chapter 3 above.

difference between the Gnostic and Christian understandings of Christ, that whereas for the latter, the human Jesus is the one who bestows identity upon the Saviour, for the Gnostic all events that are happening to Jesus have no bearing on his identity. He transcends them all and remains unaffected by them. The Christian story is about an un-substitutable person, a unique particular human being. Hence the difference from Marshall's second way. Particularity is given precisely at the point where all contingencies affect identity and are ascribed to the human person.

So far Frei seems to merge Jesus' identity completely with his story. Since Jesus is nothing other than his story, it seems that we are forced to begin and end here. This raises a problem which cannot be avoided, that of the difference between the story the gospels tell and the story of Jesus' life, or Jesus history. The historical status of the Gospels has been discussed earlier. Frei's suggestion was that whether the story is real or fictional, there is one point where the story touches down in history, namely in the passion-resurrection sequence. The difficult problems associated with reference are 'solved' in his case by the suggestion that if reference takes place at all, it is along the lines dictated by the text itself.[47] It is in the passion-resurrection sequence that to understand the identity of Jesus is to understand that the narrative itself makes a claim to reality.

It is at this point of the integration of the self by itself, the moment where Jesus is most fully himself, where his identity has been successfully rendered that we understand what that identity entails. It entails presence. This has been the master stroke of a master of hermeneutics: by giving a purely aesthetic (arguably) description of the text, he has made the transition from text to reality claim. Thus the revelatory claim of the text does not lie, as with Ricoeur, in the establishment of a moment of understanding in the reader, but it remains an intra-textual event. Here the reader understands who Jesus is and this understanding is identical with another understanding: *that* Jesus is. Frei's initial conviction is justified: that the identity and presence are indelibly connected. It is also a further vindication of his own Christological method: that the safeguarding of particularity is and must remain an intra-systematic matter. The way in which the narratives stake a claim on reality is legislated by the narratives themselves. The way in which Jesus is the Saviour, or the Son of God, or God (and so on) is not to be arrived at by independent metaphysical description, but is to follow (naturally?) from an exegesis of the text.

There is no question here of an illegitimate transition from text to reality, after the fashion of Anselm, or how he has mistakenly been interpreted. The judgements made here are purely intra-textual. There is indeed a move from text to reality, but the reality to which transition is being made is not the

---

[47] In all fairness, Frei does not consider reference to be philosophically mysterious and in need of explanation.

neutral reality of physics and science, or philosophy, but a reality which is a figure of the Scripturally-rendered world.[48] Frei argues that to understand the meaning of Christ is quite simply to understand that he lives.[49] And in this respect he declares membership to a respectable company:

> That leaves the question of the transition from the aesthetic, non-apologetic, understanding to the truth claim – historical, metaphysical, and existential. I'm not a bit sure what I can say here that Anselm or Calvin or Barth have not already said. All I can add is that to the Christian the truth of the story can present no problem, and, therefore, its meaning in formal aesthetic description is its truth. To the unbeliever, on the other hand, its meaning and its possible as well as actual truth are two totally different things.[50]

Again theology is re-description of the meanings internal to the Scriptural text. Furthermore, this is consonant with what we have called a description-based model of reference. The moves made within a religious vocabulary are always second order, where the first order language has performed the task of identification. The question of the adequacy of the first-order language, or of the fit between story and reality does not bother Frei, for he is quite content to accept the non-foundational nature of religion. There is nothing out there which would have the possibility to ground our stories about Scripture, or the Scriptural stories themselves.

Does Frei succeed in his programme? What would count as a success here? Frei is trying to use modest formal tools to allow the structure of the text to speak out, in the process of which one moves from identity to presence. The particularity of the text needs to be preserved and as a consequence the unique identity of Jesus as well, if Jesus is nothing other than his story.

Frei does not succeed in keeping theory minimal. David Kelsey observes that Frei's understanding of the biblical stories as identity depictions is backed by a particular understanding of what it means to be a human per-

---

[48] Another pressing question at this juncture: is this Scripturally formed world different in any way from Ricoeur's projected world? Arguably, the narrative world is formed by the Scriptures alone, whereas Ricoeur's is formed at the intersection of horizons, that of the reader and that of the text. But can narrative theology sustain with any seriousness such a purity of her world?

[49] But even to understand the meaning of Christ, one must be schooled to perceive the text in a certain way. This is not a natural theology, or a sort of magic initiation through the simple reading of sacred texts. That is, one must already become an insider before one understands that identity.

[50] Frei, *Theology and Narrative*, p. 43.

son.[51] This should cause some concern, for did he not aver that the move should be intra-textual rather than from outside towards the inside? Frei is apparently working with a prior anthropology in terms of which the humanity of Jesus is to be discovered. All claims to the contrary notwithstanding, Frei doesn't sufficiently do justice to the particularity of the New Testament stories themselves, precisely by imposing upon them a prior anthropology. It will be my argument, constructed as a cumulative case, that this needs not be a problem and that the imposition of such prior anthropology or indeed ontology need not pose a problem for particularity. Indeed, precisely in terms of such an ontology is particularity most able to surface. This is also what Frei is attempting to say when he writes in defence of his use of such formal categories: that we need them in order to allow the structure of the text to come out. What is being challenged in his account, however, is that such categories, or his prior anthropology is not one 'shared' by the New Testament writers,[52] and not formal enough so as to allow the text to speak. Admittedly it would be very difficult to show either that is successful or unsuccessful, because there is no independent way to the text which would then judge the success of other readings. But Frei himself argues that the success of this technique is to be established in practice. And it is in practice that it manifestly fails.

The point at which the procedure fails is in its concentration on certain aspects of a person's life to the detriment of others. It is puzzling that Frei elects not to include in his 'aesthetic interpretation' the teachings of Jesus. If there are any places in the Gospels which give us clues about the identity of Jesus it is not in the teachings themselves, writes Frei, but in the narrative parts of the Gospels[53]. The reasons for this bypassing of the teachings of Jesus are not easy to discern. In 'Remarks in Connection to a Theological Proposal' Frei mentions the futility of the questers for the historical Jesus to reach an essential body of authentic sayings of Jesus[54]. Perhaps he did not wish to rely on inauthentic material in the Gospels, against his best intuitions about the canonical shape of the narratives and the unity which is to be ascribed to them. Yet another reason is suggested by his insistence that the meaning of the Son of Man, or of Redemption, or of the Kingdom of God is given by the identity of Jesus and not the other way around. Frei

---

[51] David H. Kelsey, *The Uses of Scripture in Recent Theology*, (Philadelphia: Fortress Press, 1975), p. 46.

[52] Here Frei pushes himself into another corner by appearing to endorse some version of authorial intention hermeneutics, when in fact he rejected it in the *Eclipse*.

[53] Frei, *The Identity*, p. 87.

[54] Frei, *Theology and Narrative*, p. 36. For a historical account of the different Christological approaches since Bultmann, see Irvin Batdorf, 'Interpreting Jesus since Bultmann: selected paradigms and their hermeneutic matrix', *SBL Seminar Papers*, 23 (1984), 187-215.

may have wanted to avoid an easy slip into drawing speculative clues about the identity of the preacher, from the sermons about the Kingdom. Jesus' identity is, in Milbank's words, one operating on the surface, not in depth. He is not a person whose self remains unchanged and sovereign over the events that happen to him. Although Frei is concerned to maintain some sort of *sovereign submission* of Jesus before what is happening to him, such sovereignty is not mythical, or Gnostic.

Regardless of Frei's reasons, one cannot but agree with George Stroup's verdict about this unfortunate disjunction within the heart of the story itself.

> Yet Frei's interpretation of the dramatic reversal raises questions about a conflict between the teaching and ministry of Jesus and his self-manifestation in the passion story. Precisely what is the relation between the prophet from Galilee and the crucified and risen Christ? [...] Any theological description of Jesus' or God's identity that ignores their respective histories and their confluence in the ministry *and* passion of Jesus runs the risk of some form of docetism.[55]

Even if one granted that the sermons introduced a vertical dimension to the otherwise horizontal and temporal construal of his identity, they are still part of the story. The cost at which parts of the story are ripped from it is one which Frei should be unwilling to pay. If indeed Frei holds on to a Christological analogy according to which the identity of Jesus is his story, not simply mediated through it in allegorical fashion, then the implication of this separation within the story is a defective, possibly docetic Christology. Apparently Frei can read the Gospels as rendering the unique identity of the Saviour only at the cost of forfeiting significant parts of the text. One must seriously ask whether the end result can still stand unchanged, especially given his own affirmation of the canonical unity of the text. John Milbank has been instrumental in calling into question Frei's aesthetic exegesis. In his essay, 'The Name of Jesus', Milbank questions just about every essential turn of Frei's exegesis. Where Frei argues that the Gospels are to be read like realistic narratives, Milbank replies that they read rather more like detective stories[56]. In a realistic narrative the character evolves, there is psychological development. Here on the other hand, we are told nothing about Jesus' tastes, about his intentions and so on. His identity, in other words, is not given in particular patterns, but rather in universal terms. The Gospels are more similar to detective stories, in which the character gradually is discovered to the reader, emerging from behind the veal of universal characterisations. Milbank draws attention to the complexity of narrative. There are two fundamentally different narratives operating at distinct

---

[55] George Stroup, 'Chalcedon revisited', *Theology Today*, 35 (1978), 52-64, p. 61, emphasis mine.

[56] Milbank, 'The Name of Jesus', in *The Word Made Strange*, p. 149.

levels in the Gospel stories. First, there are the stories of Jesus, straightforward depictions of his life and ministry; second, there is the less straightforward commentary on the first one, which discloses the *secret significance of Jesus*. These stories are not parallel, the second one frequently intrudes into the first one. Milbank is echoing Lindbeck's statements about the second order claims which find their way back into the first order narratives themselves. But Milbank places this intrusion at the very level of the narrative itself, not simply at the level of reading. The stories were written, as such, in this perpetual 'alchemy'[57] of story of Jesus and human discovery of his significance. There is no separation of these stories, and there is no getting beyond the second story to the first one. Revisionist theologians have attempted precisely that, but there is no non-textual reality as such, there is no history but textual history. And given this ubiquitous textual mediation, the self is forever moving between texts, never quite finding a place to anchor down in reality. Not that Milbank would find any menace in this condition. Quite the contrary, he rejoices in the ungrounded nature of faith. It is the second narrative itself which is not grounded in the first one. The secret identity of Jesus is not traceable to the first narrative, but is to be accepted in faith together with the whole story.

The inter-penetration of these stories suggests that there has never been a case of a clear and readily available material for Frei to work on. He assumes the ready availability of the Scripture's meaning and that such a meaning is accessible outside ontological descriptions. Conversely, the rendering of Jesus' identity empties his person of all particularity. Precisely at the point where one would expect particularity to play some part, in the transition from his work to his person, it doesn't happen. I will allow Milbank himself to speak here:

> At the level of the metanarrative, we are told not only that Jesus is to be identified as virtuous through his works, and as being none other than his works, but also that the works are to be taken as signs of his unique significance. The metanarrative therefore shifts the emphasis from the works towards the person. Yet this moves us still further away from any concrete content. To identify Jesus, the gospels abandon mimetic/ diegetic narrative, and resort to metaphors: Jesus is the way, the word, the truth, life, water, bread, the seed of a tree and the fully grown tree, the foundation stone of a new temple and at the same time the whole edifice. These metaphors abandon the temporal and the horizontal for the spatial and vertical.[58]

---

[57] Milbank, *The Word Made Strange*, p. 146.
[58] Milbank, 'The Name', p. 149.

Milbank's point is a functional one: one cannot read the narratives apart from the practice that they have instantiated.[59] As a result, one cannot read the identity of Jesus as a particular person precisely because he is the founder of the Christian practice. To understand Jesus is to understand that practice and to identify the main characteristics and virtues of that practice is in fact to identify Jesus. For Milbank, then, the Gospel stories do not tell the story of Jesus except as the implication of their telling the story of a practice.[60] Milbank again: 'If we cannot describe a founder precisely in the moment of the origination of that practice, then all we can do is to identify him with the general norms of that practice, and this procedure is followed by the gospels.'[61]

This could in fact be read as a radicalisation of Frei's insight that it is only insiders that are able to read the story of Jesus and discover his identity which then leads to his presence. But where Milbank helps us get beyond Frei is in the understanding that there can be no reading without an ontology. The universality Milbank mentions is not to be confused with the universality of a neutral metaphysics, but the universality of a community which is the church. To attempt, as Frei does, to truncate the text of the Gospels and to read them from the perspective of the self-manifestation of the identity of Jesus is to forfeit access to that most original of responses to Jesus which is the Gospel itself. There is thus an ontological level besides the narrative one in the gospels.[62]

Milbank also considers the metaphors that the Gospels use to speak about Jesus. Frei would perhaps insist that it is in fact the identity of Jesus that bestows meaning upon those metaphors and not the other way around. But that would go against what Frei understands by a metaphor. In his essay on the literal reading of the Gospels, Frei asserts that metaphorical language refers creatively without creating what it refers to.[63] This would seem to involve a theory of metaphor according to which it is in the meeting, or togetherness between the metaphor and the subject matter, that meaning is created. Thus it cannot be simply a matter of Jesus bestowing identity on

---

[59] Cf. Frederic C. Bauerschmidt, 'The word made speculative? John Milbank's christological poetics', *Modern Theology*, 15 (1999), 417-432, p. 424.

[60] Just like Ricoeur (Manifestation and proclamation, in Ricoeur, *Figuring the Sacred*, pp. 56ff.), Milbank places 'Kingdom' at the centre of the Gospels' identity descriptions.

[61] Milbank, 'The Name', p. 152.

[62] Arguably, the ontological level tends to hijack the textual identification of Jesus for the purposes of a poetic ontology. Frei would argue that Milbank, just as like Ricoeur, places undue emphasis on human receptivity, through his stress on Jesus as bearer of 'Kingdom' (see Bauerschmidt, pp. 424-6).

[63] Frei, 'The Literal Reading', p. 132.

the metaphors, for that would involve the assumption of 'hollow' metaphors and no one would seriously uphold such a notion.

This discussion is also connected to the debate about Christological titles. Without entering too much in a discussion which would only betray lack of competence, the type of aesthetic interpretation that Frei upholds, has great difficulty accounting for the tradition of Christological titles. If meaning is constructed intra-textually, can the interpreter still draw on extra-textual factors such as the history of the meaning of a title such as Son of Man, in order to illumine the meaning it has in Jesus' sermons, for example? Edwin K. Broadhead has argued for a change in the usual understanding of titles. If traditionally the key to their meaning has been their historical use, the new literary approach, suggests Broadhead,[64] takes titles as formal elements which operate within a self-enclosed narrative world. The primary clue to their meaning resides not in historical or extra-textual factors, but in the way in which their meaning is constructed by the text.[65] It is the narrative itself which carries the meaning of those titles. However, as Meir Sternberg argues, it is extremely tenuous to make interpretation rely solely on intra-textual factors. Such a procedure misunderstands the very nature of language which is communal and public. The concepts it employs are themselves historical and in a very real sense extra-textual.[66] From a purely linguistic point of view, such a theory about the Christological titles is faltering at the very moment when the question is asked, why did the writer use 'Son of Man' instead of 'Son of God?' If the meaning of the titles is filled in by the narrative sequence, to the exclusion of extra-textual concerns, it makes no difference what titles or metaphors are used. Metaphor here does the uninteresting job of standing in as a billboard upon which the conceptual content is plastered.

Can metaphors still 'creatively refer' under such conditions? Does form still have any influence on meaning? It is doubtful that it still does. The only strategy left is to maintain the tensional relationship between the metaphor and that which it portrays, in a way which will be explored later on. For now, however, it is also obvious that Milbank's strategy is no less contradictory. To argue that particularity is dissipated in universality is to argue that in fact the metaphors that the Gospels employ have no real referent, but themselves, which is not the case. It is also to argue that there can be no check on the sort of metaphors that are used. If there is no particular

---

[64] See his article, 'Jesus the Nazarene: narrative strategy and Christological imagery in the Gospel of Mark', *Journal for the Study of the New Testament*, 52 (1993), 3-18, as well as *Naming Jesus: Titular Christology in the Gospel of Mark,* (Sheffield: Sheffield Academic Press, 1999).

[65] Broadhead, 'Jesus the Nazarene', p. 6.

[66] Which is not to say that the meaning of the metaphorical content is itself fixed.

content on which to perform their aesthetic function, what is to rule which metaphors are appropriate and which aren't?

There is a double lesson to be learned from this discussion of Christological titles: making sense of the Gospels involves something more than simply inhabiting a text. The text itself must be understood as part of a larger world, or text if you will. The precise nature of this correlation remains to be established, but at the very minimum any text shares a language and concepts with other texts. Hence making sense of one text always presupposes our common habitation of a world of other texts. There is no private language of any text. And the second lesson: there can be no sharp distinction between reading narratively and reading ontologically. Story and the world that story imagines presuppose each other.

Hopefully the direction of this chapter is becoming clearer. I intended to show the difficulty of separating a pure reading of the narratives of Christianity from ontological descriptions. Behind this lies a critique of the way in which postliberalism conceives the relation between story and reality. By construing stories as the only access to that reality, it runs the risk of idolatrously identifying story and the subject of the story, Gospel and Jesus. The remainder of this section will attempt to argue against such an identification by discussing the Christological analogy which guides Frei's description of the literal sense. Naturally flowing from this critique is also a critique of the incommensurability of meaning and of the dualistic distinction between insiders and outsiders to the truth.

In his *Living and Active: Scripture in the Economy of Salvation*[67], Telford Work advances a version of the Christological analogy which attempts to get beyond the impasse of the older attempts, as they have been criticised by e.g. Markus Barth or James Barr. His criticism of Gerard Loughlin's and Hans Frei's application of the Christological analogy to the Bible is instructive. For Loughlin, Work argues, Jesus is his own story and the Church's relationship to him is exhausted by its relationship to the Word, while Frei's account, as Placher suggests, 'can seem to collapse the revealed Word into Written Word, a written word that witnesses to nothing beyond itself.'[68] This is indeed a fair summarisation of the intra-textual framework. There is no access to God or to Christ except in the story of the Scriptures. However, Loughlin's and Frei's 'refusal to equivocate between Jesus and Jesus' story causes serious theological problems.'[69] The chief of these is the fact that the object is swallowed up into the text so that 'Frei's 'consuming text' consumes more than the world; it consumes God him-

---

[67] (Grand Rapids: Eerdmans, 2002).

[68] William C. Placher, 'Paul Ricoeur and postliberal theology: a conflict of interpretations?' *Modern Theology*, 4 (1987), 35-52, p. 48.

[69] Work, *Living and Active: Scripture in the Economy of Salvation*, (Grand Rapids: Eerdmans, 2002), p. 94.

self.'[70] Perhaps Work's greatest contribution is to have emphasised the need for the analogy to equivocate at some point. In fact the very nature of the incarnation, on which all postliberal theologians build, could perhaps lead us into an entirely different direction. Work comments on Barth's understanding of how incarnation revolutionises our understanding of transcendence and of the ontological difference. Traces of a change in the later Barth from a dialectical conception of divine transcendence to a more analogical conception, where, even if in a limited sense, a modest natural theology is possible, are not impossible to find.[71]

If the Christological analogy equivocates at this important point: namely that the story is not to be identified with the object of the story, then my previous arguments about the reification of the texts (and epistemic intermediaries in general) start to connect with the Christological problematic. Work argues that the analogy breaks down where one realises that the union between human words and divine words in Scripture is not hypostatic, not fleshly. There is thus more to the person of Jesus than the story is telling.

The implications of this for the issue of the incommensurability of meaning are obvious. If Jesus is more than the stories told about him in Scripture, knowing Jesus is not simply and necessarily a matter of being baptised into the world of Scripture. It is this reading of the literal sense which allows Frei to propose his own technique for reading the identity of Jesus as rendered in the gospels. However, since the foundation of this reading, the Christological analogy equivocates, one must also ask whether Jesus is indeed nothing else but his story? By identifying Jesus with his story and by requiring readers to accept the literal sense (grounded as it was in the Christological analogy) Frei effectively makes the meaning of the Gospels dependent on behavioural aspects. One could have argued that this is indeed an instance in which the meaning of the text turns on extra-textual factors such as baptism, discipleship, inhabiting a specific cultural community and so on. But I believe I have already made our point on that issue. By so connecting the meaning to behaviour, the disjunction between insiders and outsiders is solidified and with it the sense of the incommensurability of meanings.

If the argument has been correct, if the meaning of the story does indeed depict the identity of Jesus without exhausting his identity, then one may say that the debates between believer and unbeliever are not debates over incommensurable objects, but debates which can find resolution due to their common object, which is the person of Jesus Christ. To say with Frei that if one has not believed that Christ is present one has not understood the identity of Jesus is to seriously misunderstand the way reference works. Both

---

[70] Work, *Living*, p. 95.

[71] Work, *Living*, pp. 89ff.

believer and unbeliever refer to the same person, since reference is not exhausted by description but can be fixed by dubbing, by baptism, by ostensive reference and so on. Hence even though two interpreters may not agree about the specific description of Jesus, they can nonetheless share reference to him. It makes sense, then, to say that the difference between the understanding of the believer and that of the unbeliever is not one of incommensurable difference, but rather of semantic depth.[72] One may say that the understanding the believer has achieved is an intensification of what he has previously understood. The logical consequence of arguments like Loughlin's and Frei's is bibliolatry, as Work argues[73], although what bibliolatry means in each case may differ significantly.

Lindbeck and Grammatical Christology

Neither the early Marshall nor Frei are able to devise theological methods hospitable to Jesus Christ. Both perspectives turn on a dualism between narrative rendering of identity and ontological discourse. It is the story alone which is able to safeguard the uniqueness of the person. To say that the story is necessary, however, is not to say that it can be read in the absence of some ontology, as Milbank helpfully argues. The symbiosis between story and discourse is given at the very level of the creation of the story. A disjunction between narrative and ontology also turns on the distinction between insiders and outsiders to the truth, which in turn rests on a very postmodern understanding of incommensurability. I had the opportunity to dismantle various versions of the incommensurability doctrine and I have also pointed out their dualistic assumptions. This section explores the difference made by the doctrine of the incarnation to theological knowledge, following an investigation of Lindbeck's Christology. It will be argued that Lindbeck's Christology is dictated by his philosophical understanding of religion and language, rather than the other way around. At the very least this is a distinct betrayal of the postliberal emphasis on allowing one's world to be narrated Scripturally. At the worst, it represents Lindbeck's own subordination of the particularity of what Christ means to the universality of a prior understanding of religion.

Following his distinction between first order language (vocabulary) and second order theological statements (grammar), intended to provide a more lucrative model for the ecumenical dialogue, Lindbeck asserts that the Christological statements of Chalcedon and Nicaea, for example, do not

---

[72] I have already discussed semantic depth in a previous chapter, in relation to Ken Surin's work.

[73] Work, *Living*, p. 95.

make any actual truth claims, except derivatively[74]. They do not concern extra-linguistic realities. Such statements do not refer to realities out there, but only to the propositions of the first-order language. A further support is given by his suggestion that one must distinguish between the doctrine and the formulation.[75] Hence, both the first order as well as the second order propositions are separable from the forms in which they have been articulated.[76] The intention behind these distinctions is on the one hand to distinguish between the constancy of Christian practice and the diversity of doctrinal formulations, and on the other hand between the diversity of formulations and the unity of Christian truth. For Lindbeck, 'the only way to show that the doctrines of Nicaea and Chalcedon are distinguishable from the concepts in which they are formulated is to state these doctrines in different terms that nonetheless have equivalent consequences.'[77] This is more easily[78] accomplished if the doctrines are taken to be second order propositions, rather than first order truth claims.[79] He then argues that this is not in fact a new discovery. It is at this point where Lindbeck's theology starts transforming into a depth hermeneutics. Instead of being concerned purely with the description of what religious believers do, he becomes ambitious. Probing deep beneath the surface, Lindbeck actually argues that Christians have since the beginning treated such claims as second-order propositions, not about reality, but about other propositions. The Christians have learned from the Greeks the technique of second order propositions[80]. Yehuda Elkana[81] gives us an interesting insight into the reasons why such a thinking has developed. She argues that it was in fact the emergence of competing world views which claimed the right interpretation of the world which prompted the birth of thinking about thinking.[82] It is even argued that '[the] quest for transcendence is in itself a result of the soteriological wish to

---

[74] Only later, grants Lindbeck, did the full metaphysical import of the doctrines become asserted. (Lindbeck, *Doctrine*, p. 94.)

[75] Lindbeck, *Doctrine*, p. 92.

[76] I extensively criticised this model in the last chapter.

[77] Lindbeck, *Doctrine*, p. 93.

[78] Lindbeck modestly affirms that he is not proposing a true theory of religious statements. The main thesis of the book is 'concerned simply with the availability, not the superiority of a rule theory of doctrine and the associated cultural linguistic view of religion' (*Doctrine*, p. 92). Whether he does in fact treat it more than simply available is a question of a different order.

[79] Lindbeck, *Doctrine*, p. 94.

[80] Lindbeck, *Doctrine*, p. 94.

[81] Yehuda Elkana, 'The emergence of second-order thinking in classical Greece', in N. Eisenstadt, *The Origins and Diversity of Axial Age Civilizations*, (Albany: State University of New York Press, 1986).

[82] Elkana, 'Second-order thinking', p. 41.

eliminate the unbearable tensions created by competing alternative world-views, and this is already a result of second-order thinking.[83] Transcendence here becomes a construct, used to legitimate our various interpretations of the world. And up to the medieval disenchantment of the world,[84] it was the assumption of theologians that interpretations of the world had to be legitimated by some relation to the eternal, be it the eternal forms, or God, or whatever. Elkana's work helps us become aware of the danger of construing theological affirmations purely as second order statements. According to that interpretation, one which is in fact adopted by Feuerbach's criticism of religion, functionalism translates transcendence. God is but a second-order projection, serving various functions, but existing as nothing more that a useful fiction.

What is to prevent the second-order reframing of Christology from becoming a mere projection? Before we delve into that, more needs to be said about the specifics of Lindbeck's proposal. In his quest for a depth hermeneutics, he invokes Athanasius as ally:

> As a result of this logical (one might say grammatical) analysis of the data of Scripture and tradition, Athanasius expressed the meaning of 'consubstantiality' for example, in terms of the rule that whatever is said of the Father is said of the Son, except that the Son is not the Father.[85]

We are then treated to the controversial conclusion that Athanasius did not think about the statements of Nicaea and Chalcedon as first order *truths*, but as second order *rules* of speech. Thus to accept the doctrines outlined at Nicaea was *merely* to accept to speak in certain ways rather than in others. My engagement of this interpretation consists of two arguments: (a) the challenging of Lindbeck's interpretation of Lonergan's work on Athanasius; (b) my own interpretation of Athanasius. These two moments will lead us to the conclusion that while it is right to say that the doctrinal affirmations of Nicaea and Chalcedon function as rules, it is also right to say that they *may* function as rules precisely because they are grounded in reality. And secondly, the fact that such statements derive from an intra-textual interpretation of Scripture does not mean that they do not faithfully portray reality itself. At stake here is the very possibility of ontology.

The first thing that we might notice is the shallowness of Lindbeck's case. The whole discussion is extremely short and doesn't occupy more than three pages. The re-interpretation of Athanasius itself is even shorter, and given the weight it is supposed to bear in the argument itself, this is very unsatisfactory. Let us remember that Lindbeck is up to nothing less

---

[83] Elkana, 'Second-order thinking', p. 47.

[84] I am using Adorno's and Horkheimer's phrase, although with a roughly different meaning.

[85] Lindbeck, *Doctrine*, p. 94.

than a revolutionising of the way we have interpreted the Church fathers. It is in this sense that I speak of a depth hermeneutics. The reader might remember the comments several pages above about the transition from formalism to functionalism without the proper introduction of criticism. To say that theology should interpret the Bible according to the literal sense simply because it has always been the way in which the Church interpreted is to fail to distinguish between the rival ontologies (within the Church) which compete for such a privileged position. Lindbeck treats the way the Church has always interpreted the Bible, and in this case the way it has always interpreted its theological statements, as needing no further legitimation. That is in itself potentially misleading. I dit not use another more 'moderate' word, for what is at stake here is the very distance the church must create between itself and its practices. If such is the way that Athanasius, or the Church fathers, or all of the Church, have always read the Bible, or interpreted theology, that is not in itself an argument. It may be the beginning of an argument, but it is not persuasive on its own. The conviction that I have tried to outline throughout this study is that to start from a common tradition, or from a body of corporate memory and values is not to close the text, or the argument, but merely to start it. There is more than the social construction of reality, and more that the communitarian habitation of truth. To rightly understand rhetoric – in all its virtue – is to understand that the beginning of an argument is what is shared (tradition, corporate memory, canonical texts, *sensus communis*). This relieves the anxiety of beginning, but the goal of argument is nonetheless truth.

Regardless of whether it was wise to follow Lonergan in this respect, given the reception that *The Way to Nicaea* had among patristics scholars[86], there are interpreters of Lonergan who argue that Lindbeck has in fact misread him.[87] To be sure, there are indeed reasons for such a functionalist reading of Lonergan. On discussing the concept of the homoousion, Lonergan notices how the term does not first acquire its meaning in a Greek context and then is imported into Christian theology. In one context he is virulently arguing against theologians such as DeWartt, but the list of possible targets could also be extended to include von Harnack and others. Lonergan's philosophy of language is much more subtle than would allow him to believe that a concept was imported from one context to the Christian context without altering its meaning. On the contrary, the concept has been taken over metaphorically, where the metaphor did not denote any hellenic

---

[86] David Brown's comments, see the exchange in *Modern Theology* 2 (1986), esp. pp. 242f, 266f.

[87] I have in mind S. Williams, 'Lindbeck's Regulative Christology', *passim*.

concept.[88] However, Lonergan continues, if the metaphor did take some-thing from the Greek context, it was determined by the Hellenic technique of reflecting on other propositions: 'it explains the word "consubstantial" by a second level proposition to the effect that the Son is consubstantial with the Father if and only if what is true of the Father is also true of the Son, except that only the Father is Father.'[89] Lonergan is also aware of the limitations of language in relating humanity to divinity. It is safe to argue that part of the reason why he relegates the concept to the second-order level is that theological language must be treated with the appropriate res-ervations. He notes that Eusebius, Athanasius, Hilary and Basil all urged against materialistic interpretations[90]. Language had to be apophatically qualified. However, and it is at this point that Lonergan can be turned either way, he asks: 'but if we exclude all materialistic interpretations, are we even left with a metaphor?'[91] To grasp what this means is both to remember what I hinted at earlier, and to anticipate a fuller discussion: the metaphor inaugurates a moment of disclosure, or what might be called a temporal space of disclosure, where the material content of the metaphor, with all its *extra-textual* history, is overlapping with the subject matter, creating a fu-sion between them. Materiality is a necessity of the metaphor. If this is in-deed what Lonergan argues, than the fact that one uses homoousion and not, for example, 'homoiousion' is crucial to the meaning and to the func-tion it has.

Read this way, Lonergan does not dissociate like Lindbeck, between the regulative and the referential function of ontological concepts such as 'ho-moousion'. Stephen Williams asks

> But the question, it will be recalled, is whether the regulative function so developed in the early centuries as to be independent of first order refer-ence to extra-linguistic reality (such as discussions of power, temporality or creaturehood manifestly involved in Lonergan's account).[92]

Lonergan's discussion is lodged in a context of realism,[93] and it is an anach-ronism to impose upon him a scheme which does not belong there.

---

[88] Bernard Lonergan, *The Second Collection: Papers by Bernard J. Lonergan S. J*, edited by William F. J. Ryan, S. J. and Bernard J. Tyrrell, (London: Darton, Longman and Todd, 1974), p. 23.

[89] Lonergan, *Second Collection*, p. 23.

[90] Bernard Lonergan, *The Way to Nicea: The Dialectical Development of Trinitarian Theology*, translated by Conn O'Donovan, (London: Darton, Longman and Todd, 1976), p. 90.

[91] Lonergan, *The Way*, p. 90.

[92] S. Williams, 'Lindbeck's regulative Christology', p. 77.

[93] S. Williams, 'Lindbeck's regulative Christology', p. 76.

When he defends Nicaea against the accusation of executing a generic (or quantum!) leap from New Testament religion to the realm of ontology, his interest is not to deny the ontological reference of the formulation of Nicaea but to insist that the *homoousion*, read in the light of the rule, says no more and no less than the New Testament. The *homoousion*, regulatively construed, rules out ontological *innovation*, not ontological *reference* – more (for Lindbeck accepts this), the latter is ingredient in it.[94]

Lonergan's position, according to this reading, is not dissimilar to Aquinas, as we have discussed it in the first section. Aquinas distinguished between textual moves, which are grammatical statements attempting to save the *modus loquendi* of Scripture and the independent descriptive metaphysics (which Marshall accuses Barth of hijacking from the text). According to Aquinas, we remember, both descriptive metaphysics and grammatical tactics are true if they correspond to the way the reality is. But the criterion for their truth lies with the *modus loquendi* of Scripture alone. Legitimising truth claims can never be an exegesis-neutral undertaking. Which is to say, with Lonergan, that ontological concepts say nothing more and nothing less than what the New Testament already says. Williams seems to have aptly questioned Lindbeck's reading of Lonergan. But whether he does in fact incorrectly read him is not enough to dismantle his depth hermeneutics. We must next look at Athanasius himself.

Christopher Stead has argued in his *Divine Substance*[95] that Athanasius cannot be interpreted as using the 'homoousion' simply to mean that the Father and the Son are of the same species. Stead draws attention to an interesting 'built-in asymmetry in his use of the term.'[96] The term is never used of the Father, except of the Son. The reason for this being that Athanasius intends to use the term to denote an organic relationship which flows in one direction, from the Father to the Son and not the other way around. The term, then, denotes something very specific and extra-textual. Stead argues that the reading of Athanasius with which he takes issue seriously 'underrates the emphasis on shared and communicated life and light and being which is maintained in the later writings.'[97] And further down, 'There is no sign that in his later works St. Athanasius wished to withdraw the other analogies which more strongly express the organic continuity of Father and Son.'[98] There is thus something in the use of this expression which doesn't cohere with a purely regulative use. Should such a grammatical function be the sole reason behind the use of the term, there would be no point in the

---

[94] S. Williams, 'Lindbeck's regulative Christology', p. 78.

[95] (Oxford: Clarendon, 1977).

[96] Stead, *Divine Substance*, p. 260.

[97] Stead, *Divine Substance*, p. 265.

[98] Stead, *Divine Substance*, p. 265.

asymmetry. Nor would there be any reason to insist on organic metaphors. *Quite clearly, then, whilst being aware of the limitations of human analogies, Athanasius does have a referential and representative point to make.* He does intend to refer to extra-textual realities, and indeed he does intend his terms to describe something which obtains independently of us.

Is this possible, however? Does not the very use of such ontological concepts obscure the particularity of the textual event? Marshall, Frei, Lindbeck and other postliberal theologians warn us against submitting the text to foreign ontologies and external explanatory discourses. But the either/or into which they attempt to force us is unnecessary. This study has been a sustained attempt to keep the broken middle and not try to mend it. The false alternatives between foundationalism and irrationalism, or between insiders to the truth and outsiders, or between sheer nihilism and unapologetic fideism, forget the possibility of the middle. Does conceptual language still hold some promise for theology? An incipient answer to this question lies in an analysis of the role of metaphor in theology. I do not intend to provide any remotely exhaustive analysis of the philosophy of metaphor, as this is beyond the scope of this essay. The rather more modest task is to use understandings of metaphor shared by most theologians, including postliberal ones, in order to illuminate the way in which narrative and discursive knowledge co-inhabit each other.

T. F. Torrance, in his masterful essay on 'Theological Realism' provides an apt analysis of the current philosophical situation and its bearing on the way theology is done. Decrying the dualism between reality and appearance he suggests that both naïve realism and idealism have the tendency of collapsing into their opposites.

> A truly realist position will be one in which the sign differentiates itself
> from the reality on which it actually bears, and therein reveals a measure
> of disparateness or discrepancy which is an essential ingredient in its suc-
> cessful functioning as a sign. For true statements to serve the truth of be-
> ing, they must fall short of it and not be mistaken for it, for they do not
> possess their truth in themselves, but in the reality they serve: a dash of
> inadequacy therefore is necessary for their precision.[99]

Torrance's whole argument turns on the rejection of dualism between reality and the subject which apprehends it. It was 'a realist orientation of this kind which Greek patristic theology, especially from the third to the sixth century, struggled so hard to acquire and which it built into the foundations of classical theology.'[100] Unfortunately, however, it was eventually the Ar-

---

[99] T. F. Torrance, 'Theological realism', in Brian Hebblethwaite and S. Sutherland, *The Philosophical Foundations of Christian Theology: Essays Presented to D. M. MacKinnon*, (Cambridge: Cambridge University Press, 1982), p. 171.

[100] Torrance, 'Theological realism', p. 173.

istotelian-Augustinian epistemology which prevailed, with its disjunction between the thing and the mind, between which intervened the *objecta mentis*.[101] Thus the clear evidential basis that we find at the foundation of Greek patristic theology is lost when philosophy dirempts between the sensual and the super-sensible. If what is held in the mind can only arrive there by way of the senses, then knowledge of God – who is not given in the senses – can only proceed indirectly. The mind can only accede to the supra-sensual by imposing form upon the content it receives from the reality in a passive way. However, such an ascent of the mind to the supra-sensible is governed not by the power of divine reality which provides its own immediacy to the mind, but by will. The connection with Yehuda Elkana's analysis of second-order thinking and with the Scotist and modern will is evident here. The forms that the mind imposes on matter are not legitimated by anything other than the will. The way is open for a non-conceptual relation between God and man:

> So far as knowledge of God is concerned, this had the effect of detaching the understanding, even in the assent of faith, from the self-evidence of God in his own being and truth, so that in the last resort faith has to rest on moral grounds and operate only with an indirect relation to God.[102]

Theology had to find a non-conceptual way to figure out its relationship to God and in Schillebeeckx's opinion this turned theology into a second-order discipline. Theology, having no access to God, turns to faith and becomes a mere investigation of the grammar of that faith. The fact that there is no conceptual knowledge of God means that our theologies and theories about salvation have no reference in any extra-linguistic reality. In this case what is to protect theology from mere subjectivism?

Torrance shows how such a dualist epistemology has been discredited in science. This aspect of his argument, important as it is, does not bear directly on our Christological purposes here. The second aspect of his project does: it is actually Christology which (together with the new philosophy of science associated with Einstein, Polanyi et al.) overturns the dualism. Building on the writings of Barth and Anselm, Torrance writes:

> There is no non-conceptual gap between God's revealing of himself and our knowing of him, for God reveals himself to us on the ground of his own inner intelligibility which is the creative ground of all rationality in the universe and as such enables us to conceive and speak of him truly in ways that are ultimately grounded in God's supreme Being. Hence theology, interpreted as faith seeking understanding, is a humble enquiry into the intrinsic reason of things in God, and takes place as we allow the truth of God's own Being to impress itself on our understanding in its own in-

---

[101] Torrance, 'Theological realism', p. 174.
[102] Torrance, 'Theological realism', p. 176.

herent intelligibility, so that our judgements and statements about it are formed under its authority, that is, the authority of the *solida veritas* of God himself.[103]

The abolition of the dualism stems from reckoning with the reality of God's revelation. It is perhaps no surprise that the doctrine of revelation is quasi-absent from postliberal theological epistemology, with the notable exception of Ronald Thiemann. *The truth of theology, under Christological agenda, is not determined by the summoning of the will to interpret the grammar of faith, but by the gracious action of God who in revelation presents himself to us.*[104] Theological theories are not non-conceptual, which is not to say that they are to be confused with the Being of God, or with Jesus.

Herein lies one of the main differences between Torrance's Christological analogy and Frei's analogy. If for Frei the analogy identifies the story of Jesus with the identity of Jesus, for Torrance the limitations of the sign are vital to its proper functioning as a sign. To identify Jesus with the Gospels is to miss the equivocation point, as Work so compellingly argues. Neither can one identify the theological theories about Jesus with Jesus himself, for that is to miss the tension between sign and signified. There is also another distinction which must be properly underscored: both Scripture and theological theories speak about God and Jesus. But there is a qualitative difference between them. For whereas, theological theories are human words about God, the Scriptural texts as traditionally understood provide us with human and divine words about God. Yet the revelation is incomplete, which is not to say that it is unreliable. It would be beyond the scope of this book to analyse in detail the nature of the Bible,[105] yet the qualitative difference between Bible and theology remains unchallenged in postliberal quarters.

The incarnation occasioned a 'realist revolution,'[106] and the victory of the homoousion amounted to a great scientific theological act, uniting epistemology and ontology. It also meant that 'God does not merely make himself present to us in his own being in a merely passive way, but in such an active way that he grounds our knowing evidentially on the present reality of the divine being.'[107] Following the 'homoousion', theology could confidently speak about God and the disjunction between first and second-order

---

[103] Torrance, 'Theological realism', p. 178.

[104] Torrance also speaks about the homoousion of the Holy Spirit who is alone able to guarantee present theological truth ('Theological realism', pp. 186ff.).

[105] The position most consonant with our present project is that outlined by Wolterstorff in his *Divine Discourse*, as well as aspects of Work's *Living and Active: Scripture in the Economy of Salvation*.

[106] Torrance, 'Theological realism', p. 184.

[107] Torrance, 'Theological realism', p. 186.

statements can no longer hold in terms of their respective reference and non-referentiality. God is indeed an object of our knowledge, not in the sense that he is collapsable into our epistemic schemes, but that in Christ we are indeed given the whole being of God. 'It is because God has incarnated his own eternal Word and Rationality within the realities and intelligibilities of our creaturely existence in Jesus Christ, that we, creatures though we are, may grasp God conceptually in his own divine reality.'[108] To reject the conceptual reference of our theology is in fact to operate a crippled Christology, which doesn't take into account the full humanity of the Logos, or the full divinity of Jesus.

It may be argued that to some extent Torrance is also proceeding intratextually here, where Lindbeck in fact isn't. Torrance does not directly apply his critique to Lindbeck, but he would make a very appropriate target. In fact Stephen Need, in his book on *Human Language and Knowledge in the Light of Chalcedon*[109] argues more closely that notions of language are to be rooted in understandings of Christology. According to Need, the overwhelming problem in Lindbeck's arguments lies in the weak ontological roots of the cultural linguistic view[110]. His fundamental cleavage between language and ontology pays more attention to philosophies of language rather than to Christology. His regulative Christology is a direct consequence of his regulative view of language[111], when in fact the flow of interpretation should be in the opposite direction. Lindbeck himself has argued, together with Frei, that the direction of interpretation should be not from world to Scripture, but from Scripture to world. Where Lindbeck in effect denies cognitive import to theology, a proper Christological view of language would be better able to stress the tension between the 'is' and the 'is not.'[112]

This has been a failure of postliberal theology, at least Frei's and Lindbeck's, in its own terms. It has not been consistently able to read reality, involving philosophies of language as well, in light of Scripture. It thus betrays its natural condition: that we cannot help but import our own ontologies when dealing with narratives. Given this inevitability it is important to keep such theories visible, recognise their necessity as well as their transience. However, while the signs/ theories/ narratives are human constructions that is not to say that their humanity is less important. Torrance stresses the bi-polarity of the sign:

---

[108] Torrance, 'Theological realism', p. 187.

[109] American University Studies Series 7: Theology and Religion, vol. 187. (New York, Washington D.C., Baltimore, Bern, Frankfurt am Main, Berlin, Vienna, Paris: Peter Lang, 1996).

[110] Need, *Human Language*, p. 19.

[111] Need, *Human Language*, p. 20.

[112] Need, *Human Language*, p. 23.

In a realist theory of knowledge, however, we have to do with the apprehension of some object in its inner structure which is the source of our conceptions of it, and thus regard the conceptuality which arises in this way as having a bipolar character. It is grounded in the objective intelligibility of reality, but it incorporates also a subjective counterpart, since it is we the knowing subjects who conceive and express our knowledge of it.[113]

It is this union between the subjective and the objective which forms the 'tensive' character of metaphor, as Need calls it. He also speaks about the importance of togetherness in metaphor: it is the primary level (reality) in its union with the metaphorical level (the conceptual description) which provides what we have called the space of disclosure. I would also like to defend the notion of a *temporal space of disclosure* in order to point out that disclosure is a process rather than a moment, and that it involves stages of clarification, leading to greater semantic depth. Such semantic depth is in turn achieved through participation in the object, through the practices of the church. Torrance writes about the enhancement of our concepts, as they become more and more appropriate to the realities described. The process is only appropriate for Torrance if we subject our metaphors and theories to the authority of the self-validating word and reality of God.[114] What we have here, if my arguments are correct, is a view of theological knowledge which makes it commensurable to other discourses, since the materiality of its own metaphors is shared with other discourses. Such materiality, however, is modified by its application to the theological matter at hand. It retains its distinctness from the object, but it also operates creatively upon it.[115]

We do have a sense then in which theology is not only a second order activity, without any referential ability. This model of the metaphorical activity is consonant with a number of metaphorical theories, but we shall only track its reliance on John McIntyre's view of models. McIntyre distinguishes between the phenomena, which are the realities to which we are

---

[113] Torrance, 'Theological realism', p. 179.

[114] Torrance, 'Theological realism', p. 179: 'such a constant transformation of the conceptual content of our knowledge of God must take place if we are not to subject God to the control of our conceptions and representations of him. And indeed it can and does take place but, as far as I can see, only indirectly through the spiritual transformation of our lives in their relationship with God in love and within the fellowship of the church.' These last words brings Torrance's realism more in line with a pragmatic understanding of semantic depth. It is not just anyone who is able to reach it, but only 'disciples'.

[115] Cf. Ricoeur's notion that metaphors work not by perceiving a resemblance, but by creating it (Vanhoozer, *Biblical Narrative in the Philosophy of Paul Ricoeur*, pp. 66ff.).

applying metaphorical description, the model itself and the theory associated with the phenomena.[116] It is at the intersection between the model and the phenomena, that a third image is created, which is both cognitive and creative. We had in mind the same mutual inter-penetration when we have asserted the need for ontology in understanding narrative. In order to understand the rough material or the phenomena, one needs to organise it according to certain constraints, or theories. The content of those metaphors is just as essential to the resulting disclosure, as the phenomena itself. To return to Christological titles: the ontologies associated with one specific title make all the difference. It's functioning in the story does not account for its entire meaning; rather, it is both the intra-narrative use[117] as well as the extra-textual conceptual baggage that makes the metaphor.[118] McIntyre calls the Christological models, such as *homoousion*, terms in which we apprehend the person of Christ[119]. They are neither purely subjective, nor purely objective. He draws on Kemp Smith's discussion of secondary qualities, who argues that they are neither existing in reality, nor purely subjective ideas, but terms in which we apprehend the external world and describe it.[120] For McIntyre, however, what the metaphor denotes does exist in reality, otherwise there would be no point to using metaphors:[121] 'if we speak about Christ as shepherd, it is because he has certain qualities which authenticate the comparison, and it is of those qualities themselves that we are talking when we describe him as shepherd.'[122] Obviously, this is not a vision of metaphor according to which everything goes, any metaphor is appropriate, as in post-structuralist textualism. This is a perspective on metaphor according to which the ultimate tribunal for the legitimacy of metaphor are the phenomena themselves.

---

[116] John McIntyre, *The Shape of Christology,* (London: SCM, 1966), p. 56; at p. 60 he calls the last element the 'subject of disclosure'.

[117] Elisabeth Struthers Malbon argues that the titles applied to Jesus are *refracted* or bent into new meanings by Jesus' *deflection* of honour and attention from himself to God. (Elisabeth Struthers Malbon, 'Reflected Christology: an aspect of narrative 'Christology' in the Gospel of Mark', *Perspectives in Religious Studies*, 26 (1999), 127-145.)

[118] Metaphors are never 'innocent', writes Brian Wicker (Brian Wicker, *The Story-Shaped World: Fiction and Metaphysics, Some Variations on a Theme*, (London: Athlone Press, 1975), p. vii), but they always imply a certain, at least provisional, metaphysic.

[119] McIntyre, *Shape of Christology*, p. 68.

[120] McIntyre, *Shape of Christology*, p. 67.

[121] This is similar to Ricoeur's point about 'pre-configuration' or mimesis$_1$ (*Time and Narrative*, I, pp. 54-64).

[122] McIntyre, *Shape of Christology*, p. 69.

In closing this section there are two aspects which need mentioning: *the over-determination of reality by the concepts*, and the *under-determination of participation in reality by the concepts*. Torrance speaks at one point about the need to operate with signs in order better to manage the multitude of reality. Signs are 'a restricted set of more manageable things such as words, concepts, or numbers, who represent through their various combinations an unrestricted set of less manageable things... and thereby achieve a measure of rational control in our apprehension of them...'[123] There is an all-important distinction between sign and the reality signified. In order for the sign to function properly, to refer us to reality there takes place an 'over-determination' which is in fact the result of the super-imposition of the metaphor upon the phenomena. Gunton speaks of this by likening the Christological models with maps. In a map certain characteristics of the field are intensified so as to make orientation possible, the locations of the main features of the map are over-determined.[124] He then comments:

> Similarly, the Chalcedonian confession carefully mapped a number of features of what the members of the council held to be crucial truths about the person of Jesus Christ: his unity, his divinity, his humanity and the four ways in which these three were understood.[125]

Julia Kristeva, in her biography of Hannah Arendt also speaks about signs as being condensed, incomplete and atomised, giving rise to the infinite play of interpretation. She understands narratives as having the power to condense action into an *exemplary space* where a moment of accomplishment of the narrative disclosure takes place.[126] What these writers point to is that the work of the theories as well as of the narratives is simply to point us beyond them, as we shall see in the next section. Their role is not that of monopolising our attention, but with help from these features, in which understanding meets reality, we are referred beyond them. Indeed, as McIntyre sees, the test of a good metaphor is if it allows us to work on that reality, to do things with it.

To recapitulate, the relegation of Christology to the status of second-order discourse uncritically assumes the dualism between reality and appearance. Lindbeck does not allow Christology to shape his understanding of language and knowledge. In the process, Christology becomes a matter of drawing out the implications of first order language. It has become apparent that there can be no narrative reading without some sort of ontology

---

[123] Torrance, 'Theological Realism', p. 170.

[124] Colin Gunton, *Yesterday and Today: A Study of Continuities in Christology,* (Grand Rapids: Wm. B. Eerdmans, 1983), p. 153.

[125] Gunton, *Yesterday*, p. 153.

[126] Julia Kristeva, *Hannah Arendt,* translated by Ross Guberman, (New York: Columbia University Press, 2001), pp. 73, 74.

informing the reading.[127] Indeed, as Richard Allen so aptly observes, one criterion for the success of a story is that of identifiability. That is, the ability to tell a good story, or to suggest the embodiment of a virtue, depends on the ability to imagine a world in which that virtue can be identified.[128] Or, as Milbank taught us, to read a story is already to meta-narrate it. It is because ontology provides us with a setting of the story that we are able to understand the story itself. Milbank's problem is that the relationship between this ontology and the story it wants to make sense of is purely extrinsic. We are to adopt a certain ontology purely for reasons of literary taste. But if there is no truth at stake, we ask, why bother with understanding the story?

It is this fear of subjectivism which forces Kenneth Surin to react to MacKinnon's suggestion that theology is second-order language. Upon discussing the problematic concept of substance in his 'Substance in Christology – A Cross-Bench View'[129] MacKinnon rejects the modern attempts to replace metaphysics with a philosophy of event. Arguing that in the last analysis event must presuppose things which are engaged in it, the philosophy of event is in fact deconstructable into metaphysics.[130] It is a mistake, he argues, both to import metaphysical notions without qualification, as it is mistaken to believe one can do without metaphysics. MacKinnon's argument is similar to that of Oliver Davies in his *A Theology of Compassion*, where he argues that it is only against the background of universality, of the same, or Being, that the particular can be made visible.[131] The same sort of position is held by Gillian Rose[132] to the effect that the Other cannot be both affirmed and its existence denied in a philosophy that lacks a belief in agency. MacKinnon argues in this essay that we need ontological concepts

---

[127] Cf. also Brian Hebblethwaite, *The Incarnation: Collected Essays in Christology*, (Cambridge: Cambridge University Press, 1987), p. 69.

[128] Richard Allen, 'When narrative fails', *Journal of Religious Ethics*, 21 (1993), 27-67, p. 42.

[129] Donald MacKinnon, 'Substance in Christology – A cross-bench view', in Stephen Sykes and Phillip Clayton, eds., *Christ, Faith and History: Cambridge Studies in Christology*, (Cambridge: Cambridge University Press, 1972).

[130] MacKinnon, 'Substance', p. 286.

[131] Oliver Davies, *A Theology of Compassion: Metaphysics of Difference and the Renewal of Tradition*, (London: SCM, 2001), pp. 1-23, esp. 6-10. This is an idea shared with Rowan Williams and Gillian Rose: Rowan Williams, 'Between politics and metaphysics: reflections in the wake of Gillian Rose', *Modern Theology*, 11 (1995), 3-22, p. 5.

[132] Gillian Rose, *The Broken Middle: Out of Our Ancient Society*, (Oxford: Blackwell, 1992).

in order to bring out the particular[133]. Particularity without intelligibility is impossible. It is this lesson which postliberal theology needs to learn. So the question of whether theology can dispense with 'substance' is a question of whether it can dispense with propositions, which MacKinnon clearly believes it cannot.[134] However, when it comes to explaining the 'homoousion', he resorts to second-order language as well: 'its significance as an instrument for advancing our understanding to enable us to see what it is that is at issue in the simpler, more direct, more immediately moving Christological affirmations of the Gospels.'[135] There is no suspicion here that such concepts have no truth about them, but if Surin is correct, this makes theology highly vulnerable to subjectivism[136]. The danger lies in the fact that it would construe the divinity of Jesus on the basis of human textual judgements rather that on Jesus' own self-understanding, argues Surin.[137] He then casts a glancing look at the possibility of construing theological statements as semantic presuppositions, 'propositions whose truth must be presupposed in order that we may assign a truth value to other, more abstract theological propositions.'[138] It soon becomes apparent that to think of them as semantic presuppositions is not to take seriously the necessity of their truth. A semantic presupposition such as 'there is such a thing as a table' is presupposed both by the statement 'John is at the table' as well as by 'John is not sitting at the table.' Following P. F. Strawson, the assignment of a truth value to a certain proposition presupposes the truth of other propositions. Q is said to presuppose a proposition p if and only if q is neither true nor false unless p is true. Turning to Christological propositions, it could be argued that the proposition 'In Christ God reconciled all things to himself (q) presupposes the incarnational proposition 'Jesus Christ is of the same substance as the Father' (p) because it is a necessary condition of determining whether or not humanity is saved that God became incarnate in Jesus.[139] His overall argument amounts to the fact that in the absence of some ontological propositions we shall not be able to make sense of what is going on in the story, of its shocking particularity. However, a

---

[133] 'But what in the end is the service that ontology does to theology, ontology of the sort with which we have been concerned in this paper, except to tie it tightly to the concrete?', p. 292.

[134] MacKinnon, 'Substance', p. 290.

[135] MacKinnon, 'Substance', p. 291.

[136] Kenneth Surin, 'Some aspects of the 'grammar' of incarnation and 'kenosis': reflections prompted by the writings of Donald MacKinnon', in Ken Surin, ed., *Christ, Ethics and Tragedy: Essays in Honour of Donald MacKinnon*, (Cambridge: Cambridge University Press, 1989).

[137] Surin, 'Grammar', p. 97.

[138] Surin, 'Grammar', p. 97.

[139] Surin, 'Grammar', pp. 97-8.

semantic presupposition is entailed both by q and by *non-q*. Which is not what may be said about our Christological propositions: the fact that 'in Christ God did not reconcile all things in himself', or that 'in Christ it wasn't God who reconciled all things to himself' no longer assumes that 'Jesus is of the same substance with the Father.' This makes the proposition fail the test of negation. Surin consequently decides to treat such incarnational propositions as 'pragmatic presuppositions', which are those propositions which must be true in order that Christological discourse may be properly transacted.[140] Surin is also a theologian who presupposes the primacy of the intra-textual world of Scripture. But to properly understand what Scripture is saying is not to shy away from ontological affirmations, for it is these very propositions which gives to us the full force of the text. Hence, theological utterance is appropriate when incarnational propositions are (pragmatically) presupposed by those who engage in such utterance, and when what justifies the assertion of such propositions as (pragmatic) presuppositions is the *modus loquendi* of Scripture.[141] Incarnational statements and textual statements (such as those about reconciliation) mutually enforce each other. The former intensify the meaning of the latter, while textual statements are the only ones which legitimate the theological ones. Surin has succeeded in affirming the necessity of what MacKinnon calls second order statements, incarnational statements. The transition from the text to doctrine is not a second-order activity, since it is these theological statements which are 'basic' to the text. There is an interesting connection here with Alvin Plantinga's notion of basic beliefs. But whereas for Plantinga these basic statements are given in all situations and contexts, more like universal truths of reason, for Surin these statements are presupposed in a specific context and culture. Which does not take anything from their truth value, at least in Surin's eyes.

Christological Reference and Tradition as Habitus

Intra-textuality is seen as the guardian of concreteness. Milbank's narrative knowledge, Frei's identification by way of narrative rendering, or his reading of the world in light of Scripture, all of these are endorsements of a traditioned knowledge. It is a kind of knowledge that follows in the footsteps of the rhetorical tradition of Aristotle, Burke and Vico according to which the mind is always informed by prejudice. The human agent is not Descartes' punctual self, but an embedded person, living within a horizon of corporate memory. Frei himself decries the advent of modernity and the displacement of this reading of reality in light of a particular set of Scriptures. Biblical time was replaced with a real, absolute time, which in turn

---

[140] Surin, 'Grammar', p. 98.

[141] Surin, 'Grammar', p. 99.

has lead to the loss of the Bible's applicability. Modernity's revolt against all forms of tradition lead to the latter's branding as superstition, obscurantism, or infancy. The current ideal is Kant's grown-up man. Enlightenment means leaving behind the sacred texts and turning to what is natural, the universal, what is the common possession of all humanity. Richard Allen brilliantly draws the connection between the concepts of concreteness and identity. The uniqueness which derives from the particular foundational narratives of a tradition issues in a sense of identity of the author (or narratee's), and 'into the secure identity of the community, formed by the narrative.'[142] The displacement of authority brought with it the loss of certainty and the descent towards nihilism.

Frei's, Lindbeck's and Milbank's answer to this predicament is nothing less than the resuscitation of corporate memory. Theirs is the correct realisation that in the absence of any willing faith, there is nothing there to be discovered. But they are open to criticism in as much as they leave no distance between this faith and its object, on the one hand, and seek no relation between this faith and other faiths. The first is the problematic expousal of non-realism, the second is over-readiness to embrace pluralism, as opposed to plurality. Their programme tunes with the belief in the primacy of precedent, in the loss of the original in the legal tradition:

> There are, according to Burke, no principles separate from acts, no rights deracinated from history. There is nothing outside of the English legal tradition – that is, outside the various texts that compose the English constitution – that can serve as a foundation for political legitimacy.[143]

The inherent danger in such a view is that there is no distinction between what counts as a right interpretation of a narrative and what doesn't. No distance remains between the text and what the text is about, or between the text and its normative application. Legitimation is sheer rhetoric. Narratives have lost their anchoring in reality and all we are left with are texts, with no rules of deciding between them. What ensues is therefore a 'narrative frenzy'[144], as Allen calls it:

> To the extent that Lindbeck and Frei do preserve the meaning of the text, in the sense that the Scriptures are interpreted in terms of themselves and not some other things, they do so at the price of recognising that cultures can be abandoned, languages forgotten, stories rendered incomprehensible.[145]

---

[142] Allen, 'When Narrative Fails', p. 34.

[143] Allen, 'When Narrative Fails', p. 36.

[144] Allen, 'When Narrative Fails', p. 40.

[145] Allen, 'When Narrative Fails', p. 40.

By intra-textually tying meaning to these particular texts alone, and no other texts, and no other referent in reality Lindbeck and Frei open Christianity to the loss of everything together with the loss of their sacred texts. One has to agree with Allen to the extent that this results in an unnecessary removal of the text from reality and from other cultures (our two previously mentioned failures), although one need not share his willingness to celebrate life in a post-canonical era. Christianity stands or falls with its texts, but precisely because its texts are anchored in a self-evidencing reality, given in the revelation of God in Christ. Yet the diagnostic is correct: narrative frenzy results from the very concentration on the texts alone, without realising that the point of the texts is not exclusively in themselves at all.[146]

Nicholas Wolterstorff wonders, against Frei's neglect of reference, that 'What else could the point of a narrative be but the point of someone's offering us the narrative – or the point of our putting the narrative to one and another use?'[147] The point is not in the telling, as Hauerwas himself admits: 'So I think it is a fundamental and far reaching mistake to suppose that telling the story is the whole thing. What one makes of the world and of one's existence is the strength of the story: that is the pay-off.[148]' The story, then, just as models, metaphors and theories, become signs pointing to something else. Texts, to follow Edith Wyschogrod's commentary on Henry James, comprise marks and spaces whose boundaries are frangible.[149] Part of the essence of a story, then, is its proximity to that about which it is. Torrance, together with Need, as well as Telford Work, have helped assert the material difference that the doctrine of Incarnation makes. Christology has therefore been not simply a test-case for these methodological investigations into post-liberal theological epistemology, but their corrective. If we are to allow our world to be narrated by the Bible, then Christology makes a difference in how we conceive the possibility of knowledge. In dealing with epistemology, theology cannot bracket out the implications of the Incarnation and the epistemic revolution it inaugurated.

It is both surprising and understandable that postliberalism lacks a notion of revelation. Regardless of whether it is due to the fear of introducing another universal concept (with quite an aggressive pedigree), or to any other reason, it is an unfortunate omission. Mark Wallace argues that precisely such a mooring of the canonical texts in a notion of revelation would justify

---

[146] In a certain sense this is to admit some validity to Ricoeur's textual projection of a world. My discussion, however, was not in terms of meaning, but in terms of the point of the text.

[147] Wolterstorff, *Divine Discourse*, p. 234.

[148] Hauerwas, 'Why Truth Demands Truthfulness', p. 142.

[149] Edith Wyschogrod, *Saints and Postmodernism: Revisioning Moral Philosophy*, (Chicago: University of Chicago Press, 1990), p. 19.

our preference for them as opposed to other 'sacred' texts.[150] Yet Wallace also suggests the need for the openness of the Christian story. Richard Allen argues something similar when he writes that 'the only complete text is the world itself. How can any partial written text, the work of any man's hand, absorb it?'[151] Surely the following qualification matters: 'the work of any man's hand'. Should the text be in fact one which is indissolubly connected to the revelation of God, the text could not be simply dismissed and its capacity for world absorption re-established. But crucially, such a world absorption hangs on its relation to something extra-textual.[152] Hannah Arendt speaks about the danger of having the texts transformed into *mythos*, where all attention is focused on them. The text is but an exemplary sign, its existence is an effacing one, before the God to which it leads us. For Arendt, in order to guard against this self-absorbing tendency of the text, to keep the text as *energeia*, one must seek to perform it at all times. But it may be that in this performance, broken from the text's actual reference, the *mythos* is preserved under the appearance of *energeia*. In contrast, the texts' openness has to be not simply towards the reader, but more especially towards the referent.

Allen writes about the security which is offered by having one's life rendered in light of one text, or refusing the tension which might arise from opening oneself to the myriads of the texts of the world. It is in this sense that intra-textual theology, by defining the text as closed, and the world as closed, offers a false sense of security. Tyler Roberts, discussing the various narrative strategies in coping with the limitations of human knowledge, argues that both Mark C. Taylor and Stanley Hauerwas 'conceptualise narrative primarily in terms of its promises of closure and unity.'[153] Within such a closed world, reference (as I have previously argued) is a finished affair. However, this closure also means that there can be no critical revaluation of one's reading strategies. Performance lacks an original according to which it could be judged. Roberts argues that

> Although Hauerwas does claim that human beings must always question their narratives and convictions, it is unclear whether, given his faith in

---

[150] Mark I. Wallace, 'Can God be named without being known? The problem of revelation in Thiemann, Ogden, and Ricoeur', *Journal of the American Academy of Religion*, 59 (1991), 281-308, p. 282.

[151] Allen, 'When Narrative Fails', p. 40

[152] For Allen, simply telling a story is not enough; an amnesiac could do it, whereas 'to avoid narrational frenzy, one's spoken discourse must be grounded in one's perceptions, thoughts and action.' ('When Narrative Fails', p. 63.)

[153] Tyler Roberts, 'Theology and the ascetic imperative: narrative and renunciation in Taylor and Hauerwas', *Modern Theology*, 9 (1993), 181-200, p. 182.

God's power, he has shown us how historical events can lead Christians to raise serious questions about the shape of their narrative.[154]

What Roberts suggests is the opening up of a dialectical distance between story and history so that the story is never complete. There has to be a moment where this closure is broken. Mark Wallace suggests the possibility of two strategies: either a postmodern endless deferral of meaning, or a Ricoeurian deconstruction of the superiority and security of the narrative via inter-textuality.[155] Ricoeur argues that the wisdom genre of the Bible has the ability to subvert the trust we place in our stories and the unity we ascribe to them. Perhaps the more useful strategy is neither the postmodern, textualist one, nor the Ricoeurian one (since it disrupts the unity of the canon), but in fact what Tyler Roberts suggests: 'as human stories about God, the Christian narratives point beyond themselves, disrupting their own meaning and closure by continually returning to the difference between God and humanity that keeps the story going.'[156]

The consequence of this strong model of intra-textuality is a closed text, a complete and already achieved reference. Criticism is fore-closed. Ironically, as Frederic Jameson suggests, these narratives, by being closed, remember the past but only by forgetting the past. This 'narrative amnesia'[157] is the direct result of the reification of the story: 'Narrative amnesia results when a formal analysis of plot takes precedence over the events that constitute the narrative.'[158] A similar point has been made by Werner Kelber, one of a growing number of biblical scholars that start drawing attention to the oral culture in which the Gospels stories have originated. Kelber argues, following Walter J. Ong's seminal studies, that the closed model thinking (the text as closed) is only possible in the western cultural setting, when 'the technologising, objectivising impact of printing had reached a high point.'[159] For Bourdieu, writing inaugurates an economy of representation, whereas oral practice excluded reflexivity by being 'caught up in the matter at hand'. Writing exteriorises by transforming the temporal, immediate and pre-reflexive into the synchronic, reflexive and comparable.[160] Frei is able to read the gospel narratives in this way only through the anachronistic im-

---

[154] Roberts, 'Theology and the ascetic imperative', p. 187.

[155] This results in Ricoeur's healthy balancing of narrative with other literary genres. cf. Wallace, *The Second Naiveté*, p. 41.

[156] Roberts, 'Theology and the ascetic imperative', p. 194.

[157] Roberts, 'Theology and the ascetic imperative', p. 188.

[158] Roberts, p. 188.

[159] Werner Kelber, 'Gospel narrative and critical theory', *Biblical Theological Bulletin*, 18 (1988), 130-136, p. 132.

[160] Pierre Bourdieu, *Outline of a Theory of Practice*, translated by Richard Nice, (Cambridge: Cambridge University Press, 1977), pp. 187, 236 n. 41.

position upon them of canons of reading specific to the eighteenth, nineteenth and twentieth centuries. The strong idea which has informed such readings is the concept of a self-referential narrative. But there is an organic unity between narrative and tradition, or between the intra-textual and the extra-textual which implies that narrative meanings must not be immunised 'against all involvements in antecedent tradition.'[161] As the examples of Christological titles has shown, there is no need to disjunct between their intra-textual and extra-textual use.[162] To understand the oral context is to have a better sense of its transparency.

In an oral setting plot no longer functions as it does in a textual one, as is our contemporary culture. There is more of an understanding of the temporality of *disclosure*[163], rather the synchronic *presence* of meaning. The structures of the text are no longer reified units, but retreat as soon as they have been invoked, in a movement away from the text and towards what the text is all about.[164] By definition in this case reference cannot be considered an achieved result, for the story has no existence apart from its telling. Kelber speaks in another context about the non-objectifiable nature of speech and the corresponding impossibility of a dualism between sign and signified[165]. The visibility of the written sign, in a textual culture, contributed to the independence of logic from speech[166], to its formalisation and reification. Kelber is arguing for nothing else than the irrelevance of the dualism between sign and signified. The speaker and author were all part of the same continuum and spoken language effected their relationship, rather than written language breaking it. In an oral context, as Sternberg himself observes, the narrative author is a teller rather than a maker of plot.[167] If we

---

[161] Kelber, 'Gospel narrative', p. 132.

[162] Hauerwas, 'Why the truth demands truthfulness', p. 143; Michael Goldberg, *Theology and Narrative: A Critical Introduction*, (Philadelphia: Trinity Press International, 1991²) and Tilley (quoted in Hauerwas) all argue that the category of narrative may have been used in 'a far too crude manner.'

[163] See Rowan Williams' idea of 'taking time' to understand the text, in *On Christian Theology* (Oxford: Blackwell, 2000), p. 46.

[164] They become what Ricoeur calls 'mediums of discourse' (*Philosophy and the Human Sciences: Essays on Language, Action and Interpretation,* edited by John Thompson, (Cambridge: Cambridge University Press, Paris: Editions de la Maison des Sciences de l'Homme, 1981), pp. 145-149).

[165] Werner Kelber, 'In the beginning were the words: the apotheosis and narrative displacement of the Logos', *Journal of the American Academy of Religion*, 58 (1990), 69-98, p. 75.

[166] See Werner Kelber, 'Jesus and tradition: words in time, words in space', *Semeia*, 65 (1995), 139-167, p. 140.

[167] Sternberg, *Poetics*, p. 128.

grant that one cannot exaggerate the tensions inside the text[168], if we refuse the understanding of texts as compositions of reified structures we will also understand that tradition can no longer be understood as *stratification* but rather as *biosphere*.

What Kelber and Ong blame on the textual culture of modernity, Kathryn Tanner blames on the adoption of a modern anthropological model of culture in theology. She believes that Lindbeck is able to understand religion as a *verbum externum* due to such an influence. In a closed and fixed notion of culture,[169] the function of rules is to regulate behaviour, which is not what happens. Tanner objects to this interpretation of rules, believing that the weight that is placed on them is unbearable. That a set of rules exists does not mean that they do in fact legislate[170]. Furthermore, with respect to the Christological rules which Lindbeck says it is the function of doctrines to express, she argues that they in fact do not prescribe sufficiently what may or may not be said. Pierre Bourdieu writes that:

> To consider regularity, that is, what recurs with a certain statistically measurable *frequency*, as the product of a consciously laid-down and consciously respected *ruling* (which implies explaining its genesis and efficacy), or as the product of an unconscious *regulating* by a mysterious cerebral and/or social mechanism, is to slip from the model of reality to the reality of the model.[171]

Agency is completely lost in this model of culture. Those who interpret religion as a *verbum externum* omit the fact that culture and tradition is created by the movement of agents. As a result, this view 'seems to reify an abstraction.'[172] It makes little sense to construe the agents as being completely passive before the fixed system of culture. In an ironic twist, the realism which the postliberal theologians reject with respect to reality returns in a realism of culture. According to this, culture is readily available. However, *culture and tradition are not patient of description in isolation from the intentionality of those who have created them.* In fact what Tanner calls 'socialisation into the Christian culture'[173] cannot be understood as involving mere receptivity. As Surin also argues, at the point of entry into a narrative there is both a modification of the agent as well as a change of the narrative itself. Entering the Christian culture means that a whole cultural

---

[168] Kelber, 'Jesus and Tradition', p. 158.

[169] Terrence Tilley argues that such a notion is contrary to the best insights of cultural linguisticism ('Incommensurability', p. 96).

[170] Kathryn Tanner, *Theories of Culture: A New Agenda for Theology*, (Minneapolis: Fortress Press, 1997), p. 49.

[171] Bourdieu, *Outline*, p. 29;

[172] Tanner, *Culture*, p. 50.

[173] Tanner, *Culture*, p. 160.

baggage is welcomed together with the agent himself. To understand culture properly is to understand the way in which it is continually shaping agents as well as being shaped by them.

Gone is the stability of culture. Kelber's *stratification* – which operates on the assumption that culture is a continual sedimentation of fixed meanings and texts – becomes *biosphere*, or what Pierre Bourdieu calls a *habitus*: 'the durably installed generative principle of regulated improvisations'.[174] If culture is no longer understood as fixed and closed, then theology must no longer understand itself as a mere second-order activity. Tanner argues that to maintain a sharp division between first order and second order is to suffer from a hang-over of the dualism between theory and practice. We have also argued against this sharp distinction by alluding to Quine's deconstruction of the distinction between analytic and synthetic propositions. There is no such thing as a fixed practice, with a theology whose task is to 'discover' its deep grammar. This is the reason why Lindbeck's hope of providing a working model for ecumenical dialogue fails utterly: it threatens to reify the practical patterns by lifting them out of the social and intentional processes that formed them and continue to sustain them.[175]

But in the absence of such a fixed horizon, what is to guarantee the unity of the practices? According to Tanner, *the unity is conferred by their common intended reference to God*! Unity cannot be guaranteed by a fluid multitude of practices. This is indeed a very strong statement. It suggests that it is not the culture itself that controls reference to God. It is not Lindbeck's vocabulary of first-order biblical propositions, liturgy and worship that delimits what can be referred to and what cannot. Tanner's is indeed a more dialectical working of the relationship between religion and experience. She argues for a 'bringing together of the idea that the grace of Christ is universal in scope and able to find people in whatever culture, no matter how hostile.'[176] In fact it is this very Donatist-like vision of the church, according to which the practices must be correct in order for actual participation to take place, that removes postliberal theology from its Reformation bases. The very fact that, as Tanner says, postliberal theology after Lindbeck's fashion, feels constrained to secure the methodological superiority of the Word over all other secular words is a symptom of its condition. Whereas a proper understanding of the message of the Gospel would, like Barth, ascribe complete priority and agency to God, even in the absence of any contact-point, Lindbeck et. al. think that they need to methodologically supplement an implied weakness of the Gospel.

---

[174] Bourdieu, *Outline*, p. 78.

[175] Tanner, *Culture*, p. 78.

[176] Tanner, *Culture*, p. 152.

This is in fact an argument for the relativisation of the cultural constructions in light of the primacy of the Word.[177] The resulting function of theology is to remind people of the need for openness to the Word of God[178] and
that 'no matter how true and right those judgements are, one must not lose
contact with their object in a kind of self-satisfied slumber, but remain open
for new movements of faithfulness to a free Word.'[179] A remarkably different conception of the Holy Spirit is involved in these suggestions: whereas
for Lindbeck the Holy Spirit is a *verbum internum*, understood as the power
to include one's life into the narratives of Christianity, for Tanner, 'The
Holy Spirit moves over the surface of these waters [texts and practices] and
not in their depths.'[180]

The practices of Christianity and the Christian culture, the narratives that
constitute them, under-determine our participation in God. They are important in their material forms, in the content that they deliver, but they do
not exhaust either the reality of God, or our ability to perceive it. Having a
map of the terrain does not mean that once one is in the terrain itself one
cannot observe the possible mistakes inherent in the map. If our participation in God is under-determined by the narratives of Christianity this means
that the unity of those narratives and practices resides in their refrence to
God. Working with those narratives involves keeping them constantly open
to the goal of our enquiry[181], which is the self-revealing of God. It also
means taking them not as ends in themselves, but bricolating them for various purposes (reference, legitimation, meaning, dialogue). This breaks the
circle that leads us from a narrative frenzy (there are only stories and no
reality) to a narrative amnesia (we privilege parts of stories).

---

[177] Work, *Living, passim*, esp. pp. 258, 276, 316.

[178] Tanner, *Culture*, p. 155.

[179] Tanner, *Culture*, p. 155.

[180] Tanner, *Culture*, pp. 160ff.

[181] This view is also consonant with MacIntyre's understanding of justification in
terms of the goal of enquiry. See *Whose Justice? Which Rationality?* and chapter III
above.

Conclusion

Postliberal theology could be taken as an 'empowered' intellectual discourse. By this I meant an argument which assumes its own circularity and particularity, without seeing them as detrimental to its acceptability. The demise of 'foundationalism', 'metaphysics', and 'theory', viewed as totalising discourses which, in the words of Gillian Rose, are taken as 'colonising being with the garrison of thought,'[1] is taken to award a license and duty to adhere to the beliefs and identity of one's community. If therefore postliberal claims are accepted, Christian meanings and doctrines do not need to stand the test of external criteria, embedded within alien narratives. Any such engagement takes place within a pre-determined space of rhetorical force and contextual idiosyncrasies. Narrativists hold that there is no place upon which rationality could be grounded. It allows no *middle ground* where unconscious prejudices might become visible. This has arguably had the effect of weakening postliberalism's self-critical stance. With the possible exceptions of Frei, Marshall and Hauerwas, it is no longer willing to entertain a 'broken middle'. Instead, it seeks to offer theoretical solutions.

Tending to this 'middle' would involve nothing less than assuming the risks involved in judging a particular case. All too often, however, narrativists have chosen the easier way out, which is the theoretical conclusion that theory has no consequences. Rational discussion with external paradigms has been ruled out. The reason behind this is twofold: on the one hand a fear of compromising the integrity of Christian meanings; on the other a pessimistic assessment of commensurability.

Empowered faith is legitimised (in Radically Orthodox circles) by being placed within a re-written genealogy of modernity. A subterraneous philosophical heritage, running from Thomas through Vico, Hamann, Herder, Jacobi and others, undermines modernity by questioning its secular foundations. Duns Scotus is regarded as the archetypal exhibitor of the philosophical urge to ground knowledge on sure foundations. Milbank accepts without reserve the critical deconstruction of metaphysics undertaken from Heidegger onwards and the return to a late modern Judaic evasion of philosophy in ethics.

Yet many fail to recognise that the abandonment of metaphysics and ontology in the name of the Other is just as capable of permitting an even more violent power. The unreserved assumption of tradition, the 'empowered' habitation of the cultural and religious space of a community, risks

---

[1] Gillian Rose, *Mourning*, p. 8. I am also indebted to her use of 'empowered', by which she refers to e.g. liberation movements.

forgetting that the same space is public, that it betrays a basic condition of scarcity, as Rowan Williams reminds us.[2] Such scarcity results from the fact that a tradition is always situated at the intersection of rival discourses, wants, needs and interpretations. The limited number of resources within one community are regularly claimed by other meta-narratives as well. Ironically, then, the communitarianism of postliberalism and of Radical Orthodoxy idealises and absolutises space. It does so by falsely thinking space is inhabited by a single Other. But an idealised 'Other' becomes un-thinkable. Other communities, rival intellectual discourses become at best tangential and at worst remote.

Perhaps in this case the religious reverence before the Other masks an incapacity to think the Other, to include the Other in the same public space of discourse. What this involves is nothing less than having one's produc-tions (linguistic, artistic, religious, social) responsible to a number of com-mon constraints. Their meaning can remain *wholly* internal to one's tradi-tion only on pain of denying a public space. Such a space is mirrored in the public character of language, in sharing a common conceptual environment with limited resources, in employing concepts in which other traditions have a stake too.

In *nuce*, postliberals have tended to reify the conceptual scheme. By rei-fication we meant the illusion that tradition, community and culture are things, *artefacts* existing apart from the sustaining activity of agents. The postliberal city believes that it has no breaches in its walls, that its traditions have no fissures and their unity is immanently generated. Its meanings are fixed quite independently of practical activities which might include those of legitimation. The church distributes identities to its believers, it fixes the meaning of the Scriptures and determines the meaning and therefore the reference of doctrines and basic beliefs. Interpretation becomes less a mat-ter of contingent encounters with the text and more a matter of learning to perform, or rather to join an established performance.

Alien discourses remain alien, unless they are absorbed into the Christian master-story. Language is split between an *infrastructure*: the vocabulary of a religion, its practices, liturgies, hymns, Scriptures, its tradition in general, and a *superstructure*: the theological claims one makes, the grammar of a religion. No ontology is needed in order to sustain the practices, the vo-cabulary and the religion. On the contrary, ontology needs to be eschewed lest particularity is compromised and meanings are removed away from the body of texts.

Abandoning any metaphysical anxiety, postliberalism tends to reify the scheme, to relish it and to trust the appearances it generates. It assumes some holist insights, but fails to take them to their final implications. It too fails to deconstruct the scheme-content dualism by allowing a thing called

---

[2] Williams, 'Between politics and metaphysics', p. 4.

'religion', which interestingly, given Lindbeck's ecumenical concerns, is taken as unified, fixed, clearly representable, to intervene between the believer and God. It is the religion itself which either is or isn't adequate to its object, the ultimate reality. By taking 'religion' as mediating between the agent and the divine reality, it tends towards either realism or idealism. It is the religion itself whose meanings allow adherents to refer to God, or doom any such attempts to failure. The important omission, which alone makes such a deferential attitude possible, is that religion, tradition and meanings in general cannot be taken as fixed prior to processes of inquiry.

For all the apparent stability of the city, its representation, as Certeau has observed, obscures the complexity of its inner dynamic. Although apparently stable and fixed, its borders are often transgressed. A tradition appears as unified only because we thus narrate it.[3] We textualise schemes and then forget it. We tend to treat them as intermediaries between us and reality, when in fact there is no philosophical use for them, as Rorty and Davidson forcefully argue. Meaning is dependent on the contingent, practical activities of people, which include those of legitimation, grammar, seeing, pointing, speaking. There is a strong sense, then, in which difference can no longer be taken to be a semantic assumption, but a pragmatic ocurrence. This is to say that difference, just as much as identity is something which obtains in the practical (and hence public) domain of work. To say that two traditions, communities or discourses are incommensurable before the actual hard work of bringing them into conversation is to project a theoretical conclusion. And this is also to say that meaning is just as much a matter of grammar (Wittgenstein), but not only so, perhaps not even chiefly.

Meaning is a much more complex activity, which involves in varying degrees grammar, but also reference and action, as well as legitimising. Doing away with this spatial, territorial notion of meaning involves rethinking the very notion of tradition. This suggests that although meaning and truth are only available in a textual form, within the temporal disclosure of a tradition, such textuality effaces itself before the actual experience. The scheme both under-determines experience and it over-determines aspects of it (metaphorical language) for practical purposes.

Understanding the holism of meaning and truth involves rethinking some of the postliberal epistemological decisions. Hermeneutically, this holism leads to placing greater stress on the whole communicative act, rather than on texts and their immanent meanings alone. Ricoeur argues that meaning is inextricably involved with the practical creation of a textually projected world, involving a moment of critique. Stout, on the other hand, is concerned with the variety of interpretive interests rather than allowing any single notion of meaning to dominate. The meaning of the Scriptures cannot be divorced from their historical truth, although what 'historical' means

---

[3] De Certeau, 'How is Christianity Thinkable?', p. 212.

and indeed what 'meaning' is must be determined in practice. Yet the recognition that reading involves the creation of a world, that narrative presupposes ontology, is the precondition to being sensitive to ideological
distortions of theory.

The texts, moreover, do not become completely submerged beneath the
level of their performative traditions, but are recoverable in practice. Although application does condition meaning, the creation of meaning takes
place in the working space or environment between the text and the reader,
not excluding or privileging either.

Postliberals firmly place knowledge of God and of the world in the context of Scripture. Deciding about matters of faith becomes a matter of revealing the Scriptural grammar. There is no independent language of
thought which might be able to relate God in human signs, other than the
scripturally given semiotic world. The Scotist desire for univocity in effect
anchors knowledge onto an arbitrary and violently imposed metaphysic. In
contrast, postliberals argue that only by trusting the scripturally mediated
appearances is language about God possible. Such a language is analogical,
avoiding both equivocity and univocity. In light of the deconstruction of the
scheme-content dichotomy and of the relation between truth and meaning,
such a strategy falters precisely at the point where it assumes that the
meaning of the scripturally rendered universe is available apart from an
investigation into its truth. Postliberal analogy therefore suspiciously slips
back towards mere equivocation, by refusing to correlate Christian meanings with the language of the secular city.

It is at this point where, it was argued, the postliberal account of figuration provides a corrective to a deficient understanding of analogy. Milbank,
by making any such correlation a matter of rhetorical and aesthetic preference returns analogy to equivocation. Yet analogy should express both the
gap between language and the being of God, involving the risk of taking a
position, and the ability to speak positively about it. Figuration, on the other
hand, suggests that the identity of the figure is not lost through its being
absorbed by its fulfilment. This introduces a rift in the stability of the
Scriptural world, for with every newly absorbed discourse, with every con-
vert, comes a modification, an alteration of the walls of the city. The beauty
of figuration, as Frei and Marshall argue, is that it preserves identity and
particularity. World absorption should forsake its violent and manipulative
tendencies and assume the risk of finding its own discourse wanting, in
conversation with other discourses.

This turns the tables on rhetoric and rationality. Since difference is
something to be worked out, a production, the result of encounters between
paradigms cannot be prejudged. The dissolution of the scheme – content
dualism means that any account of absolute incommensurability is incoherent. The way is thus open for a good reasons approach to justification and
rational dialogue, once frustrated by the febrile search for foundations. To

quote Rose again, this 'reopens the way to conceive learning, growth and knowledge as fallible and precarious, but risk-able.'[4]

If knowledge is a matter of complex practical negotiations between beliefs, its conception as an architectonic structure no longer seems attractive. Following Quine, Davidson and Rorty, one might conceive it rather as a force field, not anchored at any single point. To conceive theology as a second order reflection on the vocabulary or a religion is to reinstate an arbitrarily imposed hierarchy. Scripture, liturgy, tradition, discipleship, ethics – to neither of these belongs the exclusive privilege of acting as absolute foundation. None of this means that knowledge is less than it ever was. But a recognition of the contingencies involved in it is a prerequisite for improvement. It also means that there is no practical stance without an ontological imagination, as Milbank helpfully points out.

At the point of the connection between a narrative world and particularity, I have re-asserted the need for ontology. Far from being obstructive to the particular, ontology provides the backdrop upon which we can conceive of 'difference'. It becomes the clarifying discourse which helps us 'see' what is involved in the political and the practical: 'and thus the political location of metaphysical discourse is not the reduction of metaphysics to functional subordination within an alien setting, but something more like the laying bare of a contemplative and non-functional dimension to the political, the element of 'seeing' that is contained in any idea of intelligible action in a world of diverse agents.'[5] Narrative without ontology risks placing the particular in a purely imaginary universe, floating above the real world.

As the final chapter tried to show, narrative theology should not shy away from ontological description, nor from reason, for that would rob it of the necessary tools for laying bare what is already at work in any linguistic practice. Furthermore, from a material Christian perspective, the incarnation occasioned a 'realist' revolution, the possibility of speech directly in world involving terms (Davidson). Christology need not be relegated to the status of second-order discourse, but it should risk describing God, while the metaphorical entanglements of any such description involve a constant balancing between the 'internal' and the 'external'. Metaphors have an ontological function to perform, even while they are applied to the narratively depicted Christ. The disclosure of meaning occurs once again in the contested middle, where Scripture intersects metaphysics, history and philosophy.

---

[4] Rose, *Mourning*, p. 13.
[5] Williams, 'Between politics and metaphysics', p. 8.

Bibliography

Abraham, Kenneth S., 'Statutory interpretation and literary theory: some common concerns of an unlikely pair' in S. Levinson and S. Mailloux (eds.), *Interpreting Law and Literature: A Hermeneutic Reader*, (Evanston: Northwestern University Press)

Abraham, W.J., Holtzer, S. W., (eds.), *The Rationality of Religious Belief: Essays in Honour of Basil Mitchell*, (Oxford: Clarendon, 1987)

Allen, Richard, 'When narrative fails', *Journal of Religious Ethics* 21 (1993), 27-67

Alliez, Eric, *Capital Times: Tales From the Conquest of Time*, trans. Georges Van Den Abbeele, (Minneapolis: University of Minnesota Press, 1996)

Alston, William, *Divine Nature and Human Language: Essays in Philosophical Theology*, (Ithaca and London: Cornell University Press, 1989)

–, 'Referring to God' in idem., *Divine Nature and Human Language: Essays in Philosophical Theology*, (Ithaca and London: Cornell University Press, 1989)

Annas, Julia, 'MacIntyre on traditions', *Philosophy and Public Affairs* 18 (1989), 388-415

Arendt, Hannah, *Eichmann in Jerusalem: A Report on the Banality of Evil*, (London: Faber, 1963)

Auerbach, Erich, *Mimesis: The Representation of Reality in Western Literature*, trans. Willard R. Trask, (Princeton: Princeton University Press, 1953)

–, 'Figura', trans. Ralph Manheim, in Wlad Godzich and Jochen Schulte-Sasse (eds.), *Scenes from the Drama of European Literature*, (Minneapolis: University of Minnesota Press, 1984)

Ayres, Lewis, 'Representation, theology and faith', *Modern Theology* 11 (1995), 23-46

Bahti, Timothy, 'Vico, Auerbach and literary history', *Philological Quarterly* 60 (1981), 239-255

Baker, Gordon P., Haker, P.M.S., *Wittgenstein: Rules, Grammar, Necessity*, (Oxford: Blackwell, 1985)

Balthasar, Hans Urs von, *The Glory of the Lord: A Theological Aesthetics*, 7 vols. Edited by Joseph Fession SJ and John Riches, (Edinburgh: T. and T. Clark, 1982-1991)

Barr, James, *Semantics of Biblical Language*, (London: SCM, 1983)

Barth, Karl, *Church Dogmatics*, vol. 1/1, trans. G. W. Bromiley, edited by G. W. Bromiley and T. F. Torrance, (Edinburgh: T. and T. Clark, 1975)

Barton, Stephen, 'New Testament interpretation as performance', *Scottish Journal of Theology* 52 (1999), 179-208.

Batdorf, Irvin, 'Interpreting Jesus since Bultmann: selected paradigms and their hermeneutic matrix', *SBL Seminar Papers* 23 (1984), 187-215

Bauerschmidt, Frederic C., 'The word made speculative? John Milbank's christological poetics', *Modern Theology* 15 (1999), 417-432

Beaumont, Daniel, 'The modality of narrative: a critique of some recent views of narrative in theology', *Journal of the American Academy of Religion* 65 (1997), 125-140

Berlin, Isaiah, *Three Critics of the Enlightenment: Vico, Herder, Hamann*, edited by Henry Hardy, (London: Pimlico, 2000)

Bernstein, Richard J., *Beyond Objectivism and Relativism: Science, Hermeneutics and Praxis*, (Oxford: Blackwell, 1983)

–, (ed.), *Habermas and Modernity*, (Cambridge: MIT Press, 1985)

Bleicher, Joseph, *Contemporary Hermeneutics: Hermeneutics As Method, Philosophy and Critique*, (London: Routledge, 1990)

Blond, Phillip (ed.), *Post-Secular Philosophy: Between Philosophy and Theology*, (London: Routledge, 1998)

Bourdieu, Pierre, *Outline of a Theory of Practice*, trans. Richard Nice, (Cambridge: Cambridge University Press, 1977)

Brenner, William H., 'Theology as grammar', *The Southern Journal of Philosophy* 34 (1996), 439-453.

Briggs, Richard, *Words in Action: Speech Act Theory and Biblical Interpretation: Towards a Hermeneutic of Self-Involvement*, (Edinburgh: T. and T. Clark, 2001)

Broadhead, Edwin K, 'Jesus the Nazarene: narrative strategy and Christological imagery in the Gospel of Mark', *Journal for the Study of the New Testament* 52 (1993), 3-18

–, *Naming Jesus: Titular Christology in the Gospel of Mark*, (Sheffield: Sheffield Academic Press, 1999)

Brown, R. Harvey, *Society As Text: Essays on Rhetoric, Reason and Reality*, (Chicago and London: University of Chicago Press, 1987)

Brown, Stuart, *Do Religious Claims Make Sense?*, (London: SCM, 1969)

Buckley, James, 'Adjudicating conflicting Christologies', *Philosophy and Theology* 6 (1991), 117-135.

Callahan, James, 'The Bible says – evangelical and postliberal biblicism', *Theology Today* 53 (1997), 449-463

Chopp, Rebecca, 'Theological persuasion: rhetoric, warrants and suffering', in William Schweiker (ed.), *Worldviews and Warrants: Plurality and Authority in Theology*, (Lanham: University Press of America, 1987)

Compier, Don, *What is Rhetorical Theology?: Textual Practice and Public Discourse*, (Harrisburg, Pa.: Trinity Press International, 1999)

Comstock, Gary, 'Truth or meaning: Ricoeur versus Frei on biblical narrative', *Journal of the American Academy of Religion* 55 (1987), 687-717

–, 'Two types of narrative theology', *Journal of the American Academy of Religion* 55 (1987)

Cosgrove, Charles H, *Appealing to Scripture in Moral Debate: Five Hermeneutical Rules*, (Grand Rapids: Eerdmans, 2002)

Cox, Harvey, *The Secular City: Secularisation and Urbanisation in Theological Perspective*, (London: Penguin, 1968)

Craigo-Snell, Shannon, 'Command performance: rethinking performance interpretation in the context of *Divine Discourse*', *Modern Theology* 16 (2000), 475-494

Cunningham, David S., *Faithful Persuasion: In Aid of a Rhetoric of Christian Theology*, (Notre Dame: University of Notre Dame Press, 1991)

Currie, Gregory, 'What is fiction?', *Journal of Aesthetics and Art Criticism* 63 (1985), 385-392

Danto, Arthur, *Analytical Philosophy of History*, (Cambridge: Cambridge University Press, 1965)

Davidson, Donald, *Inquiries into Truth and Interpretation*, (Oxford: Clarendon, 1984)

Davies, J., Harvey, G. and Watson, W.G. E. (eds.), *Words Remembered, Texts Renewed. Essays in Honour of John F. A. Sawyer*, (Sheffield: Sheffield Academic Press, 1995)

Davies, Oliver, *A Theology of Compassion: Metaphysics of Difference and the Renewal of Tradition*, (London: SCM, 2001)

–, 'Revelation and the politics of culture: a critical assessment of the theology of John Milbank', in Laurence Paul Hemming (ed.), *Radical Orthodoxy? A Catholic Enquiry*, (Aldershot: Ashgate, 2000)

Dawson, John David, *Christian Figural Reading and the Fashioning of Identity*, (Berkeley, Los Angeles and London: University of California Press, 2002)

de Certeau, Michel, 'How is Christianity Thinkable Today?' in Graham Ward (ed.), *The Postmodern God: A Theological Reader*, (Oxford: Blackwell, 1997)

de Mauro, Tullio, 'Giambattista Vico: From Rhetoric to Linguistic Historicism', in Giorgio Tagliacozzo and Hayden V. White (eds.), *Giambattista Vico: An International Symposium*, (Baltimore: The Johns Hopkins Press, 1969)

Deleuze, Gilles, *Difference and Repetition*, trans. Paul Patton, (New York: Columbia University Press, 1994)

Doppelt, Gerald, 'Kuhn's epistemological relativism: an interpretation and defense', *Inquiry* 21 (1978), 33-86

Dunleavy, Patrick and Stanyer, Jeffrey (eds.), *Contemporary Political Studies 1994: Proceedings of the Annual Conference held at the University of Wales, Swansea* 1994

Durrant, Michael, 'Reference and critical realism', *Modern Theology* 5 (1989), 133-143

Dworkin, Ronald, 'Law as interpretation', *Critical Inquiry* 9 (1982), 179-200

–, 'Objectivity and truth: you'd better believe it', *Philosophy and Public Affairs* 25 (1996), 87-139

–, *Law's Empire*, (Oxford: Hart, 1998)

Eagleton, Terry, 'The estate agent: review of Stanley Fish, *The Trouble with Principle*, Cambridge, Mass. and London: Harvard University Press, 1991', *London Review of Books*, 2 March 2000, 22 (5)

Eisenstadt, N., *The Origins and Diversity of Axial Age Civilizations*, (Albany: State University of New York Press, 1986)

Elkana, Yehuda, 'The emergence of second-order thinking in classical Greece',in N. Eisenstadt (ed.), *The Origins and Diversity of Axial Age Civilizations*, (Albany: State University of New York Press, 1986)

Envine, Simon, *Donald Davidson*, (Cambridge: Polity, 1991)

Fergusson, David and Sarot, Marcel (eds.), *The Future as God's Gift: Explorations in Christian Eschatology*, (Edinburgh: T. and T. Clark, 2000)

Fergusson, David, 'Meaning, truth and realism in Bultmann and Lindbeck', *Religious Studies* 26 (1990), 183-198

Fish, Stanley, *A Matter of Principle*, (Cambridge, Mass. and London: Harvard University Press, 1985)

–, *Doing What Comes Naturally: Change, Rhetoric and the Practice of Theory in Literary and Legal Studies*, (Durham and London: Duke University Press, 1989)

–, 'Fish vs. Fiss', in Sanford Levinson and Steven Mailloux (eds.), *Interpreting Law and Literature: A Hermeneutic Reader*, (Evanston: Northwestern University Press, 1988)

–, *Is There a Text in This Class?: The Authority of Interpretive Communities*, (Cambridge, Mass. and London: Harvard University Press, 1980)

Fiss, Owen, 'Objectivity and interpretation', Sanford Levinson and Steven Mailloux (eds.), *Interpreting Law and Literature: A Hermeneutic Reader*, (Evanston: Northwestern University Press, 1988)

Ford, David, 'On being theologically hospitable to Jesus Christ: Hans Frei's achievement', *Journal of theological studies*, NS 46 (1995), 532-546.

–, *Barth and God's Story: Biblical Narrative and the Theological Method of Karl Barth in the 'Church Dogmatics'*, (Frankfurt am Main and Berne: Verlag Peter Lang, 1981)

Fowl, Stephen and Jones, L. Gregory, *Reading in Communion: Scripture and Ethics in Christian Life*, (London: SPCK, 1991)

Fowl, Stephen, *Engaging Scripture: A Model for Theological Interpretation*, (Oxford: Blackwell, 1998)

Frei, Hans, 'Historical reference and the gospels: a response to a critique of *The Identity of Jesus Christ*' [online]. Notes edited by Mike A. Higton from the Frei archives at Yale Library. Available at: http://www.library.yale.edu/div/freidoc3.htm [June 2001].

–, *The Eclipse of Biblical Narrative: A Study in Eighteenth and Nineteenth Century Hermeneutics*, (New Haven and London: Yale University Press, 1974)

–, *The Identity of Jesus Christ: The Hermeneutical Bases of Dogmatic Theology*, (Philadelphia: Fortress, 1975)

–, *Theology and Narrative: Selected Essays*, edited by George Hunsinger and William C. Placher, (New York and Oxford: Oxford University Press, 1993)

–, *Types of Christian Theology*, edited by George Hunsinger and William C. Placher, (New Haven: Yale University Press, 1992)

Fuller, Michael B, *Making Sense of MacIntyre*, (Aldershot: Ashgate, 1998)

Gadamer, Hans-Georg, *Truth and Method*, (New York: Continuum, 1994²)

Gale, R. M, 'The fictive use of language', *Philosophy* 46 (1971), 324-339

Gianturco, Elio, 'Vico's significance in the history of legal thought', in Giorgio Tagliacozzo and Hayden V. White (eds.), *Giambattista Vico: An International Symposium*, (Baltimore: The Johns Hopkins Press, 1969)

Glock, Hans-Johann, *A Wittgenstein Dictionary*, (Oxford: Blackwell, 1996)

Godzich, Wlad and Schulte-Sasse, Jochen (eds.), *Scenes from the Drama of European Literature*, (Minneapolis: University of Minnesota Press, 1984)

Goldberg, Michael, *Theology and Narrative: A Critical Introduction*, (Philadelphia: Trinity Press International, 1991²)

Green, Garrett, *Theology, Hermeneutics, and Imagination: The Crisis of Interpretation at the End of Modernity*, (Cambridge: Cambridge University Press, 2000)

–, (ed.), *Scriptural Authority and Narrative Interpretation: Essays on the Occasion of the sixty-fifth Birthday of Hans W. Frei*, (Philadelphia: Fortress Press, 1987)

Grondin, Jean, 'Hermeneutics and relativism', in Kathleen Wright (ed.), *Festivals of Interpretation: Essays on Hans-Georg Gadamer's Work*, (Albany: State University of New York Press, 1990)

Gronkjaer, Niels (ed.), *The Return of God: Theological Perspectives in Contemporary Philosophy*, (Odense: Odense University Press, 1998)

Gunton, Colin, *Yesterday and Today: A Study of Continuities in Christology*, (Grand Rapids: Wm. B. Eerdmans, 1983)

Habermas, Jürgen, 'On systematically distorted communication', *Inquiry* 13 (1970), 360-375

–, 'Towards a theory of communicative competence', *Inquiry* 13 (1970), 205-218

Hauerwas, Stanley, Murphy, N. and Nation, M. (eds), *Theology Without Foundations: Religious Practice and the Future of Theological Truth*, (Nashville: Abingdon,1994)

Hauerwas, Stanley and Burrell, David, 'From system to story: an alternative pattern for rationality in ethics', in Stanley Hauerwas and L. Gregory

Jones (eds.), *Why Narrative? Readings in Narrative Theology*, (Grand Rapids: Eerdmans, 1989)

Hauerwas, Stanley and Jones, L. Gregory (eds.), *Why Narrative? Readings in Narrative Theology*, (Grand Rapids: Eerdmans, 1989)

Hauerwas, Stanley, 'Why the truth demands truthfulness: an imperious engagement with Hartt', *Journal of the American Academy of Religion* 52 (1984), 141-147

–, *A Community of Character*, (Notre Dame: University of Notre Dame Press, 1981)

–, *Dispatches from the Front: Theological Engagements with the Secular*, (Durham and London: Duke University Press, 1994)

–, *Unleashing the Scripture: Freeing the Bible From Captivity to America*, (Nashville: Abingdon Press, 1993)

–, *Wilderness Wanderings: Probing Twentieth Century Theology and Philosophy*, (Boulder: Westview, 1997)

Hebblethwaite, B. and Sutherland, S., *The Philosophical Foundations of Christian Theology: Essays Presented to D. M. MacKinnon* (Cambridge: Cambridge University Press, 1982)

Hebblethwaite, Brian, *The Incarnation: Collected Essays in Christology*, (Cambridge: Cambridge University Press, 1987)

Heelas, Paul and Scott, Morris, *De-Traditionalisation: Critical Reflections on Authority and Identity in a Time of Uncertainty*, (Oxford: Blackwell, 1996)

Heide, Gale Z., 'The nascent noeticism of narrative theology: An Examination of the Relationship between Narrative and Metaphysics in Nicholas Lash', *Modern Theology* 12 (1996), 459-481

Heidegger, Martin, *Being and Time*, trans. John Macquarrie and Edward Robinson, (Oxford: Blackwell, 1962)

Hedley, D., 'Should divinity overcome metaphysics? Reflections on John Milbank's theology beyond secular reason and reflections of a Cambridge Platonist', *Journal of Religion* 80 (2000), 271-298

Hemming, Laurence Paul (ed.), *Radical Orthodoxy? A Catholic Enquiry*, (Aldershot: Ashgate, 2000)

Herdt, Jennifer A., 'Alasdair MacIntyre's 'Rationality of Traditions' and tradition-transcendental standards of justification', *Journal of Religion* 78 (1998), 524-546

Higton, Mike, 'Frei's Christology and Lindbeck's cultural linguistic theory', *Scottish Journal of Theology* 50 (1997), 83-95

Hirsch, E. D., *Validity in Interpretation*, (New Haven: Yale University Press, 1967)

Holmer, Paul, *The Grammar of Faith*, (San Francisco: Harper and Row, 1978)

Hoy, David Couzens, 'Interpreting the law: hermeneutical and post-structuralist perspectives', in Sanford Levinson and Steven Mailloux (eds.), *Interpreting Law and Literature: A Hermeneutic Reader*, (Evanston: Northwestern University Press, 1988)

Hunsinger, George, 'Truth as self-involving: Barth and Lindbeck on the cognitive and performative aspects of truth in theological discourse', *Journal of the American Academy of Religion* 61 (1993), 41-56

Hütter, Reinhard, *Suffering Divine Things: Theology as Church Practice*, trans. Doug Stott, (Grand Rapids, Michigan and Cambridge: Eerdmans, 2000)

Hyman, Gavin, *The Predicament of Postmodern Theology: Radical Orthodoxy or Nihlist Textualism*, (Louisville: Westminster John Knox, 2001)

Iser, Wolfgang, *Prospecting: From Reader Response to Literary Anthropology*,)London and Baltimore: The Johns Hopkins University Press, 1989)

Jacobs, Alan, 'A tale of two Stanleys', *First Things* 44 (1994), 18-21

Jameson, Fredric, *The Political Unconscious: Narrative as a Socially Symbolic Act*, (London: Methuen, 1981)

Janik, Alan and Toulmin, Stephen, *Wittgenstein's Vienna*, (New York: Simon and Schuster, 1973)

Jasper, David, 'From theology to theological thinking: the development of critical thought and its consequences for theology', *Literature and Theology* 9 (1995), 293-305.

–, *Rhetoric, Power and Community: An Exercise in Reserve*, (Louisville: Westminster John Knox Press, 1993)

Jauss, Hans-Robert, *Towards an Aesthetic of Reception*, trans. Timothy Bahti, (Minneapolis: University of Minnesota Press, 1982)

Juhl, P. D, *Interpretation: An Essay in the Philosophy of Literary Criticism*, (Princeton: Princeton University Press, 1980)

Kallenberg, Brad, 'Unstuck from Yale: theological method after Lindbeck', *Scottish Journal of Theology* 50 (1997), 191-218

Kant, Immanuel, *Religion Within the Limits of Reason Alone*, trans. T. Greene and H. Hudson, (New York, 1960)

Keightley, Alan, *Wittgenstein, Grammar and God*, (London: Epworth, 1976)

Kelber, Werner, 'Gospel narrative and critical theory', *Biblical Theological Bulletin* 18 (1988), 18, 130-136

–, 'In the beginning were the words: the apotheosis and narrative displacement of the Logos', *Journal of the American Academy of Religion* 58 (1990), 69-98

–, 'Jesus and tradition: words in time, words in space', *Semeia* 65 (1995), 139-167

Kelsey, David H., *The Uses of Scripture in Recent Theology*, (Philadelphia: Fortress Press, 1975)

Kermode, Frank, *The Genesis of Secrecy: On the Interpretation of Narrative*, (Cambridge, Mass. and London: Harvard University Press, 1979)

Kerr, Fergus, 'Frei's Types', *New Blackfriars* 75 (1994), 184-193

–, *Theology After Wittgenstein*, (London: SPCK, 1997)

Kivy, Peter, 'Fish's consequences', *British Journal of Aesthetics* 29 (1989), 57-64

Klemm, David, 'The rhetoric of theological argument', in J.S. Nelson, A. Megill and D. N. McCloskey, *The Rhetoric of the Human Sciences*, (Madison: University of Wisconsin Press, 1987)

–, 'Toward a rhetoric of postmodern theology', *Journal of the American Academy of Religion* 55 (1987), 443-469

Kögler, Hans-Herbert, *The Power of Dialogue: Critical Hermeneutics After Gadamer and Foucault*, trans. Paul Hendrickson, (Cambridge, Mass. and London: The MIT Press, 1996)

Kort, Wesley A., *Bound to Differ: The Dynamics of Theological Discourse*, (University Park: Pennsylvania State University Press, 1992)

–, *Story, Text and Scripture: Literary Interests in Biblical Narrative*, (University Park and London: The Pennsylvania State University Press, 1988)

Köstenberger, Andreas, 'Aesthetic theology – blessing or curse? An assessment of narrative theology', *Faith and Mission* 15 (1998), 27-44

Kripke, Saul, *Naming and Necessity*, (Oxford: Blackwell, 1980)

Kristeva, Julia, *Hannah Arendt*, trans. Ross Guberman, (New York: Columbia University Press, 2001)

Kuhn, Thomas, 'Objectivity, value judgement and theory choice', in Thomas Kuhn, *The Essential Tension: Selected Studies in Scientific Tradition and Change*, (Chicago and London: University of Chicago Press, 1977)

Kuhn, Thomas, *The Essential Tension: Selected Studies in Scientific Tradition and Change*, (Chicago and London: University of Chicago Press, 1977)

Lamarque, Peter, *Fictional Points of View*, (Ithaca and London: Cornell University Press, 1996)

Lash, Nicholas, 'Not exactly politics, or power?', *Modern Theology* 8 (1992), 353-364

–, *Theology on the Way to Emmaus*, (London: SCM Press, 1986)

Lauritzen, Paul, 'Is narrative really a panacea? The use of 'narrative' in the work of Metz and Hauerwas', *Journal of Religion* 67 (1987), 322-339

Lehrer, Seth (ed.), *Literary History and the Challenge of Philology: The Legacy of Erich Auerbach*, (Stanford: Stanford University Press, 1996)

Lenttrichia, Frank, *After the New Criticism*, (London: Athlone, 1980)

Lesser, Harry, 'Political philosophy and the holocaust', in Patrick Dunleavy and Jeffrey Stanyer (eds.), *Contemporary Political Studies 1994: Proceedings of the Annual Conference held at the University of Wales, Swansea 1994*, pp. 663-671

Levene, Nancy and Ochs, Peter, *Textual Reasonings: Jewish Philosophy and Text Study at the End of the Twentieth Century*, (London: SCM, 2002)

Levinson, Sanford and Mailloux, Steven (eds.), *Interpreting Law and Literature: A Hermeneutic Reader*, (Evanston: Northwestern University Press, 1988)

Lindbeck, George, 'Confession and community: An Israel-like view of the church', *Christian Century* 107 (1990), 492-496

–, 'The story-shaped Church: critical exegesis and theological interpretation', in Garrett Green (ed.), *Scriptural Authority and Narrative Interpretation*, (Philadelphia: Fortress Press, 1987)

–, *The Nature of Doctrine: Religion and Theology in a Postliberal Age*, (London: SPCK, 1984)

Lonergan, Bernard, *Method in Theology*, (London: Darton, Longman and Todd, 1972)

–, *The Second Collection: Papers by Bernard J. Lonergan S. J*, edited by William F. J. Ryan, S. J. and Bernard J. Tyrrell, (London: Darton, Longman and Todd, 1974)

–, *The Way to Nicea: The Dialectical Development of Trinitarian Theology*, trans. Conn O'Donovan, (London: Darton, Longman and Todd, 1976)

Loughlin, Gerard, 'Using Scripture: community, and letterality', in J. Davies, G. Harvey, W. G. E. Watson (eds.), *Words Remembered, Texts Renewed. Essays in Honour of John F. A. Sawyer*, (Sheffield: Sheffield Academic Press, 1995)

–, *Telling God's Story: Bible, Church and Narrative Theology*, (Cambridge: Cambridge University Press, 1996)

Lovibond, Sabina, *Realism and Imagination in Ethics*, (Oxford: Blackwell, 1983)

Luke, Timothy, 'Identity and globalization: De-traditionalisation in postmodern time-space compression', in Paul Heelas and Morris Scott (eds.), *De-Traditionalisation: Critical Reflections on Authority and Identity in a Time of Uncertainty*, (Oxford: Blackwell, 1996)

MacIntyre, Alasdair, 'Epistemological crises, dramatic narrative and the philosophy of science', *The Monist* 60 (1977), 453-472

–, *After Virtue: A Study in Moral Theory*, (Notre Dame: Notre Dame University Press, 1994[2])

–, *Three Rival Versions of Moral Inquiry: Encyclopaedia, Genealogy, and Tradition*, (London: Duckworth, 1990)

–, *Whose Justice? Which Rationality?*, (Notre Dame: University of Notre Dame Press, 1988)

MacKinnon, Donald, 'Substance in Christology – A cross-bench view', in Stephen Sykes and Phillip Clayton (eds.), *Christ, Faith and History: Cambridge Studies in Christology*, (Cambridge: Cambridge University Press, 1972)

Malbon, Elisabeth Struthers, 'Reflected Christology: an aspect of narrative "Christology" in the Gospel of Mark', *Perspectives in Religious Studies* 26 (1999), 127-145

Malpas, J. E., *Donald Davidson and the Mirror of Meaning: Holism, Truth, Interpretation*, (Cambridge: Cambridge University Press, 1992)

Markham, Ian, 'Faith and reason: reflections on MacIntyre's tradition constituted enquiry', *Religious Studies* 27 (1991), 259-267

Marshall, Bruce D. (ed), *Theology and Dialogue: Essays in Conversation with George Lindbeck*, (Notre Dame: University of Notre Dame Press, 1990)

–, 'Aquinas as postliberal theologian', *The Thomist* 53 (1989), 353-402

–, 'We shall bear the image of the man of heaven: theology and concept of truth', *Modern* 11 (1995)

–, *Christology in Conflict: The Identity of a Saviour in Rahner and Barth*, (Oxford: Blackwell, 1987)

–, *Trinity and Truth*, (Cambridge: Cambridge University Press, 2000)

McClendon, James Wm. Jr. and Smith, J. M., *Understanding Religious Convictions*, (Notre Dame: University of Notre Dame Press, 1975)

McClendon, James Wm. Jr., 'Ludwig Wittgenstein: A Christian in philosophy', *Scottish Journal of Theology* 51 (1998), 131-161

–, *Doctrine: Systematic Theology II*, (Nashville: Abingdon: 1994)

–, *Ethics: Systematic Theology I*, (Nashville: Abingdon, 1990)

McCormick, Kathleen, 'Swimming upstream with Stanley Fish', *The Journal of Aesthetics and Art Criticism* 44 (1985), 67-76

McGee, Michael Calvin and Lyre, John R., 'What are nice folks like you doing in a place like this? Some entailments of treating knowledge claims rhetorically', in J.S. Nelson, A. Megill, and D. N. McCloskey, *The Rhetoric of the Human Sciences*, (Madison: University of Wisconsin Press, 1987)

McIntyre, John, *The Shape of Christology*, (London: SCM, 1966)

Milbank, John, Pickstock, Catherine and Ward, Graham (eds.), *Radical Orthodoxy: A New Theology*, (London: Routledge, 1999)

–, *The Religious Dimension in the Thought of Giambattista Vico 1668-1744*, 2 vols., (Lewiston, Queenston, Lampeter: The Edwin Mellen Press, 1992)

–, *The Word Made Strange: Theology, Language and Culture*, (Oxford: Blackwell, 1997)

–, *Theology and Social Theory: Beyond Secular Reason*, (Oxford: Blackwell, 1990)

Miller, Richard B., 'The reference of "God"', *Faith and Philosophy* 3 (1986), 3-15

Miner, Robert C., 'Appendix: Vico and the turn to history in recent moral thought', unpublished manuscript.

–, 'Lakatos and MacIntyre on incommensurability and the rationality of theory choice', [online], Available at: http://www.bu.edu/wcp/papers/scie/sciemine.htm [29 March 2002]

–, 'Verum-factum and practical wisdom in the early writings of Giambattista Vico', *Journal of the History of Ideas* 59 (1998), 53-73

Moores, John D., *Wrestling with Rationality in Paul: Romans 1-8 in a New Perspective*, (Cambridge: Cambridge University Press, 1995)

Murphy, Nancey and McClendon, James, 'Distinguishing modern and postmodern theologies', *Modern Theology* 5 (1989), 191-214

Murphy, Nancey, 'Illuminating skepticism', unpublished paper delivered at *Illuminations: Reason, Revelation and Science*, Oxford, July 2002

–, 'Textual relativism, philosophy of language and the Baptist vision', in S. Hauerwas, N. Murphy and M. Nation (eds.), *Theology Without Foundations: Religious Practice and the Future of Theological Truth*, (Nashville: Abingdon,1994)

Need, Stephen, *Human Language and Knowledge in the Light of Chalcedon*, (New York, Washington, D.C., Baltimore, Bern, Frankfurt am Main, Berlin, Vienna and Paris: Peter Lang, 1996)

Nelson, J.S., Megill, A. and McCloskey, D. N., *The Rhetoric of the Human Sciences*, (Madison: University of Wisconsin Press, 1987)

Neufeld, Vernon, *Earliest Christian Confessions*, (Leiden: E. J. Brill, 1963)

Noble, Paul, 'Hermeneutics and postmodernism: can we have a radical reader-response theory? Part II', *Religious Studies* 31 (1995), 1-22

O'Banion, John D., 'Narration and argumentation: Quintilian on narration as the heart of rhetorical thinking', *Rhetorica* 5 (1987), 325-351

Oakes, Edward T., 'Apologetics and the pathos of narrative theology', *Journal of Religion* 71 (1992), 37-58

–, 'The Achievement of Alasdair MacIntyre', *First Things* 65 (1996), 22-26

Ochs, Peter, 'Rabbinic pragmatism', in Bruce D. Marshall (ed), *Theology and Dialogue: Essays in Conversation with George Lindbeck*, (Notre Dame: University of Notre Dame Press, 1990)

–, *Peirce, Pragmatism and the Logic of Scripture*, (Cambridge: Cambridge University Press, 1998)

Ommen, Thomas B., 'Wittgensteinian fideism and theology', *Horizons* 7 (1980), 183-204

Patterson, Sue, *Realist Christian Theology in a Postmodern Age*, (Cambridge University Press, 1999)

Phillips, D. Z., 'Lindbeck's audience', *Modern Theology* 4 (1988), 133-154

Placher, William C., 'Paul Ricoeur and postliberal theology: a conflict of interpretations?', *Modern Theology* 4 (1987), 35-52

–, 'Gospel ends: plurality and ambiguity in biblical narrative', *Modern Theology* 10 (1994), 143-163

–, *Narratives of a Vulnerable God: Christ, Theology and Scripture*, (Louisville: Westminster John Knox, 1992)

–, *The Domestication of Transcendence: How Modern Thinking About God Went Wrong*, (Louisville: Westminster John Knox Press, 1996)

Porter, Jean, 'Openness and moral constraint: moral reflection as tradition-guided inquiry in Alasdair MacIntyre's recent works', *Journal of Religion* 73 (1993), 514-536

Prickett, Stephen, *Words and the Word: Language, Poetics and Biblical Interpretation*, (Cambridge: Cambridge University Press, 1986)

Putnam, Hilary, *Reason, Truth and History*, (Cambridge: Cambridge University Press, 1981)

–, *The Many Faces of Realism: The Paul Carus Lectures*, (LaSalle: Open Court, 1987)

Quine, W. V., *From a Logical Point of View*, (Cambridge, Mass. and London: Harvard University Press, 1964)

Ray, William, *Literary Meaning: From Phenomenology to Deconstruction*, (Oxford: Blackwell, 1984)

Rendall, S., 'Fish vs. Fiss', *Diacritics* 12 (1982), 49-56

Reno, Rusty, 'The Radical Orthodoxy Project', *First Things* 100 (2000), 37-44

Rescher, Nicholas, *Methodological Pragmatism*, (New York: New York University Press, 1977)

Ricoeur, Paul, *Figuring the Sacred: Religion, Narrative and Imagination*, trans. David Pellauer, edited by Mark I. Wallace, (Minneapolis: Fortress Press, 1995)

–, *Hermeneutics and the Human Sciences: Essays on Language, Action and Interpretation*, edited and translated by John. B. Thompson, (Cambridge: Cambridge University Press, 1981)

–, *Oneself as Another*, trans. Kathleen Blamey, (Chicago: University of Chicago Press, 1992)

–, *Symbolism of Evil*, trans. Emerson Buchanan, (Boston: Beacon Press, 1969)

–, *The Conflict of Interpretations: Essays in Hermeneutics*, edited by Don Ihde, (Evanston: Northwestern University Press, 1974)

–, *Time and Narrative*, 3 vols., trans. Kathleen McLaughlin/ Blamey and David Pellauer, (Chicago and London: The University of Chicago Press, 1984-1988)

Rigby, Paul, 'The nature of doctrine and scientific progress', *Theological Studies* 52 (1991), 669-688

Roberts, Tyler, 'Theology and the ascetic imperative: narrative and renunciation in Taylor and Hauerwas', *Modern Theology* 9 (1993), 181-200

Ronen, Ruth, 'Incommensurability and representation', [online], *Applied Semiotics/ Semiotique appliqué (A Learned Journal of Literary Research on the World Wide Web. Une Revue internationale de recherche litteraire sur Internet*, 1998, 5 (July/ juiller), 267-302. Available at: http://www.tau.ac.il/~ronnen/documents/inc-rep.html [5 May 2002]

Rorty, Richard, 'Habermas and Lyotard on Postmodernity' in Richard Bernstein (ed.), *Habermas and Modernity*, (Cambridge: MIT Press, 1985)

–, *Objectivity, Relativism and Truth*, (Cambridge and New York: Cambridge University Press, 1991)

–, *Philosophy and the Mirror of Nature*, (Princeton: Princeton University Press, 1979)

Rose, Gillian, *Mourning Becomes the Law: Philosophy and Representation*, (Cambridge: Cambridge University Press, 1996)

–, *The Broken Middle: Out of Our Ancient Society*, (Oxford: Blackwell, 1992)

Ryle, Gilbert, *Collected Papers*, Volume 2, Collected Essays, 1929-1968, (London: Hutchinson, 1971)

Saye, Scott C., 'The wild and crooked tree: Barth, Fish and interpretive communities', *Modern Theology* 12 (1996), 435-458

Scheffler, Israel, *Science and Subjectivity*, (Indianapolis: Bobbs-Merrill, 1967)

Schlink, Edmund, *The Coming Christ and the Coming Church*, trans. G. Overlach and D. B. Simmonds, (Edinburgh, 1967.)

Scholes, Robert and Kellog, Robert, *The Nature of Narrative*, (New York: Oxford University Press, 1996)

Schwartzenbrunner, Paul, 'The modesty of hermeneutics: the theological reserves of Hans Frei', *Modern Theology* 8 (1992), 181-195

Schweicker, William (ed.), *Worldviews and Warrants: Plurality and Authority in Theology*, (Lanham: University Press of America, 1987)

Searle, John, *Expression and Meaning: Studies in the Theory of Speech Acts*, (Cambridge: Cambridge University Press, 1979)

–, *The Construction of Social Reality*, (London: Penguin, 1995)

–, 'The logical status of fictional discourse', *New Literary History* 6 (1975)

Shakespeare, Steven, 'The new romantics: a critique of Radical Orthodoxy', *Theology* 103 (2000), 163-177

Soskice, Janet Martin, *Metaphor and Religious Language*, (Oxford: Clarendon, 1985)

–, 'Theological Realism', in W. J. Abraham and S. W. Holzer, *The Rationality of Religious Belief: Essays in Honour of Basil Mitchell*, (Oxford: Clarendon, 1987)

Spjuth, Ronald, 'Redemption without actuality: A critical interrelation between Eberhard Jüngel's and John Milbank's ontological endeavours', *Modern Theology* 14 (1998), 505-522

Stark, Werner, 'Giambattista Vico's Sociology of Knowledge', in Giorgio Tagliacozzo and Hayden V. White (eds.), *Giambattista Vico: An International Symposium*, (Baltimore: The Johns Hopkins Press, 1969)

Stead, Christopher, *Divine Substance*, (Oxford: Clarendon, 1977)

Stecker, Robert, 'Fish's Argument for the relativity of interpretive truth', *Journal of Aesthetics and Art Criticism* 48 (1990), 223-230

Stell, Stephen, 'Hermeneutics in theology and theology of hermeneutics: beyond Lindbeck and Tracy', *Journal of the American Academy of Religion* 61 (1993), 679-702

Stern, J. P., *On Realism*, (London: Routledge and Kegan Paul, 1973)

Sternberg, Meir, *The Poetics of Biblical Narrative: Ideological Literature and the Drama of Reading*, (Bloomington: Indiana University Press, 1985)

Stiver, Dan R., *The Philosophy of Religious Language: Sign, Symbol and Story*, (Cambridge, Mass.: Blackwell, 1996.)

–, *Theology After Ricoeur: New Directions in Hermeneutical Theology*, (Louisville: Westminster John Knox Press, 2001)

Stout, Jeffrey, 'What is the meaning of a text?', *New Literary History* 14 (1892), 1-12

–, *Ethics After Babel: The Languages of Morals and Their Discontents*, (Boston: Beacon Press, 1988)

Stroup, George W., *The Promise of Narrative Theology*, (London: SCM Press, 1984²)

–, 'Chalcedon revisited', *Theology Today* 35 (1978), 52-64

Surin, Kenneth (ed.), *Christ, Ethics and Tragedy: Essays in Honour of Donald MacKinnon*, (Cambridge: Cambridge University Press, 1989)

–, *The Turnings of Darkness and Light: Essays in Philosophical and Systematic Theology*, (Cambridge: Cambridge University Press, 1989)

Sykes, Stephen and Clayton, Phillip (eds.), *Christ, Faith and History: Cambridge Studies in Christology*, (Cambridge: Cambridge University Press, 1972)

Tagliacozzo, Giorgio and White, Hayden V. (eds.), *Giambattista Vico: An International Symposium*, (Baltimore: The Johns Hopkins Press, 1969)

Tanner, Kathryn E., 'Theology and the plain sense', in Garrett Green (ed.), *Scriptural Authority and Narrative Interpretation*, (Philadelphia: Fortress, 1987)

–, 'Scripture as popular text', *Modern Theology* 14 (1998), 279-298

–, *God and Creation in Christian Theology: Tyranny or Empowerment?*, (Oxford: Blackwell, 1988)

–, *Theories of Culture: A New Agenda for Theology*, (Minneapolis: Fortress Press, 1997)

Taylor, Charles, *Philosophical Arguments*, (Cambridge, Mass. and London: Harvard University Press, 1995)

–, *Sources of the Self: The Making of the Modern Identity*, (Cambridge: Cambridge University Press, 1989)

Thiemann, Ronald F., *Revelation and Theology: The Gospel as Narrated Promise*, (Notre Dame: University of Notre Dame Press, 1984)

Thiselton, Anthony C., Walhout, Clarence and Lundin, Roger, *The Promise of Hermeneutics*, (Grand Rapids: Eerdmans, 1999)

Thiselton, Anthony C., *The First Epistle to the Corinthians*, (Grand Rapids: Wm. B. Eerdmans, 2001)

–, 'Knowledge, myth and corporate memory', in *Believing in the Church: The Corporate Nature of Faith*, A Report by the Doctrine Commission of the Church of England, (London: SPCK, 1981)

–, 'Signs of the times: towards a theology for the year 2000 or a grammar of grace, truth and eschatology in contexts of so-called postmodernity', in David S. Fergusson and Marcel Sarot (eds.), *The Future as God's Gift: Explorations in Christian Eschatology*, (Edinburgh: T. and T. Clark, 2000)

–, *New Horizons in Hermeneutics: The Theory and Practice of Transforming Biblical Reading*, (Grand Rapids: Zondervan, 1992)

–, *The Two Horizons: New Testament Hermeneutics and Philosophical Description with Special Reference to Heidegger, Bultmann, Gadamer, and Wittgenstein*, (Carlisle and Grand Rapids: Paternoster and Eerdmans, 1980)

Tilley, Terrence F., 'Incommensurability, intratextuality, and fideism', *Modern Theology* 5 (1989), 87-117

Torrance, T. F., 'Theological realism', in B. Hebblethwaite and S. Sutherlandand (eds.), *The Philosophical Foundations of Christian Theology: Essays Presented to D. M. MacKinnon*, (Cambridge: Cambridge University Press, 1982)

Toulmin, Stephen, *Cosmopolis: The Hidden Agenda of Modernity*, (New York: Free Press, 1990)

Uhlig, Claus, 'Auerbach's "hidden" (?) theory of history', in Seth Lehrer (ed.), *Literary History and the Challenge of Philology: The Legacy of Erich Auerbach*, (Stanford: Stanford University Press, 1996)

Vaihinger, Hans, *The Philosophy of 'As If': A System of the Theoretical, Practical and Religious Fictions of Mankind*, trans. C. K. Ogden, (London: Routledge and K. Paul, 1965)

van Huysteen, Wentzel, *Essays in Postfoundationalist Theology*, (Grand Rapids: Wm. B. Eerdmans, 1997)

Vanhoozer, Kevin J., *Biblical Narrative in the Philosophy of Paul Ricoeur: A Study in Hermeneutics and Theology*, (Cambridge: Cambridge University Press, 1990)

–, *Is There a Meaning in This Text? The Bible, the Reader and the Morality of Literary Knowledge*, (Grand Rapids: Zondervan, 1998)

Vattimo, Gianni, 'History of salvation, history of interpretation', in Niels Gronkjaer (ed.), *The Return of God: Theological Perspectives in Contemporary Philosophy*, (Odense: Odense University Press, 1998)

Vidu, Adonis, 'Frei and Auerbach on the Meaning of the Gospel Narratives', *Trinity Journal* 26 NS, no. 2, Fall 2005

Wallace, Mark I., 'Can God be named without being known? The problem of revelation in Thiemann, Ogden, and Ricoeur', *Journal of the American Academy of Religion* 59 (1991), 281-308

–, *The Second Naiveté: Barth, Ricoeur, and the New Yale Theology*, (Macon: Mercer University Press, 1990)

Walton, Kendall L., *Mimesis: On the Foundations of the Representational Arts*, (Cambridge, Mass. and London: Harvard University Press, 1990)

Ward, Graham (ed.), *The Certeau Reader*, (Oxford: Blackwell, 2000)

Warnke, Georgia, *Gadamer: Hermeneutics, Tradition and Reason*, (Stanford: Stanford University Press, 1987)

Watson, Francis, *Text and Truth: Redefining Biblical Theology*, (Edinburgh: T. and T. Clark, 1997)

–, *Text, Church and World: Biblical Interpretation in Theological Perspective*, (Edinburgh: T. and T. Clark, 1994)

Webb, Stephen H., *Re-figuring Theology: The Rhetoric of Karl Barth*, (Albany: State University of New York Press, 1991)

Werpehowski, Will, 'Ad Hoc apologetics', *Journal of the American Academy of Religion* 66 (1986), 282-301

Wicker, Brian, *The Story-Shaped World: Fiction and Metaphysics, Some Variations on a Theme*, (London: Athlone Press, 1975)

Williams, Rowan, 'Between politics and metaphysics: reflections in the wake of Gillian Rose', *Modern Theology* 11 (1995), 3-22

–, *On Christian Theology*, (Oxford: Blackwell, 2000)

–, 'Trinity and revelation', *Modern Theology* 2 (1986), 197-212

–, 'The literal sense of Scripture', *Modern Theology* 7 (1991), 121-134

Williams, Stephen, 'Lindbeck's regulative Christology', *Modern Theology* 4 (1988), 172-184

Wittgenstein, Ludwig, 'Lectures on religious belief', in L. Wittgenstein, *Lectures and Conversations on Aesthetics, Psychology and Religious Belief*, edited by Cyril Barrett, (Oxford: Blackwell, 1966)

–, *Philosophical Investigations*, trans. G.E.M. Anscombe, (Oxford: Blackwell, 1997)

–, *Remarks on the Foundation of Mathematics*, edited by G. H. von Wright, R. Rhees, G. E. M. Anscombe, trans. G. E. M. Anscombe, (Oxford: Blackwell, 1978)

–, *The Blue and Brown Books*, (Oxford: Blackwell, 1969)

–, *Tractatus Logico-Philosophicus*, trans. D. F. Pears and B. F. McGuinness, (London: Routledge, 2001)

–, *Zettel*, trans. G. E. M. Anscombe, (Oxford: Blackwell, 1981)

Wolterstorff, Nicholas, *Divine Discourse: Philosophical Reflections on the Claim that God Speaks*, (Cambridge: Cambridge University Press, 1995)

–, *Works and Worlds of Art*, (Oxford: Clarendon, 1990)

Wood, Charles M., *The Formation of Christian Understanding: An Essay in Theological Hermeneutics*, (Philadelphia: Westminster Press, 1981)

–, 'Hermeneutics and the authority of scripture', in Garrett Green (ed.), *Scriptural Authority and Narrative Interpretation: Essays on the Occasion of the Sixty-Fifth Birthday of Hans W. Frei*, (Philadelphia: Fortress Press, 1987)

–, 'The Nature of doctrine: religion and theology in a postliberal age: review article', *Religious Studies Review* 11 (1985), 235-240

Work, Telford, *Living and Active: Scripture in the Economy of Salvation*, (Grand Rapids: Wm. B. Eerdmans, 2002)

Wright, Kathleen (ed.), *Festivals of Interpretation: Essays on Hans-Georg Gadamer's Work*, (Albany: State University of New York Press, 1990)

Wyschogrod, Edith, *Saints and Postmodernism: Revisioning Moral Philosophy*, (Chicago: University of Chicago Press, 1990)

Young, Frances, *The Art of Performance: Towards and Theology of Holy Scripture*, (London: Darton, Longman and Todd, 1992)

Zorn, Hans, 'Grammar, doctrine, and practice', *The Journal of Religion* 75 (1995), 509-520

Index

ad hoc, 73, 87, 95, 121, 124, 134, 149, 154, 169, 170, 171, 173, 200, 201
agency, 19, 20, 22, 24, 25, 40, 42, 68, 105, 108, 161, 172, 230, 239
Allegory, 50, 84, 205
Alliez, Eric, 4, 5, 6, 7, 111, 188, 247
Alston, William, 247
analogy, 4, 5, 57, 84, 96, 109, 163, 185, 206, 211, 215, 216, 225, 244
application, 10, 36, 38, 60, 63, 68, 69, 70-77, 101, 105, 124, 161, 165, 202, 215, 227, 233, 244
assimilative power, 152, 153
Auerbach, Erich, 36, 44, 52-58, 83, 189, 247, 254, 261
authorial intention, 71

Balthasar, Hans Urs von, 4, 6, 247
Barth, Karl, 3, 5, 40, 45, 65, 74, 106, 108, 110, 140, 147, 157, 163, 169, 171, 175, 176, 187, 194, 196-200, 204, 209, 215, 222, 224, 239, 247, 250, 253, 256, 259, 262
Berlin, Isaiah, 9, 10, 11, 14, 15, 16, 226, 248, 257
Bourdieu, Pierre, 181, 236, 238, 239, 248

Certeau, Michel de, 39, 83, 189, 243, 249, 262
charity, 126, 153, 191
Christology, x, xiv, 3, 57, 83, 162, 163, 169, 193-205, 211, 214, 217-230, 234, 245, 248, 251, 252, 255, 256, 260, 262
Christus Dominus est, 151, 174
church, v, 1, 12, 14, 22, 33, 34, 36, 43, 87, 90, 103, 106, 161, 170, 175, 176, 177, 181, 200, 203, 213, 220, 227, 239, 242, 255
comparability, 120, 121, 124, 133

Comstock, Gary, 49, 64, 80, 81, 146, 248
conceptual scheme, 89, 114, 128, 129, 242
correspondence, 11, 19, 29, 90, 91, 96, 97, 98, 99, 104, 105, 134, 137, 153, 176, 178, 199
count generation, 63
cultural linguistic, 93, 94, 95, 102, 103, 106, 158, 162, 169, 176, 218, 226, 252
Cunningham, David S., 2, 140, 143, 144, 145, 146, 249

Davidson, Donald, 39, 59, 62, 82, 94, 108, 113, 114, 115, 119, 120, 121, 125, 126, 127, 128, 129, 130, 131, 135, 136, 137, 138, 139, 146, 149, 150, 151, 152, 155, 156, 171, 177, 180, 189, 190, 243, 245, 249, 250, 256
Dawson, John David, 44, 50, 51, 52, 53, 54, 55, 56, 58, 86, 190, 205, 206, 249
diachronic, xiv, 34
dialectics, 132, 139, 140, 142, 143, 145, 146
discrimen, 109
discriminating knowledge, 81
Dworkin, Ronald, 41, 74, 75, 76, 190, 191, 250

equivocity, 5, 83, 84, 110, 244

fantasia, 15, 26
Fergusson, David S., 89, 146, 250, 261
fiction, 59, 60, 61, 62, 63, 64, 65, 66, 150, 219, 249
fideism, 1, 67, 106, 147, 150, 152, 153, 173, 223, 257, 261
figural reading, 47, 50, 52, 53, 55, 67, 68, 85, 117

figuration, xiv, 36, 43, 53, 58, 67, 85, 87, 152, 156, 244

first order language, 97, 98, 116, 162, 163, 168, 169, 172, 175, 178, 180, 186, 204, 209, 212, 217, 219, 221, 229, 239

Fish, Stanley, ix, 1, 15, 20, 21, 26-30, 34-45, 74-77, 122, 123, 145, 250, 254, 256, 258, 259, 260

formalism, 27, 45, 62, 77, 84, 90, 203, 220

forms of life, xiii, 97, 106, 167, 168, 174, 176, 186

foundationalism, 12, 15, 45, 82, 83, 107, 108, 114, 118, 120, 122, 131, 132, 148, 156, 190, 223, 241

Frei, Hans, ix, x, 27, 35, 36, 37, 44-67, 70, 72, 77-87, 90, 127, 147, 148, 150, 153, 154, 156, 157, 159, 162, 163, 167, 168, 169, 170, 171, 172, 173, 175, 178, 181, 187, 194, 195, 200-217, 223, 225, 226, 232, 233, 234, 236, 241, 244, 248, 250, 251, 252, 254, 259, 263

Gadamer, Hans-Georg, 1, 2, 10, 15-24, 29, 30, 33, 35, 39, 40, 68-78, 84, 86, 89, 116, 143, 155, 160, 161, 177-180, 251, 254, 261-263

genealogy, 2, 3, 7, 111, 241

habitus, x, 232

Hauerwas, Stanley, 1, 25, 26, 33, 34, 35, 37, 78, 80, 82, 95, 109, 143, 151, 172, 189, 197, 198, 200, 201, 234, 235, 237, 241, 251, 252, 254, 257, 258

historicism, 1, 11, 23, 39, 74, 145

holism, xiv, 20, 35, 114, 118, 119, 128, 138, 149, 156, 191, 243

Holmer, Paul, 165, 166, 172, 173, 174, 180, 252

Hunsinger, George, 36, 147, 169, 175, 176, 177, 178, 186, 251, 253

Hütter, Reinhard, 24, 89, 90, 92, 94, 102, 105, 158, 159, 169, 175, 176, 177, 187, 253

Hyman, Gavin, 2, 253

incommensurability, xiv, 11, 119-153, 171, 189, 198, 201, 215, 216, 217, 244, 257

instrumentalism, 12

interpretive community, xiv, 27, 34, 35, 38, 40, 47, 51, 76, 82

intra-textuality, 59, 172, 197, 198, 236

Janik, Alan, 14, 31, 253

justification, 2, 13, 14, 30, 39, 50, 65, 97, 106, 108, 110, 111, 114, 116, 117, 118, 119, 120, 121, 122, 123, 124, 125, 132, 133, 137, 142, 143, 145, 146, 148, 149, 150, 151, 153, 154, 156, 170, 180, 190, 240, 244, 252

Kelber, Werner, 60, 236, 237, 238, 239, 253

Kelsey, David, 26, 34, 35, 80, 95, 109, 171, 209, 210, 253

Kerr, Fergus, 94, 178, 254

Kingdom of God, 210

Kögler, Hans Herbert, 17, 18, 19, 20, 24, 25, 35, 69, 74, 178, 179, 180, 254

Kripke, Saul, 100, 254

Kuhn, Thomas, 100, 118, 119, 121, 122, 123, 124, 125, 128, 129, 131, 133, 134, 137, 146, 159, 160, 177, 181, 249, 254

language game, 76, 177

Lash, Nicholas, 22, 83, 106, 109, 155, 161, 163, 168, 172, 176, 185, 252, 254

law, ix, 11, 18, 68, 71, 74, 75, 77, 191, 247, 250, 253, 255, 259

legal positivism, 14, 51

Lindbeck, George, ix, x, 1, 68, 78, 83, 85, 86, 90-116, 146-187, 193, 194, 197, 200, 204, 205, 212, 217-223, 226, 229, 233, 234, 238, 239, 240, 243, 250, 252, 253, 255, 256, 257, 260, 262 linguistic idealism, 95, 139, 171

Lonergan, Bernard, 219, 220, 221, 222, 255

Lovibond, Sabina, 81, 101, 103, 108, 255

MacIntyre, Alasdair, ix, 1, 15, 20-30, 34, 35, 37, 39, 40, 41, 121, 123, 124, 131-146, 153, 160, 184, 187, 190, 197, 240, 247, 251, 252, 255, 256, 257, 258

MacKinnon, Donald, 223, 230, 231, 252, 255, 260, 261

Marshall, Bruce D., 2, 3, 104-106, 108, 113, 114, 120, 121, 130, 137, 148, 149, 150, 151, 152, 153, 156, 160, 171-177, 185, 186, 194-208, 217, 222, 223, 241, 244, 256, 257

McClendon, James Wm. Jr., 26-38, 61, 96, 109, 118, 162, 174, 186, 194, 198, 205, 256, 257

meaning, 27, 37, 49, 62, 66, 70, 78, 115, 130, 146, 160, 180, 243, 250, 256, 258, 259, 261

metaphor, 1, 47, 85, 103, 109, 142, 145, 152, 164, 213, 214, 220, 223, 227, 228, 229

metaphysics, 9, 161, 228, 230, 249, 252, 262

Milbank, John, 1-14, 21, 24, 30, 41, 42, 43, 55, 56, 67, 68, 82, 83, 84, 111, 117, 120, 121, 124, 132, 138-149, 153, 155, 156, 162, 163, 171, 175, 183, 185, 190, 194, 204, 207, 211-217, 230, 232, 233, 241, 244, 245, 248, 249, 252, 256, 259

Miner, Robert, 21, 23, 121, 124, 138, 142, 144, 145, 256

modus loquendi, 199, 222, 232

Murphy, Nancey, 26, 37, 38, 111, 118, 251, 257

myth, 21, 23, 28, 30, 48, 174, 179, 261

narration, 145, 257

narratives, ix, 3, 21, 23, 45, 47, 48, 49, 51, 57, 62, 65, 66, 68, 85, 129, 135, 137, 144, 146, 161, 162, 163, 164, 175, 183, 185, 188, 189, 197, 202, 204, 205, 206, 207, 208, 210, 211, 213, 215, 226, 229, 233, 235, 236, 240, 241, 242

New Criticism, 27, 36, 45, 48, 57, 80, 203, 254

Ochs, Peter, 160, 255, 257

ontology, 8, 9, 13, 20, 28, 37, 39, 56, 68, 80, 82, 84, 89, 95, 99, 110, 141, 144, 147, 176, 177, 179, 183, 185, 188, 189, 190, 193, 196, 198, 199, 205, 210, 213, 217, 219, 222, 225, 226, 228, 229, 231, 241, 242, 244, 245

participation, 3, 4, 6, 9, 11, 12, 24, 30, 68, 79, 81, 227, 229, 239, 240

particularity, 8, 13, 18, 25, 48, 51, 52, 65, 68, 70, 193, 194, 195, 196, 197, 198, 199, 200, 202, 205, 208, 209, 210, 212, 214, 217, 223, 231, 241, 242, 244, 245

pathos, 4, 24, 89, 106, 146, 168, 187, 188, 257

Patterson, Sue, 97, 110, 143, 257

performance, 18, 45, 76, 83, 105, 155, 162, 167, 174, 175, 181, 182, 183, 185, 186, 187, 188, 190, 235, 242, 248, 249

Phillips, D. Z., 165, 166, 171, 173, 175, 178, 181, 257

Placher, William, 2, 3, 5, 36, 66, 67, 147, 215, 251, 257

poetics, 62, 213, 248

poiesis, 24, 89, 94, 106, 112

positivism, 11, 12, 13, 51, 124, 155

practices, 13, 28, 30, 31, 33, 36, 37, 38, 43, 50, 51, 70, 71, 74, 75, 77, 78, 81, 82, 83, 84, 86, 94, 96, 98, 103, 105, 106, 134, 139, 149, 151, 152, 157, 161, 163, 165, 166, 167, 168, 170, 173, 174, 177, 179, 180, 181, 183, 186, 188, 189, 196, 220, 227, 239, 240, 242

pragmatic presuppositions, 232

pragmatic thesis, 151

pragmatism, 28, 32, 68, 71, 78, 160, 257

precedent, 14, 73, 77, 196, 233

prompted assent, 126, 127, 130, 131

Putnam, Hilary, 98, 100, 104, 138, 139, 258

Quine, Willard v. O., 32, 113, 118, 119, 126, 127, 129, 149, 150, 239, 245, 258

radical interpretation, 126, 127, 130, 150, 151

radical orthodoxy, 194

realism, 56, 60, 65, 76, 81, 98, 101, 103, 104, 108, 112, 117, 189, 205, 223, 229, 255, 258, 259, 260

realistic narratives, 47

receptivity, 6, 7, 91, 92, 111, 112, 199, 213, 238

reference, 3, 13, 21, 26, 36, 38, 39, 48, 49, 57, 59, 63, 64, 67, 81, 82, 85, 89, 96, 98, 99, 100, 101, 104, 109, 110, 113, 115, 121, 127, 130, 146, 154, 158, 168, 170-177, 182, 184, 185, 196, 202, 208, 209, 216, 221-226, 234-243, 250, 256

reification, xiv, 29, 30, 86, 117, 161, 163, 172, 177, 188, 216, 236, 237, 242

representation, 6, 42, 50, 52, 53, 56, 85, 91, 103, 111, 128, 189, 236, 243, 258

resurrection, 49, 50, 53, 54, 55, 56, 57, 66, 67, 85, 197, 198, 207, 208

retrospective justification, 149

revelation, 3, 4, 8, 10, 12, 33, 106, 107, 108, 110, 141, 143, 147, 148, 152, 196, 197, 225, 234, 235, 262

rhetoric, 1, 15, 24, 26, 35, 52, 121, 122, 132, 140-156, 190, 193, 196, 220, 233, 244, 248, 254

Ricoeur, Paul, 49, 50, 62, 64, 65, 67, 70, 74, 84, 139, 146, 148, 155, 202, 203, 205, 206, 208, 209, 213, 215, 227, 228, 234, 235, 236, 237, 243, 248, 257, 258, 260, 261, 262

Rorty, Richard, 3, 13, 15, 30, 43, 91, 93, 94, 111-121, 130, 151, 156, 190, 191, 243, 245, 259

Rose, Gillian, 14, 18, 19, 155, 185, 205, 230, 241, 245, 259, 262

scepticism, 5, 12, 144

scheme content dualism, 154

Scripture, v, 6, 22, 26, 33, 34, 35, 36, 37, 45, 50, 51, 59, 63, 66, 70, 71, 78, 79, 80, 81, 84, 104, 109, 160, 169, 178, 193, 197, 199, 206, 209, 210, 212, 215, 216, 219, 222, 225, 226, 232, 244, 245, 249, 250, 252, 253, 254, 255, 257, 260, 262, 263

Searle, John, 31, 61, 62, 63, 90, 259

second first language, 25, 26, 121, 136, 137, 138, 191

second order language, 162, 178

secular, 6, 7, 30, 35, 50, 52, 55, 56, 58, 111, 145, 171, 190, 239, 241, 244, 252

sedimentation, 2, 70, 71, 72, 73, 160, 164, 239

semantic depth, 72, 81, 103, 165, 217, 227

semantic presuppositions, 231

sensus communis, 10, 11, 15, 144, 149, 220

sensus literalis, 36

setting, xiii, xiv, 1, 2, 10, 23, 24, 25, 28, 30, 31, 32, 34, 35, 39, 41, 42, 43, 45, 46, 52, 68, 70, 77, 79, 83, 84, 86, 87, 89, 117, 118, 143, 144, 160, 183, 184, 185, 188, 230, 236, 237, 245

Soskice, Janet M., 100, 101, 102, 104, 127, 259

speech acts, 31, 166, 175, 186

spontaneity, 6, 91, 111

Stead, Christopher, 222, 259

Stern, David, 60, 65, 260

Sternberg, Meir, 60, 61, 62, 214, 237, 260

Stout, Jeffrey, 63, 78, 156, 243, 260

substance, 4, 28, 49, 90, 180, 205, 230

summum bonum, 23, 29, 34, 40, 134

Surin, Kenneth, 49, 80, 81, 82, 86, 98, 99, 107, 108, 194, 217, 230, 231, 232, 238, 260
synchronic, xiv, 183, 236, 237

Tanner, Kathryn, 36, 39, 70, 71, 78, 79, 80, 83, 86, 90, 159- 164, 173, 185, 186, 194, 200, 204, 238, 239, 240, 260
Thiemann, 80, 107-110, 148, 149, 153, 194, 225, 235, 260, 262
Thiselton, Anthony C., vi, xi, 20, 27, 31, 34, 62, 63, 89, 145, 166, 173, 174, 179, 188, 261
Tilley, Terrence, 106, 123, 154, 237, 238, 261
Torrance, Thomas F., 5, 106, 107, 108, 223, 224, 225, 226, 227, 229, 234, 247, 261
Toulmin, Stephen, 14, 31, 156, 253, 261
tradition, 1, 2, 4, 6, 8, 10, 13, 14, 15, 16, 17, 18, 19, 20, 21, 22, 23, 24, 25, 26, 28, 29, 33, 34, 39, 40, 42, 43, 45, 46, 47, 52, 54, 58, 67, 68, 72, 89, 110, 117, 118, 124, 125, 131, 132, 133, 134, 135, 136, 137, 138, 139, 140, 143, 145, 146, 153, 155, 161, 162, 164, 171, 173, 178, 181, 187, 189, 196, 214, 219, 220, 232, 233, 237, 238, 241, 242, 243, 245, 252, 253, 256, 258
transcendental method, 200
translation, 26, 74, 108, 129, 135, 136, 137, 138, 196
truth, xiii, xiv, 9-17, 21, 23, 24, 26, 31, 32, 46-50, 59-68, 71, 85, 89, 90, 91, 95-99, 103-106, 110-115, 120, 121, 122, 124, 125, 126, 127, 128, 132, 133, 134, 137, 139, 140, 142, 144, 145, 146, 148, 149, 150, 151, 152, 153, 155, 158, 160, 164, 167, 168, 169, 170, 171, 172, 174, 175, 176, 177, 182, 185, 186, 187, 188, 189, 190, 193, 195, 197, 199, 202, 205, 209, 212, 215, 217, 218, 220, 222, 223, 224, 225, 230, 231, 237, 243, 244, 250, 252, 253, 256, 260, 261
truth conditions, 105, 121, 125, 137
typology, 85, 103, 104

univocity: univocal, 4, 6, 50, 82, 84, 244

Vaihinger, Hans, 65, 66, 261
Vanhoozer, Kevin, vi, 37, 66, 67, 180, 203, 227, 261
verbum externum, 93, 162, 164, 168, 238
verum-factum, 8, 9, 10, 15, 16

Werpehowski, William, 154, 156, 262
Williams, Rowan, 14, 84, 86, 152, 184, 185, 193, 200, 220, 221, 222, 230, 237, 242, 245, 262
Wittgenstein, Ludwig, 10, 14, 20, 30, 31, 32, 37, 45, 82, 93, 94, 95, 101, 113, 130, 155, 165, 166, 167, 171, 172, 174, 177, 187, 243, 247, 251, 253, 254, 256, 261, 262
Wolterstorff, Nicholas, 31, 62, 63, 64, 84, 185, 225, 234, 262
world absorption, 60, 68, 82, 146, 150, 152, 155, 171, 235

Paternoster Biblical Monographs

(All titles uniform with this volume)
Dates in bold are of projected publication

Joseph Abraham
Eve: Accused or Acquitted?
A Reconsideration of Feminist Readings of the Creation Narrative Texts in Genesis 1–3
Two contrary views dominate contemporary feminist biblical scholarship. One finds in the Bible an unequivocal equality between the sexes from the very creation of humanity, whilst the other sees the biblical text as irredeemably patriarchal and androcentric. Dr Abraham enters into dialogue with both camps as well as introducing his own method of approach. An invaluable tool for any one who is interested in this contemporary debate.
2002 / 0-85364-971-5 / xxiv + 272pp

Octavian D. Baban
Mimesis and Luke's on the Road Encounters in Luke-Acts
Luke's Theology of the Way and its Literary Representation
The book argues on theological and literary (mimetic) grounds that Luke's on-the-road encounters, especially those belonging to the post-Easter period, are part of his complex theology of the Way. Jesus' teaching and that of the apostles is presented by Luke as a challenging answer to the Hellenistic reader's thirst for adventure, good literature, and existential paradigms.
2005 */ 1-84227-253-5 / approx. 374pp*

Paul Barker
The Triumph of Grace in Deuteronomy
This book is a textual and theological analysis of the interaction between the sin and faithlessness of Israel and the grace of Yahweh in response, looking especially at Deuteronomy chapters 1–3, 8–10 and 29–30. The author argues that the grace of Yahweh is determinative for the ongoing relationship between Yahweh and Israel and that Deuteronomy anticipates and fully expects Israel to be faithless.
2004 / 1-84227-226-8 / xxii + 270pp

Jonathan F. Bayes
The Weakness of the Law
God's Law and the Christian in New Testament Perspective
A study of the four New Testament books which refer to the law as weak (Acts, Romans, Galatians, Hebrews) leads to a defence of the third use in the Reformed debate about the law in the life of the believer.
2000 / 0-85364-957-X / xii + 244pp

Mark Bonnington
The Antioch Episode of Galatians 2:11-14 in Historical and Cultural Context
The Galatians 2 'incident' in Antioch over table-fellowship suggests significant disagreement between the leading apostles. This book analyses the background to the disagreement by locating the incident within the dynamics of social interaction between Jews and Gentiles. It proposes a new way of understanding the relationship between the individuals and issues involved.
2005 / 1-84227-050-8 / approx. 350pp

David Bostock
A Portrayal of Trust
The Theme of Faith in the Hezekiah Narratives
This study provides detailed and sensitive readings of the Hezekiah narratives (2 Kings 18–20 and Isaiah 36–39) from a theological perspective. It concentrates on the theme of faith, using narrative criticism as its methodology. Attention is paid especially to setting, plot, point of view and characterization within the narratives. A largely positive portrayal of Hezekiah emerges that underlines the importance and relevance of scripture.
2005 / 1-84227-314-0 / approx. 300pp

Mark Bredin
Jesus, Revolutionary of Peace
A Non-violent Christology in the Book of Revelation
This book aims to demonstrate that the figure of Jesus in the Book of Revelation can best be understood as an active non-violent revolutionary.
2003 / 1-84227-153-9 / xviii + 262pp

Robinson Butarbutar
Paul and Conflict Resolution
An Exegetical Study of Paul's Apostolic Paradigm in 1 Corinthians 9
The author sees the apostolic paradigm in 1 Corinthians 9 as part of Paul's unified arguments in 1 Corinthians 8–10 in which he seeks to mediate in the dispute over the issue of food offered to idols. The book also sees its relevance for dispute-resolution today, taking the conflict within the author's church as an example.
2006 / 1-84227-315-9 / approx. 280pp

Daniel J-S Chae
Paul as Apostle to the Gentiles
His Apostolic Self-awareness and its Influence on the Soteriological Argument
in Romans
Opposing 'the post-Holocaust interpretation of Romans', Daniel Chae competently demonstrates that Paul argues for the equality of Jew and Gentile in Romans. Chae's fresh exegetical interpretation is academically outstanding and spiritually encouraging.
1997 / 0-85364-829-8 / xiv + 378pp

Luke L. Cheung
The Genre, Composition and Hermeneutics of the Epistle of James
The present work examines the employment of the wisdom genre with a certain compositional structure and the interpretation of the law through the Jesus tradition of the double love command by the author of the Epistle of James to serve his purpose in promoting perfection and warning against doubleness among the eschatologically renewed people of God in the Diaspora.
2003 / 1-84227-062-1 / xvi + 372pp

Youngmo Cho
Spirit and Kingdom in the Writings of Luke and Paul
The relationship between Spirit and Kingdom is a relatively unexplored area in Lukan and Pauline studies. This book offers a fresh perspective of two biblical writers on the subject. It explores the difference between Luke's and Paul's understanding of the Spirit by examining the specific question of the relationship of the concept of the Spirit to the concept of the Kingdom of God in each writer.
2005 / 1-84227-316-7 / approx. 270pp

Andrew C. Clark
Parallel Lives
The Relation of Paul to the Apostles in the Lucan Perspective
This study of the Peter-Paul parallels in Acts argues that their purpose was to emphasize the themes of continuity in salvation history and the unity of the Jewish and Gentile missions. New light is shed on Luke's literary techniques, partly through a comparison with Plutarch.
2001 / 1-84227-035-4 / xviii + 386pp

Andrew D. Clarke
Secular and Christian Leadership in Corinth
A Socio-Historical and Exegetical Study of 1 Corinthians 1–6
This volume is an investigation into the leadership structures and dynamics of first-century Roman Corinth. These are compared with the practice of leadership in the Corinthian Christian community which are reflected in 1 Corinthians 1–6, and contrasted with Paul's own principles of Christian leadership.
2005 / 1-84227-229-2 / 200pp

Stephen Finamore
God, Order and Chaos
René Girard and the Apocalypse
Readers are often disturbed by the images of destruction in the book of Revelation and unsure why they are unleashed after the exaltation of Jesus. This book examines past approaches to these texts and uses René Girard's theories to revive some old ideas and propose some new ones.
2005 / 1-84227-197-0 / approx. 344pp

David G. Firth
Surrendering Retribution in the Psalms
Responses to Violence in the Individual Complaints
In *Surrendering Retribution in the Psalms*, David Firth examines the ways in which the book of Psalms inculcates a model response to violence through the repetition of standard patterns of prayer. Rather than seeking justification for retributive violence, Psalms encourages not only a surrender of the right of retribution to Yahweh, but also sets limits on the retribution that can be sought in imprecations. Arising initially from the author's experience in South Africa, the possibilities of this model to a particular context of violence is then briefly explored.
2005 / 1-84227-337-X / xviii + 154pp

Scott J. Hafemann
Suffering and Ministry in the Spirit
Paul's Defence of His Ministry in II Corinthians 2:14–3:3
Shedding new light on the way Paul defended his apostleship, the author offers a careful, detailed study of 2 Corinthians 2:14–3:3 linked with other key passages throughout 1 and 2 Corinthians. Demonstrating the unity and coherence of Paul's argument in this passage, the author shows that Paul's suffering served as the vehicle for revealing God's power and glory through the Spirit.
2000 / 0-85364-967-7 / xiv + 262pp

Scott J. Hafemann
Paul, Moses and the History of Israel
The Letter/Spirit Contrast and the Argument from Scripture in 2 Corinthians 3
An exegetical study of the call of Moses, the second giving of the Law (Exodus 32–34), the new covenant, and the prophetic understanding of the history of Israel in 2 Corinthians 3. Hafemann's work demonstrates Paul's contextual use of the Old Testament and the essential unity between the Law and the Gospel within the context of the distinctive ministries of Moses and Paul.
2005 / 1-84227-317-5 / xii + 498pp

Douglas S. McComiskey
Lukan Theology in the Light of the Gospel's Literary Structure
Luke's Gospel was purposefully written with theology embedded in its patterned literary structure. A critical analysis of this cyclical structure provides new windows into Luke's interpretation of the individual pericopes comprising the Gospel and illuminates several of his theological interests.
2004 / 1-84227-148-2 / xviii + 388pp

Stephen Motyer
Your Father the Devil?
A New Approach to John and 'The Jews'
Who are 'the Jews' in John's Gospel? Defending John against the charge of antisemitism, Motyer argues that, far from demonising the Jews, the Gospel seeks to present Jesus as 'Good News for Jews' in a late first century setting.
1997 / 0-85364-832-8 / xiv + 260pp

Esther Ng
Reconstructing Christian Origins?
The Feminist Theology of Elizabeth Schüssler Fiorenza: An Evaluation
In a detailed evaluation, the author challenges Elizabeth Schüssler Fiorenza's reconstruction of early Christian origins and her underlying presuppositions. The author also presents her own views on women's roles both then and now.
2002 / 1-84227-055-9 / xxiv + 468pp

Robin Parry
Old Testament Story and Christian Ethics
The Rape of Dinah as a Case Study
What is the role of story in ethics and, more particularly, what is the role of Old Testament story in Christian ethics? This book, drawing on the work of contemporary philosophers, argues that narrative is crucial in the ethical shaping of people and, drawing on the work of contemporary Old Testament scholars, that story plays a key role in Old Testament ethics. Parry then argues that when situated in canonical context Old Testament stories can be reappropriated by Christian readers in their own ethical formation. The shocking story of the rape of Dinah and the massacre of the Shechemites provides a fascinating case study for exploring the parameters within which Christian ethical appropriations of Old Testament stories can live.
2004 / 1-84227-210-1 / xx + 350pp

Ian Paul
Power to See the World Anew
The Value of Paul Ricoeur's Hermeneutic of Metaphor in Interpreting the Symbolism of Revelation 12 and 13
This book is a study of the hermeneutics of metaphor of Paul Ricoeur, one of the most important writers on hermeneutics and metaphor of the last century. It sets out the key points of his theory, important criticisms of his work, and how his approach, modified in the light of these criticisms, offers a methodological framework for reading apocalyptic texts.
2006 / 1-84227-056-7 / approx. 350pp

Robert L. Plummer
Paul's Understanding of the Church's Mission
Did the Apostle Paul Expect the Early Christian Communities to Evangelize?
This book engages in a careful study of Paul's letters to determine if the apostle expected the communities to which he wrote to engage in missionary activity. It helpfully summarizes the discussion on this debated issue, judiciously handling contested texts, and provides a way forward in addressing this critical question. While admitting that Paul rarely explicitly commands the communities he founded to evangelize, Plummer amasses significant incidental data to provide a convincing case that Paul did indeed expect his churches to engage in mission activity. Throughout the study, Plummer progressively builds a theological basis for the church's mission that is both distinctively Pauline and compelling.
2006 / 1-84227-333-7 / approx. 324pp

David Powys
'Hell': A Hard Look at a Hard Question
The Fate of the Unrighteous in New Testament Thought
This comprehensive treatment seeks to unlock the original meaning of terms and phrases long thought to support the traditional doctrine of hell. It concludes that there is an alternative—one which is more biblical, and which can positively revive the rationale for Christian mission.

1997 / 0-85364-831-X / xxii + 478pp

Sorin Sabou
Between Horror and Hope
Paul's Metaphorical Language of Death in Romans 6.1-11
This book argues that Paul's metaphorical language of death in Romans 6.1-11 conveys two aspects: horror and hope. The 'horror' aspect is conveyed by the 'crucifixion' language, and the 'hope' aspect by 'burial' language. The life of the Christian believer is understood, as relationship with sin is concerned ('death to sin'), between these two realities: horror and hope.

2005 / 1-84227-322-1 / approx. 224pp

Rosalind Selby
The Comical Doctrine
The Epistemology of New Testament Hermeneutics
This book argues that the gospel breaks through postmodernity's critique of truth and the referential possibilities of textuality with its gift of grace. With a rigorous, philosophical challenge to modernist and postmodernist assumptions, Selby offers an alternative epistemology to all who would still read with faith *and* with academic credibility.

2005 / 1-84227-212-8 / approx. 350pp

Kiwoong Son
Zion Symbolism in Hebrews
Hebrews 12.18-24 as a Hermeneutical Key to the Epistle
This book challenges the general tendency of understanding the Epistle to the Hebrews against a Hellenistic background and suggests that the Epistle should be understood in the light of the Jewish apocalyptic tradition. The author especially argues for the importance of the theological symbolism of Sinai and Zion (Heb. 12:18-24) as it provides the Epistle's theological background as well as the rhetorical basis of the superiority motif of Jesus throughout the Epistle.

2005 / 1-84227-368-X / approx. 280pp

Kevin Walton
Thou Traveller Unknown
The Presence and Absence of God in the Jacob Narrative
The author offers a fresh reading of the story of Jacob in the book of Genesis through the paradox of divine presence and absence. The work also seeks to make a contribution to Pentateuchal studies by bringing together a close reading of the final text with historical critical insights, doing justice to the text's historical depth, final form and canonical status.
2003 / 1-84227-059-1 / xvi + 238pp

George M. Wieland
The Significance of Salvation
A Study of Salvation Language in the Pastoral Epistles
The language and ideas of salvation pervade the three Pastoral Epistles. This study offers a close examination of their soteriological statements. In all three letters the idea of salvation is found to play a vital paraenetic role, but each also exhibits distinctive soteriological emphases. The results challenge common assumptions about the Pastoral Epistles as a corpus.
2005 / 1-84227-257-8 / approx. 324pp

Alistair Wilson
When Will These Things Happen?
A Study of Jesus as Judge in Matthew 21–25
This study seeks to allow Matthew's carefully constructed presentation of Jesus to be given full weight in the modern evaluation of Jesus' eschatology. Careful analysis of the text of Matthew 21–25 reveals Jesus to be standing firmly in the Jewish prophetic and wisdom traditions as he proclaims and enacts imminent judgement on the Jewish authorities then boldly claims the central role in the final and universal judgement.
2004 / 1-84227-146-6 / xxii + 272pp

Lindsay Wilson
Joseph Wise and Otherwise
The Intersection of Covenant and Wisdom in Genesis 37–50
This book offers a careful literary reading of Genesis 37–50 that argues that the Joseph story contains both strong covenant themes and many wisdom-like elements. The connections between the two helps to explore how covenant and wisdom might intersect in an integrated biblical theology.
2004 / 1-84227-140-7 / xvi + 340pp

Stephen I. Wright
The Voice of Jesus
Studies in the Interpretation of Six Gospel Parables
This literary study considers how the 'voice' of Jesus has been heard in different
periods of parable interpretation, and how the categories of figure and trope may
help us towards a sensitive reading of the parables today.
2000 / 0-85364-975-8 / xiv + 280pp

Paternoster:
thinking faith

Paternoster
9 Holdom Avenue,
Bletchley,
Milton Keynes MK1 1QR,
United Kingdom
Web: www.authenticmedia.co.uk/paternoster

Paternoster Theological Monographs

(All titles uniform with this volume)
Dates in bold are of projected publication

Emil Bartos
Deification in Eastern Orthodox Theology
An Evaluation and Critique of the Theology of Dumitru Staniloae

Bartos studies a fundamental yet neglected aspect of Orthodox theology: deification. By examining the doctrines of anthropology, christology, soteriology and ecclesiology as they relate to deification, he provides an important contribution to contemporary dialogue between Eastern and Western theologians.

1999 / 0-85364-956-1 / xii + 370pp

Graham Buxton
The Trinity, Creation and Pastoral Ministry
Imaging the Perichoretic God

In this book the author proposes a three-way conversation between theology, science and pastoral ministry. His approach draws on a Trinitarian understanding of God as a relational being of love, whose life 'spills over' into all created reality, human and non-human. By locating human meaning and purpose within God's 'creation-community' this book offers the possibility of a transforming engagement between those in pastoral ministry and the scientific community.

2005 / 1-84227-369-8 / *approx. 380 pp*

Iain D. Campbell
Fixing the Indemnity
The Life and Work of George Adam Smith

When Old Testament scholar George Adam Smith (1856–1942) delivered the Lyman Beecher lectures at Yale University in 1899, he confidently declared that 'modern criticism has won its war against traditional theories. It only remains to fix the amount of the indemnity.' In this biography, Iain D. Campbell assesses Smith's critical approach to the Old Testament and evaluates its consequences, showing that Smith's life and work still raises questions about the relationship between biblical scholarship and evangelical faith.

2004 / 1-84227-228-4 / xx + 256pp

Tim Chester
Mission and the Coming of God
Eschatology, the Trinity and Mission in the Theology of Jürgen Moltmann
This book explores the theology and missiology of the influential contemporary theologian, Jürgen Moltmann. It highlights the important contribution Moltmann has made while offering a critique of his thought from an evangelical perspective. In so doing, it touches on pertinent issues for evangelical missiology. The conclusion takes Calvin as a starting point, proposing 'an eschatology of the cross' which offers a critique of the over-realised eschatologies in liberation theology and certain forms of evangelicalism.
2006 / 1-84227-320-5 / approx. 224pp

Sylvia Wilkey Collinson
Making Disciples
The Significance of Jesus' Educational Strategy for Today's Church
This study examines the biblical practice of discipling, formulates a definition, and makes comparisons with modern models of education. A recommendation is made for greater attention to its practice today.
2004 / 1-84227-116-4 / xiv + 278pp

Darrell Cosden
A Theology of Work
Work and the New Creation
Through dialogue with Moltmann, Pope John Paul II and others, this book develops a genitive 'theology of work', presenting a theological definition of work and a model for a theological ethics of work that shows work's nature, value and meaning now and eschatologically. Work is shown to be a transformative activity consisting of three dynamically inter-related dimensions: the instrumental, relational and ontological.
2005 / 1-84227-332-9 / xvi + 208pp

Stephen M. Dunning
The Crisis and the Quest
A Kierkegaardian Reading of Charles Williams
Employing Kierkegaardian categories and analysis, this study investigates both the central crisis in Charles Williams's authorship between hermetism and Christianity (Kierkegaard's Religions A and B), and the quest to resolve this crisis, a quest that ultimately presses the bounds of orthodoxy.
2000 / 0-85364-985-5 / xxiv + 254pp

Keith Ferdinando
The Triumph of Christ in African Perspective
A Study of Demonology and Redemption in the African Context
The book explores the implications of the gospel for traditional African fears of occult aggression. It analyses such traditional approaches to suffering and biblical responses to fears of demonic evil, concluding with an evaluation of African beliefs from the perspective of the gospel.

1999 / 0-85364-830-1 / xviii + 450pp

Andrew Goddard
Living the Word, Resisting the World
The Life and Thought of Jacques Ellul
This work offers a definitive study of both the life and thought of the French Reformed thinker Jacques Ellul (1912-1994). It will prove an indispensable resource for those interested in this influential theologian and sociologist and for Christian ethics and political thought generally.

2002 / 1-84227-053-2 / xxiv + 378pp

David Hilborn
The Words of our Lips
Language-Use in Free Church Worship
Studies of liturgical language have tended to focus on the written canons of Roman Catholic and Anglican communities. By contrast, David Hilborn analyses the more extemporary approach of English Nonconformity. Drawing on recent developments in linguistic pragmatics, he explores similarities and differences between 'fixed' and 'free' worship, and argues for the interdependence of each.

***2006** / 0-85364-977-4 / approx. 350pp*

Roger Hitching
The Church and Deaf People
A Study of Identity, Communication and Relationships with Special Reference to the Ecclesiology of Jürgen Moltmann
In *The Church and Deaf People* Roger Hitching sensitively examines the history and present experience of deaf people and finds similarities between aspects of sign language and Moltmann's theological method that 'open up' new ways of understanding theological concepts.

2003 / 1-84227-222-5 / xxii + 236pp

John G. Kelly
One God, One People
The Differentiated Unity of the People of God in the Theology of
Jürgen Moltmann
The author expounds and critiques Moltmann's doctrine of God and highlights
the systematic connections between it and Moltmann's influential discussion of
Israel. He then proposes a fresh approach to Jewish–Christian relations building
on Moltmann's work using insights from Habermas and Rawls.
2005 / 0-85346-969-3 / approx. 350pp

Mark F.W. Lovatt
Confronting the Will-to-Power
A Reconsideration of the Theology of Reinhold Niebuhr
Confronting the Will-to-Power is an analysis of the theology of Reinhold
Niebuhr, arguing that his work is an attempt to identify, and provide a practical
theological answer to, the existence and nature of human evil.
2001 / 1-84227-054-0 / xviii + 216pp

Neil B. MacDonald
Karl Barth and the Strange New World within the Bible
Barth, Wittgenstein, and the Metadilemmas of the Enlightenment
Barth's discovery of the strange new world within the Bible is examined in the
context of Kant, Hume, Overbeck, and, most importantly, Wittgenstein.
MacDonald covers some fundamental issues in theology today: epistemology,
the final form of the text and biblical truth-claims.
2000 / 0-85364-970-7 / xxvi + 374pp

Keith A. Mascord
Alvin Plantinga and Christian Apologetics
This book draws together the contributions of the philosopher Alvin Plantinga to
the major contemporary challenges to Christian belief, highlighting in particular
his ground-breaking work in epistemology and the problem of evil. Plantinga's
theory that both theistic and Christian belief is warrantedly basic is explored and
critiqued, and an assessment offered as to the significance of his work for
apologetic theory and practice.
2005 / 1-84227-256-X / approx. 304pp

Gillian McCulloch
The Deconstruction of Dualism in Theology
With Reference to Ecofeminist Theology and New Age Spirituality
This book challenges eco-theological anti-dualism in Christian theology, arguing that dualism has a twofold function in Christian religious discourse. Firstly, it enables us to express the discontinuities and divisions that are part of the process of reality. Secondly, dualistic language allows us to express the mysteries of divine transcendence/immanence and the survival of the soul without collapsing into monism and materialism, both of which are problematic for Christian epistemology.
2002 / 1-84227-044-3 / xii + 282pp

Leslie McCurdy
Attributes and Atonement
The Holy Love of God in the Theology of P.T. Forsyth
Attributes and Atonement is an intriguing full-length study of P.T. Forsyth's doctrine of the cross as it relates particularly to God's holy love. It includes an unparalleled bibliography of both primary and secondary material relating to Forsyth.
1999 / 0-85364-833-6 / xiv + 328pp

Nozomu Miyahira
Towards a Theology of the Concord of God
A Japanese Perspective on the Trinity
This book introduces a new Japanese theology and a unique Trinitarian formula based on the Japanese intellectual climate: three betweennesses and one concord. It also presents a new interpretation of the Trinity, a co-subordinationism, which is in line with orthodox Trinitarianism; each single person of the Trinity is eternally and equally subordinate (or serviceable) to the other persons, so that they retain the mutual dynamic equality.
2000 / 0-85364-863-8 / xiv + 256pp

Eddy José Muskus
The Origins and Early Development of Liberation Theology in Latin America
With Particular Reference to Gustavo Gutiérrez
This work challenges the fundamental premise of Liberation Theology, 'opting for the poor', and its claim that Christ is found in them. It also argues that Liberation Theology emerged as a direct result of the failure of the Roman Catholic Church in Latin America.
2002 / 0-85364-974-X / xiv + 296pp

Jim Purves
The Triune God and the Charismatic Movement
A Critical Appraisal from a Scottish Perspective
All emotion and no theology? Or a fundamental challenge to reappraise and realign our trinitarian theology in the light of Christian experience? This study of charismatic renewal as it found expression within Scotland at the end of the twentieth century evaluates the use of Patristic, Reformed and contemporary models of the Trinity in explaining the workings of the Holy Spirit.
2004 / 1-84227-321-3 / xxiv + 246pp

Anna Robbins
Methods in the Madness
Diversity in Twentieth-Century Christian Social Ethics
The author compares the ethical methods of Walter Rauschenbusch, Reinhold Niebuhr and others. She argues that unless Christians are clear about the ways that theology and philosophy are expressed practically they may lose the ability to discuss social ethics across contexts, let alone reach effective agreements.
2004 / 1-84227-211-X / xx + 294pp

Ed Rybarczyk
Beyond Salvation
Eastern Orthodoxy and Classical Pentecostalism on Becoming Like Christ
At first glance eastern Orthodoxy and classical Pentecostalism seem quite distinct. This ground-breaking study shows they share much in common, especially as it concerns the experiential elements of following Christ. Both traditions assert that authentic Christianity transcends the wooden categories of modernism.
2004 / 1-84227-144-X / xii + 356pp

Signe Sandsmark
Is World View Neutral Education Possible and Desirable?
A Christian Response to Liberal Arguments
(Published jointly with The Stapleford Centre)
This book discusses reasons for belief in world view neutrality, and argues that 'neutral' education will have a hidden, but strong world view influence. It discusses the place for Christian education in the common school.
2000 / 0-85364-973-1 / xiv + 182pp

Hazel Sherman
Reading Zechariah
The Allegorical Tradition of Biblical Interpretation through the Commentary of Didymus the Blind and Theodore of Mopsuestia
A close reading of the commentary on Zechariah by Didymus the Blind alongside that of Theodore of Mopsuestia suggests that popular categorising of Antiochene and Alexandrian biblical exegesis as 'historical' or 'allegorical' is inadequate and misleading.
2005 / 1-84227-213-6 / approx. 280pp

Andrew Sloane
On Being a Christian in the Academy
Nicholas Wolterstorff and the Practice of Christian Scholarship
An exposition and critical appraisal of Nicholas Wolterstorff's epistemology in the light of the philosophy of science, and an application of his thought to the practice of Christian scholarship.
2003 / 1-84227-058-3 / xvi + 274pp

Damon W.K. So
Jesus' Revelation of His Father
A Narrative-Conceptual Study of the Trinity with Special Reference to Karl Barth
This book explores the trinitarian dynamics in the context of Jesus' revelation of his Father in his earthly ministry with references to key passages in Matthew's Gospel. It develops from the exegeses of these passages a non-linear concept of revelation which links Jesus' communion with his Father to his revelatory words and actions through a nuanced understanding of the Holy Spirit, with references to K. Barth, G.W.H. Lampe, J.D.G. Dunn and E. Irving.
2005 / 1-84227-323-X / approx. 380pp

Daniel Strange
The Possibility of Salvation Among the Unevangelised
An Analysis of Inclusivism in Recent Evangelical Theology
For evangelical theologians the 'fate of the unevangelised' impinges upon fundamental tenets of evangelical identity. The position known as 'inclusivism', defined by the belief that the unevangelised can be ontologically saved by Christ whilst being epistemologically unaware of him, has been defended most vigorously by the Canadian evangelical Clark H. Pinnock. Through a detailed analysis and critique of Pinnock's work, this book examines a cluster of issues surrounding the unevangelised and its implications for christology, soteriology and the doctrine of revelation.
2002 / 1-84227-047-8 / xviii + 362pp

Scott Swain
God According to the Gospel
Biblical Narrative and the Identity of God in the Theology of Robert W. Jenson
Robert W. Jenson is one of the leading voices in contemporary Trinitarian theology. His boldest contribution in this area concerns his use of biblical narrative both to ground and explicate the Christian doctrine of God. *God According to the Gospel* critically examines Jenson's proposal and suggests an alternative way of reading the biblical portrayal of the triune God.
2006 / 1-84227-258-6 / approx. 180pp

Justyn Terry
The Justifying Judgement of God
A Reassessment of the Place of Judgement in the Saving Work of Christ
The argument of this book is that judgement, understood as the whole process of bringing justice, is the primary metaphor of atonement, with others, such as victory, redemption and sacrifice, subordinate to it. Judgement also provides the proper context for understanding penal substitution and the call to repentance, baptism, eucharist and holiness.
2005 / 1-84227-370-1 / approx. 274 pp

Graham Tomlin
The Power of the Cross
Theology and the Death of Christ in Paul, Luther and Pascal
This book explores the theology of the cross in St Paul, Luther and Pascal. It offers new perspectives on the theology of each, and some implications for the nature of power, apologetics, theology and church life in a postmodern context.
1999 / 0-85364-984-7 / xiv + 344pp

Adonis Vidu
Postliberal Theological Method
A Critical Study
The postliberal theology of Hans Frei, George Lindbeck, Ronald Thiemann, John Milbank and others is one of the more influential contemporary options. This book focuses on several aspects pertaining to its theological method, specifically its understanding of background, hermeneutics, epistemic justification, ontology, the nature of doctrine and, finally, Christological method.
2005 / 1-84227-395-7 / approx. 324pp

Graham J. Watts
Revelation and the Spirit
*A Comparative Study of the Relationship between the Doctrine of Revelation
and Pneumatology in the Theology of Eberhard Jüngel and of
Wolfhart Pannenberg*
The relationship between revelation and pneumatology is relatively unexplored.
This approach offers a fresh angle on two important twentieth century
theologians and raises pneumatological questions which are theologically crucial
and relevant to mission in a postmodern culture.
2005 / 1-84227-104-0 / xxii + 232pp

Nigel G. Wright
Disavowing Constantine
*Mission, Church and the Social Order in the Theologies of John Howard Yoder
and Jürgen Moltmann*
This book is a timely restatement of a radical theology of church and state in the
Anabaptist and Baptist tradition. Dr Wright constructs his argument in dialogue
and debate with Yoder and Moltmann, major contributors to a free church
perspective.
2000 / 0-85364-978-2 / xvi + 252pp

Paternoster
9 Holdom Avenue,
Bletchley,
Milton Keynes MK1 1QR,
United Kingdom
Web: www.authenticmedia.co.uk/paternoster